RESOURCE REDEPLOYMENT AND CORPORATE STRATEGY

ADVANCES IN STRATEGIC MANAGEMENT

Series Editor: Brian S. Silverman

Recent Volumes:

Volume 26: Economic Institutions of Strategy
Edited by: Jackson A. Nickerson and Brian S. Silverman

Volume 27: The Globalization of Strategy Research
Edited by: Joel A.C. Baum and Joseph Lampel

Volume 28: Project-based Organizing and Strategic Management
Edited by: Gino Cattani, Simone Ferriani, Lars Frederiksen and Florian Täube

Volume 29: History and Strategy
Edited by: Steven J. Kahl, Brian S. Silverman and Michael A. Cusumano

Volume 30: Collaboration and Competition in Business Ecosystems
Edited by: Ron Adner, Joanne E. Oxley and Brian S. Silverman

Volume 31: Finance and Strategy
Edited by: Belén Villalonga

Volume 32: Cognition and Strategy
Edited by: Giovanni Gavetti and William Ocasio

Volume 33: Business Models and Modelling
Edited by: Charles Baden-Fuller and Vincent Mangematin

Volume 34: Strategy Beyond Markets
Edited by: John M. de Figueiredo, Michael Lenox, Felix Oberholzer-Gee and Richard G. Vanden Bergh

ADVANCES IN STRATEGIC MANAGEMENT VOLUME 35

RESOURCE REDEPLOYMENT AND CORPORATE STRATEGY

EDITED BY

TIMOTHY B. FOLTA

University of Connecticut, Storrs, CT, USA
University of Strasbourg Institute for Advanced Study, Strasbourg, France

CONSTANCE E. HELFAT

Dartmouth College, Hanover, NH, USA

SAMINA KARIM

Northeastern University, Boston, MA, USA

Emerald

United Kingdom – North America – Japan
India – Malaysia – China

Emerald Group Publishing Limited
Howard House, Wagon Lane, Bingley BD16 1WA, UK

First edition 2016

British Library Cataloguing in Publication Data
A catalogue record for this book is available from the British Library

ISBN: 978-1-78635-508-9
ISSN: 0742-3322 (Series)

CONTENTS

LIST OF CONTRIBUTORS

Gautam Ahuja	University of Michigan, Ann Arbor, MI, USA
Jaideep Anand	The Ohio State University, Columbus, OH, USA
Josep M. Argilés-Bosch	Universitat de Barcelona, Barcelona, Spain
Joel Blit	University of Waterloo, Waterloo, ON, Canada
Robert P. Bremner	Stanford University, Palo Alto, CA, USA
Ari Dothan	Interdisciplinary Center Herzliya (IDC), Herzliya, Israel
Gary Dushnitsky	London Business School, London, UK
Kathleen M. Eisenhardt	Stanford University, Palo Alto, CA, USA
Timothy B. Folta	University of Connecticut, Storrs, CT, USA; University of Strasbourg Institute for Advanced Study, Strasbourg, France
Josep Garcia-Blandon	Universitat Ramon Llull, Barcelona, Spain
Douglas P. Hannah	University of Texas at Austin, Austin, TX, USA
Constance E. Helfat	Dartmouth College, Hanover, NH, USA
Samina Karim	Northeastern University, Boston, MA, USA
Hyunseob Kim	The Ohio State University, Columbus, OH, USA
Thomas Klueter	IESE Business School, Barcelona, Spain
Dovev Lavie	Technion – Israel Institute of Technology, Haifa, Israel

Gwendolyn K. Lee	University of Florida, Gainesville, FL, USA
Christopher C. Liu	University of Toronto, Toronto, ON, Canada
Shaohua Lu	Tulane University, New Orleans, LA, USA
Mónica Martinez-Blasco	Universitat Ramon Llull, Barcelona, Spain
Luis L. Martins	University of Texas at Austin, Austin, TX, USA
Patia J. McGrath	University of Pennsylvania, Philadelphia, PA, USA
Douglas J. Miller	Rutgers, The State University of New Jersey, New Brunswick, NJ, USA
Will Mitchell	University of Toronto, Toronto, ON, Canada
Elena Novelli	City University London, London, UK
Srikanth Parachuri	The Pennsylvania State University, State College, PA, USA
Violina P. Rindova	University of Texas at Austin, Austin, TX, USA
Harbir Singh	University of Pennsylvania, Philadelphia, PA, USA
Hsiao-shan Yang	University of Illinois at Urbana-Champaign, Champaign, IL, USA
Adrian Yeow	SIM University, Singapore

EXAMINING RESOURCE REDEPLOYMENT IN MULTI-BUSINESS FIRMS

Timothy B. Folta, Constance E. Helfat and Samina Karim

ABSTRACT

This paper introduces the volume on Resource Redeployment and Corporate Strategy, which is devoted to exploring a relatively new justification for how multi-business firms create value – having flexibility to internally redistribute non-financial resources across their businesses. We clarify how a theory around resource flexibility differs from other theories of how multi-business firms create value. We then synthesize the collection of papers in this volume and describe how they contribute to this line of inquiry. Finally, we offer our own views on opportunities for elaboration of this theory.

Keywords: Inter-temporal economies of scope; resource redeployment; corporate strategy; multi-business firms; corporate advantage; corporate flexibility

Resource Redeployment and Corporate Strategy
Advances in Strategic Management, Volume 35, 1–17

ISSN: 0742-3322/doi:10.1108/S0742-332220160000035002

INTRODUCTION

A coherent corporate strategy explains how a firm's multiple businesses exist within a single firm to create a corporate advantage. Several rationales exist, including garnering economies of scope (Penrose, 1959; Rumelt, 1974), diversifying risk (Lewellen, 1971), filling institutional voids (Khanna & Palepu, 1997), and reallocating capital efficiently (Matsusaka & Nanda, 2002; Williamson, 1975). This volume is devoted to exploring a relatively new justification for how multi-business firms create value – having flexibility to internally redistribute non-financial resources across their businesses. This explanation is receiving increased attention since a series of papers have emphasized it is different from economies of scope tied to simultaneous sharing of resources across businesses (Helfat & Eisenhardt, 2004; Levinthal & Wu, 2010, Sakhartov & Folta, 2014). Our goals in extending the call for papers are to encourage even greater clarity about the uniqueness of this theory relative to other theories of the multi-business firm, gain a better understanding of how to empirically test this theory, and illuminate opportunity for elaboration. This, we believe, will enhance research in corporate strategy because it will whet the discriminative edge of each theory.

The papers selected for the special issue greatly expand the volume of work on the emerging topic of resource redeployment and contribute to the literature in several important ways. Several papers empirically explore the extent to which market inducements inspire resource redeployment. Prior work has only theorized about the importance and the types of inducements and emphasized that an absence of them might support explanations of redeployment centered on agency costs, information efficiencies, or political processes. These empirical treatments also illuminate how inducements might be measured, a welcome contribution in a literature that has been largely theoretical. Other papers address the factors dictating the efficiency of internal or external resource markets. This is critical because internal resource redeployment only creates value if it is more efficient than external resource acquisition for the same purpose. Another common theme is the extent to which resource constraints at the overall firm level (e.g., size and financial constraints) affect resource redeployment. This empirical work relates to the arguments of Levinthal and Wu (2010), who theorize that specific types of resources that are constrained in their use (non-scale-free resources) are the prime candidates for redeployment, because they can only be used productively in one setting at a time. These are only a few of the themes fundamental to the topic of resource redeployment explored in this volume. A number of theoretical perspectives are represented in the volume, including resource-based theory, real options theory, dynamic capabilities, and behavioral theory.

This introductory paper accomplishes four broad objectives. First, it clarifies what is meant when firms have the flexibility for resource redeployment. Our hope is that this clarity will unite the field in the use of terminology going forward. Second, it clarifies how a theory around resource flexibility differs from other theories of how multi-business firms create value. We synthesize the collection of papers in this volume and describe how they contribute to this line of inquiry. Finally, we offer our own views on opportunities for elaboration.

MULTI-BUSINESS FIRMS ARE ALIVE AND WELL

To be clear, this volume addresses a fundamental issue in strategic management research – how a corporate headquarter adds to firm value. Given the extra costs of the headquarter unit, and the coordination costs tied to creating spillovers across business units, it should not be assumed that internalizing businesses adds to corporate advantage, even if doing so is quite common. Villalonga (2004) reports that between 1978 and 1997, around one-third of all firms in her COMPUSTAT sample are in more than one four-digit SIC segments. Our analysis of COMPUSTAT data between 1997 and 2014 suggests that the percentage of multi- segment firms remains large, but has decreased since 1997.[1] Table 1 also suggests that multi-business firms constitute around half of all assets, revenues, and

Table 1. Distribution of Multi-Business Firms between 1997 and 2014.*

	1997	2007	2014
# of single segment firms	1,563	1,765	1,433
# of multi-segment firms	887	926	662
% of multi-segment firms	36.2%	34.4%	31.6%
% of sample assets owned by multi-segment firms	57.0%	61.5%	48.8%
% of sample revenues generated by multi-business firms	54.3%	59.6%	49.7%
% of sample market value generated by multi-business firms	52.9%	55.6%	41.6%

*Sample derived by authors from COMPUSTAT Segment database, using the same criteria as Villalonga (2004).

market value. Although these values have declined since 2007, they indicate that decisions around corporate scope remain non-trivial.

There is less clarity on our understanding of how much corporate diversification enhances value. Research using variance decomposition techniques suggest that the corporate unit contributes somewhere between 4.3 and 18.0 percent to business segment profitability.[2] Bowman and Helfat (2001) caution that these numbers represent averages, and some firms create far more value with their corporate units. Another stream of research documents that the average multi-business firm trades at a slight discount relative to single business firms (Berger & Ofek, 1995; Lang & Stulz, 1994), but a more recent study suggests that the average multi-business firm trades at a slight premium when accounting for the data limitations of COMPUSTAT and the possibility that poor performance induces diversification (Villalonga, 2004). All of this points to a greater need for understanding how and when corporate units create value.

CORPORATE FLEXIBILITY THROUGH RESOURCE REDEPLOYMENT

In this section we explain the emerging theory around corporate flexibility through resource redeployment. The argument is that corporate value derives from having discretion to partially or completely withdraw resources from one business and reallocate them to another business. This benefit has been referred to as "inter-temporal economies of scope" (Helfat & Eisenhardt, 2004) or "redeployability" (Sakhartov & Folta, 2014), and is available when resources have the potential to be internally reallocated across business units, products, or even business models. When firms have such discretion, there is greater potential to escape from declining prospects in a business, an option particularly attractive when a firm's alternative businesses offer large discrepancies in the current or future payoffs (Anand & Singh, 1997; Matsusaka, 2001). It should be more valuable in turbulent and unpredictable environments.

Surely, internal resource transfer (i.e., redeployment) is only one available alternative when a resource is not in its highest and best use. The firm could also (a) expand use of the resource in its current use, (b) share the resource with another business, (c) transfer the resource via the external market (i.e., through acquisitions, divestments, alliances), (d) or no longer use the resource. So, it is imperative that resource redeployment be compared against these alternative forms of resource reconfiguration (Karim & Capron, 2015). Research has studied the first two applications in depth, finding that expanded resource use often results in economies of scale, and sharing resources may result in synergies. Significant work has also explored the decisions to externally reconfigure resources with parties outside the firm.[3] We have made far less progress in understanding how, when, and why firms internally transfer resources across businesses, products, or business models which, for purposes of this volume, we refer to as redeployment.

It is worth discriminating between *resource redeployment* and *having the potential for resource redeployment*. Resource redeployment enables the alternative business to benefit from greater efficiency or higher willingness-to-pay than is available through acquisition of external resources. Having potential to redeploy, however, is the essence of flexibility and underlies why the potential to achieve inter-temporal economies of scope is important for understanding the multi-business firm. Accordingly, while resource redeployment may or may not occur, the absence of redeployment does not disavow the potential for multi-business firms to create value through inter-temporal economies of scope.

Several elements of this theory are unique from alternative theories of value creation by the multi-business firm. However, ascertaining theoretical and empirical uniqueness is challenging in the absence of clear criteria for differentiating alternative hypotheses. To promote fertility in the research process, we begin by clarifying several important theoretical criteria relative to alternative theories explaining corporate value.

Inter-Temporal Economies of Scope versus Intra-Temporal Economies of Scope

Contributions to the theory of inter-temporal economies of scope are growing, particularly since Helfat and Eisenhardt (2004) clarify that inter-temporal economies are a different explanation for corporate advantage than the way scope economies are typically imagined – where resources are contemporaneously shared across businesses. They emphasize that inter-temporal economies are especially relevant for firms with related businesses, where resources can be redeployed at low adjustment costs. Sakhartov and Folta (2014) extend this logic by suggesting that lower adjustment costs amount to lower sunk re-entry costs, and develop a formal model to value the option to redeploy resources and the path dependence associated with it. It is implied in their model that firms pursuing intra-temporal economies do not incur re-entry costs, but neither can they switch resources between businesses. Sakhartov and Folta (2014) show that lower adjustment costs increase the value of inter-temporal economies of scope, and this advantage is accentuated when a firm's business opportunities are more uncertain. In studying the telecommunications industry, Lieberman, Lee, and Folta (forthcoming) argue that firms with more related businesses should be quicker to exit poorly performing businesses, because they have fewer sunk costs coming from more options to redeploy. This argument is counter-intuitive to the idea that greater portfolio relatedness should decrease exit because of greater intra-temporal economies of scope.

Levinthal and Wu (2010) suggest that the types of resources used to capture inter-temporal economies should be different than those used for intra-temporal economies. They argue that inter-temporal economies require that resources have capacity constraints, such that use in one business precludes it from use in another business. Allocations of resources with capacity constraints, termed non-scale-free resources, incur opportunity costs. In contrast, scale-free resources can be allocated contemporaneously across businesses without opportunity cost.

Organizational structure and control systems are expected to differ substantially across organizations pursuing inter-temporal economies versus intra-temporal economies (Helfat & Eisenhardt, 2004). One implication from this insight is that it might not be easy to switch between strategies because changing structure and control is costly.

The argument that both inter-temporal and intra-temporal economies increase when corporate portfolios are more related is curious in several respects. First, as noted by Sakhartov and Folta (2014), the relatively strong evidence that more related diversification creates more value has been interpreted as evidence of intra-temporal economies, when perhaps it should be attributable to inter-temporal economies, or both. Second, it suggests developing a more nuanced understanding about the theoretical determinants of both. Finally, we need more clarity about how to empirically disentangle one type of economy from another.

Inter-Temporal Economies of Scope versus Internal Capital Markets

The theory of internal capital markets advocates that multi-business firms might have advantages in allocating capital more efficiently than the external market. This will be the case if the firm has better information than outsiders about a business opportunity, and is more willing to allocate capital to the opportunity. Fundamentally, the theory is about one type of resource – capital. A theory of inter-temporal economies of scope is similar in one important respect: it is pertinent when internal markets are more efficient than external markets. If there are no efficiency differences between internal and external markets, then inter-temporal economies do not exist and firms could instead acquire resources from the external market. The theory of inter-temporal economies of scope is different from the theory of internal capital markets in that it focuses on non-financial resources. This is pertinent because it encompasses drivers of corporate value beyond information asymmetry. Redeployment of non-financial resources usually requires adjustment to resources, whereas cash does not. As noted earlier, adjustment costs invite consideration of path dependence. Whether adjustment costs are a function of resource characteristics or firm capability should be given stronger consideration in the literature.

Inter-Temporal Economies of Scope versus Institutional Voids

Khanna and Palepu (1997) argue that diversified firms might have higher returns in emerging markets where their internal markets are more efficient than external markets because of institutional voids in the economy. For example, when an economy has weak education or certification institutions for training potential employees, a firm might be able to replace these institutions with a strong training program that creates a robust internal labor market. There are strong similarities between this theory and the theory around inter-temporal economies of scope. Both emphasize that corporate scope might be extended when internal resource markets are more efficient than external resource markets. Emerging markets are certainly one context where such discrepancies are likely to exist, and institutional voids are a helpful framework with which to pinpoint them. A key difference is that the theory of institutional voids does not explicitly concern itself with when resources might be redeployed across businesses, and does not incorporate adjustment costs and inducements.

Inter-Temporal Economies of Scope versus Diversification of Risk

Lewellen (1971) argues that firms might benefit from diversification if it lowers the corporation's variability in earnings such that it reduces borrowing costs. This theory portrays an indirect relationship between risk and value creation: risk reduction lowers borrowing costs which creates value. Sakhartov and Folta (2014) found that when firms have portfolios that are more inversely correlated, their inducements for switching resources between businesses are greater because if one business declines, another will be increasing. Instead, if businesses are positively correlated, a decline in one business does not present opportunities to profitably redeploy to similarly declining businesses. Portfolios with inversely correlated businesses will generally have lower risk associated with them, but the theory of inter-temporal economies of scope suggests a direct relationship between risk reduction and corporate value.

In summary, this section has explained how inter-temporal economies of scope create value for the multi-business firm and compared it to existing theories that inform when corporate advantage might occur.

THE CONTRIBUTIONS IN THIS VOLUME

The papers following this introduction represent significant extensions to the theory and empirical understanding of inter-temporal scope economies. Here we present the rationale for our enthusiasm for each. You will note that the majority of papers directly speak to the topic of resource redeployment. Others consider alternative forms of reconfiguration, and have indirect implications for a theory of resource redeployment.

The paper by Hannah, Bremner, and Eisenhardt (2016) is noteworthy because it helps build understanding of how ecosystem firms – whose components have "consumption-side" inter-dependence – might benefit from inter-temporal economies of scope. This context is important and fascinating because such firms often have components that are positively correlated, a condition that prior work has noted should lead to few inducements for resource redeployment. Through an inductive case study of an entrepreneurial firm in the U.S. residential solar industry, they uncover that ecosystem firms might have two unique forms of inducements – improving the capabilities of lagging components and relieving bottlenecks. Moreover, like Miller and Yang (2016), they provide evidence that resource-constrained firms are likely to redeploy, and suggest inter-temporal economies may be particularly valuable for entrepreneurial firms because of their limited resources.

Miller and Yang (2016) develop some much-needed stylized facts for the study of resource redeployment. While they do not measure resource redeployment directly, they look for empirical evidence in Corptech data in cases of product turnover – where a firm simultaneously dropped and added a product in the same year. Such simultaneous events, they reason, are likely to be at least partially the result of managers seeking efficient resource allocation through redeployment. To buttress these claims, they run multivariate models to identify whether inducements for resource redeployment are related to product turnover. Prior work has only theorized about this relationship. Moreover, they find some evidence that resource-constrained firms are most likely to exploit inducements, and that some scale-free resources may in fact be redeployed rather than shared contemporaneously, providing an important qualification to the arguments of Levinthal and Wu (2010). The approach taken by these authors to develop stylized facts is sorely needed in the theory of inter-temporal economies of scope.

Lee and Parachuri (2016) offer another empirical contribution to the understanding of how inducements contribute to inter-temporal economies of scope. The threat of technological substitution creates an inducement for resource redeployment to alternative opportunities, and the authors use content analysis of media announcements to identify such threats in the internet infrastructure industry. This approach offers a novel way to empirically identify inducements. Their finding that inducements take on more importance for entry into related markets offers empirical evidence consistent with prior work. They also offer evidence that resource commitments in an industry escalate a firm's proclivity to respond to inducements.

Ahuja and Novelli (2016) consider that the theory of redeployment might be applicable to single business firms that have potential to switch between business models that target different consumer types. This emphasis is similar to other work that considers that inter-temporal economies exist in a less-aggregated context than a business unit, such as the product type (Miller & Yang, 2016) or the patent class (Blit, Liu, & Mitchell, 2016; Dothan & Lavie, 2016). Their emphasis on consumption-side economies rather than production-side economies is similar to that of Hannah et al. (2016).

Anand, Kim, and Lu (2016) offer a comprehensive framework for diagnosing the factors determining the preference for resource sharing versus resource redeployment. Consequently, they address a considerable gap in the literature that is struggling to develop a comprehensive understanding of when to share and when to redeploy. Four resource characteristics are fundamental to their framework: fungibility, scale-free nature, decomposability, and tradability. The framework is not only important for directing practitioners in their resource decisions, but it also provides an agenda for researchers.

The following three papers are generally concerned with resource reconfiguration, but have strong implications for redeployment.

Blit et al. (2016) suggest that redeployment is evident not only in the breadth of firm scope but also in its turnover of activities as embodied in how actively a firm reconfigures its resource base. The idea that corporate scope should affect the potential for resource redeployment is noted in prior work. However, these authors emphasize that two firms with the same scope over time might have two completely different profiles for how resources are reconfigured. They provide examples with patenting activities in the consumer electronics and pharmaceutical industries.

McGrath and Singh (2016) contribute to our understanding of the relative efficiency of internal versus external resource transfers. In particular, they provide some context for when external transfers are efficient because they have an external reconfiguration capability. It is implied that resource redeployment, which involves internal transfers, is less suitable for firms with such capabilities. They suggest that resource-based theory, dynamic capabilities, and transaction cost theory help to illuminate how firms might develop external reconfiguration capabilities.

Rindova, Martins, and Yeow (2016) track how Google and Yahoo build capabilities in their first 10 years, serving as platforms for growth. In their paper, resource redeployments are an important complement to external resource acquisition strategies. As such, a key contribution is that they consider how firms manage their portfolio of "sensing" and "seizing" activities to position themselves for growth. Through an inductive case study, they also note how resource reconfiguration strategies differ across time.

The following two papers explore whether behavioral theory might explain resource redeployment and reconfiguration.

Dushnitsky and Kleuter (2016) challenge the assumption that corporate strategists are always aware of opportunities to redeploy resources. This is relevant because a theory of inter-temporal economies of scope breaks down if managers do not know the extent to which resources can be redeployed. They look for evidence of their claims in how many commercial applications firms deploy their patented technology. Their key argument is that routines may create a behavioral bias that may limit a firm's awareness of where to deploy general technologies, and find evidence in support of this with interesting data. This finding certainly invites consideration that behavioral theory has something to say about reaping inter-temporal economies.

Dothan and Lavie (2016) explore whether resource reconfiguration is driven by performance relative to behavioral aspirations. As such, the paper is important because it is only a small leap to suggest that the behavioral theory of the firm may have some import in the study of redeployment. Noteworthy is their attempt to empirically measure redeployment of intellectual property and tease apart whether the performance feedback works differently for redeployment versus co-deployment, where the latter represents resource sharing or synergy. They find empirical evidence consistent with their theory.

Argilés-Bosch, Garcia-Blandon, and Martinez-Blasco (2016) develop a basic hypothesis that less-constrained resources are easier to redeploy. This is consistent with the view that resources requiring more adjustment will decrease their flexibility and value associated with redeployment. Accordingly, they expect that less-constrained resources will lead to higher profitability. They find evidence of this in a large sample from Compustat.

EDITORIAL PERSPECTIVE

In this section we reflect on the collection of work in the volume and offer our own views on directions needed to clarify how a theory of resource redeployment contributes to our understanding of the multi-business firm.

A critical starting point is to develop stylized facts around resource redeployment. Because they represent internal transactions, it is extraordinarily difficult to observe redeployments in secondary data. This represents a considerable obstacle in empirical testing of this theory. Noteworthy are the indirect approaches using product turnover by Miller and Yang (2016) and Blit et al. (2016) to triangulate when redeployments might be occurring. To the extent that redeployment is an unobservable choice preferred when internal switching costs are lower than external acquisition costs, future work might consider the method used by Masten, Meehan, and Snyder (1991) to diagnose the determinants of unobservable internal transaction costs. While additional indirect approaches are encouraged to empirically test the theory, direct observations of redeployments are preferable. Doing so may initially require in-depth case studies, as provided by Hannah et al. (2016) and Rindova et al. (2016). This process may yield insight about measurement that can then be extended to secondary data. It is clear that much needs to be done in this domain to understand the extent to which redeployment is used. We emphatically encourage scholars to uncover simple descriptive analysis of redeployment. If we gain clarity on when redeployment is used, we can pursue with more confidence why and how it is different from alternative explanations of value creation by the multi-business firm.

A theme emerging in several papers is the role of inducements that encourage resource redeployment. These efforts contribute by offering novel ideas for how to operationalize inducements. For example, Hannah et al. (2016) look at changing regulation as an inducement for redeploying human capital across state operations. Miller and Yang (2016) consider that there are greater inducements to redeploy the further a product's growth rate exceeds the growth rates of a firm's other products. Lee and Parachuri (2016) consider that technological discontinuities are an inducement to redeploy to new businesses, and collect evidence of discontinuities through content analysis of media announcements. These approaches might be adopted and expanded in future research to better understand the role of inducements in spurring redeployment. To the extent that inducements do not drive redeployment, we should look to alternative explanations through agency theory or behavioral theory.

Another common theme among the papers is whether an argument for resource redeployment applies only to non-scale-free resources, as argued by Levinthal and Wu (2010). Miller and Yang (2016) find evidence that resource-constrained firms are more likely to be induced to simultaneously exit and enter product markets, an activity they believe signals redeployment. Smaller firms and private firms are shown to be more likely to have product turnover when there is greater divergence in product growth rates, even though firms with lower financial slack do not respond similarly to such inducements. This suggests that smaller and private firms redeploy scale-free resources, even though these are the types of resources that Levinthal and Wu (2010) suggest would be shared contemporaneously. The paper by Argilés-Bosch et al. (2016) finds that firms perform better when they have less-constrained resources. The inductive case study of the solar industry by Hannah et al. (2016) also reveals that more entrepreneurial firms, which generally have more resource constraints, are more likely to redeploy resources. These three studies represent the first attempts to empirically examine the relationship between resource constraints and redeployment, and, accordingly make an important contribution. A more direct test of the theory elaborated by Levinthal and Wu (2010) would focus on whether non-scale-free or scale-free resources are redeployed and under which conditions.

In aggregate, the volume speaks to the potential breadth of the theory of inter-temporal economies of scope. It is clear that redeployment is not merely a feature of firms with multiple business units, where resources are transferrable across business units, but also a feature of multi-product firms (Blit et al., 2016; Miller & Yang, 2016), multi-technology firms (Lee & Parachuri, 2016), multi-geography firms (Hannah et al., 2016), and firms with multiple business models (Ahuja & Novelli, 2016). All these scenarios offer flexibility to internally transfer resources over time, depending on adjustment costs and inducements for doing so.

The theory has been cast as pertinent to multi-business firms, but it is certain that all multi-business firms began as single business firms. Might gaining the potential for inter-temporal economies of scope induce entry into a second business. The combination of adjustment costs and inducements will be the basis for gaining such inter-temporal economies (Sakhartov & Folta, 2015), along with the condition that firms are differentially positioned to benefit from such economies. It is not an extreme leap to consider that these same criteria might induce entry into a third or a fourth business. Or to consider that changing criteria might induce exit from a business. This suggests that the pursuit of inter-temporal economies of scope has potential to explain firm evolution (Rindova et al., 2016). Much more research is needed here.

A vitally important theme is understanding the locus of inter-temporal economies of scope. What is the extent to which it is tied to the characteristics of a firm's resources (Anand et al., 2016), the markets a firm occupies (Blit et al., 2016; Miller & Yang, 2016), or a firm's capability to transfer resources or scout opportunities for redeployment (Dushnitsky & Kleuter, 2016)? Future work should more explicitly enlighten the sources of differential firm ability to manage adjustment costs and position the firm to capitalize on inducements.

CONCLUSION

Resource redeployment is an emerging topic in corporate strategy, and underlies inter-temporal economies of scope. While inter-temporal economies are pertinent in both single and multi-business firms, we emphasize the uniqueness of this theory from alternative explanations of how multi-business firms create value and influence firm evolution. The 11 papers following this one offer valuable extensions to this literature and a guidepost for scholars seeking to enrich it further.

NOTES

1. We adopt the same criteria for sample inclusion as Villalonga (2004).

2. While McGahan and Porter (1997) uncover that only 4.3 percent of business segment profitability is attributable to the corporate parent, the total corporate effect is actually around 10 percent when including the interaction effect (of 5.51 percent) between the corporate parent and the industry. By comparison, the majority of business segment profitability is attributable to the business segment (31.7 percent) and the industry (18.7 percent). Roquebert, Phillips, and Westfall (1996) find a corporate effect of 18 percent when excluding single business firms, because their effects are otherwise attributable to the business.

3. Reconfiguration involves the choices made by firms to add (either through internal development, acquisitions, or alliances), delete, or recombine resources and businesses (Karim & Capron, 2015). This body of work has emphasized how, and under what conditions, the proactive process of reconfiguration may benefit firms. For example, Capron (1999), Capron, Dussauge, and Mitchell (1998), and Karim and Mitchell (2000) show how resource reallocation between targets and acquirers can create value subsequent to acquisitions. Karim (2009) and Karim and Kaul (2015) examine how business unit recombinations (and the bringing together of their underlying resources) may impact innovation and the creation of new patent resources. Other resources that may be reconfigured in their use are executives; Karim and Williams (2012) explore how executives both within the firm and newly joining the firm via acquisition may be transferred within the organization and influence structural reorganization. While redeployment is one form of internal reconfiguration, the two are not synonymous. Other forms of internal reconfiguration may involve, for example, recombination within the firm.

ACKNOWLEDGMENTS

We gratefully acknowledge the University of Strasbourg Institute for Advanced Study (USIAS), which recognized Professor Folta as a 2013–2016 USIAS Fellow. USIAS generously provided financial and administrative resources to host a November 2015 conference titled "Corporate Strategy and Resource Redeployment" in Strasbourg France for all volume participants. Special gratitude also goes to BETA (Bureau d'Economie Théorique et Appliquée), which regularly hosted Professor Folta, and especially Patrick Llerena, Robin Cowan, Bertrand Koebel, and Thierry Burger-Helmchen. USIAS colleagues Rifka Weehuizen and Etienne Franchineau also provided valuable assistance throughout this project. Monique Flasaquier created a flawless conference program. The editors also acknowledge the support and encouragement of Brian Silverman.

REFERENCES

Ahuja, G., & Novelli, E. (2016). Incumbent responses to an entrant with a new business model: Resource co-deployment and resource re-deployment strategies. In T. B. Folta, C. E. Helfat, & S. Karime (Eds.), *Resource redeployment and corporate strategy* (Vol. 35). Advances in Strategic Management. Bingley, UK: Emerald Group Publishing Limited.

Anand, J., Kim, H., & Lu, S. (2016). Resource characteristics and redeployment strategies: Towards a theoretical synthesis. In T. B. Folta, C. E. Helfat, & S. Karime (Eds.), *Resource redeployment and corporate strategy* (Vol. 35). Advances in Strategic Management. Bingley, UK: Emerald Group Publishing Limited.

Anand, J., & Singh, H. (1997). Asset redeployment, acquisitions and corporate strategy in declining industries. *Strategic Management Journal*, Summer Special Issue, *18*(S1), 99–118.

Argilés-Bosch, J., Garcia-Blandón, J., & Martínez-Blasco, M. (2016). The impact of absorbed and unabsorbed slack on firm profitability: Implications for resource redeployment. In T. B. Folta, C. E. Helfat, & S. Karime (Eds.), *Resource redeployment and corporate strategy* (Vol. 35). Advances in Strategic Management. Bingley, UK: Emerald Group Publishing Limited.

Berger, P. G., & Ofek, E. (1995). Diversification's effect on firm value. *Journal of Financial Economics*, *37*, 39–65.

Blit, J., Liu, C. C., & Mitchell, W. (2016). What goes on beneath the surface of reconfiguration? The impact of redeployment via activity addition and subtraction on firm scope and turnover. In T. B. Folta, C. E. Helfat, & S. Karime (Eds.), *Resource redeployment and corporate strategy* (Vol. 35). Advances in Strategic Management. Bingley, UK: Emerald Group Publishing Limited.

Bowman, E. H., & Helfat, C. E. (2001). Does corporate strategy matter? *Strategic Management Journal*, *22*(1), 1–23.

Capron, L. (1999). The long-term performance of horizontal acquisitions. *Strategic Management Journal*, *20*(11), 987–1018.

Capron, L., Dussauge, P., & Mitchell, W. (1998). Resource redeployment following horizontal acquisitions in Europe and North America, 1988–1992. *Strategic Management Journal*, *19*(7), 631–661.

Dothan, A., & Lavie, D. (2016). Resource reconfiguration: Learning from performance feedback. In T. B. Folta, C. E. Helfat, & S. Karime (Eds.), *Resource redeployment and corporate strategy* (Vol. 35). Advances in Strategic Management. Bingley, UK: Emerald Group Publishing Limited.

Hannah, D. P., Bremner, R. P., & Eisenhardt, K. M. (2016). Resource redeployment in business ecosystems. In T. B. Folta, C. E. Helfat, & S. Karime (Eds.), *Resource redeployment and corporate strategy* (Vol. 35). Advances in Strategic Management. Bingley, UK: Emerald Group Publishing Limited.

Helfat, C. E., & Eisenhardt, K. M. (2004). Inter-temporal economies of scope, organizational modularity, and the dynamics of diversification. *Strategic Management Journal*, *25*(13), 1217–1232.

Khanna, T., & Palepu, K. (1997). Why focused strategies may be wrong for emerging markets. *Harvard Business Review*, *July–August*, 3–10.

Karim, S. (2009). Business unit reorganization and innovation in new product markets. *Management Science*, *55*(7), 1237–1254.

Karim, S., & Capron, L. (2015). Reconfiguration: Adding, redeploying, recombining, and divesting resources and business units. *Strategic Management Society Virtual Special Issue Introduction*. Retrieved from http://onlinelibrary.wiley.com/journal/10.1002/(ISSN)1097-0266/homepage/reconfiguration_vsi_introduction.htm

Karim, S., & Kaul, A. (2015). Structural recombination and innovation: Unlocking internal knowledge synergy through structural change. *Organization Science*, *26*(2), 439–455.

Karim, S., & Mitchell, W. (2000). Path-dependent and path-breaking change: reconfiguring business resources following acquisitions in the US medical sector, 1978–1995. *Strategic Management Journal*, *21*(10–11), 1061–1081.

Karim, S., & Williams, C. (2012). Structural knowledge: How executive experience with structural composition affects intrafirm mobility and unit reconfiguration. *Strategic Management Journal*, *33*(6), 681–709.

Kleuter, T., & Dushnitsky, G. (2016). Linking technologies to applications – Insights from online markets for technology. In T. B. Folta, C. E. Helfat, & S. Karime (Eds.), *Resource redeployment and corporate strategy* (Vol. 35). Advances in Strategic Management. Bingley, UK: Emerald Group Publishing Limited.

Lang, L. H. P., & Stulz, R. M. (1994). Tobin's Q, corporate diversification, and firm performance. *Journal of Political Economy*, *102*, 1248–1280.

Lee, G. K., & Parachuri, S. (2016). Resource redeployment through exit and entry: Threats of substitution as inducements. In Folta, Helfat, & Karim (Eds.), *Resource redeployment and corporate strategy* (Vol. 35). Advances in Strategic Management. Bingley, UK: Emerald Group Publishing Limited.

Levinthal, D. A., & Wu, B. (2010). Opportunity costs and non-scale free capabilities: Profit maximization, corporate scope, and profit margins. *Strategic Management Journal*, *31*, 780–801.

Lewellen, W. G. (1971). A pure financial rationale for the conglomerate merger. *Journal of Finance*, *26*, 521–537.

Lieberman, M., Lee, G., & Folta, T. B. (forthcoming). Entry, exit, and potential for resource redeployment. *Strategic Management Journal*.

Masten, S. E., Meehan, J. W., & Snyder, E. A. (1991). Costs of organization. *Journal of Law, Economics and Organization*, *7*(1), 1–25.

Matsusaka, J. G. (2001). Corporate diversification, value maximization, and organizational capabilities. *Journal of Business*, *74*(3), 409–431.

Matsusaka, J. G., & Nanda, V. (2002). Internal capital markets and corporate refocusing. *Journal of Financial Intermediation*, *11*(2), 176–211.

Mcgahan, A. M., & Porter, M. E. (1997). How much does industry matter, really? *Strategic Management Journal*, *18*, 15–30.

McGrath, P. J., & Singh, H. (2016). Resource reconfiguration and transactions across firm boundaries: The roles of firm capabilities and market factors. In T. B. Folta, C. E. Helfat, & S. Karime (Eds.), *Resource redeployment and corporate strategy* (Vol. 35). Advances in Strategic Management. Bingley, UK: Emerald Group Publishing Limited.

Miller, D. J., & Yang, H. (2016). Product turnover: Simultaneous product market entry and exit. In T. B. Folta, C. E. Helfat, & S. Karime (Eds.), *Resource redeployment and corporate strategy* (Vol. 35). Advances in Strategic Management. Bingley, UK: Emerald Group Publishing Limited.

Penrose, E. T. (1959). *The theory of the growth of the firm*. New York, NY: Wiley.
Rindova, V. P., Martins, L. L., & Yeow, A. (2016). The hare and the fast tortoise: Dynamic resource reconfiguration and the pursuit of new growth opportunities by Yahoo and Google (1995–2007). In T. B. Folta, C. E. Helfat, & S. Karime (Eds.). *Resource redeployment and corporate strategy* (Vol. 35). Advances in Strategic Management. Bingley, UK: Emerald Group Publishing Limited.
Roquebert, J. A., Phillips, R. L., & Westfall, P. A. (1996). Markets vs. management: What 'Drives' profitability? *Strategic Management Journal, 17*(8), 653–664.
Rumelt, R. P. (1974). *Strategy, structure and economic performance*. Boston, MA: Division of Research, Harvard Business School.
Sakhartov, A. V., & Folta, T. B. (2014). Resource relatedness, redeployability, and firm value. *Strategic Management Journal, 35*, 1781–1797.
Sakhartov, A. V., & Folta, T. B. (2015). Getting beyond relatedness as a driver of corporate value. *Strategic Management Journal, 36*(13), 1939–1959.
Villalonga, B. (2004). Does diversification cause the "diversification discount"? *Financial Management, 59*(2), 5–27.
Williamson, O. (1975). *Markets and hierarchies*. New York, NY: Free Press.

RESOURCE REDEPLOYMENT IN BUSINESS ECOSYSTEMS

Douglas P. Hannah, Robert P. Bremner and Kathleen M. Eisenhardt

ABSTRACT

This paper addresses resource redeployment in ecosystems. Prior research examines the value of resource redeployment across product markets in multi-business firms. In contrast, resource redeployment across ecosystems is an important corporate strategy employed by both single- and multi-business ecosystem firms that has received little attention. To address this gap, we present a case study of resource redeployment by an entrepreneurial firm in the US residential solar industry. We propose that the value creation mechanisms (i.e., improving capabilities, bottleneck relief) are fundamentally different when resources are redeployed in ecosystems. We identify "consumption-side" interdependence of components and "production-side" resource relatedness as playing critical roles in both types of value creation and propose conditions under which resource redeployment is most valuable. Overall, we contribute insights into the literatures on resource redeployment and strategy in business ecosystems.

Keywords: Redeployment; ecosystems; bottlenecks; capabilities; case study; solar

Resource Redeployment and Corporate Strategy
Advances in Strategic Management, Volume 35, 19–48

ISSN: 0742-3322/doi:10.1108/S0742-332220160000035003

INTRODUCTION

While it has long been recognized that firms create value through the deployment of resources, scholars have only recently explored the *redeployment* of resources. Redeployment is the partial or complete withdrawal of resources from one business followed by the reallocation, rather than divestment, of those resources into another business (Helfat & Eisenhardt, 2004). Redeployment allows firms to create value by allocating resources to their most productive applications (Galunic & Eisenhardt, 1996, 2001). A key driver of value creation via redeployment is inter-temporal economies of scope – that is, cost savings associated with reassigning existing resources to new uses, rather than obtaining entirely new resources (Helfat & Eisenhardt, 2004). Building on this concept, research recently unpacks the mechanisms by which resource redeployment create value and the conditions under which resource redeployment is most valuable (Sakhartov & Folta, 2014, 2015). This work confirms that resource redeployment allows firms to maximize returns by entering and exiting markets such that they capture the relative returns advantages of one market over another. Overall, redeployment is an important source of value creation over time in multi-business firms, particularly when product markets are uncertain and their resources are related (Helfat & Eisenhardt, 2004).

But resource redeployment may also be an important strategy in ecosystem firms. Ecosystems are networks of firms that offer discrete products or services that collectively form a valuable solution (Adner, 2012; Jacobides, Knudsen, & Augier, 2006). The smartphone ecosystem, for example, includes operating systems, handset manufacturers, network carriers, and applications developers – each of which provides a key component of the smartphone. Central to ecosystems is what we term "consumption-side" interdependence.[1] By consumption-side interdependence, we mean that the value of one firm's product depends on the availability and performance of complementary products or services that collectively comprise a valuable solution. If a single component falters, then the other components suffer because there is no longer an adequate complete solution. As a result, the performance of firms in one component depends on to the performance of firms in other components (Adner, 2012; Adner & Kapoor, 2010; Ozcan & Eisenhardt, 2009).

The extant literature examines redeployment in multi-business firms where product markets are largely independent, their returns may be negatively correlated, and their resources are often related (Anand & Singh, 1997; Galunic & Eisenhardt, 1996; Sakhartov & Folta, 2014). A next step is to explore redeployment in a novel and contrasting context: ecosystem firms where components have "consumption-side" interdependence, their returns are often positively correlated, and their resources likely have varied relatedness. Ecosystems present distinctive strategic challenges because successful strategy requires envisioning the entire ecosystem (Ozcan & Eisenhardt, 2009), or what Adner (2012) terms the "wide lens" rather than simply a single business. With this in mind, we ask: *How and when does resource redeployment influence firm value in ecosystems?*

We examine our question using an in-depth, inductive case study of an entrepreneurial firm in the US residential solar industry. Inductive case methods are particularly appropriate when theory and evidence are limited, and the research addresses a process question (Eisenhardt & Graebner, 2007). The US residential solar industry is a prototypical ecosystem composed of multiple distinct components. Combining fieldwork and archival data, we track our focal firm from its founding in 2007 through 2014, a period of extreme industry uncertainty. Since our focal firm engaged in multiple redeployments with varying success, we can likely isolate value creation mechanisms underlying resource redeployment in ecosystems.

We contribute to the literatures on resource redeployment and ecosystems. First, we identify the unique inducements for resource redeployment within ecosystems. Prior research on the inducements focuses on comparing market returns in multi-business firms: current returns, volatility of returns, and negatively correlated returns (Helfat & Eisenhardt, 2004; Sakhartov & Folta, 2015). In contrast, inducements in ecosystems turn on how redeployment improves returns in the focal component by: improving the capabilities of lagging components and relieving bottlenecks. Second, we clarify the conditions under which resource redeployment is likely to be of greatest value such as evolving markets, and when it is likely to be most effective. Third, we introduce a key concept, "consumption-side" interdependence, and distinguish it from "returns" interdependence and "production-side" resource relatedness. We add the insight that resource-constrained firms are particularly likely to engage in redeployment. Overall, we contribute to theory on both resource redeployment and strategy in business ecosystems. Despite conditions like varied resource relatedness and correlated market returns that should diminish redeployment, we outline how redeployment is an effective corporate strategy in ecosystem firms.

THEORETICAL BACKGROUND

Resource redeployment is the partial or complete withdrawal of resources from one business followed by the reallocation of those resources into another business (Helfat & Eisenhardt, 2004). Redeployment allows firms to capture "inter-temporal economies of scope" – that is, the cost savings that result from sharing resources over time by exiting one business and entering a more attractive one, rather than developing entirely new resources. Since it allows firms to apply resources in their most productive product-market uses over time, redeployment is an important corporate strategy when firms operate in uncertain industries – that is, where product markets are frequently emerging, growing, splitting and declining (Galunic & Eisenhardt, 1996, 2001). Redeployment contrasts with synergy, a standard approach to corporate value creation (Helfat & Eisenhardt, 2004; Martin & Eisenhardt, 2010; Sakhartov & Folta, 2014). Synergy relies on the well-known concept of "intra-temporal economies of scope" – that is, the cost savings associated with sharing resources *simultaneously* across businesses. In contrast, redeployment relies on sharing resources *over time* by exiting and entering businesses.

The literature offers several empirical examples of resource redeployment. This work typically conceptualizes redeployment as a strategy by which firms can maximize performance by continually realigning their business unit portfolios with the most attractive product-market opportunities and simultaneously reallocating resources among the business units to fit this alignment (Eisenhardt & Brown, 1999). For example, Karim and Mitchell (2004) find that Johnson & Johnson purposefully reconfigured its existing business units in order to search for new business opportunities. Similarly, Karim (2006) studies 250 medical industry firms and finds that medical industry firms engage in substantial reconfiguration in order to reallocate internal resources, while Kaul (2012) observes the same in a sample of about 5,000 US manufacturing firms. A key insight is that modular organization through a multiple business M-form makes redeployment easier as firms can more readily exit one business and enter another (Helfat & Eisenhardt, 2004).

Redeployment is particularly relevant in *uncertain markets* where product-market opportunities frequently emerge, change, combine, split, and disappear (Galunic & Eisenhardt, 1996; Karim, 2009; Karim & Kaul, 2014). For example, Galunic and Eisenhardt (2001) examine the "charter change" process by which executives frequently realigned business-units and their resources to address rapidly changing product-market opportunities. In this extraordinarily successful Fortune 100 technology firm, executives reassigned resources to address new business opportunities, realigned their match of business-unit resources with product markets, and moved resources from declining businesses. These redeployments enabled the firm to match its resources with superior product-market opportunities even as those opportunities changed. Similarly, Karim,

Carroll, and Long (2015) track 46 medical device firms, and find that executives engaged in redeployment when industry uncertainty was high in order to improve fit with the environment.

Redeployment is also particularly relevant for specific types of *resources*. When resources have greater "production-side" relatedness across product markets, they are likely to be highly useful across applications and so relevant to redeployment (Sakhartov & Folta, 2014). This relatedness ensures low readjustment costs of resources between product markets and so makes redeployment advantageous over other approaches to obtaining resources such as acquisition or building from scratch (Helfat & Eisenhardt, 2004). Relatedness also enables reversibility by which firms can move resources back and forth among uses. Such reversibility is helpful when temporary redeployments are germane (Sakhartov & Folta, 2014). Finally, resource redeployment is relevant for "non-scale-free" resources (i.e., those that cannot be deployed simultaneously across uses because of limited capacity or scalability) (Bryce & Winter, 2009; Levinthal & Wu, 2010), Examples include employees, location-specific assets, and equipment. In contrast, "scale-free" resources such as brands and intellectual property can be simultaneously shared across multiple uses (Panzar & Willig, 1981), and so are relevant to corporate value creation via synergy.

Redeployment creates value when *strong inducements* exist – that is, settings where the relative performance advantages between markets are high (Anand, 2004; Penrose, 1959; Silverman, 1999). Helfat and Eisenhardt (2004) highlight current-returns differences between two markets as a strong inducement. Sakhartov and Folta (2015) analyze data from the US medical device industry and develop a simulation model to unpack further when strong inducements exist. They find that a greater expected returns disparity exists between two markets (i.e., strong inducement) when the new market has: higher current returns (as anticipated by prior research), higher volatility, and higher negatively correlated returns. Interestingly, these three conditions characterize the canonical case of redeployment (Helfat & Eisenhardt, 2004) – that is, related diversified firms in which resources are redeployed as product markets evolve from mature markets to new ones: ones with higher current returns, more volatile returns than mature markets, and negatively correlated returns with mature markets.

Overall, resource redeployment is an important corporate strategy that creates value for firms by allowing them to allocate their resources to their most attractive use over time (Galunic & Eisenhardt, 2001; Helfat & Eisenhardt, 2004; Sakhartov & Folta, 2014). Redeployment is particularly valuable in settings with (1) high uncertainty such that product markets are fluid and evolving, (2) non-scale-free resources with high "production-side" relatedness (low readjustment costs and high reversibility), (3) modular business-unit (M-form) organization, and (4) strong inducements (i.e., high disparity in expected market returns) to enter new markets. To date, redeployment research has focused on multi-business firms in evolving product markets. A next step is to explore redeployment in a contrasting context: ecosystem firms.

Competing in Ecosystem Industries

Ecosystems are networks of firms producing distinct products or services that together comprise a valuable solution (Adner, 2012; Jacobides et al., 2006). Examples include personal computers (hardware, software, and peripherals), smartphones (carriers, handset makers, operating systems, and applications developers), and 3D printing (scanners, materials, modeling software and printers). Ecosystems are characterized by high consumption-side interdependence. That is, the value of any individual component depends on the performance, availability, and interface with the other components of the ecosystem (Adner, 2012; Moore, 1993).

Ecosystems are shaped by an *industry architecture* that defines the roles and relationships among firms (Jacobides et al., 2006). This architecture is, in effect, the "blueprint" for interactions among component firms (Ozcan & Eisenhardt, 2009). Firms in different components often come from diverse industries, and as such may rely on resources that exhibit little "production-side" resource relatedness (Bremner, Eisenhardt, & Hannah, 2016). For example, the resources of carriers, handset makers, and game developers are largely unrelated in the smartphone ecosystem.

Ecosystems are characterized by both cooperation *and* competition. Since ecosystem firms are highly interdependent, they must work together to create value. As a result, there may be substantial co-specialization and alignment among firms (Bremner et al., 2016). For example, Ozcan and Eisenhardt (2009) describe how a game publisher, carrier, and software platform provider engaged in substantial co-specialization and alignment. This self-named "unholy trinity" ultimately came to dominate the nascent mobile gaming ecosystem. Interdependence also drives the emergence of bottleneck components that can impede the performance of the entire ecosystem (Adner, 2012). For example, Adner and Kapoor (2010) find that technological bottlenecks in complementary components blocked innovation across the photolithography ecosystem. These bottlenecks allowed the rivals of leading innovators to catch up before the leaders could exploit the advantages of their innovations. In contrast to waiting, firms may also mobilize their resources to address bottlenecks in complementary components. For example, Hannah and Eisenhardt (2016) find that high-performing firms in the nascent residential solar industry ecosystem devoted substantial effort to reducing the innovation challenges faced by their partners or to enter bottlenecks themselves. Similarly, Ethiraj (2007) finds that firms in the PC ecosystem allocate R&D resources (measured by patents) to mitigate bottlenecks in complementary components. A key insight is that, within ecosystems (unlike independent product markets), the ability of a firm to succeed in one component depends on both the success in their own component *and* the success of their partners.

Third, while ecosystem partners cooperate to create value, they also compete to capture value (Hannah, 2016). For example, they may jockey to become the "kingpin" firm that dominates the ecosystem (Jacobides & Tae, 2015). This simultaneous collaboration and competition among partners, as well as the importance of complementarity and co-specialization, complicate strategy within ecosystems. Yet despite the likelihood of positively correlated financial returns and weak resource relatedness that should diminish redeployment in ecosystems (Sakhartov & Folta, 2015), the shifting attractiveness of ecosystem components, emergence of bottlenecks, and opportunities for co-innovation across components all suggest that resource redeployment may play a valuable role in ecosystems. A next step is to examine *how* and *when* (if at all) resource redeployment creates corporate value in ecosystem firms. Below, we take this step via a detailed case study of an entrepreneurial firm that competes in the US residential solar ecosystem.

METHODS

Given the limited theory and evidence regarding resource redeployment within ecosystems, we conduct a detailed case study of a single firm (Consumer Solar) competing in the US residential solar industry from 2007 to 2014. We combine both theory-building and theory-elaboration. Case studies are appropriate for under-theorized settings as well as for process research questions such as ours (Eisenhardt, 1989; Langley, 1999). Although single cases sacrifice some generalizability, they also enable rich exploration of a specific setting (Yin, 1994).

We study the US residential solar industry for several reasons. First, this industry is a prototypical ecosystem composed of multiple, distinct components. Specifically, the ecosystem consists of several components which together comprise the overall consumer solar product (i.e., grid-connected solar PV system): (1) solar photovoltaic panels, (2) racking, which is the hardware on which the panels are mounted, (3) sales, including system design, (4) installation, including permitting and supply logistics, and (5) consumer finance (Fig. 1). As in all ecosystems, these components have high "consumption-side" interdependence such that they depend on one another to create a valuable solution. Second, we chose the residential solar industry because of substantial media coverage due to public interest in climate change and well-publicized events (e.g., Solyndra failure). This coverage enabled us to develop a rich history of the industry, from its re-emergence in 2007 through 2014. Third, the residential solar industry is highly uncertain and evolving during our study, making redeployment likely to be an attractive strategy (Helfat & Eisenhardt, 2004; Sakhartov & Folta, 2014). Bottlenecks, for example, shifted. In 2007, finance was the bottleneck with, as an illustration, one analyst calling the lack of consumer financing *"the biggest barrier to adoption."* By 2010, the bottleneck was the sales component, and then

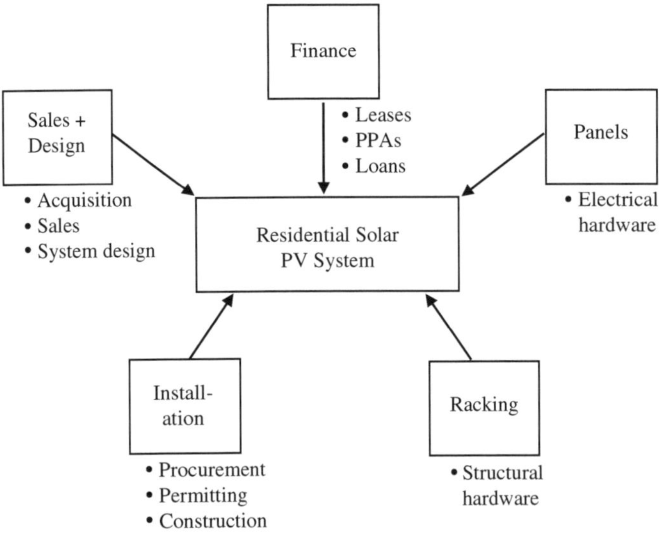

Fig. 1. Residential Solar Photovoltaic (PV) Ecosystem.

installation in 2013. PV panels dramatically dropped in price, and technical innovations in sales and installation occurred. States enacted (and sometimes withdrew) various incentive programs and utility connection policies (e.g., net metering). The industry grew by over 1,500% during our study. But while the industry grew consistently at the national level, the growth of individual state markets was highly uncertain. Overall, the industry was characterized by a highly uncertain evolutionary path.

We study a single entrepreneurial firm, Consumer Solar (pseudonym). We chose this firm for several reasons. First, the firm engaged in several instances of resource redeployment across components and geographies, making it useful for illuminating resource redeployment within ecosystems. Second, it is an entrepreneurial firm, which allows us to track redeployment since birth, and thus avoid left-censoring. Finally, Consumer Solar was a key player in the resurgent US residential solar industry, and so received unusually rich media coverage that we could use to complement our fieldwork. Several founders were particularly active in engaging with the media.

Data Sources

We rely on several data sources, including (1) semi-structured interviews with firm executives, (2) interviews with industry experts, journalists, and competitors, (3) informal follow-up interviews with key respondents, and (4) archival materials, including press releases, recorded interviews, books, analyst reports, and internet resources. These data allowed triangulation among multiple sources, which strengthened data accuracy and inference quality. A particularly valuable source was archival interviews performed by journalists with firm executives from 2007 through 2012. These and other archival sources provided real-time data, relatively free of retrospective bias.

Semi-structured interviews were also a major data source. During 2013 and 2014, we conducted eight in-depth interviews (in waves) with Consumer Solar executives about their company's history, strategy, and key strategic actions. These informants included Consumer Solar's founders and other key executives such as the finance director and a vice-president. We also gathered data from external informants, including both individuals in the industry (e.g., investors and rivals' executives) as well as those with more general industry expertise (e.g., analysts and technology journalists). These external informants provided a highly informed outsider perspective on Consumer Solar, its competitors and the industry that gave us a richer and more complete picture of events.

The interviews had three sections. The first covered informants' background, work history, and role or familiarity with the company. The second section consisted of a detailed narrative of Consumer Solar's history from founding (or last interview) to the time of the interview. This section focused on specific actions, motivations, and implications vis-à-vis the ecosystem. The goal was to understand how and why Consumer Solar addressed each component over time. The third section explored specific issues that arose during the interview or in archival research, and the informant's performance assessment of Consumer Solar and its competitors. Each interview lasted 1−2 hours, and were recorded and transcribed within a day. Follow-up interviews and emails were also used to examine explore particular events more fully.

We took multiple steps to ensure the validity of our data and to minimize informant bias. Interviews were structured to gather specific information and were conducted using techniques such as event tracking and non-directive questioning, which yield more accurate information (Huber, 1985; Huber & Power, 1985). For event tracking, informants walked through the history of the firm to produce a detailed chronology of events (Eisenhardt, 1989). For non-directive questioning, informants were asked to focus on specific facts and events, rather than speculation. We avoided leading questions (e.g., "was the market attractive?"). Furthermore, as described above, we interviewed a wide range of internal and external informants. This diversity of viewpoints provides a more complete and accurate perspective than single informants (Kumar, Stern, & Anderson, 1993). Moreover, all informants were ensured anonymity, which allowed them to speak candidly about the firm's motivations and failures.

Finally, we triangulated between interview and archival data, enabling a rich combination of real-time and retrospective information. The residential solar industry received extensive press coverage throughout the study period. In total, we collected 302 articles (788 pages) and 32 press releases on Consumer Solar, from sources such as the New York Times, Green Tech Media, and Businessweek. These archival data confirmed the interview-based histories and also generated new insights. In combination, our data sources yield a comprehensive and accurate history of Consumer Solar and the US residential solar industry from 2007 to 2014.

Consumer Solar, Inc.

Consumer Solar was founded in 2007 by environmental activists and an investment banker who were motivated to launch a residential solar company to address climate change. In particular, the founders believed that improving the quality and cost of the sales and design component was critical for industry growth. At the time, the sales component was performed by *"mom and pop"* home contractors. As one Consumer Solar executive described, *"There was just nothing simple about it if you were a customer. It was confusing. It was very do-it-yourselfy."* Another executive concurred,

> It's a bunch of men who love their machinery and think that the solar industry is all about the hardware on the roof, whereas it's all about the customer and the service they get. That's the original and blinding insight.

Consumer Solar's vision was to specialize in the sales and design component, which the founders believed would be the most critical component of the ecosystem over the long term. The founders also believed that focus on a single component (i.e., a component strategy) would pay-off. As one stated, *"Installers love to install, sales people love to sell, differentiate, division of labor, do what you're good at."* Thus, their strategy was to rely on partners to provide the remaining hardware, finance, and installation ecosystem components while Consumer Solar was *"using the Internet to change the way solar is sold."* They did the latter by developing an extremely novel, web-enabled sales and design technology that used satellite imagery from Google Earth to create and price solar system designs for homeowners. This greatly streamlined the sales process. Other firms relied on a sales and design process that was largely manual and involved home visits: driving to a prospective customer's house, taking measurements, designing a proposed system, and returning to the "kitchen table" to sell the project. By contrast, Consumer Solar's use of the Internet and satellite imagery enabled the firm to design the system and provide a sales quote in a few hours with no home visit. This drastically cut the cost of sales and design, and the number of necessary sales staff. It freed up the company's limited resources for redeployment to other components.

Consumer Solar maintained this same strategic focus on the sales and design component throughout our study. At the same time, they also engaged in several resource redeployments driven by changes in the residential solar industry. Some addressed emergent bottlenecks in the ecosystem while others addressed the changing geographic attractiveness of various states. Despite these redeployments, Consumer Solar remained committed its sales component strategy. As one executive described:

> [We have] been remarkably true to the original vision. We've had a crew when we need a crew even though we knew we didn't want crews. We've built funds when we needed funds because no one will give us tax equity without our own financial operation. We've gone from that to back to our original vision ... We changed and morphed as required.

By the end of the study, Consumer Solar had emerged as a successful firm in the residential solar industry, ranking among the top 10 in the United States for cumulative sales. In 2014, the company had deployed 20,000 installations, operated in 10 states with approximately 300 employees, and was consistently ranked by experts as being a major player in the industry.

Resource Redeployment at Consumer Solar

Table 1 lists Consumer Solar's redeployment initiatives along with details regarding the resources and ecosystem components involved, rationale for redeployment, and performance. We describe these initiatives in depth below, first focusing on redeployments across ecosystem components over time and then the company's geographic redeployments.

Consumer Solar's 2007 Entry and 2009 Exit from Installation

Although founded to address an innovation opportunity in sales and design, Consumer Solar quickly entered the installation component as well as sales when the company launched in 2007. The founders believed that the installation and sales components were tightly linked such that the payoff from co-innovating across these two components was likely to be high (Hannah, 2016). In other words, performing installations in-house would be essential to improve Consumer Solar's web-based satellite imagery technology for sales and design, and realize its full value. As one executive stated,

> We had to ground proof and test out the remote solar design to make sure it would work. We started with this lab and ran crews for about a year, which allowed us to hone the tool and make sure that the installation systems were feeding back into the design process.

By 2009, Consumer Solar had succeeded in refining its sales and design product (with help from its own installation experience) such that it was

Table 1. Consumer Solar Resource Redeployment Initiatives.

Redeployment Initiative	Logic Type	Resources	From/To	Rationale	Outcome	Representative Quotes
2009 Installation exit	Ecosystem	Installation crew managers	Installation/ sales and design	Improve component	Success	*"You don't get to millions of units of household installation owning your own trucks and ladders."*
2010 Finance entry	Ecosystem	Founding partner, finance and sales associates	Sales and design/ finance	Bottleneck relief	Failure	*"We've built funds when we needed funds because no one would give us tax equity without our own financial operation."* *"We've never believed you build a brand and a customer relation business that is also fundamentally a financial operation. Those two things are different."*
2014 Installation re-entry	Ecosystem	Supply chain facilities and personnel, operations managers	Sales/ installation	Bottleneck relief	Success	*"We drifted too far from the execution, so we now have our own installers, one on each coast that are basically learning labs."*
2011 entry into various state markets, 2011 Colorado exit	Multi-business	Sales, marketing and design teams	Multiple states/ multiple states	Maximize returns	Success	*"When Colorado's subsidy runs out, we just shift our marketing resources to Southern California and that's the end of that. If you then buy distribution centers and trucks and 40 W-2 employees, it gets a much more complicated world to live in."*

superior to that of rivals. As one executive described, *"it (Consumer Solar's sales & design product) is better than if you send the guy on the roof. It's the rules-based software. We've gone through tons of thousands of iterations."* This co-innovation success allowed Consumer Solar to exit the installation component in 2009 and return to its original vision of partnering for the installation component.

This installation exit also freed resources that were previously used for installation for redeployment into sales. Senior managers, on-the-roof installers, and permitting specialists as well as supply chain infrastructure (e.g., procurement and hardware distribution) were redeployed from installation to sales, rather than divested. For example, staff that had previously performed installations were integrated into the sales teams, where they coordinated with their installation partners and ensured a high-quality customer experience. As one executive described, *"we spoke to every single customer on the phone about how their installer experience was. We also inspected every single install."* Other redeployed staff improved operational efficiency in sales. For example, these staff "pre-wrapped" customers for their installation partners, which allowed these installers to concentrate on the "on-the-roof" activities. Ultimately, the redeployment of installation resources to sales allowed Consumer Solar to improve the quality and capacity of its sales and design business.

How did the redeployment of installation resources into sales improve the sales component and create value? First, once the sales and design component was refined, dedicating resources to installation was not as value-creating for sales as it had been. The product was unique and superior to that of rival firms, and additional installation experience was not providing new insights into further improvements. Second, the redeployed staff were able to exploit their acquired knowledge from installation to improve the overall sales experience. This enhanced the Consumer Solar brand through improved quality control, facilitating additional sales growth through referrals. As one executive described, *"It swung around from our core competency being providing a fast quote to providing an all- around good experience, then leveraging our software platform to encourage people to refer their friends."* Third, the redeployed staff also used their knowledge acquired from installation to improve the interface of installation with sales by orchestrating high value-creating partnerships with the installers. Simply put, the redeployed staff's extensive knowledge of installation enabled the company to select better installation partners and work more effectively with them, thereby improving the sales component, its returns, and the overall strength of the ecosystem. Moreover, a key point is that this staff was likely mispriced in the market – that is, these individuals are particularly valuable to Consumer Solar because of their knowledge of the two components and the company itself, and yet Consumer Solar does not have to pay for this additional value.[2] This adds to the attractiveness of redeployment.

Consumer Solar's 2010 Entry and 2014 Exit from Finance

Similar to Consumer Solar's entry into the installation component, the company's 2010 entry into the finance component was motivated by the aim of competing effectively at the sales component and ecosystem levels. However, whereas the entry into installation was driven by an opportunities to co-innovate across the sales and installation components and the redeployment back to sales further improved the sales component with valuable installation knowledge, its entry into finance was driven by finance's role as the key bottleneck to industry growth.

The US residential solar industry experienced a stunning resurgence with the passage of the federal Energy Policy Act of 2005, which allowed firms to claim a 30% tax credit on the installation of residential solar systems. At this time, residential solar systems cost upwards of $20,000, and homeowners paid up front or arranged their own financing. As one industry executive said, "*not being able to pay as you go was the number one most important buying obstacle for customers.*" Another claimed, lack of consumer finance was "*the biggest barrier to adoption.*" Enabled by this tax law change, many firms like Consumer Solar entered the industry. But only a few firms mastered the new ecosystem component, finance. The finance product involved providing solar equipment leases to homeowners, and bundling those leases for investors. This financing eliminated the upfront costs of "going solar" and sparked an industry resurgence that attracted entrepreneurial firms like Consumer Solar.

As early as 2007, Consumer Solar's executives realized that the lack of consumer finance was a bottleneck. However, they chose to focus on the sales and design component because they thought finance would quickly commoditize. As one executive stated, "*This is a new asset class and it's bumpy right now, but over time it's going to be just like anything else .... How are you going to differentiate? Dollars are fungible.*" Moreover, Consumer Solar's executives believed that the finance and sales businesses were too disparate to manage together. As another executive stated, "*We knew right upfront we weren't a financial operation. Notwithstanding [founder]'s acumen, which is great – he is a banker from hell – we didn't want to be a mini-bank.*" Thus, although Consumer Solar had a founder with finance expertise, they chose to wait for partners to develop the finance component.

By 2010, it was clear that finance was not commoditizing as Consumer Solar's executives expected. In fact, it turned out that the finance component was *"phenomenally complex"* – or as another executive described, *"totally mind-numbingly complicated."* Only two firms had succeeded in developing a consumer finance product that took advantage of the 2005 tax law change. These successful finance entrants developed complex instruments that enabled homeowners to lease their solar equipment while investors purchased securitized bundles of these leases. As a result, these firms became sought after partners by firms like Consumer Solar because they provided a zero-cost path for homeowners to buy a solar system. Moreover, this near-monopoly in the bottleneck component allowed the two finance participants to place exorbitant demands on their ecosystem partners like Consumer Solar and capture disproportionate value within the ecosystem.

Wishing to escape the onerous terms of its finance partners, Consumer Solar entered the finance component in 2010. They did so by hiring a CFO who had experience in consumer finance. Apart from this senior hire, however, the finance team was assembled by redeploying Consumer Solar employees. Specifically, the Consumer Solar's investment banker-founder was shifted from being CEO to overseeing the development of the finance component, and some sales staff was redeployed into finance. While redeployment was effective from installation to sales, it was not for sales to finance. Although there was high consumption interdependence (i.e., consumers highly valued finance and sales together) within the residential solar ecosystem, the finance component was highly technical, and drew on capabilities and resources (e.g., investment fund management, tax law) that were mostly unrelated to sales. Sales and finance thus had low resource relatedness. As one executive conceded, *"We didn't invest in building a world class tax equity team because we didn't believe that was where the long term value was."* As a result, Consumer Solar developed an inferior finance component that did not competitively address the finance bottleneck.

More importantly, since finance and sales were interdependent as ecosystem components, offering a non-competitive finance product limited Consumer Solar's success despite its excellent sales and design component. Thus, this redeployment failure in finance ended up limiting the growth of the sales and design component, not just finance. This highlights a distinctive feature of ecosystem strategy: performance depends on assembling a complete ecosystem of valuable components, not just producing a superior single component. As one executive lamented, *"Because of difficulties on the project finance side, it certainly stopped us while we got our tax equity sorted out."* Similarly, a media outlet reported, *"a very significant number of solar systems are installed on customer rooftops but are not yet energized because Consumer Solar does not have the funding."*[3] Looking back, Consumer Solar executives described their failure to build a more competent finance team as their *"biggest fundamental error"* and the mistake that *"almost killed us."*

Why did the resource redeployment from sales to finance fail to create value? First, Consumer Solar's finance product was late. Since Consumer Solar executives expected finance to be a *"temporary arbitrage,"* they initially assumed that the finance component would be unimportant, and that they would be able to choose from many potential finance partners in a commoditized component. While this eventually happened, the timing was several years later than Consumer Solar expected. This limited Consumer Solar's growth in its sales business because the firm lacked a competitive finance product for its potential customers for several years as the ecosystem took off. When Consumer Solar partnered with the few viable finance firms, their extractive terms limited value capture by Consumer Solar in its sales business.

Second, Consumer Solar introduced a weak finance product. Executives assumed that redeploying existing sales resources (rather than investing in new finance resources) would be sufficient. But consumer finance was more difficult than they expected, and its resource requirements were quite different from sales, a point which they ironically understood but ignored. As one executive observed, *"We've never believed you build a brand and a customer relation business that is also fundamentally a financial operation. Those two things are different."* So while redeployment allowed Consumer Solar to avoid many costs associated with developing finance resources, it also led to a weak finance component – one that had delays in raising investment funds, a high cost of capital due to skepticism in the financial community, and problems in managing its securitized leases and funds. These problems put Consumer Solar well-behind its rivals in the sales component. By the time Consumer Solar developed a competitive finance product, the finance component no longer had attractive returns because it had commoditized (as Consumer Solar predicted) and the bottleneck had shifted from finance.

In 2014, Consumer Solar exited the finance component. As one executive stated, *"As soon as we could, we started to diversify away from running our own tax equity fund."* There were now many companies in the finance component, which enabled Consumer Solar to pick among many potential partners and gain attractive terms. Moreover, unlike Consumer Solar, these partners had heavily invested in the finance, accounting, and legal resources necessary to operate effectively in the finance component. Consumer Solar's finance resources, including the staff associated with its tax equity fund management, were redeployed back into the company into various roles, and the company exited the finance component in 2014.

Consumer Solar's participation in the installation and finance components provides an intriguing comparison. Resource redeployment created value for Consumer Solar and the focal solar component in the former, but not the latter, for several reasons. First, although the installation component was not attractive in and of itself, it offered strong inducements that are unique and relevant in ecosystems – that is, the opportunity to co-innovate and acquire knowledge that could improve the capabilities of the focal sales component. The firm gained hands-on installation knowledge that proved essential to improving the quality of the sales and design product. When installation resources redeployed back to sales, the firm benefitted from employees' acquired knowledge about installation that further improved the sales component (creating component-level value) and the interface between the two components, (creating value at the ecosystem-level). In contrast, while there was also high consumption interdependence between finance and sales (i.e., customers wanted viable finance, sales and installation components), there were no clear opportunities to co-innovate with finance or to acquire knowledge from finance to benefit the sales component and vice versa. Overall, resource relatedness was much higher between sales and installation than between sales and finance. This created readjustment costs in finance that were overwhelming and precluded the effective use of redeployment.

Second, Consumer Solar's executives initially entered installation with better resources, including external resources, than they did for finance. For example, one executive described two early installation hires as, *"the experts, if experts even existed."* Part of the rationale for investing in additional high-quality resources was that they correctly understood that resources developed to compete in installation could be effectively redeployed into sales. In contrast, since Consumer Solar's executives undervalued finance and miscalculated its difficulty, they acquired few external resources. Instead, they relied mostly on redeployed sales resources that were not up to the task. So while the finance component itself was highly attractive (i.e., highest returns, strategic bottleneck), opportunities for co-innovation and knowledge acquisition that would improve component capabilities were too limited for resource redeployment to succeed.

Consumer Solar's 2014 Re-Entry into Installation

From 2009 to 2014, Consumer Solar worked with installation partners to put the systems that it designed and sold on rooftops. This allowed Consumer Solar to focus on sales. However, as the industry evolved with dramatically declining PV panel prices and sales costs, installation became the bottleneck in 2014. Consumer Solar's integrated rivals who competed in installation were quick to innovate and drive down their installation costs. In contrast, Consumer Solar's fragmented and small, local installer partners lacked the resources to do the same. As one Consumer Solar executive lamented, *"We're getting beaten on install efficiency."* Because of its own ongoing resource constraints, however, Consumer Solar could not abandon its installation partners and perform its own installation, particularly since it now operated at a national scale. As one executive stated, *"You don't get to millions of units owning your own trucks and ladders."*

To address the installation bottleneck, Consumer Solar embarked on an "improving strategy" (Hannah, 2016) to upgrade the capabilities of its installation partners. Specifically, it redeployed some existing sales and design resources (e.g., operations and supply chain managers, procurement facilities) into the installation component. The firm used these resources to create two installation *"learning centers"* where it experimented to develop new equipment and novel installation processes, which it made available to its installation partners. These installation experiments allowed Consumer Solar to upgrade its installation partners' capabilities. An unexpected benefit was co-innovation: Consumer Solar improved its solar system designs to have better installation efficiency. As one executive described the interdependence, *"Can we trim 1 or 2% off that really complicated array, or just not put the extra array on the north side of the roof? These are things we've got to think through (in our design process)."*

How did the redeployment of sales resources into installation improve the solar component and create value? As in all ecosystems, lack of performance in a complementary component limits performance in the focal component. By redeploying resource *back* into installation, Consumer Solar created value by (1) improving the capabilities of its installer partners and (2) unexpectedly co-innovating to improve its own design product vis-à-vis greater installation efficiency of its solar system designs. Moreover, this successful redeployment was enabled by the high "production-side" resource relatedness that lowered readjustment costs. Both sales and installation require extensive knowledge of the underlying solar technology and systems design which create high production-side resource relatedness such that people, intellectual property and other resources were easily redeployable across these components.

Consumer Solar's Entry and Exit into State Markets

During our study, the attractiveness of the US residential solar industry varied widely by state. For example, in 2007 California accounted for nearly 70% of new residential installations, but fell to 30% by 2010 as other states adopted incentives to promote solar system usage. By 2010, New Jersey, New York, Pennsylvania, and Massachusetts ranked among the top states. But while the industry grew rapidly at a national level (e.g., 76% in 2011, 60% in 2013), the state markets varied widely. For example, New Jersey implemented a renewable energy credit trading program in which subsidies fluctuated. High subsidies attracted entrants, but then prices crashed such that many entrants failed. In other states, uncertainty was driven by lack of clarity regarding what the incentive policies would actually be. For example, an anticipated incentive program in Texas prompted several solar firms to invest heavily in installation resources (i.e., crews and distribution infrastructure) in the state, only to divest these resources when the state legislature did not approve the program.

Consumer Solar entered and exited these state markets according to their varying attractiveness. The company initially operated in three Western states that offered plentiful sunshine and favorable policy incentives (i.e., California, Colorado, and Arizona). In 2011, the company then entered five Northeastern states when new incentive programs made these states attractive. Consumer Solar did so by redeploying sales staff from a California call center (a non-scale-free resource) and sharing sales software with each state (a scale-free resource). This redeployment and related use of synergy allowed Consumer Solar to scale rapidly while minimizing its investment in state-specific resources such as permitting expertise, installation crews, and supply chain infrastructure whose deployment would be difficult to reverse. Rather, it obtained these less reversible resources from its installation partners.

Consumer Solar also exited state markets and redeployed their resources rapidly when they became unfavorable. For example, when the incentive program in Colorado ended in 2011 due to lobbying by the state's largest utility, Xcel Energy, Consumer Solar redeployed its Colorado resources to more attractive states. The company laid off one employee, whose job had been to oversee the company's ten installation partners in Colorado.

The remainder of the Colorado resources – sales, business development, and marketing teams – were not state-specific, and thus redeployed to other states at very little cost.[4] As one executive described,

> You know, when Colorado's subsidy runs out, we just shifted our marketing dollars to Southern California and that's the end of that. But if you buy distribution centers and trucks and 40 W-2 employees, it gets to be a much more complicated world to live in.

In contrast, its rivals who also competed in the installation component (with its more irreversible resources) were more damaged by Colorado's decline. An executive at one such rival lamented, *"This (competing in Colorado) is an existential struggle."* A Consumer Solar executive explained, their rivals who also competed in installation had *"bought and hired hundreds of people, and were now facing closure, layoffs, and all that and the black eye, lost morale and discontinuity."*

How did the redeployment of resources across state markets create corporate value? Much like value creation in multi-business firms, Consumer Solar created value by continually redeploying its resources into the most attractive state markets over time – markets that lacked high consumption-side interdependence. Further, Consumer Solar's redeployment was effective because its resources such as sales and marketing staff were largely redeployable across states at low cost – for example, production-side resource relatedness existed. At the same time, it relied on installation partners – often local home improvement contractors – to provide the state-specific (and thus less reversible) resources. This ensured that Consumer Solar's own resources could be readily redeployed, a feature that is particularly useful when uncertainty is high (Sakhartov & Folta, 2014). In other words, the company benefited from lower adjustment costs driven by resource relatedness (Helfat & Eisenhardt, 2004). An executive confirmed this insight: *"We felt that our business model was more appropriate for the lumpy, on again, off again, nature of the market as it grew."*

DISCUSSION

This paper contributes to the resource redeployment and ecosystems literatures. Prior research examines *resource redeployment* in multi-business firms (e.g., Chandler, 1962; Galunic & Eisenhardt, 2001; Helfat & Eisenhardt, 2004; Karim, 2006), but has yet to explore redeployment in ecosystem firms. Similarly, prior research on *ecosystems* addresses how firms collaborate and compete in ecosystems, settings characterized by consumption-side interdependence among multiple components (e.g., Adner, 2012; Hannah & Eisenhardt, 2016; Kapoor & Furr, 2014; Ozcan & Eisenhardt, 2009), but has yet to clarify how resource redeployment plays a strategic role in such settings.

To address these gaps, we conducted an in-depth case study of Consumer Solar, a firm in the US residential solar ecosystem. We make several contributions. First, we add insights into the strategic differences that motivate redeployment (i.e., inducements) in multi-business v. ecosystem firms. Second, we introduce the concept of "*consumption-side*" interdependence that drives these differences across settings, and distinguish it from "returns" interdependence and "production-side" resource relatedness. Third, we sharpen the conditions under which resource redeployment is likely and effective: market evolution and uncertainty, firm constraints, and resource relatedness (Table 2).

Value Creation through Resource Redeployment

Resource redeployment is undertaken to increase returns in uncertain and evolving markets. In these situations, redeployment attempts to allocate resources to their "most attractive use" (Sakhartov & Folta, 2014, p. 1793). In *multi-business firms*, redeploying resources is motivated by comparison of the current and future returns of distinct markets. The canonical situation is redeploying resources by exiting maturing businesses and entering new ones: ones where current returns are higher, future returns are more volatile, and returns are negatively correlated (Sakhartov & Folta, 2015). The key point is that the inducement to redeploy resources rests on maximizing returns by *comparing returns across markets* (Helfat & Eisenhardt, 2004; Karim, 2006).

Consumer Solar's redeployment between geographic markets reflects this multi-business logic. For example, when the Colorado tax incentives expired, returns were projected to wane. This prompted Consumer Solar to exit and redeploy its Colorado resources to more attractive states. Redeployment was facilitated by Consumer Solar's management such that its "portfolio" of states could be readily re-arranged and its resources redeployed to match evolving markets and changing returns. The states possessed "production-side" related resources that were easily redeployed, but had little (if any) consumption-side interdependence. Indeed, Consumer Solar's portfolio of geographic businesses resembled the business

Table 2. How and When Resource Redeployment Creates Value.

	Ecosystem Firms	Multi-Business Firms (Product or Geographic Markets)
Mechanisms *(How is value created?)*	*Capability improvement* – Firms allocate resources to improve weak capabilities in focal or complementary components, thereby increasing focal component returns *Bottleneck relief* – Firms allocate resources to relieve bottlenecks, thereby increasing focal component returns	*Maximize returns* – Firms allocate resources from lower return markets to higher return markets
Conditions *(When is redeployment most likely?)*	*High disparity in component capabilities in evolving and uncertain markets drives redeployment* *High rate of technological or regulatory change* – Increases frequency with which component quality is out of synch, lowering focal component returns – Increases frequency with which bottleneck components emerge, lowering focal component returns *High resource constraints*	*High disparity in market returns across evolving and uncertain markets drives redeployment* *High current return advantage* – Increases marginal return gained by redeployment into new market *High return volatility* – Increases likelihood of better returns in new market *Low return correlation* – Increases likelihood of divergent returns between markets (return advantage in new market)
Conditions *(When is redeployment most effective?)*	*High resource relatedness* – Reduces readjustment cost of redeployment because of high resource similarity – Due to diverse industries, resource relatedness is often varied across ecosystem components *High interdependence* – Amplifies the positive effects of capability improvement and bottleneck relief on focal component returns	*High resource constraints* *High resource relatedness* – Reduces readjustment cost of redeployment because of high resource similarity – Due to similar industries (related diversifiers), resource relatedness is often high across businesses

portfolio of Omni, a key exemplar in the original statement of intertemporal economies of scope in multi-business firms (Helfat & Eisenhardt, 2004).

In contrast, since ecosystem components have high consumption-side interdependence, returns in a given component depend on capabilities in that component *and* in the other ecosystem components. Failure in one component affects all components. Thus, in *ecosystem firms*, effective redeployment considers both the focal component and the entire ecosystem (Ozcan & Eisenhardt, 2009) or as Adner (2012) terms the "wide lens." Redeployment attractiveness rests *on improving the capabilities in the focal component* (either directly or through effects on complementary components) to improve returns, not just on comparison of returns in the focal v. new market. This introduces two additional mechanisms that provide strong inducements for redeployment in ecosystems: capability improvement and bottleneck relief.

Capability Improvement

Since consumers use a solution that combines ecosystem components, *capability improvement* in components can increase value creation in the ecosystem and enhance the performance of the focal component. It can, for example, be beneficial for a firm to redeploy resources into complementary components in order to improve them – that is, to learn about both the capabilities in that component and how that component interacts with the component of the focal firm. Successful product design and execution in one component is enhanced by capabilities knowledge acquired about other components (Adner & Kapoor, 2010; Hannah & Eisenhardt, 2016; Kapoor & Adner, 2012). Moreover, the human capital associated with these improved capabilities is likely to be under-priced in the market (relative to the value the focal firm receives).

For example, Consumer Solar's capabilities to produce products in sales and design depended on its understanding of other components such as underlying panel and racking technologies as well as installation. The firm improved its novel sales and design technology by temporarily participating in the installation component in 2007–2008. When Consumer Solar then redeployed installation resources back to sales in 2009, it again improved its sales and design capabilities via knowledge acquired about how to choose better installers and to integrate the two components better to achieve higher quality and superior customer experience. So although installation was itself a fragmented and low-margin business, participation in installation and redeployment of installation resources into sales improved Consumer Solar's capabilities and ultimately performance in its focal sales and design business.

Bottleneck Relief

Given the interdependence of ecosystems, bottlenecks often emerge due to poor quality, lagging innovation, and insufficient capacity (Jacobides et al., 2006; Jacobides & Tae, 2015). Bottlenecks limit the performance of both the entire ecosystem and individual components (Hannah & Eisenhardt, 2016). Therefore, it can be advantageous to *relieve bottlenecks*, even if participation in the bottleneck component is not attractive in the long run. For example, Consumer Solar redeployed resources to mitigate bottlenecks twice: first by entering finance in 2010, and again when it re-entered installation in 2014. In both cases, the underlying logic was to enter the bottlenecks in order to mitigate them and increase the returns to the sales and design component. Both moves were effective from a value creation perspective although the former failed due to low resource relatedness between finance and sales. Finally, given that firms in bottleneck components can become "kingpins" in the ecosystem and capture disproportionate value (Hannah & Eisenhardt, 2016; Jacobides & Tae, 2015), redeployment into bottlenecks can lead to superior performance if the firm can become a "kingpin." In these situations, the comparative returns logic of multi-business firms holds – that is, the bottleneck component per se is more attractive (higher returns) than the current market.

In summary, redeployment can create value in ecosystem firms in three ways: (1) achieve superior returns through entry into a more attractive component (i.e., traditional multi-business logic), (2) improve capabilities in complementary or focal components to increase the returns of the focal component (ecosystems logic), and (3) relieve bottlenecks to increase the returns of the focal component (ecosystems logic).

Key Conditions: Uncertain and Evolving Markets, Related Resources, and Resource Constraints

We also contribute insights into the conditions that favor redeployment in ecosystems. We consider the nature of the market, relevance of firm-level resource constraints, and relatedness of resources across markets. First, in both multi-business and ecosystem firms, redeployment is likely to occur when markets are evolving and uncertainty is high. However, these market conditions play out differently in the two settings. In the case of multi-business firms, redeployment is particularly likely in multi-business firms when they participate in markets at varying stages of maturity. This creates greater disparity in the returns across markets, motivating redeployment. The canonical case of the related diversifier is an exemplar of such firms (Helfat & Eisenhardt, 2004).

In contrast, *evolution and uncertainty* across ecosystem components is often driven by differential rates of technological and regulatory change. These changes create disparities in the capabilities across components or to the emergence of bottlenecks, leading to greater use of resource redeployment to ensure that the focal component and its partners are successfully offering viable components that comprise the complete ecosystem. For example, Consumer Solar faced regulatory change with the 2005 tax law enactment that created the opportunity to relieve the consumer finance bottleneck via resource redeployment. Later, technological improvements that dramatically lowered costs in sales and PV panels created the opportunity to redeploy resources to the lagging installation component to improve the capabilities of its installer-partners, creating greater value for Consumer Solar.

Second, firms with *resource constraints* are more likely to engage in resource redeployment because they are less able to acquire or build resources from scratch. For example, like many entrepreneurial firms, Consumer Solar was resource constrained throughout our study. Entrepreneurial firms generally operate under substantial resource constraints (Chatterji, 2009; Katila, Rosenberger, & Eisenhardt, 2008) and their performance often significantly depends on effectively using their limited resources. This makes redeployment particularly salient for them and for resource-constrained firms more broadly. Moreover, archival sources indicate that Consumer Solar deliberately chose to be resource-constrained. Executives implemented a "*capital light business model*," and raised only $2.5M in venture capital during their first two years, compared to the $10M raised by their closest competitor. Thus, constrained resources made resource redeployment a critical part of the Consumer Solar strategy.

Finally, ecosystem firms with *related resources* vis-à-vis other components are more likely to use redeployment and to be effective in doing so. Here, the readjustment costs of re-purposing resources from one use to another are germane (Helfat & Eisenhardt, 2004). These costs typically turn on the underlying production-side relatedness of the resources (Sakhartov & Folta, 2014). Specifically, when resources are related across uses, they have lower readjustment costs and greater reversibility between uses. The importance of resource relatedness for creating value through redeployment holds true for both multi-business and ecosystem firms (although ecosystems may have varied relatedness since component firms are often from diverse industries). That is, resource relatedness influences the value creation of redeployment and thus returns in both ecosystem and non-ecosystem settings by reducing adjustment costs and the related specificity of required investments (Sakhartov & Folta, 2014). So even when there is a strong inducement to redeploy resources to improve returns, high readjustment costs can preclude redeployment and instead favor another alternative for obtaining resources such as acquisition or building from scratch.

For example, Consumer Solar's resource redeployment into the finance component primarily failed because of high readjustment costs driven by the unrelated resources needs in finance v. sales. So while there was substantial inducement to relieve the bottleneck in finance, unrelated resources made readjustment costs too high. In contrast, resource relatedness between the installation and sales components facilitated successful redeployment across these two components in support of the performance in focal sales and design business.

CONCLUSION

Resource redeployment is a key corporate strategy for creating value by continually reallocating resources to their most productive uses (Helfat & Eisenhardt, 2004; Sakhartov & Folta, 2014). Prior work examines redeployment in the context of multi-business firms. We contribute by identifying how ecosystem firms can also corporate create value through redeployment. Through our study of Consumer Solar and the US residential ecosystem, we argue that the inducements that underlie resource redeployment across ecosystem components differ from those of multi-business firms. Comparison of returns across markets drives redeployment in multi-business firms. In contrast, both comparison of returns and increases in returns to the focal market from redeployment to and from complementary markets can drive redeployment. Furthermore, the likelihood of resource redeployment depends on market evolution and uncertainty as well as firm-level resource constraints. Its effectiveness depends on related resources. Overall, despite sometimes weak resource relatedness and positively correlated returns, ecosystems are a key setting for resource redeployment as an effective corporate strategy.

NOTES

1. We appreciate Gautam Ahuja's insightful suggestions for sharpening this concept.

2. We appreciate Harbir Singh's helpful insight on the market failure associated with mispriced human capital.

3. Delays in part occurred because the financial institutions that purchased the funds typically issued one tranche per time period, so that a customer might have to wait for their installed system to be operational. Having multiple open tax equity funds minimized this issue.

4. This experience repeated in other states as well. When Arizona incentives were similarly removed, one executive remarked, *"Arizona incentives went away, and we basically do nothing there. If we had lots of employees, it would have been very painful."*

ACKNOWLEDGMENTS

We would like to express gratitude to our colleagues at the McCombs School of Business and the Stanford Technology Ventures Program for their insight and helpful feedback. We also thank the editors of this special issue, and the executives without whom this research would not have been possible. Research support provided by the Stanford Technology Ventures Program and the Mackenzie Family Fellowship Fund at Stanford University. All errors are our own.

REFERENCES

Adner, R. (2012). *The wide lens: A new strategy for innovation*. New York, NY: Portfolio/Penguin.

Adner, R., & Kapoor, R. (2010). Value creation in innovation ecosystems: How the structure of technological interdependence affects firm performance in new technology generations. *Strategic Management Journal*, *31*(3), 306–333.

Anand, J. (2004). Redeployment of corporate resources: A study of acquisition strategies in the US defense industries, 1978–1996. *Managerial and Decision Economics*, *25*(6-7), 383–400.

Anand, J., & Singh, H. (1997). Asset redeployment, acquisitions and corporate strategy in declining industries. *Strategic Management Journal*, *18*(S1), 99–118.

Bremner, R. P., Eisenhardt, K. M., & Hannah, D. P. (2016, forthcoming). Business ecosystems. In L. Mesauita, J. J. Reuer, & R. Ragozzino (Eds.), *Collaborative strategy: A guide to strategic alliances*. Cheltenham: Edward Elgar Publishing.

Bryce, D. J., & Winter, S. G. (2009). A general interindustry relatedness index. *Management Science, 55*(9), 1570–1585.

Chandler, A. D. (1962). *Strategy and structure: Chapters in the history of the American enterprise*. Cambridge, MA: Massachusetts Institute of Technology Press.

Chatterji, A. K. (2009). Spawned with a silver spoon? Entrepreneurial performance and innovation in the medical device industry. *Strategic Management Journal, 30*(2), 185–206.

Eisenhardt, K. M. (1989). Building theories from case study research. *Academy of Management Review, 14*(4), 532–550.

Eisenhardt, K. M., & Brown, S. L. (1999). Patching. Restitching business portfolios in dynamic markets. *Harvard Business Review, 77*(3), 72–82.

Eisenhardt, K. M., & Graebner, M. E. (2007). Theory building from cases: Opportunities and challenges. *Academy of Management Journal, 50*(1), 25–32.

Ethiraj, S. K. (2007). Allocation of inventive effort in complex product systems. *Strategic Management Journal, 28*(6), 563–584.

Galunic, D. C., & Eisenhardt, K. M. (1996). The evolution of intracorporate domains: Divisional charter losses in high-technology multidivisional corporations. *Organization Science, 7*(3), 255–282.

Galunic, D. C., & Eisenhardt, K. M. (2001). Architectural innovation and modular corporate forms. *Academy of Management Journal, 44*(6), 1229–1249.

Hannah, D. (2016). *Value creation and capture in a world of bottlenecks*. Working Paper. Retrieved from SSRN: http://ssrn.com/abstract=2808036. Accessed on April 12, 2016.

Hannah, D., & Eisenhardt, K. M. (2016). *How firms navigate cooperation and competition in nascent ecosystems*. Working Paper. Retrieved from SSRN http://ssrn.com/abstract=2808034. Accessed on February 20, 2016.

Helfat, C. E., & Eisenhardt, K. M. (2004). Inter-temporal economies of scope, organizational modularity, and the dynamics of diversification. *Strategic Management Journal, 25*(13), 1217–1232.

Huber, G. P. (1985). Temporal stability and response-order biases in participant descriptions of organizational decisions. *Academy of Management Journal, 28*(4), 943–950.

Huber, G. P., & Power, D. J. (1985). Retrospective reports of strategic-level managers: Guidelines for increasing their accuracy. *Strategic Management Journal, 6*(2), 171–180.

Jacobides, M. G., Knudsen, T., & Augier, M. (2006). Benefiting from innovation: Value creation, value appropriation and the role of industry architectures. *Research Policy, 35*(8), 1200–1221.

Jacobides, M. G., & Tae, C. J. (2015). Kingpins, bottlenecks, and value dynamics along a sector. *Organization Science, 26*(1), 128–152.

Kapoor, R., & Adner, R. (2012). What firms make vs. what they know: How firms' production and knowledge boundaries affect competitive advantage in the face of technological change. *Organization Science, 23*(5), 1227–1248.

Kapoor, R., & Furr, N. R. (2014). Complementarities and competition: Unpacking the drivers of entrants' technology choices in the solar photovoltaic industry. *Strategic Management Journal, 36*(3), 416–436.

Karim, S. (2006). Modularity in organizational structure: The reconfiguration of internally developed and acquired business units. *Strategic Management Journal, 27*(9), 799–823.

Karim, S. (2009). Business unit reorganization and innovation in new product markets. *Management Science, 55*(7), 1237–1254.

Karim, S., Carroll, T., & Long, C. (2015). Delays on the road to prosperity: How firms realign through structural recombination when faced with turbulence. *Academy of Management Journal*, forthcoming.

Karim, S., & Kaul, A. (2014). Structural recombination and innovation: Unlocking intraorganizational knowledge synergy through structural change. *Organization Science*, *15*(5), 555–568.

Karim, S., & Mitchell, W. (2004). Innovating through acquisition and internal development: A quarter-century of boundary evolution at Johnson & Johnson. *Long Range Planning*, *37*(6), 525–547.

Katila, R., Rosenberger, J. D., & Eisenhardt, K. M. (2008). Swimming with sharks: Technology ventures, defense mechanisms and corporate relationships. *Administrative Science Quarterly*, *53*(2), 295–332.

Kaul, A. (2012). Technology and corporate scope: Firm and rival innovation as antecedents of corporate transactions. *Strategic Management Journal*, *33*(4), 347–367.

Kumar, N., Stern, L. W., & Anderson, J. C. (1993). Conducting interorganizational research using key informants. *Academy of Management Journal*, *36*(6), 1633–1651.

Langley, A. (1999). Strategies for theorizing from process data. *Academy of Management Review*, *24*(4), 691–710.

Levinthal, D. A., & Wu, B. (2010). Opportunity costs and non-scale free capabilities: Profit maximization, corporate scope, and profit margins. *Strategic Management Journal*, *31*(7), 780–801.

Martin, J. A., & Eisenhardt, K. M. (2010). Rewiring: Cross-business-unit collaborations in multibusiness organizations. *Academy of Management Journal*, *53*(2), 265–301.

Moore, J. F. (1993). Predators and prey: A new ecology of competition. *Harvard Business Review*, *71*(3), 75–83.

Ozcan, P., & Eisenhardt, K. M. (2009). Origin of alliance portfolios: Entrepreneurs, network strategies, and firm performance. *Academy of Management Journal*, *52*(2), 246–279.

Panzar, J. C., & Willig, R. D. (1981). Economies of scope. *The American Economic Review*, *71*(2), 268–272.

Penrose, E. T. (1959). *The theory of the growth of the firm*. Hoboken, NJ: Wiley.

Sakhartov, A. V., & Folta, T. B. (2014). Resource relatedness, redeployability, and firm value. *Strategic Management Journal*, *35*(12), 1781–1797.

Sakhartov, A. V., & Folta, T. B. (2015). Getting beyond relatedness as a driver of corporate value. *Strategic Management Journal*, *36*, 1939–1959.

Silverman, B. S. (1999). Technological resources and the direction of corporate diversification: Toward an integration of the resource-based view and transaction cost economics. *Management Science*, *45*(8), 1109–1124.

Yin, R. K. (1994). *Case study research: Design and methods*. Thousands Oaks, CA: International Educational and Professional Publisher.

PRODUCT TURNOVER: SIMULTANEOUS PRODUCT MARKET ENTRY AND EXIT

Douglas J. Miller and Hsiao-shan Yang

ABSTRACT

Resource redeployment may occur when a firm exits from one line of business and enters another. We suggest that when multiproduct firms identify opportunities in new high-growth markets, their entry will occur alongside exit from low-growth markets when the firm is resource-constrained. For our sample of over 47,000 high-tech US firms in CorpTech from 1993 to 2004, 5% of the firm-years include simultaneous entry and exit at the product market level, which we term "product turnover." Firms are more likely to engage in product turnover when there is a larger spread between the highest and lowest growth rates for the product markets in the firm's portfolio. This effect is strongest for small- and medium-sized firms, which tend to be privately held. Therefore, future research on resource redeployment might find fruitful ground in samples of mid-size firms.

Keywords: Market entry and exit; resource redeployment; multiproduct firms; product turnover

Resource Redeployment and Corporate Strategy
Advances in Strategic Management, Volume 35, 49–87

ISSN: 0742-3322/doi:10.1108/S0742-332220160000035004

Research taking an explicitly evolutionary perspective to corporate diversification has addressed how and why firms reallocate resources across businesses over time (Helfat & Eisenhardt, 2004), either to respond to changes in consumer demand (Chandler & Hikino, 1990) or to learn and develop new capabilities (Chang, 1996). A firm's resource base in one period can either enable or constrain its growth in subsequent periods (Wernerfelt, 1989) in a path dependent manner, a theme central to Penrose's seminal work (1959). As identified by Kor and Mahoney (2004), there is an inherent tension in Penrose's (1959) thinking about path dependence. On the one hand, it is not just the presence of resources, but the way they are used that matters for success in markets. Thus, with sufficient managerial attention, expertise, and teamwork, firms can grow by reusing or recombining their resources in new ways. More resources yield more potential for recombination, so history facilitates growth. On the other hand, continuing use of resources requires ongoing management. Given the constraints of managerial attention and expertise, and the varying efficiency of hierarchical structures for coordinating different scopes of tasks, firms cannot simply add new resources or activities without working to relax these human resource and structural constraints. In the short run, history limits growth. Growth is not constant, nor do managers conduct the same growth-oriented processes in every period. Therefore, firms grow in an evolutionary pattern as managers recognize new opportunities, experiment with new combinations, and search for new resources (Nelson & Winter, 1982).

Yet what if the firm faces opportunities to grow quickly? Must the rate of growth be fixed based on the firm's past decisions? Or can the firm free up managerial resources for the new growth opportunities by abandoning existing products, lines of business, or more fundamentally, resources of any type? Indeed, although Penrose's (1959) main thesis is that change is difficult, she writes: "There are many examples of firms with vigorous and creative management which have substantially altered their range of products, sometimes completely abandoning their original products and expanding their total output in spite of unfavorable demand conditions for the old products" (Penrose, 1959, p. 36). There is a crucial need to understand how a firm's complete product portfolio is managed, including both adding and subtracting products (Villalonga & McGahan, 2005). For instance, Berry (2010) develops a resource-based approach to divestment decisions (Mahoney & Pandian, 1992) finding evidence that firms sometimes exit existing businesses precisely to free capacity for allocation to better opportunities.

The emerging literature on resource redeployment addresses these and other questions, such as whether the ability to convert resources back to their original use affects the firms' propensity to experiment in applying those resources to new uses (Lee, Folta, & Lieberman, 2012); how demand uncertainty influences the choice of entering closely related markets to pursue synergy versus entering slightly less related markets where redeployment costs may be lower (Sakhartov & Folta, 2014b); and the environmental contexts in which quickly reconfiguring the firm's portfolio of businesses creates the most value (Eisenhardt & Brown, 1998). Theorizing about redeployment suggests hypotheses about how redeployment costs relate to firm value (Sakhartov & Folta, 2014a), in conjunction with internal synergy and external uncertainty, and to what extent having more redeployable resources creates firm value, considering differences between new and existing markets in which the firm participates (Sakhartov & Folta, 2014b). Given an assumption about firms being profit-seeking, such insights could lead to tests of the incidence of redeployment, its direction (i.e., into *which* new uses), its persistence as a corporate strategy, and other observable outcomes. Good measures of resources and their redeployability are necessary for this empirical research.

In this paper, we abstract away from the specific firm's resources to document the extent to which firms exit one line of business and enter another (Helfat & Eisenhardt, 2004), which may indicate redeployment of resources. In fact, recent research confirms that *concurrent* entry and exit into product markets is a frequent phenomenon. Bernard, Redding, and Schott (2010) define their dependent variable – product "switching" – as a change of product portfolio that involves at least one entry or exit in a time period (after aggregating establishment-level data to the product market level). They find more than half of US manufacturing firms "switch" products between each national census, which is taken every five years. We define "product turnover" as a firm having at least one entry *and* one exit within the same period. This is less common than switching, but still a quarter of US manufacturing firms turnover their mix of products in a five-year span (Bernard et al., 2010). For our extensive sample of over 47,000 firms in high-tech industries (described below), over 5% of firms turnover products *in a single year*.

We develop and test hypotheses about the interaction between industry dynamics and firm characteristics that suggest product turnover occurs when firms must free up constrained resources in order to take advantage of high-growth opportunities. A key insight is that even relatively scale-free resources, which could be leveraged as synergy in related businesses, may instead be redeployed if the firm's private ownership structure or small size place constraints on growth in general. Overall, our results suggest that future research on redeployment would benefit from including small, private firms in the sample.

THEORY AND HYPOTHESES

Early economic research seeking to explain product market entry, exit, and "turnover" (i.e., changes in which firms are part of an industry) generally focused on how industry-level factors affect the behavior of single-product firms (de Figueiredo & Silverman, 2007; Gort & Klepper, 1982; Jovanovic, 1982; Klepper, 1996). The common interpretation in this "industry dynamics" literature is that entering a market is a result of a firm's success, while exiting a market is a signal of failure, since market demand is exogenous to firm decisions. More recently, Bernard et al. (2010) revealed that most market entry and exit is conducted by multiproduct firms. The economics literature emphasizes consumers' evolving preferences across industries as the fundamental factor driving firms to adapt and adjust their product portfolios. Penrose explained these industry demand factors as "inducements" to enter new markets (Penrose, 1959; Sakhartov & Folta, 2014b). Exogenous uncertainty at the market level includes such factors as the timing of widespread adoption in the product life cycle, demand shocks, technological breakthroughs from other industries, changes in government regulation, or increased competition due to lower international trade barriers (Audretsch, 1995a; Klepper, 1997). Thus, market entry and exit could occur even without resource synergy or redeployment if the firm acts as a holding company or unrelated diversifier. The firm would simply respond to industry dynamics, seeking higher profit through exiting declining markets and entering growing markets (Christensen & Montgomery, 1981; Porter, 1980), perhaps through acquisitions and divestitures.

From a resource-based perspective (Barney, 1986; Rumelt, 1974; Wernerfelt, 1984), a firm changes over time either because the firm acquires new resources, or because it recombines existing resources into new capabilities (Makadok, 2001). Furthermore, a firm could apply its resources and capabilities (hereafter, "resources") to various product markets in a dynamic fashion (Helfat & Eisenhardt, 2004; Sakhartov & Folta, 2014a; Wernerfelt, 1984). In general, any resource may be more or less specific to a certain use and have a certain capacity. The more specific (i.e., less fungible) a resource is, the less its value as applied in its second-best use, such as a new product market (Montgomery & Wernerfelt, 1988). If resources were perfectly fungible, firms could always reallocate their resources to the most profitable markets (Chandler & Hikino, 1990). Physical assets often have a fixed capacity, while intangible assets such as technological know-how and brand identity can be re-applied to additional uses without being exhausted – they are more scalable or "scale-free" (Levinthal & Wu, 2010). Also, excess capacity (i.e., slack) can develop over time as the firm becomes more efficient through learning-by-doing, thereby freeing some portion of a resource to be re-applied to another use. Utilizing scalable resources and excess capacity by producing additional products leads to economies of scope (Panzar & Willig, 1977), thereby lowering the average cost of production, and providing economic incentives to diversify. Over time, resources that a firm controls and protects lead the firm to develop a particular portfolio of business units (Karim & Mitchell, 2000). Firms then differ not only in the extent of their diversification, but also the way in which that diversification is intended to create value (Jovanovic, 1993; Mahoney & Pandian, 1992; Teece, 1982). Thus, while diversification has been considered an important decision for firms since the first writings about corporate strategy (Ansoff, 1957; Penrose, 1959), resource-based theory has developed to explain which industries a firm will enter to leverage its resources (Capron, Mitchell, & Swaminathan, 2001; Gort, 1962; Silverman, 1999) and how that affects firm financial performance (Markides & Williamson, 1994; Miller, 2006; Robins & Wiersema, 1995).

The matching of firm resources to external opportunities under uncertainty is the essence of strategy. However, due to the complexity of the problem, prior literature on diversification or product market entry and exit has tended to focus either on the industry- or firm-level dynamics. For example, de Figueiredo and Kyle (2006) study the interaction between industry evolution and product changes, analyzing the level of competition in a market, firm market share, and firm innovative capability to explain entry and exit separately. While they consider firm heterogeneity, the dynamics are only at the industry level. Similarly, a growing literature on "demand-side" theory emphasizes external drivers of value dynamics (Adner, 2002; Adner & Zemsky, 2006; Priem, Li, & Carr, 2012). In contrast, Wu (2013) emphasizes the firm level, investigating the effect of a firm's pre-existing capabilities on its decision to diversify in subsequent periods. Exemplars of research that consider dynamics at both levels are de Figueiredo and Silverman (2007) and Lee et al. (2012). Sakhartov and

Folta (2014a) theorize that firm resource characteristics and industry-level uncertainty interact to affect firm value, while Sakhartov and Folta (2014b) explicate how comparative returns, volatility, and correlation of returns between industries would affect the value of having redeployable resources, in complex ways. Yet the extant literature still lacks large-scale empirical evidence on simultaneous entry and exit by the same firm (Helfat & Eisenhardt, 2004), which may imply that firms are redeploying resources across businesses, given industry-level dynamics.

Industry Dynamics through the Lens of the Firm's Product Portfolio

Industry dynamics are an external force that affects a firm's incentive to simultaneously enter and exit product markets. For an operating company, one which manages resources to create and sell products, it does not make sense to try to scan the entire landscape to identify growth opportunities because the firm's resources are only useful in some markets. Managers may not even recognize some opportunities unless they are already involved in the product market, or a closely related market. Therefore, managers interpret changes in demand and other sources of exogenous uncertainty through the lens of the firm's existing product portfolio. The incidence of product turnover implies that a firm has some resources (or capabilities) that are relevant for different product markets, even if it needs to acquire additional resources to enter a given new market. Thus, a behavioral theory of strategy implies that firms will evolve their product market portfolios in a manner influenced by information about markets in which they already participate. Moreover, even if managers are scanning broadly, the firm may establish a foothold in a new industry prior to expanding into multiple markets within that industry or exiting an existing market in a different industry. What does this suggest for when firms will simultaneously enter and exit markets?

Market growth is a central aspect of industry "attractiveness" and profitability. If a firm were in only in markets that decline in demand, it might primarily exit some of those markets to refocus on fewer, although it could engage in some search for entirely new, high-growth opportunities (Helfat & Eisenhardt, 2004). On the other hand, if a firm were in only markets with increasing demand, it might primarily add products in those markets or ones closely related, without being motivated to exit any. However, a firm that is in both high-growth and low-growth markets could reconfigure its resources toward the high-growth opportunities. The firm's existing activity in high-growth markets gives it a foothold to redeploy resources and capabilities, while its presence in low-growth markets means it has some resources and capabilities in place that could be used to take advantage of new opportunities. The greater the difference between the profitability of the markets, the more likely the firm would completely exit the low-growth market to emphasize the high-growth market or closely related markets. This movement could be gradual. One would not expect firms to enter and exit entire industries within a few months, especially if exit requires divestiture of a large division.

Indeed, traditional approaches to corporate portfolio management, such as Boston Consulting Group's "Growth-Share Matrix," emphasized expanding in high-growth markets while retaining the cash flow benefits, at least for a time, of having a unit with large market share in a slow-growth market. Similar to our approach, the Growth-Share Matrix highlighted investment in existing portfolio businesses in high-growth markets, not exploring entirely new industries. A key difference between the approaches is that the Growth-Share Matrix stressed the firm's performance (in market share) relative to competitors in the same markets, whereas we emphasize the firm's comparison of future prospects in one of its existing businesses relative to other of its businesses. Information on competitors would influence a firm's aspirations and perception of opportunities, but our data provide detail on market activity at a fine-grained level, somewhat at the expense of detail on firm performance in a given market.

Therefore, we need to define a level of activity at which we would expect to see rapid firm changes, in response to exogenous uncertainty that affects a set of activities. Foreshadowing our empirical method, we define four levels of market definition. An industry would be Clothing Retail or Vehicle Manufacturing. A sub-industry would be Shoe Retail or Heavy Truck Manufacturing. A product market would be Children's Shoe Retail or Dump Truck Manufacturing. A product would be a particular style of shoe trademarked or patented under a specific brand or a model of dump truck. A firm can alter and update its products within a product market without major disruption to its resource configuration. Changes at the product level are often minor and tactical in nature, such as the addition of a single feature or a new color scheme; thus, most productive assets will carry over with minor adaptation. The literature on resource redeployment considers even these incremental changes, but also applies to more strategic changes. At the other extreme, some sources of uncertainty affect an entire industry, but unexpected demand shifts probably occur at the level of the sub-industry or product market. Thus, we define product turnover as simultaneous entry and exit into distinct product markets. We then estimate growth rates of sub-industries and impute these rates to each product market. The intuition is that a firm with even a foothold in a high-growth product market will tend to enter more product markets in the same sub-industry, while exiting product markets in a low-growth sub-industry, without necessarily exiting the sub-industry entirely in the short run.

In sum, managers respond to demand growth in the product markets in which the firm already participates. When a firm is in both high-growth and low-growth markets, and the difference in growth across those markets is substantial, managers will be willing to exit a low-growth market in order to redeploy resources to a high-growth market (Helfat & Eisenhardt, 2004) and markets closely related to it (same sub-industry). Therefore, we state our baseline hypothesis as:

> **Hypothesis 1.** Ceteris paribus, a firm is more likely to engage in product turnover if its product market portfolio exhibits greater distance between market growth in its high growth markets and its low growth markets.

Constraints on Growth and Resource Redeployment

Citing Bryce and Winter (2009), Sakhartov and Folta (2014a) state that "redeployability is only pertinent for resources with limited capacity" (2014a, p. 1783). Examples of such "non-scale free" resources have included skilled personnel and a factory of defined capacity (Levinthal & Wu, 2010). Wu (2013) includes managerial attention in the list of non-scale free capabilities, consistent with the literature since Penrose (1959). Noting this emphasis, we suggest that the statement above can be refined as follows: redeployability is only pertinent for resources whose capacity is constrained by the characteristics of those resources themselves *or* necessary complementary resources. Most simply, even a scale-free resource like brand name can only be redeployed if there is sufficient managerial attention; this is consistent with Barney's emphasis on adding "organization" (VRIO) to his resource-based VRIS framework (Barney, 1991; Barney & Wright, 1997). As another example, a production facility could be highly modular in design, such that expansion to match minimum efficient scale in a new line of business is feasible; but if the firm is not able to raise the capital for such investment, the scalability embedded in the resource by the architect cannot be realized. Similarly, if the firm's location caps how many employees with an advanced skill they can hire affordably, then leveraging the firm's scalable IT infrastructure into new businesses will be constrained. This insight about complementary resources suggests that it may not be necessary to measure the precise resources of firms to understand when they might redeploy resources, rather than seek synergy. Rather, we can identify firms under more general constraints on growth. Here, we develop hypotheses about constraints due to private ownership, size, and financial slack.

The logic common to each of the remaining hypotheses is that a firm will more readily respond to the inducement of portfolio spread by engaging in product turnover when the firm faces a general constraint on growth. Managers want to pursue high growth opportunities, but must exit some market in order to free up the complementary resources necessary to employ key resources in the new market; whether those key resources are redeployed or the firm acquires new resources while shedding old ones. Thus, firm characteristics interact with industry dynamics to stimulate product turnover. The more often a firm enters new markets, the more likely it is to also exit a market in the same time period, even if exiting is random or unrelated to resource issues. This product turnover may indicate some extent of resource redeployment. We do not hypothesize about direct effects, although we will discuss them in the results section. Instead, we propose that the general constraint moderates the effect of portfolio spread on product turnover.

The first constraint exists when a firm is privately held. Private ownership might affect market dynamics because incentives for private firm managers differ from those for public firm managers (Jensen, 1989). Agency issues arise in private firms as well as public firms, but as Schultze, Lubatkin, and Dino (2003) write: "Although private ownership thus engenders fiscal conservatism, all else being the same, we deduce from a behavioral agency view that directors are willing to incur debt to pursue the investments that they perceive to be the best ones, particularly when the directors expect their firm's market to grow" (2003, p. 187). Perhaps the most extensive evidence on differences in investment behavior between private and public firms is offered in Asker, Farre-Mensa, and Ljungqvist (2012). They find that private firms invest more than comparable public firms, and are more responsive to changes in investment opportunities.[1] Asker et al. (2012) interpret these findings to indicate that a major agency problem in public firms is managers underinvesting in the short term in order to smooth earnings and signal further growth potential in future earnings (Stein, 1989). The more long-term orientation of private firm managers is shown in the self-reported behaviors of managers in public and private firms when they faced financial constraints due to the recent economic crisis (Campello, Graham, & Harvey, 2010). Public firms planned to respond to the tighter conditions by cutting tech spending, whereas private firms were more likely to cut marketing and capital expenditures.

Research in entrepreneurship also suggests private firms more efficiently allocate resources and combine them to create more value (Baker & Nelson, 2005; George, 2005). This process of bricolage exploits value from resources that others might have overlooked. The ability to create opportunities suggests that private firm managers will keep less excess capacity on hand of various types. Also, family-owned private firms tend to add and divest businesses in line with strategic and family goals, rather than purely financial goals (Chung & Luo, 2008). Thus, we expect private firms to pursue high-growth opportunities, but to be reluctant to dispose of existing businesses, and thus less likely to engage in product turnover than public firms. However, when already active in both high-growth and low-growth markets, such that they can reallocate people and other resources without having to acquire and divest, private firms will be even more aggressive about market entry and exit than public firms. Overall, this logic implies that the direct effect of private ownership on product turnover will be negative, but that private ownership will positively moderate the effect of portfolio spread on product turnover.

Hypothesis 2. Ceteris paribus, the positive effect of portfolio distance on product turnover is stronger for private firms.

The second constraint is firm size. Certainly, larger firms that are present in more product markets could end up conducting more market entry and exit, even at the same time, than smaller firms that are focused on a few markets. Nevertheless, being a small- or medium-sized enterprise (e.g., under 500 employees) has additional implications for corporate strategy than just those due to the number of business units. Around the world, small firms face greater difficulties than large firms in "obtaining finance, accessing legal systems, or dealing with corruption" (Beck, Demirguc-Kunt, & Maksimovic, 2005, p. 148). Similarly, Bercovitz and Mitchell (2007) suggest that as firms grow, they develop organizational capital in terms of financial resources, organizational routines, and external ties. For very small firms, an owner-manager is probably too stretched to deal with rapid expansion (Ocasio, 1997). Even for medium-sized firms, increasing both technological knowledge and market knowledge (Danneels, 2002) at the same time is difficult; they probably have to decide whether to focus on certain customers or certain capabilities. Our approach to inducements requires firms to be present in multiple product markets and small firms may simply not have enough scope to experience vast differences in growth rates across their product markets. However, if they do, small firms will be more likely than large firms to exit one market as a way to expand further into another market.

> **Hypothesis 3.** Ceteris paribus, the positive effect of portfolio distance on product turnover is stronger for small firms.

Finally, the lack of financial resources could prevent a firm from responding to inducements in new markets. Financial resources are highly fungible, and while they are not unlimited (in the short term), their presence can serve to alleviate constraints in other types of resources. Any venture into a new product market requires some financial resources. Cash and cash-equivalent assets are perfectly fungible, but not available in unlimited quantities, at least in the short term. Thus, even when capital markets are highly efficient, and money eventually flows to the most worthwhile projects, in practice firms have a pecking order of sources of capital (Myers, 2001; Simerly & Li, 1999). A firm reporting large cash amounts on its balance sheet might seem to be free to enter any industry in which an acquisition is feasible. However, managers have reasons to retain some financial slack, such as to maintain a solid credit rating, with its concomitant lower costs of capital (Opler & Titman, 2012). Further, in high-technology industries, cash reserves are used to fund R&D without having to reveal valuable knowledge to the market (Myers & Majluf, 1984; O'Brien, 2003). Therefore, a firm that has more financial slack than another firm can use it to facilitate the acquisition or redeployability of other assets, even managerial human resources (Mishina, Pollock, & Porac, 2004). For instance, a firm that enters a new market through acquisition could pay more to retain acquired managerial talent if it has more financial slack. Or, a firm with high slack could pay consultants to bridge the gap until its managerial team adapts to the new firm size and scope. If nothing else, greater financial slack allows a firm to move into a new market as soon as opportunity arises or defer exiting a market (or adapting in various ways; Kraatz & Zajac, 2001), because the firm can afford to lose some money in the short term. Thus, unabsorbed financial slack is a perfectly redeployable resource – "cash is king" in any business – that facilitates either synergy or redeployment.

It may seem that privately held and small firms would have difficulty accessing capital (Carpenter & Petersen, 2002); however, detailed survey evidence suggests that private status and small firm size are poor indicators of financial constraints (Campello et al., 2010). For example, although private firms rely more on debt than public firms (Brav, 2009), private firms considering an acquisition may plan ahead to hold more cash reserves. Then, the fact that they are paying in cash, and can credibly commit to a walkaway price, contributes to them paying lower premiums than public acquirers (Bargeron, Schlingenmann, Stulz, & Zutter, 2008). Instead, a shortness of cash on hand is distinct from the previous sources of constraints. Firms with high financial slack do not face as many constraints on use of other, scalable resources as do firms with minimal financial slack. Therefore, they can respond to inducements to enter new markets without having to exit existing markets. This logic leads to the following hypothesis:

Hypothesis 4. Ceteris paribus, the positive effect of portfolio distance on product turnover is weaker for firms with high financial slack.

METHODS

Data

CorpTech covers more than 49,000 private and public firms active across 17 high-tech industries, 258 sub-industries, and 2,600 product markets in the United States between 1989 and 2004 annually. It is a directory of high-tech industry manufacturers (Lavin, 1992) including contact information, managers, employment, firm-level sales, year of establishment, and a hierarchical product classification system developed by CorpTech.[2] Research related to market evolution, entry/exit, and diversification has relied heavily on similar directories with detailed product classifications such as the Thomas Register of American Manufactures (Agarwal & Gort, 1996; Gort & Klepper, 1982; Klepper & Graddy, 1990) or the Business Information Tracking Series (BITS) data (Villalonga, 2004). CorpTech provides a greater level of detail in product classification than earlier databases such as the FTC Line of Business Data (available 1974–1977) or TRINET (biannually from 1981–1989), which employed SIC or NAICS codes. In Strategic Management, CorpTech has provided the empirical basis for research on acquisitions (Lee & Lieberman, 2010; Puranam & Srikanth, 2007), entry timing (Lee, 2006, 2008, 2009; Lee & Paruchuri, 2008), and exit (Lee et al., 2012). Its extensive coverage of small firms has also made it useful for studies of venture capital (Freear, 1990), entrepreneurial management structure (Baron, 1999; Sine, 2006), and product development

(Markham, 1998). For all CorpTech-derived measures, we aggregate subsidiaries up to the corporate level, and collect corresponding financial information from Compustat.

We define the most detailed product category classified by CorpTech as a *product market*. The 2,600 product markets are aggregated into 17 *industries*. The 17 industries in CorpTech are Factory Automation, Biotechnology, Chemicals, Computer Hardware, Defense, Energy, Environmental, Manufacturing Equipment, Advanced Materials, Medical Equipment, Pharmaceuticals, Photonics, Computer Software, Subassemblies and Components, Test and Measurement, Telecommunications and Internet, and Transportation. Thus, while CorpTech's commercial purpose was as a directory of "high-tech" firms, the database covers nearly all the manufacturing sector of the US economy, and firms' service offerings are also reported. The format of CorpTech's classification system is IN-SUB-PRM where IN is one of the 17 industries, PRM is the product market, and SUB is an intermediate level of classification that we call *sub-industry*. The sub-industry level is roughly equivalent to a three-digit SIC code or four-digit NAICS code. For example, "MED-IM-OJ" is the code for "Medical-Implants/Prostheses-Joints." The "IM" sub-industry is defined as "substances or artificial body parts" and comprises 15 product markets. A firm can offer many distinct products within a product market – for example, artificial hips, shoulders, knees, and various parts to install these implants, at different sizes and using different materials. Thus, entry or exit into a product market is not merely adding or dropping a single product, such as a new version of software or flavor of breakfast cereal, but is a substantive change in the firm's offerings.

Sample size for various analyses depends on whether we employ any variables that are lagged one year or measured over a four-year rolling time window. The database from 1990 to 2004 forms an unbalanced panel of 472,722 firm-year observations, whereas the sample using a four-year rolling time window includes 456,728 firm-year observations from 1993 to 2004. Regression models exclude observations with missing values, with 285,010 firm-year observations remaining, of which 34,883 are public firms with data available in Compustat; thus, the vast majority of firms in CorpTech are private.

Description of the Phenomenon

Dependent Variables

Product turnover is the number of product markets simultaneously added and dropped within the product portfolio. For example, if a firm adds three product markets and drops two others, the value of product turnover is 2. In effect, the value of product turnover is the minimum of the number of product markets entered or exited in a given period. Most of our reported results use a period of one year.

We also estimate models with *Gross Entry* and *Gross Exit* as dependent variables to investigate the two components of product turnover. *Gross Entry (Exit)* is the number of added (dropped) product markets in the focal year.

Incidence of Product Turnover

Fig. 1 reveals the frequency of product turnover over time. The solid line indicates the percentage of firms that engage in product turnover in each year. This line somewhat reflects the underlying behaviors of product market entry and exit; for comparison, the dashed line shows the percentage of firms that have any change in their product portfolio in each year. Further, product turnover moves in contrast to the business cycle; the dotted line indicates US real GDP growth in each year. Emerging out of recession in 1991, turnover decreases. Then, when GDP falls, product turnover tends to rise in the following year. For this brief time series, the correlation between product turnover and real GDP growth lagged one year is −0.33. Overall,

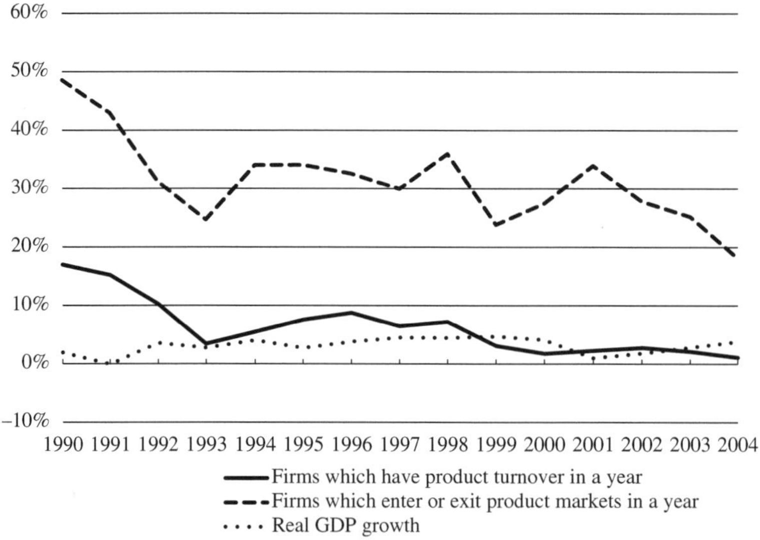

Fig. 1. The Percentage of Firms with Product Turnover.

product turnover decreases through the early 2000s, to a low of 1% of firms in 2004, while 18% of those firms still entered or exited at least one product market that year. Therefore, product turnover is a frequent activity, and relates to the business cycle, but decreased over a 15-year period. Next, we provide some descriptive statistics to further clarify the phenomenon, before moving to regression analysis.

Table 1 reports the frequency and distribution of product turnover at various levels of classification and time windows. The first column employs our primary definition: both entry and exit into product markets within a one-year time window. For the sample of 472,722 firm-years, 5.11% show product turnover. Using a four-year time window, the incidence approaches 9%. In comparison, using a different classification system, Bernard et al. (2010) found 25% of manufacturing firms both entered and exited markets in a five-year time window. Product turnover can be broken down into its components: on average, 20% of firms enter a new product market in a given year, whereas only 10% exit a product market (not shown in the table). Thus, the incidence of product turnover is more constrained by market exit, because firms are more regularly entering markets.

Returning to the one-year column in Table 1, the mean value of the product turnover variable is 0.065; that is, the average firm-year saw turnover of 7/100ths of a product. This value is slightly higher than the percentage of firms that had product turnover, consistent with other statistics that indicate the typical activity involved in product turnover is to drop one product market while entering one or more. However, the maximum value

Table 1. Summary of Product Turnover at Three Levels.

Time Window	Product Market Level	Sub-Industry Level One-year	Industry Level	Product Market Level Four-year
Observations		472,722		456,728
Percentage of firms that turnover products	5.11%	2.94%	1.23%	8.89%
Product turnover mean	0.065	0.031	0.011	0.134
Std. dev.	0.398	0.209	0.107	0.848
Max	34	14	3	62
Skewness	15.609	9.964	10.088	19.910
Kurtosis	540.480	181.039	112.404	603.467
Transition probability	13.70%	9.27%	3.51%	64.06%

of 34 indicates that one firm both added at least 34 product markets and dropped at least 34 others in the same year. Using a four-year time window, the mean of product turnover doubles, to 13.4%. As shown in the second and third columns, product turnover occurs even at the sub-industry (3%) and industry (1%) levels, using the one-year time window. The maximum value at the industry level (column 3) indicates that a firm entered three of the 17 CorpTech industries and exited three others in the same year. Change at this level likely results from substantial corporate activity, such as acquisitions and restructuring, and is only possible for large, highly diversified firms. Later regression analysis will control for firm size and diversification. The transitional probability in the final row is the conditional probability that a firm experienced product turnover in the focal period given that it experienced product turnover in the immediate prior period. For the product-market level analysis, 13.7% of those firms that had turnover in one year also had it in the next year. Since this percentage is higher than the unconditional probability, some firms are more likely than others to engage in simultaneous entry and exit.

By Firm Size

Larger firms are active in more product markets than smaller firms. Therefore, Table 2 also gives the breakdown of product market changes for small- (≤24 employees), medium- (25–499 employees), and large- (≥500 employees) sized firms. In Table 2, we again report the mean values for product turnover, adding a two-year time window for comparison to the other windows, and showing the underlying market entry and exit behavior. For example, considering a two-year period, the average sample firm is adding at least one new product market per period and dropping a little less than half of a product.

By Industry

Product turnover occurs in all industries. Fig. 2 graphs turnover rates by industry using two definitions. Different from what has been reported above, the product turnover *rate* is the count of product turnover divided by the firm's total number of product markets. Fig. 1a reports a firm's overall product turnover rate, regardless of which industry in which the product markets were added or dropped, and averages the firm rate into the mean value for each industry in which the firm operates. Thus, each firm and its value of product turnover rate can appear multiple times in the figure. Using this approach, each industry sees a turnover rate between

Table 2. Summary of Firm Dynamics within 1-, 2-, and 4-Year Time Window.

Time Window	One-Year	Two-Year	Four-Year
All firms	(N = 472,722)	(N = 470,754)	(N = 456,728)
Product market added	0.626 (1.886)	1.132 (2.599)	1.892 (3.538)
Product market dropped	0.282 (1.192)	0.461 (1.708)	0.548 (2.045)
Product Turnover	0.065 (0.398)	0.092 (0.570)	0.134 (0.848)
Small firms	(N = 212,039)	(N = 196,233)	(N = 177,529)
Product market added	0.561 (1.510)	1.035 (1.991)	1.742 (2.476)
Product market dropped	0.086 (0.483)	0.151 (0.669)	0.225 (0.824)
Product turnover	0.043 (0.248)	0.050 (0.286)	0.062 (0.334)
Medium firms	(N = 174,114)	(N = 158,868)	(N = 142,288)
Product market added	0.550 (1.462)	1.044 (2.007)	1.765 (2.578)
Product market dropped	0.127 (0.590)	0.228 (0.819)	0.333 (1.010)
Product turnover	0.062 (0.309)	0.082 (0.370)	0.115 (0.464)
Large firms	(N = 33,526)	(N = 30,733)	(N = 27,706)
Product market added	1.415 (3.918)	2.632 (5.619)	4.606 (8.592)
Product market dropped	0.514 (2.202)	0.937 (3.416)	1.389 (4.958)
Product turnover	0.230 (0.968)	0.442 (1.590)	0.753 (2.475)

The statistics reported are mean (Std. Dev.).
The median number of employees is 24. Thus, small firms are those with ≤24 employees, medium firms have 25–499 employees, and large firms have ≥500 employees.

1.1% and 2.1%. For a one-year window, the lowest turnover rates occur for firms in chemicals (CHE) and manufacturing equipment (MAN), two industries with high fixed costs. The highest turnover rates occur in computer hardware and subassemblies. Four-year turnover rates are higher, with a notable deviation from the parallel shift upwards in the graph: manufacturing equipment has the highest turnover rate using a four-year window, perhaps reflecting that firms enter and exit this industry in service of broader corporate strategies, such as vertical integration during a part of the industry life cycle. Other industries in which the difference between four-year and one-year rates is higher than average are defense (DEF), photonics (PHO), and software (SOF). In contrast, there is no substantial increase in turnover rate from the one-year to the four-year window for the environmental (ENV), subassemblies and components (SUB), and transportation (TRN) industries.

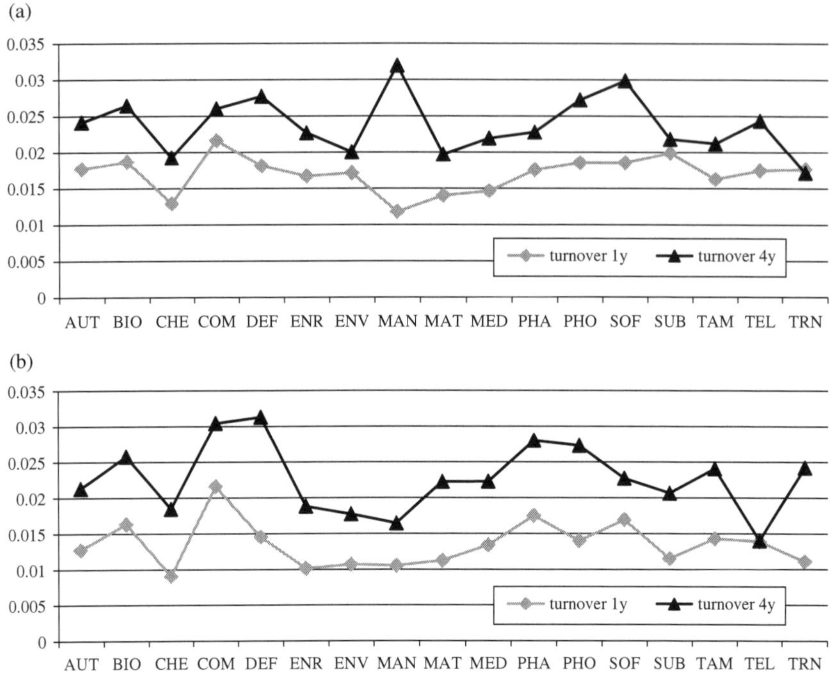

Fig. 2. Product Turnover Rate by Industry. (a) Operating Industry; (b) Primary Industry.

Fig. 2b assigns each firm to a single primary industry, as defined within CorpTech. The primary industry may not be the one in which the firm started, or in which it has the most products. Primary industry is coded according to the expertise of CorpTech staff, whose goal in compiling the database was to facilitate business-to-business sales to these firms. Again, product turnover rates are similar across industries, with chemicals and computer hardware on the low and high ends. However, using the primary industry, the greatest difference between the four-year and one-year rates occurs in defense (DEF), whereas the lowest difference is in telecommunications and Internet (TEL).

Table 3 breaks product turnover in each industry into two components: extensive product turnover and intensive product turnover. Extensive Product Turnover is the minimum of a firm's entries into product markets in CorpTech industries in which the firm has not operated and all exits

Table 3. Summary of Entry/Exit by Primary Industry (One-Year Time Window).

	All Firm-Years				Firm-Years with Exit		All Firm-Years	
	Gross entry	Gross extensive entry	Gross intensive entry	Gross exit	Gross extensive entry	Gross intensive entry	Extensive product turnover	Intensive product turnover
Factory automation	0.362	0.255	0.107	0.092	0.460	0.827	0.017	0.017
Biotechnology	0.532	0.362	0.170	0.122	0.403	0.704	0.019	0.022
Chemicals	0.407	0.266	0.141	0.146	0.353	1.022	0.015	0.028
Computer hardware	0.570	0.373	0.197	0.164	0.450	1.088	0.023	0.044
Defense	0.866	0.438	0.428	0.316	0.905	3.114	0.051	0.099
Energy	0.448	0.332	0.116	0.119	0.372	0.805	0.015	0.017
Environmental	0.383	0.276	0.107	0.088	0.417	0.669	0.015	0.012
Manufacturing equipment	0.361	0.279	0.082	0.065	0.439	0.623	0.012	0.010
Advanced materials	0.463	0.292	0.171	0.151	0.376	1.166	0.018	0.030
Medical equipment	0.440	0.298	0.142	0.113	0.385	0.707	0.014	0.019
Pharmaceuticals	0.665	0.401	0.264	0.212	0.430	1.336	0.024	0.067
Photonics	0.521	0.333	0.188	0.139	0.436	0.952	0.023	0.036
Computer software	0.588	0.383	0.205	0.130	0.287	1.085	0.013	0.036
Subassemblies and components	0.465	0.299	0.166	0.135	0.447	1.197	0.019	0.032
Test and measurement	0.437	0.293	0.144	0.124	0.517	1.081	0.023	0.023
Telecom and internet	1.239	0.944	0.295	0.116	0.991	1.224	0.020	0.024
Transportation	0.550	0.351	0.199	0.188	0.496	1.640	0.019	0.040

Notes: Gross extensive entry = count of a firm's entries into product markets in CorpTech industries in which the firm has not operated; gross intensive entry = count of a firm's entries into product markets in CorpTech industries in which the firm already operates; gross entry − gross extensive entry = gross intensive entry; extensive product turnover = minimum of a firm's extensive entries and all exits; intensive product turnover = minimum of a firm's intensive entries and all exits.

from any of the firm's industries. Intensive Product Turnover is the minimum of a firm's entries into product markets within industries in which the firm already operates and all exits. Intensive Product Turnover represents cases in which a firm might be taking resources from one product market in an industry and redeploying them to another product market in the same industry. Additional tables with more detail on the panel by year and industry are provided in the Appendix.

Hypothesis Testing

Statistical Estimation

Because each of the dependent variables – Product Turnover, Gross Entry, and Gross Exit – is a natural number and also an integer, we estimate random-effects, Poisson regression models.[3] We select firms that are reported in CorpTech for at least two consecutive years. In total, the data form an unbalanced panel of 285,010 firm-year observations. The vast majority of firms in CorpTech are private. Regression models including Compustat variables generally include 34,883 firm-year observations.

Independent and Control Variables

We use four independent variables to test the present study's hypotheses. The first independent variable is *Portfolio Spread* of industry growth, a measure of the distance between the highest and lowest growth rates for the markets in the firm's product portfolio. A limitation of the CorpTech data is that they do not report sales by product, but only for the firm as a whole. Therefore, we cannot directly measure growth of a product market by tracking sales across firms in that market. Instead, we regress firm-level year-to-year sales growth on 258 sub-industry dummies, with the dummies weighted by the number of product markets the firm has in that sub-industry. In this way, we estimate the effect of participating in any sub-industry on growth for the average firm. The estimated coefficient of a subunit is higher if the market is growing faster. Next, we assign the sub-industry coefficients of the 258 dummies to each product market in a firm's portfolio, and find the 90th percentile and 10th percentile of the growth coefficients within a firm's product market portfolio. Portfolio Spread is the difference between the growth rates at the 90th and 10th percentiles for the focal firm. A portfolio with higher spread includes markets with a greater distance between high and low investment opportunities, which we suggest motivates managers to consider implementing changes to the product portfolio. The industry growth variable is lagged one period behind the dependent variable and we take the natural log; as such we can capture the causal relationship between past industry attributes and current product market activity.

A *Private* firm is one that does not have stock traded on a public exchange in the focal year. Since the model is non-linear, we use split sample analysis to test for statistical significance of the moderating effect of private status on the relationship between Portfolio Spread and Product Turnover.

Firm size and scope is incorporated through multiple measures. For hypothesis testing, we split the sample by number of employees into small ($\leq$24), medium (25–499), and large ($\geq$500) firms, and propose that the effect of Portfolio Spread on Product Turnover is greater for small firms. This test is performed after controlling for the (natural log of the) number of product markets in a firm's portfolio (i.e., *Product Scope*), and the (natural log of the) firm's total *Sales* in millions of $US. Another control variable that correlates highly with firm size is the *Diversification Index*, a Herfindahl measure given by $1 - \sum_{j=1}^{17} {r_{ijt}}^2$, where r_{ijt} denotes the percentage of product count manufactured by firm i in the industry j at time t.

Financial *Slack* is measured as current assets minus current liabilities with a one-year lag. The data for this variable are drawn from Compustat and merged with the CorpTech data using firms' ticker symbols. Adding this variable reduces the number of observations significantly because the data are limited to public firms. *Slack* is highly correlated with cash on hand ($\rho = 0.818$), which we use in some robustness checks.

Additional controls are at the level of the firm and the industry. First, 17 industry-dummy variables and 12 year-dummy variables are generated to control for industry-specific and time-specific effects for the period 1993 to 2004. Second, a firm's age is likely to affect its experience and capability. Numerous studies, including Evans (1987), Hall (1987), Dunne, Roberts, and Samuelson (1989), Audretsch (1991, 1995b), Agarwal (1997), and Audretsch and Mahmood (1995) find that survival rate increases with firm age. *Market Competition* is the average number of competitors in each of the product markets in which the firm participates. The more competitors in a product market, the lower the barriers to entry, in general. *Adding in the Previous Period* and *Dropping in the Previous Period* are dummy variables that equal 1, respectively, if the firm adds or drops any product market in the previous year. We employ the terms "adding" and "dropping" for the dummy control variables based on a one-year lag, to distinguish them from the count dependent variables of "Gross Entry" and "Gross Exit" in the focal year.

RESULTS

Table 4 reports the correlations and descriptive statistics. The bivariate correlations between the hypothesized variables and other variables suggest a lack of multicollinearity issues.

The results of the main Poisson regression models are presented in Table 5. In Models 1–3 the dependent variable is Product Turnover. Models 4–6 and 7–9 report the results of the regressions with Gross Entry and Gross Exit as dependent variables separately. We will refer to the separate entry and exit models for more details as we discuss each hypothesis. Looking at the controls, Model 1 reveals that firms with higher sales, more products, and more diversified product portfolios have more product turnover, and older firms and those in markets with higher numbers of competitors have less product turnover. Recent changes, whether adding or dropping products, relate to lower counts of product turnover in the focal period.

In Model 1, Portfolio Spread provides a test of H1, which suggests that having a product portfolio covering both low-growth and high-growth industries drives firms to turnover products. The positive coefficient is consistent with H1. The economic magnitude of this effect is small: a change from the mean of portfolio spread to one standard deviation above the mean only raises the predicted value of product turnover by 2%. Still, firms engage in more product turnover if their portfolio has a greater spread between high growth and low growth markets. In non-tabulated models, we repeat Model 1, but split Product Turnover into its two components, using Extensive Product Turnover and Intensive Product Turnover as the dependent variables, respectively. Results for both models are consistent with the estimates using overall Product Turnover; however, the coefficient and economic magnitude of the effect of Portfolio Spread is about three times as large for Extensive as for Intensive Product Turnover. Thus, industry inducements have a stronger effect on firms entering new industries than entering new product markets within their current set of industries. Table 5 also shows that Portfolio Spread encourages entry and discourages exit, with clear statistical significance, as seen in Models 4 and 7.

Table 4. Correlations and Descriptive Statistics.

		Mean	S.D.	1	2	3	4	5	6	7	8	9	10	11	12
1	Turnover	0.07	0.40	1.00											
2	Gross entry	0.29	1.32	0.50	1.00										
3	Gross exit	0.15	0.88	0.62	0.26	1.00									
4	Log (product scope)	1.05	0.80	0.18	0.18	0.23	1.00								
5	Diversification Index	0.29	0.33	0.13	0.15	0.14	0.49	1.00							
6	Log (market competition)	5.58	1.36	−0.01	0.02	0.00	0.20	0.25	1.00						
7	Log (sales)	1.84	1.83	0.16	0.22	0.18	0.31	0.43	0.11	1.00					
8	Log (firm age)	2.90	0.80	0.02	0.02	0.04	0.07	0.19	−0.09	0.31	1.00				
9	Portfolio variance	1.91	4.44	0.04	0.09	0.04	0.26	0.26	0.17	0.17	−0.02	1.00			
10	Adding in the previous	0.23	0.42	0.09	0.10	0.09	0.19	0.16	0.09	0.11	−0.17	0.11	1.00		
11	Dropping in the previous	0.08	0.27	0.11	0.10	0.11	0.15	0.12	−0.02	0.15	0.03	0.05	0.29	1.00	
12	Slack – Lagged $US Billion	0.0001	0.001	0.16	0.18	0.11	0.22	0.15	−0.01	0.27	0.10	0.03	0.11	0.10	1.00

N = 285,010 for all variables except Slack, which is available for 40,363 observations.

Table 5. Poisson Regressions (One-Year Window).

	Product Turnover			Gross Entry			Gross Exit		
	(1) All firms	(2) Public	(3) Private	(4) All firms	(5) Public	(6) Private	(7) All firms	(8) Public	(9) Private
Ln (product scope)	0.599***	0.858***	0.513***	–0.445***	–0.293***	–0.602***	1.302***	1.373***	1.362***
	(0.014)	(0.026)	(0.017)	(0.008)	(0.014)	(0.011)	(0.012)	(0.022)	(0.015)
Diversification Index	1.074***	0.146 +	1.240***	0.212***	–0.190***	0.216***	1.134***	0.134*	1.548***
	(0.037)	(0.077)	(0.044)	(0.021)	(0.037)	(0.026)	(0.031)	(0.060)	(0.037)
Ln (market competition)	–0.107***	0.076***	–0.126***	0.013*	–0.010	0.059***	–0.143***	0.074***	–0.196***
	(0.009)	(0.021)	(0.011)	(0.006)	(0.010)	(0.007)	(0.008)	(0.016)	(0.009)
Ln (sales)	0.120***	0.023*	0.105***	0.337***	0.195***	0.268***	0.021***	–0.065***	0.036***
	(0.006)	(0.011)	(0.009)	(0.004)	(0.008)	(0.006)	(0.005)	(0.009)	(0.007)
Ln (firm age)	–0.275***	–0.088***	–0.303***	–0.231***	–0.001	–0.231***	–0.194***	–0.023	–0.223***
	(0.013)	(0.025)	(0.016)	(0.010)	(0.018)	(0.011)	(0.012)	(0.021)	(0.014)
Portfolio spread	0.004**	–0.001	0.007***	0.026***	0.014***	0.037***	–0.016***	–0.000	–0.034***
	(0.002)	(0.003)	(0.002)	(0.001)	(0.001)	(0.001)	(0.002)	(0.002)	(0.003)
Adding in the previous period	–0.053**	–0.045	–0.076**	–0.103***	–0.028*	–0.195***	–0.158***	–0.106***	–0.192***
	(0.019)	(0.032)	(0.023)	(0.009)	(0.014)	(0.012)	(0.013)	(0.020)	(0.016)
Dropping in the previous period	–0.120***	–0.042	–0.216***	–0.097***	–0.064***	–0.166***	–0.261***	–0.205***	–0.327***
	(0.022)	(0.032)	(0.032)	(0.011)	(0.015)	(0.017)	(0.015)	(0.021)	(0.022)
Constant	–2.039***	–2.976***	–1.786***	–0.991***	–0.161*	–1.163***	–1.691***	–2.988***	–1.269***
	(0.065)	(0.141)	(0.075)	(0.042)	(0.079)	(0.051)	(0.055)	(0.111)	(0.064)
Industry dummies	Yes	Yes	Yes	Yes	Yes	Yes	Yes	Yes	Yes
Time dummies	Yes	Yes	Yes	Yes	Yes	Yes	Yes	Yes	Yes
Firms	47,833	5,929	43,326	47,833	5,929	43,326	47,833	5,929	43,326
N	285,010	34,883	250,127	285,010	34,883	250,127	285,010	34,883	250,127

Standard errors in parentheses; $^{+}p < 0.10$, $^{*}p < 0.05$, $^{**}p < 0.01$, $^{***}p < 0.001$.

H2 states that the effect of Portfolio Spread should be higher for private firms, due to their constraints on growth. The distinction appears in Models 2 and 3. The coefficient for Portfolio Spread is positive and statistically significant for the private firms (Model 3) but not for the public firms (Model 2). However, a Chow test demonstrates the difference between these coefficients is not statistically significant (p-value = 0.125).[4]

To further understand the relationship between ownership type and market dynamics, note that Portfolio Spread is positively associated with Gross Entry for both public and private firms (Models 5 and 6), but the negative association between Portfolio Spread and Gross Exit only holds for private firms (Models 8 and 9). Perhaps one reason the Portfolio Spread effect on Product Turnover is not significantly different for the public and private subsamples is that the difference between these types of firms is strongly captured by the control variables. For instance, Market Competition correlates 0.17 with Portfolio Spread, consistent with the idea that low barriers to entry often exist in high growth stages of industry evolution. Private firms are much more likely to enter contested markets (Model 6), and less likely to exit from them (Model 9) than public firms (Models 5 and 8). Moreover, diversification and total sales have stronger positive effects, and adding or dropping in the previous period have stronger negative effects on Product Turnover for private firms than public firms. Thus, private firms that have recently changed their product market portfolio may need more time to adapt before initiating more changes, particularly if they are fairly focused and small, and this reduces their sensitivity to Portfolio Spread. Indeed, being private has the direct effect of reducing the count of all three dependent variables (seen when we add a Private dummy to Models 1, 4, and 7; estimates not reported in a table).

This discussion leads naturally to the models to test H3, about the moderating effect of firm size, presented in Table 6. In the first three columns, we split the sample by number of employees. As expected, the coefficient for Portfolio Spread is positive and statistically significant for the small firms, but not for the large firms. The Chow test result shows the difference is significant (p-value = 0.036). Notably, the coefficient is similar for the medium-sized firms as the small firms (Chow test p-values for small vs. medium = 0.707; medium vs. large = 0.024). Models 4 through 6 present similar estimations using firm sales as an alternative way to split the sample according to size, with cutoff values of the median value for sales, $3 Million, and the round figure of $50 Million. As shown in Models 4 through 6, Portfolio Spread again has a much higher effect on Product

Table 6. Poisson Regressions of Product Turnover (One-year Window) – Split Sample Analyses for Size.

	(1) Small firms (employee)	(2) Median firms (employee)	(3) Large firms (employee)	(4) Small firms (sales)	(5) Median firms (sales)	(6) Large firms (sales)	(7) Small public firms (employee)	(8) Small private firms (employee)	(9) Single industry firms
Ln (product scope)	0.422***	0.560***	1.020***	0.433***	0.536***	0.982***	0.435*	0.425***	0.493***
	(0.027)	(0.022)	(0.031)	(0.026)	(0.024)	(0.028)	(0.212)	(0.028)	(0.022)
Diversification Index	1.618***	0.925***	−0.002	1.558***	0.877***	0.116	0.662	1.615***	2.308***
	(0.070)	(0.053)	(0.097)	(0.068)	(0.059)	(0.083)	(0.485)	(0.071)	(0.059)
Ln (market competition)	−0.170***	−0.052***	0.136***	−0.182***	−0.033*	0.077**	−0.025	−0.170***	−0.180***
	(0.016)	(0.014)	(0.030)	(0.016)	(0.015)	(0.024)	(0.112)	(0.017)	(0.014)
Ln (sales)	0.170***	0.026^{+}	0.056***	0.271***	−0.015	0.043**	0.083	0.168***	0.032**
	(0.021)	(0.014)	(0.015)	(0.023)	(0.019)	(0.014)	(0.106)	(0.021)	(0.011)
Ln (firm age)	−0.299***	−0.324***	−0.082**	−0.315***	−0.330***	−0.085***	0.052	−0.304***	−0.319***
	(0.026)	(0.020)	(0.026)	(0.025)	(0.022)	(0.023)	(0.210)	(0.027)	(0.023)
Portfolio spread	0.011***	0.009***	−0.002	0.011***	0.013***	−0.001	−0.005	0.011***	−0.016***
	(0.003)	(0.002)	(0.003)	(0.003)	(0.003)	(0.003)	(0.027)	(0.003)	(0.005)
Adding in the previous period	−0.084*	−0.089**	−0.040	−0.056	−0.144***	−0.022	−0.716**	−0.066^{+}	−0.089**
	(0.037)	(0.029)	(0.036)	(0.035)	(0.032)	(0.032)	(0.261)	(0.038)	(0.034)
Dropping in the previous period	−0.239***	−0.245***	0.012	−0.233***	−0.207***	−0.047	−0.837*	−0.225***	−0.163***
	(0.054)	(0.039)	(0.034)	(0.051)	(0.043)	(0.032)	(0.341)	(0.054)	(0.047)

Constant	−1.561***	−1.813***	−3.932***	−1.496***	−1.779***	−3.526***	−2.081*	−1.564***	−2.436***
	(0.117)	(0.097)	(0.208)	(0.110)	(0.109)	(0.170)	(0.837)	(0.118)	(0.146)
Industry dummies	Yes	Yes	Yes	Yes	Yes	Yes	Yes	Yes	Yes
Time dummies	Yes	Yes	Yes	Yes	Yes	Yes	Yes	Yes	Yes
Firms	25,973	24,838	4,650	28,817	23,602	7,026	769	25,318	30,138
N	123,336	135,038	24,708	132,946	117,194	34,867	2,056	121,280	157,158

Standard errors in parentheses; $^{+}p < 0.10$, $^{*}p < 0.05$, $^{**}p < 0.01$, $^{***}p < 0.001$.

Turnover for small and medium firms than large firms, when determined by sales.

However, given the cutoff value of less than 25 employees, nearly all the small firms (97%) are private. Is the size split sample result really just the public/private difference? In Models 7 and 8 of Table 6, we run regressions for public small firms and private small firms. Results echo the findings for the overall comparison between public and private firms: the coefficient for Portfolio Spread is only positive and statistically significant for the small private firms, but the coefficients are not significantly different at standard levels of statistical analysis. This evidence suggests that the constraint on growth of being small relates to private ownership.

Note that even small firms can have product market portfolios that span industries. In Model 9, we report results for firms that only have products in one of the 17 CorpTech industries. All control variables retain their same effects as for the full sample, but Portfolio Spread has a negative effect. Therefore, the positive relationship between Portfolio Spread and Product Turnover for small firms (e.g., Model 1) is not explained away because small firms might typically be limited to a single industry (Model 9). Instead, Portfolio Spread appears to drive Product Turnover only when the high growth and low growth markets are in distinct industries; specifically, when small, private firms are diversified.

In H4, we propose that ample financial slack would help firms overcome the constraints that might make them opt for Product Turnover when they want to grow. Table 7 reports models for the public firms that have information on Slack. The lagged Slack measure has a positive direct effect on Product Turnover (Model 1) and Gross Entry (Model 2), and a negative effect on Gross Exit (Model 3). Results are consistent using cash rather than our measure of financial slack, but these effects disappear if we use instead the ratio of financial slack over total assets. The split at the median value of Slack (approximately $30M) is shown in Models 4 and 5 of Table 7. Contrary to the hypothesis, there is no significant difference in the effects of Portfolio Spread across the two subsamples. Financial slack may facilitate Product Turnover, but does not make firms more or less likely to respond to inducements from external industry dynamics.

CONCLUSION

The present study presents panel data suggesting that multiproduct firms alter their product portfolios frequently. The diversification literature has focused mainly on explaining why firms expand product scope and in

Table 7. Poisson Regressions (One-Year Window) – Split Sample Analyses for Slack.

	(1) Turnover	(2) Gross entry	(3) Gross exit	(4) Turnover: high slack	(5) Turnover: low slack
Ln (product scope)	0.946***	−0.295***	1.518***	1.079***	0.684***
	(0.040)	(0.022)	(0.035)	(0.053)	(0.068)
Diversification Index	0.032	−0.168**	−0.093	−0.051	0.256
	(0.121)	(0.055)	(0.093)	(0.174)	(0.182)
Ln (market competition)	0.099**	−0.040**	0.119***	0.068	0.108*
	(0.034)	(0.015)	(0.026)	(0.048)	(0.051)
Ln (sales)	0.025	0.221***	−0.057***	0.025	0.045
	(0.017)	(0.012)	(0.014)	(0.026)	(0.028)
Ln (firm age)	−0.099**	0.091**	−0.056+	−0.156***	0.016
	(0.038)	(0.028)	(0.032)	(0.047)	(0.064)
Portfolio spread	−0.001	0.008***	0.000	−0.007	0.010
	(0.004)	(0.002)	(0.003)	(0.006)	(0.007)
Adding in the previous period	−0.042	−0.019	−0.064*	−0.061	−0.025
	(0.046)	(0.020)	(0.029)	(0.057)	(0.085)
Dropping in the previous period	−0.087*	−0.122***	−0.203***	−0.036	−0.260**
	(0.044)	(0.020)	(0.028)	(0.052)	(0.096)
Slack-lagged	31.937*	46.871***	−91.721***		
	(14.564)	(6.282)	(12.123)		
Constant	−3.239***	−0.367**	−3.556***	−3.278***	−2.993***
	(0.219)	(0.120)	(0.173)	(0.303)	(0.344)
Industry dummies	Yes	Yes	Yes	Yes	Yes
Time dummies	Yes	Yes	Yes	Yes	Yes
Firms	3,024	3,024	3,024	1,747	1,832
N	16,823	16,823	16,823	8,502	7,631

Standard errors in parentheses; $^{+}p < 0.10$, $*p < 0.05$, $**p < 0.01$, $***p < 0.001$.

which direction firms tend to diversify based on their specific resources. We consider entry and exit as a whole and explain that they often occur simultaneously, and that this could be the result of managers seeking efficient resource reallocation (Helfat & Eisenhardt, 2004). We use a longitudinal database with precise product category definitions to examine firm behaviors of market entry and exit, and define product turnover as a firm both entering and exiting in the same time period. We find that product turnover increases when firms participate in both high-growth and low-growth markets. This tendency to reallocate resources by exiting some (if not all) product markets and entering others simultaneously is particularly strong for small- and medium-sized firms, which tend to be privately owned firms. Some evidence supports our contention that general constraints on growth due to fixed capacity of complementary assets could tip the scales toward resource redeployment rather than synergy even if the firm has valuable, scale-free resources.

We identify several patterns that other researchers should note when choosing different product category systems, time windows, and samples to study diversification and related behaviors. Not only are there differences between broad classification systems like SIC codes and more precise product categories, but also the incidence of net adding, net dropping, and product turnover vary by industry and time window. Theory about resource redeployment suggests the need for empirical research at the resource level. Our analysis at the product market level suggests that such research might find fruitful ground in samples of mid-size firms. Findings may well still generalize to large, established firms or small, startup firms, but the phenomenon may be most evident for the mid-size firms.

The present study has limitations. While the CorpTech data enables us to estimate some models for thousands of firms, including smaller ones often excluded from academic analysis, it does lack product-level sales data. We estimate a firm's investment opportunities using sample-wide patterns of sales growth, but perhaps a better measure of Portfolio Spread of industry growth, using firm-specific sales data, would yield different results than our sample provided. Furthermore, we generate a diversification index by assuming that each product is of equivalent importance to the firm. The estimated effects of this control variable, and that of number of products, are as one would expect, yet more refined sales data would permit a measure of diversification that better matches the literature.

In addition, further research questions are worth investigating. First, our theory and results corroborate the idea that exiting a product market is not necessarily a signal of failure, but can be a strategic means to free up resources for redeployment to more profitable uses (Lee et al., 2012). Other data may permit the distinction between exit through divesting a subsidiary or facility, closing it down, or repurposing it. Second, the industry dynamics that affect product swapping may stem from international competition (Moreno-Badia, Miranda, & Van Beveren, 2008); thus, future research could investigate the relationship between resource redeployability and international diversification or product diversification in specific regions. Third, the executive succession literature suggests that a change in CEO is often associated with a change in strategy. The conduct of the top management team under a new CEO could be investigated to examine how distinct managerial skills and decision making processes affect the timing of shifts in the business portfolio, such as whether entry and exit are simultaneous (Greiner & Bhambri, 1989; Kiesler & Sproull, 1982; Wiersema & Bantel, 1993). Fourth, echoing the development of the literature on diversification, future research could move from the study of the incidence of product turnover to its direction (Capron, et al., 2001; Silverman, 1999). Which divisions are likely to be sold off when the firm is also actively entering new markets? As Chandler and Hikino (1990) suggested, technology often drives diversification, and technology relatedness affects the direction of diversification. For product turnover, industry-level factors and firm-level resources should both determine direction. Sakhartov and Folta (2014b) provide several testable hypotheses about the value of redeployability, and the direction would stem from similar factors. In sum, many rich possibilities exist for multi-level exploration of the interactions between different types of corporate strategy decisions.

NOTES

1. Since these authors only consider private firms that can be matched to public firms, they exclude very small private firms. Therefore, their sample of private firms is different from ours, and not only because they use a different data source.
2. Readers may be familiar with the CorpTech product classifications from their integration into the CapitalIQ database.
3. Hausman test statistics on the full sample and various subsamples yield test statistics that are not significant at $\alpha = 0.05$; therefore, we cannot reject the null hypothesis that the unobserved effect is uncorrelated with the explanatory variables, and the fixed-effect model is not consistent. For these tests, we use the Stata module "xtpqml" to estimate fixed-effect Poisson regressions, because "xtpoisson, fe" computes robust standard errors, as described by Wooldridge (1999) in the *Journal of Econometrics* (pp. 77–97). We also estimate negative binomial models as robustness checks, with similar results.
4. We use the Stata suest command to test for differences in coefficients across subsamples. However, this command is not available for panel Poisson models. Therefore, the Chow tests we report are based on comparison of coefficients from Poisson models that do not take firm random effects into account. Those coefficients can be slightly different from the ones reported in the tables.

ACKNOWLEDGMENT

We gratefully acknowledge insights from conversations about corporate strategy with Deepak Somaya, adjustments to the CorpTech data provided by Phil Anderson, and feedback from participants at the 2015 special conference in Strasbourg, France, sponsored by USIAS.

REFERENCES

Adner, R. (2002). When are technologies disruptive? A demand-based view of the emergence of competition. *Strategic Management Journal, 23*(8), 667–688.

Adner, R., & Zemsky, P. (2006). A demand-based perspective on sustainable competitive advantage. *Strategic Management Journal, 27*(3), 215–239.

Agarwal, R. (1997). Survival of firms over the product life cycle. *Southern Economic Journal, 63*(3), 571–584.

Agarwal, R., & Gort, M. (1996). The evolution of markets and entry, exit and survival of firms. *Review of Economics and Statistics, 78*(3), 489–498.

Ansoff, H. I. (1957). Strategies for diversification. *Harvard Business Review, 35*(5), 113–124.

Asker, J., Farre-Mensa, J., & Ljungqvist, A. (2012). *Comparing the investment behavior of public and private firms*. NBER Working Paper 17394.

Audretsch, D. B. (1991). New-firm survival and the technological regime. *The Review of Economics and Statistics, 73*(3), 441–450.

Audretsch, D. B. (1995a). Firm profitability, growth, and innovation. *Review of Industrial Organization, 10*(5), 579–588.

Audretsch, D. B. (1995b). *Innovation and industry evolution*. Cambridge, MA: MIT Press.

Audretsch, D. B., & Mahmood, T. (1995). New firm survival: New results using a hazard function. *The Review of Economics and Statistics, 77*(1), 97–103.

Baker, T., & Nelson, R. (2005). Making do with what's at hand: Entrepreneurial bricolage. *Administrative Science Quarterly, 50*(3), 329–366.

Bargeron, L. L., Schlingenmann, F. P., Stulz, R. M., & Zutter, C. J. (2008). Why do private acquirers pay so little compared to public acquirers? *Journal of Financial Economics, 89*, 375–390.

Barney, J. B. (1986). Strategic factor markets: Expectations, luck and business strategy. *Management Science, 32*(10), 1231–1241.

Barney, J. B. (1991). Firm resources and sustained competitive advantage. *Journal of Management, 17*(1), 99–120.

Barney, J. B., & Wright, P. M. (1997). On becoming a strategic partner: The role of human resources in gaining competitive advantage. *Human Resource Management, 37*(1), 31–46.

Baron, J. N. (1999). Building the iron cage: Determinants of managerial intensity in the early years of organizations. *American Sociological Review, 64*(4), 527–547.

Beck, T., Demirguc-Kunt, A., & Maksimovic, V. (2005). Financial and legal constraints to growth: Does firm size matter? *Journal of Finance, 60*(1), 137–177.

Bercovitz, J., & Mitchell, W. (2007). When is more better? The impact of business scale and scope on long-term business survival, while controlling for profitability. *Strategic Management Journal*, *28*, 61–79.

Bernard, A. B., Redding, S. J., & Schott, P. K. (2010). Multiple-product firms and product switching. *American Economic Review*, *100*(1), 70–97.

Berry, H. (2010). Why do firms divest? *Organization Science*, *21*(2), 380–396.

Brav, O. (2009). Access to capital, capital structure, and the funding of the firm. *Journal of Finance*, *64*, 263–308.

Bryce, D. J., & Winter, S. G. (2009). A general interindustry relatedness index. *Management Science*, *55*, 1570–1585.

Campello, M., Graham, J. R., & Harvey, C. R. (2010). The real effects of financial constraints: Evidence from a financial crisis. *Journal of Financial Economics*, *97*, 470–487.

Capron, L., Mitchell, W., & Swaminathan, A. (2001). Asset divestiture following horizontal acquisitions: A dynamic view. *Strategic Management Journal*, *22*(9), 817.

Carpenter, R. E., & Petersen, B. C. (2002). Is the growth of small firms constrained by internal finance? *Review of Economics and Statistics*, *84*(2), 298–309.

Chandler, A. D., & Hikino, T. (1990). *Scale and scope: The dynamics of industrial capitalism*. Harvard, MA: Belknap Press.

Chang, S. J. (1996). An evolutionary perspective on diversification and corporate restructuring: Entry, exit, and economic performance during 1981–89. *Strategic Management Journal*, *17*(8), 587–611.

Christensen, H. K., & Montgomery, C. A. (1981). Corporate economic performance: Diversification strategy versus market structure. *Strategic Management Journal*, *2*(4), 327–343.

Chung, C., & Luo, X. (2008). Institutional logics or agency costs: The influence of corporate governance models on business group restructuring in emerging economies. *Organization Science*, *19*(5), 766–784.

Danneels, E. (2002). The dynamics of product innovation and firm competences. *Strategic Management Journal*, *23*(12), 1095–1121.

de Figueiredo, J., & Silverman, B. (2007). Churn, baby, churn: Strategic dynamics among dominant and fringe firms in a segmented industry. *Management Science*, *53*(4), 632–650.

de Figueiredo, J. M., & Kyle, M. K. (2006). Surviving the gales of creative destruction: The determinants of product turnover. *Strategic Management Journal*, *27*(3), 241–264.

Dunne, T., Roberts, M. J., & Samuelson, L. (1989). The growth and failure of U. S. manufacturing plants. *The Quarterly Journal of Economics*, *104*(4), 671–698.

Eisenhardt, K. M., & Brown, S. L. (1998). Patching: Restitching business portfolios in dynamic markets. *Harvard Business Review*, *77*(3), 72–82.

Evans, D. S. (1987). Tests of alternative theories of firm growth. *The Journal of Political Economy*, *95*(4), 657–674.

Freear, J. (1990). Who bankrolls high-tech entrepreneurs? *Journal of Business Venturing*, *5*(2), 77–89.

George, G. (2005). Slack resources and the performance of privately held firms. *Academy of Management Journal*, *48*, 661–676.

Gort, M. (1962). *Diversification and integration in American industry*. Princeton, NJ: Princeton University Press.

Gort, M., & Klepper, S. (1982). Time paths in the diffusion of product innovations. *The Economic Journal*, *92*(367), 630–653.

Greiner, L. E., & Bhambri, A. (1989). New CEO intervention and dynamics of deliberate strategic change. *Strategic Management Journal*, *10*, 67–86.

Hall, B. H. (1987). The relationship between firm size and firm growth in the US manufacturing sector. *The Journal of Industrial Economics*, *35*(4), 583–606.

Helfat, C. E., & Eisenhardt, K. M. (2004). Inter-temporal economies of scope, organizational modularity, and the dynamics of diversification. *Strategic Management Journal*, *25*(13), 1217–1232.

Jensen, M. C. (1989). Eclipse of the public corporation. *Harvard Business Review*, *67*(5), 61–74.

Jovanovic, B. (1982). Selection and the evolution of industry. *Econometrica*, *50*(3), 649–670.

Jovanovic, B. (1993). The diversification of production. *Brookings Papers on Economic Activity*, *1*, 197–247.

Karim, S., & Mitchell, W. (2000). Path-dependent and path-breaking change: Reconfiguring business resources following acquisitions in the U.S. medical sector. *Strategic Management Journal*, *21*(10/11), 1061–1081.

Kiesler, S., & Sproull, L. (1982). Managerial response to changing environments: Perspectives on problem sensing from social cognition. *Administrative Science Quarterly*, *27*(4), 548–570.

Klepper, S. (1996). Entry, exit, growth, and innovation over the product life cycle. *American Economic Review*, *86*(3), 562–583.

Klepper, S. (1997). Industry life cycles. *Industrial and Corporate Change*, *6*(1), 145–182.

Klepper, S., & Graddy, E. (1990). The evolution of new industries and the determinants of market-structure. *Rand Journal of Economics*, *21*(1), 27–44.

Kor, Y. Y., & Mahoney, J. T. (2004). Edith Penrose's (1959) contributions to the resource-based view of the firm. *Journal of Management Studies*, *41*(1), 183–191.

Kraatz, M. S., & Zajac, E. J. (2001). How organizational resources affect strategic change and performance in turbulent environments: Theory and evidence. *Organization Science*, *12*(5), 632–657.

Lavin, M. R. (1992). *Business information: How to find it, how to use it* (2nd ed.). Phoenix, AZ: Oryx Press.

Lee, G. K. (2006). The significance of network resources in the race to enter emerging product markets: The convergence of telephony communications and computer networking, 1989–2001. *Strategic Management Journal*, *28*(1), 17.

Lee, G. K. (2008). Relevance of organizational capabilities and its dynamics: What to learn from entrants' product portfolios about the determinants of entry timing. *Strategic Management Journal*, *29*(12), 1257–1280.

Lee, G. K. (2009). Understanding the timing of 'fast-second' entry and the relevance of capabilities in invention vs. commercialization. *Research Policy*, *38*(1), 86–95.

Lee, G. K., Folta, T. B., & Lieberman, M. B. (2012). *Relatedness and market exit.* Working Paper No. 1920922.

Lee, G. K., & Lieberman, M. B. (2010). Acquisition vs. internal development as modes of market entry. *Strategic Management Journal*, *31*(2), 140–158.

Lee, G. K., & Paruchuri, S. (2008). Entry into emergent and uncertain product-markets: The role of associative rhetoric. *Academy of Management Journal*, *51*(6), 1171–1188.

Levinthal, D. A., & Wu, B. (2010). Opportunity costs and non-scale free capabilities: Profit maximization, corporate scope, and profit margins. *Strategic Management Journal*, *31*(7), 780–801.
Mahoney, J. T., & Pandian, J. R. (1992). The resource-based view within the conversation of strategic management. *Strategic Management Journal*, *13*(5), 363–380.
Makadok, R. (2001). Toward a synthesis of the resource-based and dynamic-capability views of rent creation. *Strategic Management Journal*, *22*(5), 387–401.
Markham, S. K. (1998). The breakfast of champions: Associations between champions and product development environments, practices and performance. *Journal of Product Innovation Management*, *15*(5), 436–454.
Markides, C. C., & Williamson, P. J. (1994). Related diversification, core competences and corporate performance. *Strategic Management Journal*, *15*(S2), 149–165.
Miller, D. (2006). Technological diversity, related diversification, and firm performance. *Strategic Management Journal*, *27*, 601–619.
Mishina, Y., Pollock, T. G., & Porac, J. (2004). Are more resources always better for growth? Resource stickiness in market and product expansion. *Strategic Management Journal*, *25*(12), 1179–1197.
Montgomery, C. A., & Wernerfelt, B. (1988). Diversification, Ricardian rents, and Tobin-q. *Rand Journal of Economics*, *19*(4), 623–632.
Moreno-Badia, M., Miranda, V., & Van Beveren, I. (2008). Globalization drives strategic product switching. *SSRN eLibrary*.
Myers, S. C. (2001). Capital structure. *Journal of Economic Perspectives*, *15*(2), 81–102.
Myers, S. C., & Majluf, N. S. (1984). Corporate financing and investment decisions when firms have information that investors do not have. *Journal of Financial Economics*, *13*(2), 187–221.
Nelson, R. R., & Winter, S. G. (1982). *An evolutionary theory of economic change*. Harvard, MA: Harvard University Press.
O'Brien, J. P. (2003). The capital structure implications of pursuing a strategy of innovation. *Strategic Management Journal*, *24*(5), 415–431.
Ocasio, W. (1997). Towards an attention-based view of the firm. *Psychology*, *1*, 403–404.
Opler, T. C., & Titman, S. (2012). Financial distress and corporate performance. *Journal of Finance*, *49*(3), 1015–1040.
Panzar, J. C., & Willig, R. D. (1977). Economies of scale in multi-output production. *Quarterly Journal of Economics*, *91*(3), 481–493.
Penrose, E. T. (1959). *The theory of the growth of the firm*. Oxford: Oxford University Press.
Porter, M. E. (1980). *Competitive strategy*. New York, NY: Free Press.
Priem, R. L., Li, S., & Carr, J. C. (2012). Insights and new directions from demand-side approaches to technology innovation, entrepreneurship, and strategic management research. *Journal of Management*, *38*(1), 346–374.
Puranam, P., & Srikanth, K. (2007). What they know vs. what they do: How acquirers leverage technology acquisitions. *Strategic Management Journal*, *28*(8), 805–825.
Robins, J. A., & Wiersema, M. (1995). A resource-based approach to the multibusiness firm. *Strategic Management Journal*, *16*, 277–299.
Rumelt, R. P. (1974). *Strategy, structure, and economic performance*. Harvard, MA: Harvard Business School Press.
Sakhartov, A. V., & Folta, T. B. (2014a). Resource relatedness, redeployability, and firm value. *Strategic Management Journal*, *35*, 1781–1797.

Sakhartov, A. V., & Folta, T. B. (2014b). Getting beyond relatedness as a driver of corporate value. *Strategic Management Journal*, *36*, 1939–1959.

Schultze, W. S., Lubatkin, M. H., & Dino, R. N. (2003). Exploring the agency consequences of ownership dispersion among the directors of private family firms. *Academy of Management Journal*, *46*(2), 179–194.

Silverman, B. S. (1999). Technological resources and the direction of corporate diversification: Toward an integration of the resource-based view and transaction cost economics. *Management Science*, *45*(8), 1109–1124.

Simerly, R. L., & Li, M. (1999). Environmental dynamism, capital structure and performance: A theoretical integration and an empirical test. *Strategic Management Journal*, *21*(1), 31–49.

Sine, W. D. (2006). Revisiting burns and stalker: Formal structure and new venture performance in emerging economic sectors. *Academy of Management Journal*, *49*(1), 121–132.

Stein, J. C. (1989). Efficient capital markets, inefficient firms: A model of myopic corporate behavior. *The Quarterly Journal of Economics*, *104*(4), 655–669.

Teece, D. J. (1982). Towards an economic theory of the multiproduct firm. *Journal of Economic Behavior and Organization*, *3*(1), 39–63.

Villalonga, B. (2004). Diversification discount or premium? New evidence from the business information tracking series. *Journal of Finance*, *59*, 479–506.

Villalonga, B., & McGahan, A. M. (2005). The choice among acquisitions, alliances, and divestitures. *Strategic Management Journal*, *26*, 1183–1208.

Wernerfelt, B. (1984). A resource-based view of the firm. *Strategic Management Journal*, *5*(2), 171–180.

Wernerfelt, B. (1989). From critical resources to corporate-strategy. *Journal of General Management*, *14*(3), 4–12.

Wiersema, M. F., & Bantel, K. A. (1993). Top management team turnover as an adaptation mechanism: The role of the environment. *Strategic Management Journal*, *14*(7), 485–504.

Wooldridge, J. M. (1999). Distribution-free estimation of some nonlinear panel data models. *Journal of Econometrics*, *90*(1), 77–97.

Wu, B. (2013). Opportunity costs, industry dynamics, and corporate diversification: Evidence from the cardiovascular medical device industry, 1976–2004. *Strategic Management Journal*, *34*, 1265–1287.

APPENDIX

Table A1. Summary of Product Turnover by Primary Industry.

	Product Market Level	Sub-Industry Level One-year	Industry Level	Product Market Level Two-year	Product Market Level Four-year
Factory automation	0.042 (0.287)	0.021 (0.160)	0.009 (0.099)	0.073 (0.453)	0.120 (0.613)
Biotechnology	0.053 (0.285)	0.029 (0.184)	0.010 (0.099)	0.092 (0.401)	0.149 (0.611)
Chemicals	0.052 (0.350)	0.025 (0.196)	0.008 (0.094)	0.112 (0.656)	0.212 (1.237)
Computer hardware	0.076 (0.446)	0.038 (0.227)	0.014 (0.122)	0.124 (0.687)	0.190 (0.971)
Defense	0.161 (0.834)	0.067 (0.350)	0.020 (0.147)	0.302 (1.399)	0.465 (1.926)
Energy	0.043 (0.334)	0.024 (0.183)	0.011 (0.109)	0.090 (0.593)	0.135 (0.698)
Environmental	0.038 (0.249)	0.012 (0.118)	0.006 (0.082)	0.061 (0.318)	0.089 (0.398)
Manufacturing equipment	0.028 (0.202)	0.014 (0.132)	0.008 (0.095)	0.043 (0.280)	0.071 (0.416)
Advanced materials	0.061 (0.464)	0.027 (0.232)	0.010 (0.100)	0.124 (0.758)	0.225 (1.232)
Medical equipment	0.044 (0.275)	0.020 (0.152)	0.008 (0.089)	0.082 (0.440)	0.134 (0.668)
Pharmaceuticals	0.091 (0.497)	0.050 (0.286)	0.011 (0.104)	0.167 (0.790)	0.205 (0.232)
Photonics	0.065 (0.367)	0.025 (0.185)	0.009 (0.099)	0.123 (0.620)	0.292 (1.295)
Computer software	0.059 (0.348)	0.028 (0.194)	0.006 (0.076)	0.094 (0.508)	0.205 (0.975)
Subassemblies and components	0.060 (0.420)	0.025 (0.195)	0.009 (0.095)	0.117 (0.714)	0.131 (0.770)
Test and measurement	0.058 (0.360)	0.028 (0.195)	0.012 (0.111)	0.103 (0.585)	0.195 (1.138)
Telecommunications and Internet	0.057 (0.363)	0.031 (0.209)	0.013 (0.114)	0.082 (0.524)	0.166 (0.871)
Transportation	0.081 (0.638)	0.034 (0.235)	0.009 (0.096)	0.165 (0.964)	0.107 (0.821)

Table A2. Diversifying Activities from Firms' Primary Industry.

Primary/Diversifying industry	AUT	BIO	CHE	COM	DEF	ENR	ENV	MAN	MAT	MED	PHA	PHO	SOF	SUB	TAM	TEL	TRN
Factory automation	4,526	14	35	275	32	140	191	867	183	72	11	169	492	815	724	221	109
Biotechnology	38	2,878	285	36	3	12	92	56	88	444	628	20	119	26	180	22	2
Chemicals	75	204	1,484	21	19	59	176	125	602	43	105	29	29	56	109	36	19
Computer hardware	336	11	18	7,039	33	67	44	234	37	67	2	196	3,603	517	273	2,745	52
Defense	109	11	19	204	529	43	67	176	50	24	3	119	298	262	157	364	315
Energy	181	17	107	84	20	1,478	246	184	129	25	2	60	159	388	251	143	54
Environmental	179	94	158	69	22	225	4,816	317	141	42	20	18	192	193	374	106	59
Manufacturing equipment	834	28	48	158	45	140	292	5,379	346	152	18	190	296	775	369	206	143
Advanced materials	211	97	423	47	40	92	170	556	3,666	87	38	151	67	407	156	62	98
Medical equipment	100	353	124	123	25	33	94	135	82	4,569	269	141	269	227	334	142	28
Pharmaceuticals	17	548	168	12	5	0	20	29	68	287	2,128	4	64	10	43	45	3
Photonics	236	16	17	123	36	62	25	221	88	134	1	3,194	144	333	328	258	44
Computer software	213	25	15	2,914	43	86	125	255	20	93	19	77	38,803	236	208	5,545	70
Subassemblies and components	878	30	40	693	127	447	262	1,065	319	194	9	632	418	9,249	1,361	1,045	366
Test and measurement	771	122	64	227	54	182	392	334	104	299	32	416	343	880	4,419	265	131
Telecommunications and internet	205	14	10	3,851	123	87	67	273	30	51	12	465	8,077	942	328	56,089	199
Transportation	135	4	25	91	109	97	95	203	97	33	4	84	152	335	265	145	932

Note: Each cell indicates the number of times in which a firm in the primary industry shown in the first column entered into a new product market in the industry shown across the top row. For example, there were 38 instances of a firm entering a product market in the Factory Automation industry when that firm's primary industry was biotechnology.

Table A3. Summary of Product Turnover by Primary Industry and Firm Size (One-Year Time Window).

	Product Turnover			Gross Extensive Entry			Gross Redeployment Entry		
	Small	Median	Large	Small	Median	Large	Small	Median	Large
Factory automation	0.181	0.040	0.029	0.529	0.227	0.225	0.137	0.026	0.016
Biotechnology	0.104	0.060	0.040	0.479	0.359	0.406	0.090	0.047	0.029
Chemicals	0.240	0.024	0.026	0.448	0.223	0.203	0.172	0.015	0.013
Computer hardware	0.250	0.072	0.050	0.598	0.381	0.371	0.355	0.051	0.031
Defense	0.588	0.070	0.031	0.836	0.389	0.229	0.495	0.032	0.018
Energy	0.118	0.030	0.024	0.539	0.292	0.262	0.066	0.015	0.013
Environmental	0.130	0.041	0.024	0.465	0.249	0.247	0.115	0.030	0.015
Manufacturing equipment	0.098	0.029	0.019	0.531	0.270	0.269	0.066	0.016	0.010
Advanced materials	0.181	0.036	0.028	0.459	0.251	0.228	0.096	0.030	0.023
Medical equipment	0.123	0.039	0.028	0.443	0.293	0.267	0.083	0.031	0.021
Pharmaceuticals, photonics	0.315	0.059	0.030	0.471	0.340	0.451	0.249	0.055	0.019
Photonics	0.383	0.079	0.038	0.557	0.331	0.308	0.366	0.056	0.028
Computer software	0.200	0.075	0.039	0.561	0.468	0.351	0.252	0.079	0.040
Subassemblies and components	0.249	0.040	0.026	0.517	0.248	0.274	0.196	0.026	0.016
Test and measurement	0.386	0.050	0.040	0.612	0.285	0.256	0.450	0.026	0.021
Telecommunications and internet	0.251	0.063	0.034	0.882	0.890	1.178	0.269	0.051	0.022
Transportation	0.360	0.037	0.023	0.629	0.302	0.233	0.188	0.018	0.017
Other	0.078	0.078	0.078	0.640	0.640	0.640	0.044	0.044	0.044
Total	0.206	0.053	0.034	0.584	0.400	0.470	0.180	0.042	0.025

Notes: Product turnover = minimum of entries and exits; Gross extensive entry = count of a firm's entries into product markets in CorpTech industries in which the firm has not operated; gross redeployment entry = count of a firm's entries into product markets in CorpTech industries in which the firm left some product market(s) in the same year.

RESOURCE REDEPLOYMENT THROUGH EXIT AND ENTRY: THREATS OF SUBSTITUTION AS INDUCEMENTS

Gwendolyn K. Lee and Srikanth Parachuri

ABSTRACT

The purpose of this original research is to explore whether firms redeploy the resources that were withdrawn from existing businesses and use them to enter an emerging product market. We studied 244 firms that have exited from at least one business and analyzed whether the firms entered the emerging product market as a new business. The inducements of resource redeployment vary with information cues in media rhetoric about emerging and shifting threats of substitution between the firm's existing businesses and the new one. Through our hazard rate analysis of entries of firms that exited existing businesses, we examined the hypotheses that resource redeployment through exit and entry may be driven by an interaction of the volume of substitution rhetoric with the resource commitments that the firm had made in the domain of the new business as well as the market relatedness between the firm's existing businesses and the new one. Our study makes conceptual and methodological

Resource Redeployment and Corporate Strategy
Advances in Strategic Management, Volume 35, 89–124

ISSN: 0742-3322/doi:10.1108/S0742-332220160000035005

contributions to the research on inducements, by theorizing how performance advantages of new over existing businesses vary with product evolution and by characterizing emerging and shifting threats of substitution with content analysis of media rhetoric. Our study suggests that prior work investigating corporate diversification provides an incomplete picture of the contribution of resource relatedness to firm value and firm decision-making.

Keywords: Resource redeployment; entry; exit; substitution threats

INTRODUCTION

Inter-temporal economies of scope involve redeploying firm resources – withdrawing firm resources from original businesses and reallocating them to new businesses – through exiting and entering different businesses (Helfat & Eisenhardt, 2004). Resource redeployment through exit and entry may potentially play an important role in a firm's strategic renewal (Agarwal & Helfat, 2009). While resource redeployment from existing businesses to new ones has been acknowledged since Penrose (1959), only recently have researchers started to clarify more in depth what she referred to as inducements. The extant research on the inducements of resource redeployment has examined the inducements that push resources away from a declining market (Helfat & Eisenhardt, 2004) and the inducements that pull resources from existing businesses to new businesses (Sakhartov & Folta, 2014).

While a declining market and the performance advantages of new over existing businesses may induce resource redeployment, whether a firm that has exited from an existing business would enter a new product at a stage of emergence as its new business is not clear. Both uncertainty and ambiguity are high about the new business because the technology and the market of a new product at a stage of emergence are still evolving. As the technology and the market evolve, the emerging product may pose a threat of substitution to a declining product, if the advancements in technology and the shifts in price-performance trade-off favor the emerging product.[1] However, the threat of substitution may shift in strength and even disappear. The threat diminishes when the technology and the price-performance ratio of the emerging product fail to meet expectations. Even when the technology and the price-performance ratio exceed expectations, product attributes, usage conditions, and benefits may change in the course of evolution such that the emerging product shifts its disruptive force elsewhere. Therefore, the performance advantages of new over existing businesses vary with the emerging and shifting threats posed by the new business as a substitute for the existing businesses.

We submit that resource redeployment through exit and entry is driven by an interaction between the threats of substitution that a firm's existing businesses face from a newly emerging product and specific firm characteristics. The signals about threats of substitution are not unambiguous and managers have to make entry decisions under uncertainty and ambiguity. Cues such as customer/supplier defections, factor price increases, price reduction pressures, and sales displacements indicate the extent of substitution that has occurred. However, these cues are at best transient signals because product attributes, usage conditions and benefits evolve over the course of a product's development. As the volume of the substitution threat signals increases, decision-makers' awareness increases along with the saliency of this substitution potential, prompting the firms to take action. Yet, these signals continue to suggest uncertainty and ambiguity, because the newly emerging product market is still evolving (Daft & Lengel, 1986; Weick, 1979). In this paper, we focus on two firm characteristics that will allow us to predict how likely the decision-makers may act by entering the new business: resource commitments in the domain of new business and the market relatedness between the firm's existing businesses with the newly emerging one.

We propose that the more resource commitments a firm has in the domain, the more actively the firm conducts purposeful experimentation and searches for new opportunities in the domain. A firm's purposeful experimentation and search for new opportunities is the essence of resource reconfiguration (Karim, 2006; Karim & Mitchell, 2004).[2] Increase in volume of substitution threat signals will prompt the firm with high resource commitments in the domain of the new business to engage in purposeful experimentation and find new opportunities in the domain, thereby increasing the likelihood of entering the new business. In contrast, the firm with little or no resource commitment in the domain is relatively less inclined to perform purposeful experimentation and search in the domain. Therefore, we hypothesize that, the firm's resource commitments in the domain of the new business may moderate the effect of volume of substitution threat signals on entry decision.

Additionally, we propose that the market relatedness of the firm's existing businesses with the newly emerging one also helps assess how likely the firm may act in response to increasing volume of substitution threat signals. The firm with more relatedness will have more awareness of and saliency to the these signals than the firm with less relatedness. This is so because relatedness enhances a firm's absorptive capacity (Cohen & Levinthal, 1990). Moreover, compared to firms with less relatedness, firms with more relatedness may also have lower entry costs making their future success relatively more feasible. Therefore, we also hypothesize that the market relatedness of the firm's existing businesses may moderate the effect of volume of substitution threat signals on entry decisions.

To test our hypotheses, we conducted an empirical analysis in the context of emerging and shifting threats of substitution. The empirical context of substitution involving a new product at a stage of emergence is ideal for studying resource redeployment through exit and entry. It is so, because "[i]nter-temporal economies of scope have implications for the evolution of related diversified corporations over time, *particularly in markets where technologies and demand are in flux. As these sorts of markets emerge, grow, split, combine with other markets, and mature*, managers must make frequent strategic decisions about *whether and when to enter or exit product-markets*" (Helfat & Eisenhardt, 2004, pp. 1217–1218, emphasis added).

We study 244 firms in the industry of computer networking and communications equipment over a fifteen-year period during the boom and the bust in the 1990s and the early 2000s. These firms exited from at least one of the existing products in this industry. Twenty percent of the firms entered the product market of "network switches," which is the new product and its domain is the Internet infrastructure. The domain of Internet infrastructure covers a subset of the products in the computer networking and communications equipment industry (Fig. 1). As the new product evolved, it posed emerging and shifting threats of substitution to the existing products in the industry, according to the professional judgments of journalists that are reported in the media rhetoric. In essence, our empirical test is on firms that were deciding, under uncertainty and ambiguity, whether to redeploy the resources that were withdrawn from the exits and use them to enter the new product market that was at a stage of emergence.

Our study on resource redeployment through exit and entry has implications for the conceptual and the empirical challenges of linking inducements to resource redeployment. One implication is in regards to the temporal variations in inducements. As mentioned earlier, the performance advantages of new over existing businesses are not fixed. We use our empirical context of emerging and shifting threats of substitutions between new and existing products to demonstrate the temporal variations in performance advantages.

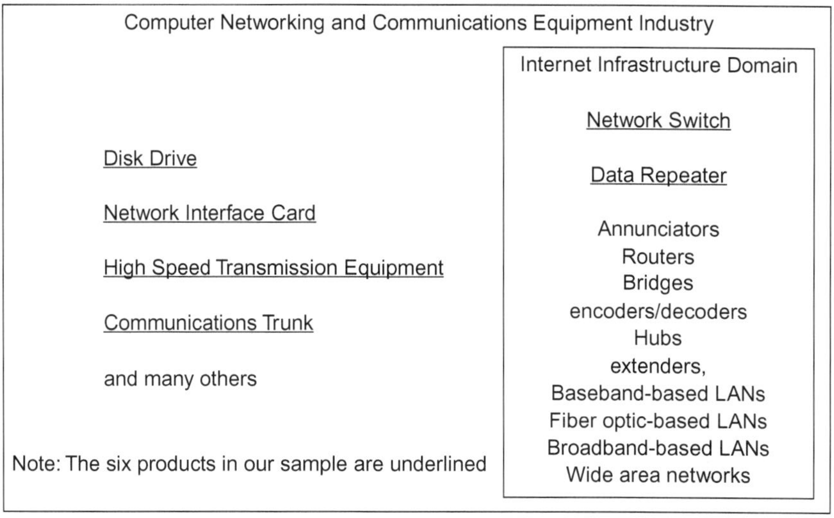

Fig. 1. The Domain of Internet Infrastructure Covers a Subset of the Products in the Computer Networking and Communications Equipment Industry.

And we show how to use content analysis of media rhetoric as signals of such temporal variations and how to incorporate the variations in an empirical analysis of exit and entry. Hence, we extend Sakhartov and Folta's (2014) insights on performance advantages of new over existing businesses, by contributing both conceptually and methodologically how inducements change as product attributes, usage conditions and benefits evolve over the course of a product's development. This contribution allows us to reflect on one of the questions raised in the Special Issue Call for Papers. We offer our answer to the question about resource relatedness, firm value, and firm decision-making in the "Discussion" section.

THEORETICAL BACKGROUND AND DEVELOPMENT

Notion of Inducements

Starting from Penrose (1959), researchers have highlighted the role of inducements for firm growth and technical change. She conceptualized the inducements to expand as "growing demand for particular products, changes in technology which call for production on a larger scale than before, *discoveries and inventions the exploitation of which seems particularly promising or which open up promising fields in supplementary directions*, special opportunities to obtain a better market position or achieve some monopolistic advantage, and similar conditions and opportunities" (Penrose, 1959; Chapter V, emphasis added). While she used the notion of internal and external inducements to explain the direction of expansion, researchers have distinguished inducements along three dimensions. The three dimensions are current return advantages of new markets (Anand, 2004; Levinthal & Wu, 2010; Silverman, 1999; Wu, 2013), return volatility (Helfat & Eisenhardt, 2004; Kogut & Kulatilaka, 1994; Sakhartov & Folta, 2014; Triantis & Hodder, 1990), and return correlation between markets (Triantis & Hodder, 1990).

However, as Sakhartov and Folta (2014) point out, the research frontier should consider more complex notions of inducements. Conceptualizing redeployment as real options to switch the use of resources across markets, Sakhartov and Folta (*ibid.*) identify inducements as a combination of interdependent dimensions of current resource advantages, return volatility, and return correlation. The more complex notions of inducements are shown to modify the conventional wisdom about the effect of relatedness on corporate value. In addition to generating novel insights about inducements, Sakhartov and Folta (*ibid.*) opens up possibilities for further reconceptualization and identification of inducements. Our study builds on their work on inducements by emphasizing the uncertainty and the ambiguity in interpreting emerging and shifting threats of substitution.

Emerging and Shifting Threats of Substitution

Product attributes, usage conditions and benefits evolve over the course of a product's development. Products with no overlap in product attributes, usage conditions and benefits may subsequently emerge into substitutes. Yet, products with some overlap may not materialize into actual substitutes. As such, cues indicating the extent of substitution that has occurred are at best transient signals. Without less ambiguous cues, managers looking for inter-temporal economies of scope often fail to categorize a product as an emerging substitute until it is too late to take action (Peteraf & Bergen, 2003).

Identifying substitution threats involving an emerging product is particularly important for those managers who are looking for inter-temporal economies of scope because early identification allows them to capture greater returns from reallocating resources to the newly emerging product. In order to identify and understand the looming threats of emerging substitute, managers need to evaluate the extent of overlap between the firm's products and all newly emerging products. However, such evaluation requires managers to exhaustively compare all pairs of products across all attributes, usage conditions and benefits. The combinatorial explosion and its associated cognitive complexity create serious challenges for managers.

Despite the challenges, the research on a socio-cognitive view of product markets and technology evolution suggests that media stories help market actors make sense of a product market by constructing meaning about the product market with respect to a system of existing product markets (for a socio-cognitive view of product markets, see Fligstein, 1996; Garud & Rappa, 1994; Kennedy, 2008; Rosa, Porac, Runser-Spanjol, & Saxon, 1999; White, 1981, 2002; for that of technology evolution, see Kaplan, 2011). According to this research, media stories enable a large number of different actors to share their understanding. They facilitate market actors' sensemaking and meaning construction by associating one product with other products and classifying and positioning it in a network vis-à-vis other products (Rosa & Porac, 2002; Rosa et al., 1999).

The research on socio-cognitive view further posits that frames are constructed to create awareness, saliency and legitimacy for audiences. Frames are the "schemata of interpretation" (Goffman, 1974, p. 21), as devices that organize information and package them for their audiences, providing "persistent patterns of cognition, interpretation, and presentation, of selection, emphasis, and exclusion" (Gitlin, 1980, p. 7). By building frames, the media reduces the complexity of an issue and provides structures of meaning (Reese, 2007; Scheufele & Tewksbury, 2007).

Through frames, awareness is created by bringing to audiences' attention the information about comparisons of attributes, usage conditions, and benefits collected from different constituents (Abrahamson, 1996). Salience is created by making audiences realize that this information is very important (Deephouse, 2000). Lastly, legitimacy is created around this information such that firms have incentives and pressures to act (Pollock & Rindova, 2003; Suchman, 1995). If in fact the media stories on threats of substitution create this awareness, saliency and legitimacy, we expect managers to pay attention to an increasing rhetoric of substitution, as firms look for inter-temporal economies of scale.

Resource Redeployment through Exit and Entry

As mentioned earlier, signals of threats of substitution are uncertain and ambiguous. As the amount of rhetoric in the media stories about substitution between a firm's existing product markets and the newly emerging one increases, the awareness and saliency of potential substitution increase. Further, given that substitution threats emerge and shift over time, increase in the volume of media rhetoric about threats of substitution does not necessarily reduce uncertainty and ambiguity for decision-makers.

However, firms with specific characteristics may be in a better position than others to act under such uncertainty and ambiguity (Daft & Lengel, 1986; Weick, 1979). We focus on two characteristics: resource commitments in the domain of the new business and the market relatedness between the firm's existing businesses and the newly emerging one. Domain-specific resource commitments make firms prone to purposeful experimentation in the domain and prompt them to act in response to high volume of substitution threat signals. Market relatedness between the firm's existing businesses and the newly emerging one increases the pressure as well as the incentive to act in response to substitution threat signals.

Resource Commitments in a Domain

As mentioned earlier, the more resource commitments a firm has in a domain, the more actively the firm conducts purposeful experimentation and searches for new opportunities in the domain (Karim, 2006; Karim & Mitchell, 2004). Through the process of purposeful experimentation and search for new opportunities, the firm deepens its commitment to the domain.

As the volume of substitution threat signals increases, the decision-makers become more aware of the substitution potential between their existing products and the new one. The substitution potential also becomes more salient (Abrahamson, 1996; Deephouse, 2000). This increased awareness and saliency put pressure on the decision-makers to act in response to those signals (Pollock & Rindova, 2003; Suchman, 1995). However, while the awareness and saliency increase with the volume of signals, the uncertainty and ambiguity associated with the emerging and shifting substitution threats do not go away. Even if the media declares that one product will be substituted, the underlying technologies, customer tastes, product features, and its usages may evolve in such a way that the substitution may switch its direction or completely vanish later in the future. In short, even with increasing awareness and saliency, the ambiguity and uncertainty will not be resolved.

We propose that firms with high resource commitments to the domain of the new business act differently from those with low resource commitments, as the volume of substitution threat signals increases. While the ambiguity and uncertainty remain unresolved, firms with high resource commitments are prone to conduct purposeful experimentation and search for new opportunities in the domain. So, as awareness and saliency of the substitution potential increase, firms more committed to the domain are likely construe the new business as an opportunity for them to do purposeful experimentation, thereby increasing the likelihood of entry. That is, for firms with high resource commitments, the likelihood of entry increases with awareness and saliency. In contrast, for firms with low resource commitments, the likelihood of entry decreases with awareness and saliency. Low resource commitment to the domain suggests that the firms are not as enthusiastic about experimentation.

In sum, we hypothesize the following interaction effect (H1): the volume of substitution rhetoric in the media stories and the resource commitments of a firm in a domain will jointly influence the firm's entry into a newly emerging business in the domain. The increased likelihood of entry with increasing substitution rhetoric would be much higher for firms with higher resource commitments than for firms with no/little resource commitments.

Market Relatedness between a Firm's Existing Businesses and the New One

Market relatedness may moderate the effect of substitution rhetoric on entry for two reasons. First, the knowledge about how markets are related in the underlying science and technology increases the firm's ability to identify and assess external information signals (Cohen & Levinthal, 1989). In addition, market relatedness enhances a firm's absorptive capacity with respect to the application of knowledge to commercial ends and the development of products and markets (Cohen & Levinthal, 1990, 1994). As suggested by the research on entry to new market niches (Helfat & Lieberman, 2002), market relatedness across product generations, industry segments, or subfields plays a significant role in entry decisions. We propose that firms with more market relatedness act differently from those with less market relatedness, as the volume of substitution rhetoric increases. The absorptive capacity with respect to the new business suggests that the awareness and saliency of the signals are much heightened for firms with more market relatedness than firms with less market relatedness. As such, the pressure to act in response to substitution threat signals is higher on firms with more market relatedness.

The second reason is that, with more market relatedness, firms can more easily leverage activities, processes, and competencies from one market to another, thus reducing the costs of entering the new business. As such, with increasing pressure to act arising from increasing volume of substitution threat signals, the reduced entry cost would increase the likelihood of entry even more, because even if the entry turns out to be a mistake, the mistake is less costly for firms with more market relatedness. In addition, the chance of succeeding in the new business is higher for firms with more market relatedness, because more resources and experiences can be transferred. Therefore, market relatedness increases not only the pressure but also the incentive to act in response to substitution threat signals.

In sum, we hypothesize the following interaction effect (H2): The volume of substitution rhetoric in the media stories and market relatedness of a firm with respect to a new business jointly influence the firm's entry into the new business. The increased likelihood of entry with increasing substitution rhetoric would be much higher for firms with more market relatedness than for firms with less market relatedness.

RESEARCH METHODS

Sampling Frame and Empirical Setting

To better understand whether a firm would exit an existing business and enter a new one, hence, redeploy resources through exit and entry, we study emerging and shifting threats of substitution as our empirical context. In this context, a firm conducts purposeful experimentation and search for new opportunities in the domain of Internet infrastructure. Specifically, the firm applies multi-media communications technology to the development of network components, for the build-out of Internet infrastructure (Lee, 2008). The domain covers many products, including annunciators, routers, bridges, encoders/decoders, hubs, repeaters, extenders, local area networks (LANs are built with network components for short distance, high speed, interconnection between computers), baseband-based LANs, broadband-based LANs, fiber optic-based LANs, wide area networks (WANs), and network switches.

A sample of products was randomly selected from the industry of computer networking and communications equipment, where the industry is broader than the domain of Internet infrastructure, as illustrated in Fig. 1 earlier. This sampling frame allowed us to analyze a firm's exit from an existing product and entry into a new one. Given that seemingly unrelated products could become substitutes and seemingly substitutable products could become unrelated products, a random sampling frame ensures that a firm's products have varying potential in substituting and being substituted by the new product. Among a sample of six products, we designated "network switch" as the new product because it was the last one to emerge. We referred to the other five – "network interface card," "data repeater," "disk drive," "communications trunk," and "high speed transmission equipment" – as existing products. Resource redeployment through exit and entry is thus reusing the resources from exiting at least one of the existing products to "network switches."

A firm became at risk of entering the new product market when it exited from at least one of the five products between 1990 and 2002; it fell out of the risk set after entering the new product market or at the end of our 15-year observation period that completed in 2003. In total, our analysis of exit and entry covered 244 firms and 813 firm-year observations. Among the risk set, 49 firms entered the new product market, while 195 didn't. Only forty-one percent of the 244 firms have resource commitments in the domain of Internet infrastructure.

Data Sources

Our sample of products and firms was drawn from the CorpTech directory on "Who Makes What" organized by firm, product code, and year. For the coding of exit and entry events, we examined how the product portfolios of our sample firms changed over time. For each firm, the CorpTech directory also provided data on the number of employees and the year of founding. Based on which, we calculated firm size and firm age. To collect data about market size and market growth rates, we used product revenue reported by the United States Census Bureau.

The media rhetoric characterizes emerging and shifting threats of substitution between two products by describing the overlap between the two in attributes, usage conditions, and benefits. We assess the overlap between the new product and the existing products espoused in the media's substitution rhetoric by tracking news articles that offered professional judgments of journalists covering the computer and telecommunications industry. The data source for the news articles is the LexisNexis Academic database, a common source used by researchers (Abrahamson & Fairchild, 1999; Ghaziani & Ventresca, 2005; Pollock & Rindova, 2003).

Justification for using media story is provided by Rosa et al. (1999, p. 75): "Careful and systematic analysis of the public discourse that surrounds emerging and established product categories yields measures that can be almost as detailed and precise as those collected through other methods …." Media stories serve as a source of primary information and collective sensemaking for several audiences including managers, customers, and investors (*ibid.*).

Capturing Emerging and Shifting Substitution Threat with Content Analysis of Media Rhetoric

We developed the following procedure for measuring the rhetoric of substitution in the media. First, we identified a set of articles for content analysis by selecting those that co-mention in the same article the keywords of the new product and the firm's existing product. The keywords came from the CorpTech directory for describing the products. To ensure that the keywords are comprehensive and representative descriptions, we asked a technical expert with more than ten years of experience in communications engineering to independently verify the keywords. Following Rosa et al. (1999), we posit that when products are co-mentioned, the nature of relationship between the products is revealed by the type of association characterized in the media story.

Second, we employed four raters to independently analyze the content of the identified articles. The raters' task was to assess how professional journalists discussed in each article the extent of overlap between products in their attributes, usage conditions, and benefits. After the articles were analyzed, we verified the extent to which the raters agreed on the assessments. Our inter-rater agreement index measured with r_{wg} (James, Demaree, & Wolf, 1993) suggested that the within-article agreement among the raters was adequate (mean = .70). Although there are no absolute standards regarding acceptable levels of inter-rater agreement, a mean agreement index of .70 is typically used as the threshold, above which the raters are in agreement (George, 1990; Janz, Colquitt, & Noe, 1984, 1997). For articles about which raters disagreed, the assessment was based on a consensus that was achieved after extensive discussions in a meeting with all the raters.

The final step was to measure the amount of media characterization relevant for each firm each year by matching the product that the firm produced in the publication year with the product co-mentioned with network switch. For firms producing more than one of the five existing products we sampled, the count of articles was normalized by the number of a firm's existing products.

Dependent Variable and Analytical Technique

The dependent variable, which is coded for each annual spell of a firm, takes the value of 1 if the firm entered the new product market in year *t*, and 0 otherwise. In estimating the hazard rate of market entry with a duration model, we use the proportional-hazard specification known as the Cox model (1972). The advantage of the commonly adopted Cox model is that it releases us from making assumptions about the form of duration dependence in the hazard rate. The independent and control variables are measured with a one-year lag. Additionally, robust standard errors are estimated so as to account for multiple spells of the same firm.

Primary Variables of Theoretical Interest

Our hypothesis posits that a firm's resource redeployment through exit and entry – exiting from existing products and entering into a new one – is a function of two interactions. One interaction is between volume of substitution rhetoric in the media and a firm's resource commitments in a domain. The other interaction is between volume of substitution rhetoric in the media and the market relatedness between a firm's existing products and the new one.

Volume of Substitution Rhetoric

The larger the volume of substitution rhetoric, the higher the awareness and saliency about the potential threats of substitution. We measure the volume annually, so we can track the threats as they emerge and shift over time. One scenario may suggest that the new product poses a substitution threat against a firm's existing products, but another scenario may suggest the opposite, where the firm's existing products pose a substitution threat against the new product. To be thorough, we account for both scenarios with the normalized count of the number of articles with substitution rhetoric.

The Firm's Resource Commitments in the Domain of Internet Infrastructure
We measure the firm's resource commitments in a domain by counting the number of products the firm has that are in the same domain as the new product, which is the domain of Internet infrastructure. We use CorpTech's classification system to define the domain with the root category of product codes beginning with TEL-NW (e.g., TEL-NW-W: Wide area networks, as shown in Fig. 1 earlier). These products specific to the domain represent a purposeful experimentation and search for opportunities with respect to the build-out of Internet infrastructure. This is only one aspect of the firm's product portfolio, albeit a strategic one.

Market Relatedness between the Firm's Existing Businesses and the New One
We measure market relatedness with the similarity between the firm's existing products and the new one. The existing products in our sample cover a diverse set of products including those inside the domain of Internet Infrastructure and those outside, since the sample is randomly drawn from the industry of computer networking and communications equipment, which is broader than the domain of Internet Infrastructure. The measure of market relatedness is the average of the inter-market similarity index across the market pairs between the firm's existing product markets and the new one. The inter-market similarity index is developed with the pattern of Who Makes What in the industry of computer networking and communications equipment. Please see Lee (2008, 2009) for further details about the methodology.

Control Variables

We used a set of firm-level variables to control for characteristics that may affect market entry. Larger firms are likely to have more resources for market entry. So, we controlled for firm size by using the natural log of a firm's employee headcount in year $t-1$. Older firms are less likely to respond to environmental changes, such as threats of substitution. So, we controlled for firm age by using the number of years since the firm's founding. We also controlled for the number of existing products the firm has, since, for some firms, resource redeployment through exit and entry may involve more than one of the five existing products in the sample. When the firm exits from more than one existing product, the momentum to redeploy the resources released from the exits may become stronger. As such, we controlled for the number of products a firm had among the five existing products we sampled. In addition, we controlled for how diverse the firm's entire product portfolio is, using the Blau's (1977) heterogeneity index. When each of the firm's products belongs to a distinct industry sector, the index reaches its maximum value of 1; when the firm's products all belong to the same industry sector, the index reaches its minimum value of 0. Finally, we controlled for the number of technology classes the firm has as well as the average number of patents per technology class in the firm's patent profile, since firms with patents may be able to enter the new product market faster.

We also used a set of market-level variables to control for characteristics of the new product market that may affect entry. First, we controlled for the growth rate of the exited product market, because the lower the growth rate, the high the likelihood that the firm would be in search for a new market to enter. Next, we controlled for the growth rate and the size of the new product market, which are indicators for the amount of business activity in the new market. The amount of business activity may affect future market opportunity. As the size of the new market grows faster and becomes larger, the entry rate increases, until the market becomes saturated. In addition, we controlled for the number of firms entering into and exiting from the new market. A large number of entries suggests to the firms that have been waiting an attractive market condition, whereas a large number of exits suggests deteriorating market condition. Finally, we controlled for media forecasts about the new product market. The nature of business forecasts may affect entry because they provide informational stimuli to managerial decision making. We used a random sample of articles (four articles per month) that made business forecasts about the new product market. Business forecasts that reported facts, cited research, or provided analysis about the outlook of the new product market were coded as optimistic, neutral, or pessimistic forecast. Based on the random sample, we estimated the probability of optimistic, neutral, or pessimistic media forecast, and used the estimated probabilities in year $t-1$ as control variables.

Furthermore, we used a set of control variables at the firm-market level. First, we controlled for associative rhetoric in media story linking the firm's existing product markets and the new one, because associative rhetoric has been shown to affect entry. Following Lee and Paruchuri (2008), we control for the volume of positive or neutral associative rhetoric. The association is positive if the media story described the relationship between the two products/markets as complementary or synergistic, and neutral if the relationship between the two was not explicitly stated. Moreover, we controlled for the sequence in which the firms exited and entered with a dummy variable. The purpose of this control variable is to identify the cases where the exit and entry events may coincide. We identify the sequence with a dummy variable by comparing the year of the entry event and that of the exit event. The dummy variable takes the value of 1 if the exit and the entry events occurred in the same year. Otherwise, the dummy variable takes the value of 0. Furthermore, we controlled for market entry inertia and market entry momentum, accounting for the firm's history of market entry. Entry inertia is measured with the number of years that has elapsed since the firm's most recent entry event by the firm into any market. Entry momentum is measured with the cumulative number of product markets a firm had entered from the first year the firm is in the risk set through year $t-1$. Finally, we controlled for the firm's technological capabilities most similar to those required by the new product and the technological relatedness between the firm's existing product and the new product. Both measures are constructed with a technology similarity index with respect to the new product market, ranking a list of technology classes.[3] The technology classes were ranked according to their similarity to "Class 370 – multiplex communications," which is the focal technology class for network switches. The firm's technological capabilities most similar to those required by the new product is the measured with the highest rank of the firm's patent classes, representing the nearest point corresponded to the most similar technology class in the firm's patent portfolio each year. By contrast, the technological relatedness between the firm's existing product and the new product is measured with the average of the interclass similarity index across the existing-new technology class pairs. These two measures are not correlated statistically, capturing distinct features of the firm's technology that may be applicable to the new product.

CONTENT ANALYSIS

In the "Research Methods" section, we developed an approach for capturing emerging and shifting threats of substitution through media rhetoric. In this section, we present concrete examples from our content analysis on the media rhetoric that espouses emerging and shifting threats of substitution. Here are the findings from our qualitative analysis of substitution rhetoric involving the new product, which is the "network switches."

Emerging and Shifting Substitution Rhetoric Involving the New Product

First, the media rhetoric provides frames in which two products are interpreted as substitutes when the *product attributes* of two products are compared and discussed as overlapping. For example, one media story noted: "**As a technology, switching has put** older, shared-bandwidth hubs and **repeaters out to pasture**. The bottom line: The more state-of-the-art your switched network becomes, the more likely it will incorporate vendor-proprietary capabilities and features. The trade-off for advanced functionality, then, is interoperability" (*Network World*, August 11, 1997, emphasis bolded). The patterns of emphasis suggest that the attributes of one product such as the technology are superior to those of the other. Such discussion of overlapping product attributes provides a frame of substitution, illuminating a classic case of substitution as articulated by Christensen (1997) where one product based on next generation technology displaces another product based on earlier generation technology. A similar comparison is also evident in the following: "The 1G-AnyLAN technology is expected to reach the draft standard stage this spring, said Daniel Dove, principal engineer at HP's Roseville Networks Division in Roseville, Calif. HP **repeaters** and LAN **switches based on the pumped-up VG-AnyLAN technology** could be out in the next 18 to 24 months, he said ... However, he said a 1G bit/sec **switch would be considerably more expensive**" (*Network World*, January 8, 1996; emphasis bolded).

Another way the media rhetoric provides frames of substitution between two products is by discussing their overlap in *usage conditions* (Tripsas, 2009 for importance of customer preferences), as in when one product's usage conditions overlap with the other product's usage. For example, one media story noted: "**Customers will need the repeater products early on, followed by high-end enterprise switches** .... The switch can support as many as 240 Fast Ethernet ports and 24 Gigabit Ethernet links, with FDDI, ATM and frame relay interfaces **planned for the future**. The device boasts a backplane capacity of 56G bit/sec and provides full Layer 3 routing at wire speed, according to Daines [president and CEO of Packet Engines]" (*Network World*, July 28, 1997, emphasis bolded). The patterns of emphasis suggest that repeaters will be replaced by switches because their usage conditions overlap as enterprise customers become sophisticated in future planning for capacity and speed. Another illustration of this pattern is: "By **providing ports with multiple bandwidths** at a low price per port, the LANCAST Desktop **Switch is an extremely attractive alternative to the less effective single-speed repeaters** .... The requirements of computer networks are constantly changing even as new bandwidth-hungry applications are introduced, added Bob Cellucci [Vice President of Sales for LANCAST]" (*PR Newswire*, October 8, 1997; emphasis bolded).

The media rhetoric also provides frames of substitution when the *benefits* of two products are compared, as in when price and performance of one product are characterized as more attractive than those of the other. For example, one media story noted: "Texas Instruments, Inc. last week unveiled a new Ethernet processor, dubbed ThunderSwitch, that will allow LAN switch vendors to **build switches that support advanced features** such as virtual LANs and built-in Remote Monitoring, but **at the price of repeaters**" (*Network World*, March 11, 1996, emphasis bolded). This pattern of emphasis suggests that an innovation in a component of switches is projected to increase performance without adding cost such that the price of higher-performance switches will have the same price as repeaters. As such, switches can be interpreted as becoming a substitute of repeaters, representing a classic case of substitution articulated in Porter (2008 [1985]) where the price-performance trade-off is tipping in favor of the substitute. Another illustration of such price-performance comparison is inherent in the following: "3Com's switches are very **aggressively priced because they are going after** the repeater market," [Glenn Gabriel Ben-Yosef, president of Clear Thinking Research, Inc. in Boston] said (*Network World*, May 8, 1995; emphasis bolded).

An additional point of interest in the media stories is that they typically identified which product is substituting/is substituted by which product. For example, consider the earlier media story about substitution between switch and repeater: "**As a technology, switching has put** [...] **repeaters out to pasture**. [...]" (*Network World*, August 11, 1997, emphasis bolded). The patterns of emphasis suggest that switch has substituted/is substituting repeaters.

Moreover, these media stories about product categorization comprised conversations among diverse groups of actors. In the context of substitution, we observed that information is drawn from different actors, including customers, producers, engineers, end users, analysts, researchers, etc. For example, in one media story, the **president** of Clear Thinking Research, Inc. in Boston articulated that "3Com's switches are very aggressively priced because they are going after the repeater market" (*Network World*, May 8, 1995). In a different media story, information is gathered from **security analysts**: "Some analysts questioned whether the price differential will be enough to entice customers to choose a repeater over a switch" (*Network World*, March 3, 1997). In yet another media story, information was gathered from **users**: "Dubiel's [manager of planning for Boston Edison] solution was to put multiple network interface cards (NIC) into key servers so they could reside on multiple LAN segments. However, it soon became apparent that he needed a better fix. This year, Dubiel began deploying combination 10M/100M bit/sec Ethernet switches at the work-group level" (*Network World*, March 4, 1996).

RESULTS

Estimating Resource Redeployment through Exit and Entry

The descriptive statistics are presented in Table 1. Firm size and firm age were highly correlated, so they were orthogonalized with a modified Gramm-Schmidt procedure. This procedure removes high correlations among the variables without affecting their correlations with other variables (Golub & Van Loan, 1989). The Gramm-Schmidt procedure was also applied to remove the high correlation between the number of technology classes that the firm has in its patents and the average number of patents the firm has per technology class. In addition, the procedure applied to remove the high correlation among the growth rate of the exited product market, the growth rate of the new product market, the size of the new product market, the number of firms exiting from the new product market, and the number of firms entering the new product market. The pair-wise correlations among the variables are presented in Table 2, reporting no other high correlations that require further attention.

The results of the Cox proportional hazards regression analysis are presented in Table 3. All the control variables are presented in model 3-1. The primary variables of theoretical interest are added in model 3-2. The first and the second interaction effects that we hypothesize are introduced in models 3-3 and 3-4, respectively. Model 3-5 presents both interaction effects. However, the collinearity between the two interaction terms is high, because the two share a common base variable, which is the volume of substitution rhetoric. As such, we focus on models 3-3 and 3-4.

As shown in model 3-3, the interaction effect we hypothesize between volume of substitution rhetoric in the media and a firm's resource commitments in a domain is statistically significant. For visualizing and interpreting the interaction effect, we present our estimation graphically in Fig. 2. The y-axis is the multiplier of entry hazard, and the x-axis is the volume of substitution rhetoric. The top graph of Fig. 2 focuses on firms with low resource commitments in the domain of Internet infrastructure, while the bottom graph of the same figure focuses on those with high commitments.

Table 1. Descriptive Statistics.

813 Firm-Year Observations	Mean	S.D.	Min	Max
(1) Entry to the new product market				
(2) Volume of substitution rhetoric	0.44	0.82	0	5
(3) Volume of substitution rhetoric, in favor of the new product market	0.36	0.71	0	4
(4) Volume of substitution rhetoric, in favor of the exited product market	0.07	0.35	0	2
(5) The firm's resource commitments in the domain of Internet infrastructure	0.72	1.04	0	5
(6) Market relatedness between the firm's existing businesses and the new one.	0.14	0.04	0	0.2
(7) Firm size	4,306	18,101	219	275,930
(8) Firm age, divided by 100	0.18	0.18	0.01	1.5
(9) The number of existing products the firm has	1.16	0.41	1	3
(10) Product diversification	0.40	0.25	0	0.84
(11) The number of technology classes the firm has in its patents	4.99	18.38	0	150
(12) Average number of patents the firm has per technology class	1.01	3.42	0	28.36
(13) The growth rate of the exited product market	0.10	0.15	−0.38	0.33
(14) The growth rate of the new product market	0.03	0.11	−0.29	0.19
(15) The size of the new product market	4,659	819	3,096	6,120
(16) The number of firms exiting from the new product market in the prior year	10.95	9.75	0	31
(17) The number of firms entering the new product market in the prior year	0.76	0.42	0	1
(18) Amount of positive or neutral associative rhetoric in media story	27.56	27.35	0	123
(19) Media forecasts projecting optimistic or neural views about the new product market	61.53	37.50	20.57	126.24
(20) Media forecasts projecting pessimistic views about the new product market	13.54	14.73	0	56.60
(22) The sequence of exit and entry	0.08	0.27	0	1
(23) Market entry inertia	3.94	3.05	1	15
(24) Market entry momentum	3.74	6.61	0	67
(25) The firm's technological capabilities most similar to those required by the new product	0.21	0.35	0	1
(26) Technological relatedness between the firm's existing product and the new product	0.41	0.12	0	0.61

Table 2. Pair-wise Correlations.

	(1)	(2)	(3)	(4)	(5)	(6)	(7)	(8)	(9)	(10)	(11)	(12)
(1)	1											
(2)	−0.09*	1										
(3)	−0.08*	0.90*	1									
(4)	−0.04	0.50*	0.09*	1								
(5)	0.39*	0.05	0.05	0.01	1							
(6)	−0.002	0.14*	0.10*	0.13*	−0.02	1						
(7)	−0.01	0.04	0.04	0.005	0.15*	−0.05	1					
(8)	0.03	−0.002	−0.0002	−0.006	0.02	−0.02	0	1				
(9)	−0.01	0.009	0.01	−0.001	0.14*	−0.17*	0.13*	0.03	1			
(10)	−0.03	0.01	0.01	0.02	0.04	−0.01	0.24*	0.04	−0.04	1		
(11)	0.02	−0.04	−0.04	−0.02	0.03	−0.06	0.34*	0.23*	0.04	0.04	1	
(12)	0.01	0.01	0.00	0.002	−0.05	0.09	0.25*	0.10*	−0.06	−0.08	0	1
(13)	0.09*	0.10*	0.07*	0.09*	0.02	0.01	0.02	−0.07*	0.004	0.01	0.05	0.07*
(14)	−0.05	−0.11	0.02	−0.31*	−0.10*	−0.26*	0.02	−0.01	0.03	0.04	0.03	−0.10*
(15)	−0.004	0.31*	0.37*	−0.03	0.02	0.21*	−0.02	−0.04	−0.04	−0.08*	−0.01	0.03
(16)	0.10*	0.07*	−0.001	0.16*	0.09*	0.15*	0.01	−0.008	0.01	−0.001	−0.01	−0.02
(17)	0.04	−0.05	0.07*	−0.29*	0.007	−0.08*	−0.005	−0.001	−0.02	0.02	−0.03	−0.01
(18)	−0.14*	0.57*	0.42*	0.48*	−0.14*	0.34*	−0.01	−0.004	−0.06	0.06*	−0.001	0.08*
(19)	−0.03	0.10*	−0.02*	0.29*	−0.07*	0.11*	0.01	0.04	−0.05	0.02	0.04	−0.02
(20)	0.02	0.21*	0.17*	0.14*	−0.03	0.17*	−0.06	−0.007	−0.02	0.06	0.03	0.04
(22)	0.70*	−0.12*	−0.11*	−0.06	0.32*	−0.05	−0.06	0.03	−0.01	−0.04	0.03	0.02
(23)	0.07*	0.07*	0.04	0.07*	0.04	0.12*	0.09*	0.01	−0.05	−0.07*	−0.02	0.01
(24)	0.05	0.06	0.08*	−0.006	0.10*	−0.11*	0.32*	0.05	0.007	0.24*	0.11*	−0.08*
(25)	0.11*	−0.11*	−0.09*	−0.07*	0.08*	−0.10*	0.12*	0.09*	0.04	−0.04	0.55*	0.17*
(26)	0.01	0.14*	0.11*	0.11*	0.30*	0.41*	0.01	−0.02	0.14*	0.01	−0.07*	0.09*

Table 2. *(Continued)*

	(13)	(14)	(15)	(16)	(17)	(18)	(19)	(20)	(22)	(23)	(24)	(25)	(26)
(13)	1												
(14)	0	1											
(15)	0	0	1										
(16)	0	0	0	1									
(17)	0	0	0	0	1								
(18)	0.08*	−0.23*	0.20*	0.07*	0.12*	1							
(19)	0	0	0	0	0	0.13*	1						
(20)	0	0	0	0	0	0.22*	0	1					
(22)	0.08*	0.05	−0.08*	0.02	−0.002*	−0.20*	0.001	−0.03	1				
(23)	−0.04	−0.19*	0.25*	0.10*	−0.03	0.05	0.301	−0.03	0.02	1			
(24)	−0.04	−0.08*	0.02	0.05	0.03	0.05	−0.05	0.08*	0.003	−0.28*	1		
(25)	0.04	0.05	−0.03	−0.07*	−0.07*	−0.13*	−0.001	0.02	0.22*	−0.05	0.07*	1	
(26)	−0.001	−0.37*	0.29*	0.01*	−0.04	0.16*	−0.03	−0.006*	−0.03	0.14*	−0.08*	−0.06	1

*$p < 0.05$.

Table 3. A Hazard Model of Estimating the Likelihood of Entering the Product Market of Network Switches.

	Model (3-1)	Model (3-2)	Model (3-3)	Model (3-4)	Model (3-5)
Primary variables of theoretical interest					
Volume of substitution rhetoric		−0.37	−1.34**	−5.03*	−5.56*
		(0.24)	(0.44)	(2.47)	(2.80)
The firm's resource commitments in the domain of Internet infrastructure		0.44***	0.41***	0.44***	0.41***
		(0.12)	(0.11)	(0.12)	(0.11)
Interaction effect (H1)					
Volume of substitution rhetoric XThe firm's resource commitments in the domain of Internet infrastructure			**0.44****		0.35*
			(0.17)		(0.17)
Market relatedness between the firm's existing businesses and the new one.		5.12	4.76	3.37	3.34
		(5.25)	(5.26)	(5.05)	(5.06)
Interaction effect (H2)					
Volume of substitution rhetoric XMarket relatedness between the firm's existing businesses and the new one.				**28.57***	26.78
				(14.45)	(16.80)
Control variables					
Firm-level variables					
Firm size	0.13	−0.07	−0.11	−0.09	−0.13
	(0.16)	(0.22)	(0.22)	(0.22)	(0.22)
Firm age	0.02	0.04	0.04	0.06	0.06
	(0.07)	(0.08)	(0.08)	(0.08)	(0.08)
The number of existing products the firm has	−0.31	−0.28	−0.34	−0.15	−0.21
	(0.35)	(0.39)	(0.39)	(0.40)	(0.40)
Product diversification	−0.28	−0.47	−0.44	−0.46	−0.42
	(0.56)	(0.54)	(0.53)	(0.54)	(0.54)

Table 3. (*Continued*)

	Model (3-1)	Model (3-2)	Model (3-3)	Model (3-4)	Model (3-5)
The number of technology classes the firm has in its patents	−0.01	0.003	0.01	0.002	0.01
	(0.01)	(0.01)	(0.02)	(0.01)	(0.01)
Average number of patents the firm has per technology class	0.03	−0.06	−0.09	−0.05	−0.08
	(0.06)	(0.08)	(0.09)	(0.08)	(0.09)
Market-level variables					
The growth rate of the exited product market	2.83	2.41	1.91	2.22	1.89
	(2.71)	(3.40)	(3.40)	(3.34)	(3.34)
The growth rate of the new product market	−3.21	-4.22^{+}	−3.77	−3.95	−3.60
	(2.26)	(2.50)	(2.36)	(2.53)	(2.42)
The size of the new product market	−0.0004	−0.0006	−0.0004	−0.0007	−0.0006
	(0.0009)	(0.0009)	(0.0009)	(0.0009)	(0.0009)
The number of firms exiting from the new product market	0.01	−0.03	−0.01	−0.03	−0.02
	(0.04)	(0.04)	(0.04)	(0.04)	(0.04)
The number of firms entering the new product market in the prior year	0.05	0.07	0.05	0.07	0.06
	(0.05)	(0.05)	(0.05)	(0.05)	(0.05)
Media forecasts projecting optimistic or neural views about the new product market	−0.01	−0.01	−0.01	−0.01	−0.01
	(0.01)	(0.01)	(0.01)	(0.01)	(0.01)
Media forecasts projecting pessimistic views about the new product market	0.01	0.01	0.01	0.01	0.01
	(0.01)	(0.01)	(0.01)	(0.01)	(0.01)
Firm-market-level variables					
Volume of positive or neutral associative rhetoric in media story between the firm's existing product markets and the new one	0.006	−0.01	−0.002	−0.02	−0.01
	(0.01)	(0.01)	(0.01)	(0.01)	(0.01)

The sequence of exit and entry	4.47***	3.78***	3.72***	3.76***	3.70***
	(0.42)	(0.42)	(0.41)	(0.41)	(0.41)
Market entry inertia	0.01	0.02	0.04	0.02	0.04
	(0.03)	(0.04)	(0.04)	(0.04)	(0.04)
Market entry momentum	0.04*	0.03	0.04^{+}	0.03	0.04
	(0.02)	(0.02)	(0.02)	(0.02)	(0.02)
The firm's technological capabilities most similar to the new product	−0.17	−0.45	−0.47	−0.45	−0.47
	(0.23)	(0.32)	(0.31)	(0.33)	(0.32)
Technological relatedness between the firm's existing product and the new product	1.38	−0.14	−0.04	0.12	0.20
	(1.44)	(1.25)	(1.26)	(1.27)	(1.26)
Observations	813	813	813	813	813
Chi-square test	365.9	466.3	569.8	614.9	633.6
Log likelihood	−165.7	−160.8	−160.2	−159.8	−159.4

Robust standard errors in parentheses.
***$p < 0.001$, **$p < 0.01$, *$p < 0.05$, $^{+}p < 0.10$.

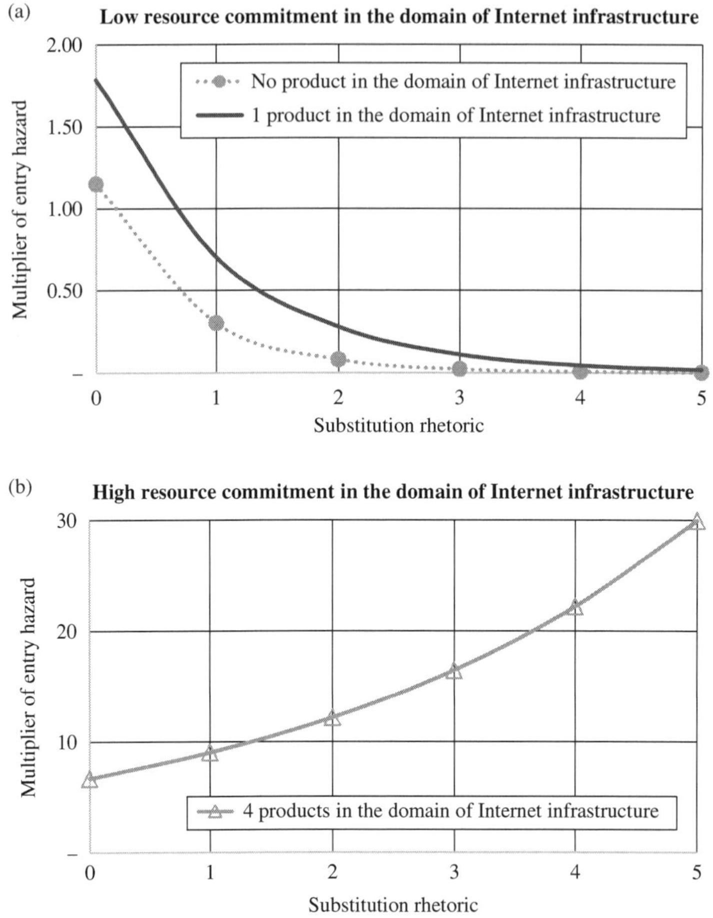

Fig. 2. The Interaction Effect between Substitution Rhetoric and the Firm's Resource Commitments in the Domain of Internet Infrastructure.

As the volume of substitution rhetoric increases, the multiplier of entry hazard decreases for firms with low resource commitments in the domain, but increases for firms with high resource commitments. That is, firms with fewer products in the domain of Internet infrastructure are less likely to enter the product market of network switches, while firms with more products in the domain of Internet infrastructure are more likely to enter. However, while the interaction term appears to have a statistically significant coefficient, the log likelihood ratio test does not show enough improvement in model fit at the normal level of statistical proof (model 3-3 compared to model 3-2). As such, we do not have strong enough evidence to support our first hypothesis.

Model 3-4 shows that the interaction effect we hypothesize between volume of substitution rhetoric in the media and the market relatedness between a firm's existing products and the new one is statistically significant. For visualizing and interpreting the interaction effect, we present our estimation graphically in Fig. 3. The *y*-axis is the multiplier of entry hazard,

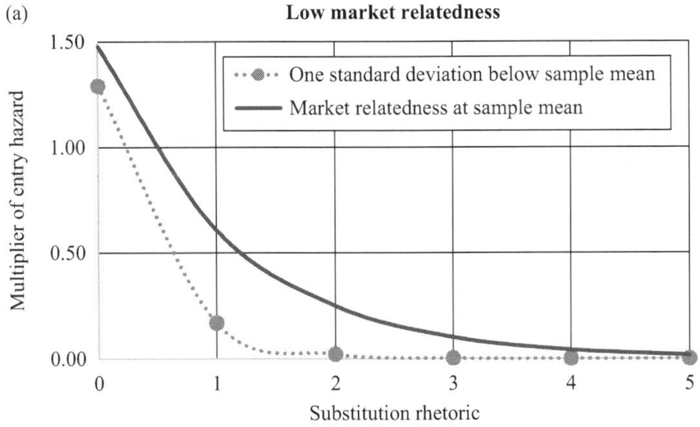

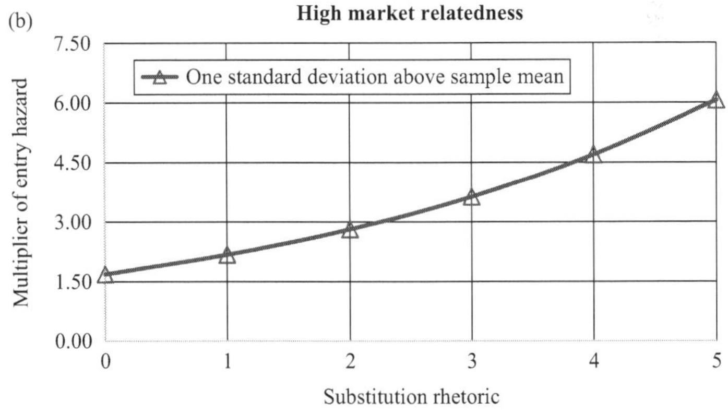

Fig. 3. The Interaction Effect between Substitution Rhetoric and Market Relatedness of the Firm with Respect to the New Product.

and the x-axis is the volume of substitution rhetoric. The top graph of Fig. 3 focuses on firms with low market relatedness, while the bottom graph of the same figure focuses on those with high market relatedness. As the volume of substitution rhetoric increases, the multiplier of entry hazard decreases for firms with low market relatedness, but increases for firms with high market relatedness. That is, firms with existing markets not very similar to that of network switches are less likely to enter, while firms with existing markets that are very similar to that of network switches are more likely to enter. However, while the interaction term appears to have a statistically significant coefficient, the log likelihood ratio test does not show enough improvement in model fit at the normal level of statistical proof (model 3-4 compared to model 3-2). As such, we do not have strong enough evidence to support our second hypothesis.

DISCUSSIONS

Resource redeployment through exit and entry creates corporate value by providing discretion or flexibility to partially or completely withdraw resources from one business and reallocate them to another business. When resources can be redeployed in this manner, firms have greater potential to escape from declining prospects in a business (Anand & Singh, 1997), and adapt in turbulent environments (Eisenhardt & Brown, 1999). Our paper highlights the inducements to redeploy resources through exit and entry, by connecting the inducements with industry evolution such as forces of substitution in the competitive environment.

Our study builds on Sakhartov and Folta's (2014) work on inducements by emphasizing the uncertainty and the ambiguity in interpreting emerging and shifting threats of substitution. We submit that the performance advantages of new over existing businesses are not fixed. As products evolve in their course of development, their relative performance reflects emerging and shifting threats of substitution. Threats of substitution are uncertain and ambiguous, particularly when a new product is in its phase of emergence. As the volume of substitution threat signals increases, firms have more awareness and saliency of the substation potential. However, the uncertainty and ambiguity remain unresolved because the substitution threat may continue to shift over time. So, we examined specific characteristics of firms that allow us to predict their responses to the increasing volume of substitution threat signals. The two characteristics we focused on are the resource commitments to the domain of the new business and the market relatedness between a firm's existing businesses and the new one.

Our study contributes to one of the questions posed in the Special Issue Call for Papers asks, "Is it possible that existing work provides an incomplete picture of the contributions of resource relatedness to firm value and firm decision-making?" Our study suggests that the answer is yes. The existing work provides an incomplete picture because the conventional wisdom in corporate strategy explaining why related diversification creates more value than unrelated diversification has focused on the idea that relatedness reduces the costs of redeploying resource inside the firm. Yet, as Sakhartov and Folta (2014) points out, the theory about value deriving from diversification is incomplete. The theory is incomplete because the effect of relatedness on value critically depends on inducements, the performance advantages of new over existing businesses. The effect of relatedness is important only when inducements are strong, as demonstrated in their computer simulations. When inducements are weak, the effect may completely vanish. Hence, without paying attention to inducements as a boundary condition, the theory cannot answer satisfactorily why related diversification does not guarantee high value or why unrelated diversification can create value through redeploying resources.

We emphasize the resource commitments in the domain of the new product and the relatedness of a firm's existing product markets with the new one. The resource commitments in the domain are distinct from the relatedness between the new and the existing products, since the existing products were randomly sampled and thus would not necessarily be in the same domain as the new product. In comparison, the theory about value deriving from diversification has not focused on the domain as a unit of examination. And the theory has narrowly focused on the role of relatedness in reducing the costs of resource redeployment. By contrast, we highlight the role of relatedness in aiding the firm's decision-making under uncertainty and ambiguity.

Finally, our study enriches the research on resource redeployment, which tends to draw from the economics literature, by bringing in a socio-cognitive view of product markets (Porac & Thomas, 1990; Porac, Thomas, & Baden-Fuller, 1989, 2011; Rosa & Porac, 2002; Rosa et al., 1999; also see Kaplan & Tripsas, 2008 on a cognitive view of technology evolution). A socio-cognitive view of product markets maintains that product categorizations are a form of cognitive representations that link attributes, usage conditions, and benefits into a product's definition. Drawing from a socio-cognitive view, we develop an empirical approach for evaluating emerging and shifting threats of substitution between two products. By analyzing the characterization of overlap between products in attributes, usage conditions, and benefits in media stories, we captured temporal variations in the performance advantages of new over existing products. This allowed us to advance the frontier on the research on inducements.

Limitations and Future Research Directions

As with any paper, there are a number of limitations here that could form avenues for future research. First, the firm's resource commitments in a domain is only one moderator that attenuates/strengthens the link between inducements and resource redeployment. Whether a firm withdraws resources from one business and reallocates them to a new business also depends on many other factors such as existing capabilities, behavioral routines, and cognitive frames.[4] Each factor may potentially moderate the link between inducements and resource redeployment. Moreover, a firm's decision on when to enter the market of a substitute also depends on many other factors beyond what our empirical model entails. As shown in prior research, entry is delayed if the substitute can be easily imitated (Katz & Shapiro, 1987) or the firm has complementary assets that afford it to wait (Teece, 2007). But entry is not delayed if the firm's product that is threatened is its core product (Mitchell, 1989), the market of the substitute is highly competitive (D'Aveni, 1994), or the substitute is based on disruptive technologies (Christensen, 1997).

Second, we do not examine the process via which media stories are produced. The process potentially may drive the substitution rhetoric. Prior research has shown that media story itself may be culturally produced in the process of negotiation among different constituents (Kaplan & Tripsas, 2008; Lounsbury & Rao, 2004), so media story may not be completely exogenous. Future studies can explore the interplay between media and firm behavior in generating media story. Also, we have considered only established and reputable journals, as is common in media studies. While this approach helps test our hypothesis, it ignores nascent journals that emerge with the rise of new industries. Future research studies could incorporate journals' reputational ranking to examine the co-evolution of media and industries. Lastly, since our study does not examine news-collecting or information-processing structures inside the firm, future studies may explore how media story affects the way the structure of organizations grows toward news sources. The structure of organizations features prominently in Stinchcombe's (1990) research on information and organizations, but the internal workings of an organization have not been systematically linked to the external information sources in affecting managers' attention focus and decision-making.

CONCLUSIONS

In conclusion, the resource commitments that the firm had made in the domain of the new business as well as the market relatedness between the new business and the firm's existing businesses may serve as boundary conditions moderating the effect of inducements on resource redeployment. Our hypotheses contribute to both the resource redeployment theory and the socio-cognitive view of product markets. The methodology employed in our empirical investigation potentially opens up new avenues of research at the intersection of these two streams of literature, advancing our knowledge about resource redeployment through exit and entry.

NOTES

1. As an example, flash computer memory is an emerging product, which is a substitute for low-capacity hard-disk drives. Similarly, videoconferencing is a substitute for travel, plastic is a substitute for aluminum, and e-mail is a substitute for express mail (Porter, 2008, p. 17). Diagnostic imaging equipment based on computed-tomography, magnetic resonance, and digital-radiography is a substitute for that based on X-ray (Mitchell, 1989).

2. "Resource reconfiguration" refers to the retention, deletion, addition, and recombination of resources (Karim, 2006; Karim & Mitchell, 2004). Rooted in the resource-based and dynamic capabilities theories of business strategy (Helfat et al., 2007; Penrose, 1959; Wernerfelt, 1984), the research on resource reconfiguration explains why and how firms reconfigure their resource base. Firms reconfigure their resource base because doing so regularly helps the firms sustain the value of their resources (Amit & Schoemaker, 1993; Capron, Dussauge, & Mitchell, 1998). By "adding, splitting, transferring, exiting or combining chunks of businesses," firms remap their divisional structure, realign their businesses, and transfer some resources from one business to another (Eisenhardt & Brown, 1999, p. 73). By adding new resources (Teece, 1982), eliminating underperforming resources (Capron, Mitchell, & Swaminathan, 2001), and employing existing resources in new business applications (Penrose, 1959), firms reconfigure their resource base.

3. Specifically, we generated the technology similarity index with a market-wide pattern in Who Patents What: the patent profile by firm, technology class, and application year. The index was a normalized count of organizations that have accumulated patents in both the focal technology class and a certain technology class, where the basis of similarity is shared knowledge between the pair of technology classes (cf. Jaffe, 1989; Nerkar, Paruchuri, & Khaire, 2007). The index was constructed with the patent portfolios of 1,514 organizations that held at least one patent in Class 370 during the period of 1985–2003. As an example, "Class 375 – pulse or digital communication" had the highest value in the index; organizations with patents in Class 370 were more likely to have patents in Class 375 than other classes.

4. As exemplified by the case of "the digital photography company" (Tripsas, 2009, p. 441), what made a firm successful under an earlier technological regime may become inertial forces, limiting adaptive flexibility toward a different regime (Benner & Tushman, 2002; Christensen & Bower, 1996; Henderson & Clark, 1990; Kaplan, 2008; Tripsas & Gavetti, 2000; Tushman & Anderson, 1986).

ACKNOWLEDGMENTS

We would like to thank Editors Tim Folta, Connie Helfat, Samina Karim, and participants at the Special Conference on Corporate Strategy and Resource Redeployment for their feedback and suggestions.

REFERENCES

Abrahamson, E. (1996). Management fashion. *Academy of Management Review, 21*(1), 254–285.

Abrahamson, E., & Fairchild, G. (1999). Management fashion: Lifecycles, triggers and collective learning processes. *Administrative Sciences Quarterly, 44*, 708–740.

Agarwal, R., & Helfat, C. E. (2009). Strategic renewal of organizations. *Organization Science, 20*(2), 281–293.

Amit, R., & Schoemaker, P. J. H. (1993). Strategic assets and organizational rents. *Strategic Management Journal, 14*(1), 33–46.

Anand, J. (2004). Redeployment of corporate resources: a study of acquisition strategies in the US defense industries, 1978–1996. *Managerial and Decision Economics, 25*(6–7), 383–400.

Anand, J., & Singh, H. (1997). Asset redeployment, acquisitions and corporate strategy in declining industries. *Strategic Management Journal*, Summer Special Issue, *18*(S1), 99–118.

Benner, M. J., & Tushman, M. (2002). Process management and technological innovation: A longitudinal study of the photography and paint industries. *Administrative Science Quarterly, 47*(4), 676–707.

Blau, P. M. (1977). *Inequality and heterogeneity: A primitive theory of social structure.* New York, NY: Free Press.

Capron, L., Dussauge, P., & Mitchell, W. (1998). Resource redeployment following horizontal acquisitions in Europe and North America, 1988–1992. *Strategic Management Journal, 19*(7), 631–661.

Capron, L., Mitchell, W., & Swaminathan, A. (2001). Asset divestiture following horizontal acquisitions: A dynamic view. *Strategic Management Journal, 22*(9), 817–844.

Christensen, C. M. (1997). *The innovator's dilemma: When new technologies cause great firms to fail.* Boston, MA: Harvard Business Press.

Christensen, C. M., & Bower, J. L. (1996). Customer power, strategic investment, and the failure of leading firms. *Strategic Management Journal, 17*(3), 197–218.

Cohen, W. M., & Levinthal, D. A. (1989). Innovation and learning: the two faces of R & D. *The Economic Journal, 99*(397), 569–596.

Cohen, W. M., & Levinthal, D. A. (1990). Absorptive capacity: A new perspective on learning and innovation. *Administrative Science Quarterly, 35*, 128–152.

Cohen, W. M., & Levinthal, D. A. (1994). Fortune favors the prepared firm. *Management Science, 40*(2), 227–251.

Cox, D. R. (1972). Regression models and life tables. *Journal of the Royal Statistical Society Series B, 34*, 187–220.

Daft, R. L., & Lengel, R. H. (1986). Organizational information requirements, media richness and structural design. *Management Science, 32*(5), 554–571.

D'Aveni, R. A. (1994). *Hypercompetition: Managing the dynamics of manoeuvring.* New York, NY: Free Press.

Deephouse, D. L. (2000). Media reputation as a strategic resource: An integration of mass communication and resource based theories. *Journal of Management, 26*, 1091–1112.

Eisenhardt, K. M., & Brown, S. L. (1999). Patching: Restitching business portfolios in dynamic markets. *Harvard Business Review, 77*(3), 72–82.

Fligstein, N. (1996). Markets as politics: A political-cultural approach to market institutions. *American Sociological Review, 61*, 656–673.

Garud, R., & Rappa, M. A. (1994). A socio-cognitive model of technology evolution: The case of cochlear implants. *Organization Science, 5*, 344–362.

George, J. M. (1990). Personality, affect, and behavior in groups. *Journal of Applied Psychology, 75*(2), 107–116.

Ghaziani, A., & Ventresca, M. J. (2005). Keywords and cultural change: Frame analysis of business model public talk 1975–2000. *Sociological Forum, 20*(4), 523–559.

Gitlin, T. (1980). *The whole world is watching: Mass media in the making and unmaking of the new left.* Berkeley, CA: University of California Press.

Goffman, E. (1974). *Frame analysis: An essay on the organization of experience.* Cambridge, MA: Harvard University Press.

Golub, G. H., & Van Loan, C. F. (1989). *Matrix computations* (2nd ed.). Baltimore, MD: The Johns Hopkins University Press.

Helfat, C. E., & Eisenhardt, K. M. (2004). Inter-temporal economies of scope, organizational modularity, and the dynamics of diversification. *Strategic Management Journal, 25*(13), 1217–1232.

Helfat, C. E., Finkelstein, S., Mitchell, W., Peteraf, M., Singh, H., Teece, D., & Winter, S. G. (2007). *Dynamic capabilities: Understanding strategic change in organizations.* Hoboken, NJWiley.

Helfat, C. E., & Lieberman, M. B. (2002). The birth of capabilities: Market entry and the importance of pre-history. *Industrial and Corporate Change*, *11*(4), 725–760.

Henderson, R. M., & Clark, K. B. (1990). Architectural innovation: The reconfiguration of existing product technologies and the failure of established firms. *Administrative Science Quarterly*, 9–30.

Jaffe, A. B. (1989). Characterizing the 'technological position' of firms, with application to quantifying technological opportunity and research spillovers. *Research Policy*, *18*(2), 87–97.

James, L. R., Demaree, R. G., & Wolf, G. (1993). r_{wg}: An assessment of within-group interrater agreement. *Journal of Applied Psychology*, *78*(2), 306–309.

Janz, B. D., Colquitt, J. A., & Noe, R. A. (1984). Estimating within-group interrater reliability with and without response bias. *Journal of Applied Psychology*, *69*, 85–98.

Janz, B. D., Colquitt, J. A., & Noe, R. A. (1997). Knowledge worker team effectiveness: The role of autonomy, interdependence, team development, and contextual support variables. *Personnel Psychology*, *50*(4), 877–904.

Kaplan, S. (2008). Framing contests: Strategy making under uncertainty. *Organization Science*, *19*(5), 729–752.

Kaplan, S. (2011). Research in cognition and strategy: Reflections on two decades of progress and a look to the future. *Journal of Management Studies*, *48*(3), 665–695.

Kaplan, S., & Tripsas, M. (2008). Thinking about technology: Applying a cognitive lens to technical change. *Research Policy*, *37*(5), 790–805.

Karim, S. (2006). Modularity in organizational structure: The reconfiguration of internally developed and acquired business units. *Strategic Management Journal*, *27*(9), 799–823.

Karim, S., & Mitchell, W. (2004). Innovating through acquisition and internal development: A quarter-century of boundary evolution at Johnson & Johnson. *Long Range Planning*, *37*(6), 525–547.

Katz, M. L., & Shapiro, C. (1987). R&D rivalry with licensing or imitation. *American Economic Review*, *77*, 402–420.

Kennedy, M. T. (2008). Getting counted: Markets, media and reality. *American Sociological Review*, *73*(2), 270–295.

Kogut, B., & Kulatilaka, N. (1994). Operating flexibility, global manufacturing, and the option value of a multinational network. *Management Science*, *40*(1), 123–139.

Lee, G. K. (2008). Relevance of organizational capabilities and its dynamics: What to learn from entrants' product portfolios about the determinants of entry timing. *Strategic Management Journal*, *29*(12), 1257–1280.

Lee, G. K. (2009). Understanding the timing of 'fast-second'entry and the relevance of capabilities in invention vs. commercialization. *Research Policy*, *38*(1), 86–95.

Lee, G. K., & Paruchuri, S. (2008). Entry into emergent and uncertain product-markets: The role of associative rhetoric. *Academy of Management Journal*, *51*(6), 1171–1188.

Levinthal, D. A., & Wu, B. (2010). Opportunity costs and non-scale free capabilities: Profit maximization, corporate scope, and profit margins. *Strategic Management Journal*, *31*, 780–801.

Lounsbury, M., & Rao, H. (2004). Sources of durability and change in market classifications: A study of the reconstitution of product categories in the American mutual fund industry: 1945–1985. *Social Forces*, *82*(3), 969–1033.

Mitchell, W. (1989). Whether and when? Probability and timing of incumbents' entry into emerging industrial subfields. *Administrative Science Quarterly*, *34*, 208–230.

Nerkar, A., Paruchuri, S., & Khaire, M. (2007). Business method patents as real options: Value and disclosure as drivers of litigation. In J. J. Reuer & T. W. Tong (Eds.), 2007, *Real options theory* (Vol. 24, pp. 247–274). of Baum, J. A.C. (series editor), Advances in Strategic Management, Oxford: Elsevier JAI.

Penrose, E. T. (1959). *The theory of the growth of the firm*. New York, NY: Wiley.

Peteraf, M. A., & Bergen, M. E. (2003). Scanning dynamic competitive landscapes: A market-based and resource-based framework. *Strategic Management Journal*, *24*(10), 1027–1041.

Pollock, T. G., & Rindova, V. P. (2003). Media legitimation effects in the market for initial public offerings. *Academy of Management Journal*, *46*(5), 631–642.

Porac, J. F., & Thomas, H. (1990). Taxonomical mental models in competitor definition. *Academy of Management Review*, *15*(2), 224–240.

Porac, J. F., Thomas, H., & Baden-Fuller, C. (1989). Competitive groups as cognitive communities: The case of Scottish knitwear manufacturers. *Journal of Management*, *26*(4), 397–416.

Porac, J. F., Thomas, H., & Baden-Fuller, C. (2011). Competitive groups as cognitive communities: The case of Scottish knitwear manufacturers revisited. *Journal of Management Studies*, *48*(3), 646–664.

Porter, M. E. (2008 [1985]). The five competitive forces that shape strategy. In *On competition*. Boston, MA: Harvard Business School Publishing.

Reese, S. D. (2007). The framing project: A bridging model for media research revisited. *Journal of Communication*, *57*(1), 148–154.

Rosa, J. A., & Porac, J. F. (2002). Categorization bases and their influence on product category knowledge structure. *Psychology & Marketing*, *19*(6), 503–531.

Rosa, J. A., Porac, J. F., Runser-Spanjol, J., & Saxon, M. S. (1999). Sociocognitive dynamics in a product market. *Journal of Marketing*, Special Issue, *63*, 64–77.

Sakhartov, A. V., & Folta, T. B. (2014). Resource relatedness, redeployability, and firm value. *Strategic Management Journal*, *35*, 1781–1797.

Scheufele, D. A., & Tewksbury, D. (2007). Framing, agenda setting, and priming: The evolution of three media effects models. *Journal of Communication*, *57*(1), 9–20.

Silverman, B. S. (1999). Technological resources and the direction of corporate diversification: Toward an integration of the resource-based view and transaction cost economics. *Management Science*, *45*(8), 1109–1124.

Stinchcombe, A. L. (1990). *Information and organizations*. Berkeley, CA: University of California Press.

Suchman, M. C. (1995). Managing legitimacy: Strategic and institutional approaches. *Academy of Management Review*, *20*(3), 571–610.

Teece, D. J. (1982). Towards an economic theory of the multiproduct firm. *Journal of Economic Behavior and Organization*, *3*, 39–63.

Teece, D. J. (2007). Explicating dynamic capabilities: The nature and microfoundations of (sustainable) enterprise performance. *Strategic Management Journal*, *28*(13), 1319–1350.

Triantis, A. J., & Hodder, J. E. (1990). Valuing flexibility as a complex option. *Journal of Finance*, *45*(2), 549–565.

Tripsas, M. (2009). Technology, identity, and inertia through the lens of "the digital photography company". *Organization Science*, *20*(2), 441–460.

Tripsas, M., & Gavetti, G. (2000). Capabilities, cognition, and inertia: Evidence from digital imaging. *Strategic Management Journal*, *21*, 1147–1161.

Tushman, M. L., & Anderson, P. (1986). Technological discontinuities and organizational environments. *Administrative Science Quarterly*, 439–465.

Weick, K. E. (1979). Cognitive processes in organizations. *Research in Organizational Behavior*, *1*(1), 41–74.

Wernerfelt, B. (1984). A resource-based view of the firm. *Strategic Management Journal*, *5*(2), 171–180.

White, H. C. (1981). Where do markets come from? *American Journal of Sociology*, *87*, 517–547.

White, H. C. (2002). *Markets from networks: Socioeconomic models of production*. Princeton, NJ: Princeton University Press.

Wu, B. (2013). Opportunity costs, industry dynamics, and corporate diversification: Evidence from the cardiovascular medical device industry, 1976–2004. *Strategic Management Journal*, *34*(11), 1265–1287.

INCUMBENT RESPONSES TO AN ENTRANT WITH A NEW BUSINESS MODEL: RESOURCE CO-DEPLOYMENT AND RESOURCE RE-DEPLOYMENT STRATEGIES

Gautam Ahuja and Elena Novelli[☆]

ABSTRACT

The constructs of re-deployment and co-deployment have been central to discussions of scope economies in diversified firms. We argue however that these constructs are also significant in the context of single-business firms. Increasingly, changes in technology and demand preferences have provided opportunities for entrants to attack incumbents with a different business model, one that may neutralize the incumbent's advantage for at least some set of customers (e.g., Netflix vs. Blockbuster). In such a

[☆]Both authors contributed equally to this work. Authors' names are listed in alphabetical order.

Resource Redeployment and Corporate Strategy
Advances in Strategic Management, Volume 35, 125–153

ISSN: 0742-3322/doi:10.1108/S0742-332220160000035006

context incumbents often respond by modifying their business model. We note that several of the business model-altering responses of the incumbent can be characterized in terms of co-deployment and re-deployment benefits and costs, where co-deployment benefits/cost apply to the scope economies/diseconomies in running multiple business models within the same firm and re-deployment benefits/costs apply to the implications of moving assets from one business model to another. We then examine the set of strategic choices faced by the incumbent in competing with an entrant with a different business model. We identify five set of factors that are likely to influence the decision to choose between these alternatives – uncertainty spawned by the new business model, market segment targeted by the new model, the within-business-across-business-model co-deployment and re-deployment benefits and costs, the across-business co-deployment and re-deployment benefits and costs, and the incumbent's prior performance history. Although some of these choices have seen some work, most remain relatively underexplored in the strategy literature. We highlight the potential for research in this area with a set of propositions that identify key conditions that should hold true for a particular strategic choice to be picked by an incumbent.

Keywords: Business models; economies of scope; re-deployment; synergies; incumbents' response

INTRODUCTION

Historically, the construct of scope economies has been used to explain firm performance in the context of research on diversification and firms' entry into multiple businesses. In such analyses scope economies usually emerge in two forms, synergy – the contemporaneous sharing of resources across markets leading to super-normal returns (Panzar & Willig, 1981) – and resource re-deployment benefits – the benefits originating from the withdrawal of a resource from a context to use it in a different one (Helfat & Eisenhardt, 2004). These constructs have been – implicitly or explicitly – referred to as the core mechanisms to explain the antecedents and effects of various managerial choices in multiple literatures (Helfat & Eisenhardt, 2004; Karim & Mitchell, 2000; Sakhartov & Folta, 2014, 2015). For instance, the mechanism of resource re-deployment has been referred to in the context of research on the performance of acquisitions (Capron, 1999; Capron, Dussauge, & Mitchell, 1998; Capron & Mitchell, 1998; Capron, Mitchell, Swaminathan,

2001); on the impact of prior experience or preadaptation when entering new settings (Cattani, 2006; Klepper & Simons, 2000) and on the reuse of complementary assets in new contexts (Mitchell, 1989, 1991; Rosenbloom & Christensen, 1994); research on performance heterogeneity between de novo and de alio firms (Carroll, Bigelow, Seidel, Tsai, 1996; Ganco & Agarwal, 2009; Sosa, 2013). Similarly, the construct of resource co-deployment and the achievement of synergies has been a core mechanism identified as underlying the relationship between firm diversification and performance (Bettis, 1981; Bettis & Hall, 1982; Grant & Jammine, 1988; Rumelt, 1974, 1982).

Yet, the constructs also have important implications for single-business firms. The possibility of sharing resources across multiple value chains (i.e., co-deployment) or withdrawing resources from one use and applying them to another (i.e., re-deployment) are in fact very meaningful mechanisms in the context of a single-business firm as well. In particular in this paper we suggest that the constructs of co- and re-deployment might be particularly relevant when we recognize that, increasingly, firms offer their services through multiple business models. We define business models here as a set of connected activity choices used by a company to serve a given product market (Amit & Zott, 2001; Baden-Fuller & Haefliger, 2013; Casadesus-Masanell & Ricart, 2010; Lanzolla & Markides, 2015[1]). To clarify the distinction between this context and the more commonly studied context of multi-business diversification we note that a firm in multiple product markets might be targeting different customers/customer needs. Instead, different business models might be targeting the same market and might rather imply different ways of engaging with the customers.

For instance, a company in the airline industry could conduct business both (1) with a model based on low fares, flying to secondary airports, no meals, short-haul flights and high standardization and (2) with a model based on added comfort and differentiated offers that is based on reducing the number of seats in planes, providing additional offers of food, baggage transfer and flights to primary airports (Casadesus-Masanell & Ricart, 2010; Rivkin, 2000). In this setting we can see that there could be resource co-deployment possibilities between the two business models (e.g., procurement or technology could be shared across the two models), as well as opportunities for resource re-deployment (e.g., personnel could be moved from one model to another).

In many industries, technology (on the supply side) and customer preferences (on the demand side) are making possible – and sometimes even demanding – a reconsideration of existing business models (Casadesus-Masanell & Zhu, 2010; Markides & Charitou, 2004). Commonly, entrants introduce new business models – often enabled by technological advancements – in attempts to challenge incumbents. For instance, in 1997 Netflix challenged the Blockbuster business model – based on the physical renting of VHS or DVDs from one of the thousand retail locations of the company – by advancing a mail-based online "rent from home" model. Whereas the Blockbuster model was mainly sustained by the offering of hit new movies available in limited selections from physical stores with the payment of late rent fees by its customers as an incentive to rotate the limited inventory, Netflix operated a subscription-based model, which did away with late fees but also presented far fewer new movies but made up for it with a much larger selection and a recommendation engine and "queue" that helped to stimulate demand.

In this paper we focus on the context of an incumbent faced with the challenge from an entrant with a new business model and we address the following research question: what are the strategies available to incumbents to respond to the emergence of new business models and what are the antecedents of this strategic choice?

Recognizing the possibility of multiple business models in a single product firm we argue that the constructs of re-deployment and co-deployment and the prior work on this literature can help us understand the strategic choices faced by an incumbent so challenged. We draw upon the prior literature to identify the main strategic alternatives facing an incumbent that has been confronted by an entrant with a different business model. Having highlighted the strategic choices before the incumbent we develop a set of propositions identifying some of the conditions under which an incumbent will select each of the main strategic choices.

PRIOR RESEARCH

Incumbents and Business Model Disruption

One of the core themes in technology strategy research concerns the phenomenon of new entrants displacing incumbent firms in the context of radical technological change (Adner, 2002; Henderson & Clark, 1990; Tripsas & Gavetti, 2000; Tushman & Anderson, 1986). Research in this area emphasizes how the emergence of a new technology in an industry or market often requires new capabilities, assets and resources as well as new cognitive schema or even new business models to be dealt with

(Henderson & Clark, 1990; Tripsas, 1997; Tripsas & Gavetti, 2000). In this context, incumbents often find themselves trapped in their own prior experiences and competences, which slow their adaptation attempts.

In this paper we emphasize that another situation in which incumbents are at risk of being displaced by new entrants is the case in which new business models emerge in the market. New business models do not necessarily imply a change in technological competences. For instance, the new business model advanced by Netflix did not involve a substantial technological change, but it rather led to a redefinition of the targeted customers (e.g., the Netflix model targeted regular movie watchers while the Blockbuster's model targeted occasional movie watchers); of the value offered to the customers (e.g., a varied and customized selection in the case of Netflix versus a selection focused on new releases in the case of Blockbuster); of the way in which the value is appropriated (e.g., via a subscription-based fee in the case of Netflix versus a per-movie fee in the case of Blockbuster).

The notion of competing business models has gained considerable recognition in recent years. Several studies have emphasized that many business models can coexist in the same market and have investigated the conditions under which one business model can be more successful than another (Bonaccorsi, Giannangeli, & Rossi, 2006; Casadesus-Masanell & Ghemawat, 2006; Casadesus-Masanell & Yoffie, 2007; Chesbrough & Appleyard, 2007). Within this context, the competitive dynamics between actors operating under different models and in particular the choice made by incumbents and new entrants on the adoption of competing business models have been identified as a particularly relevant and complex managerial problem (Casadesus-Masanell & Hervas-Drane, 2010; Casadesus-Masanell & Yoffie, 2007; Economides & Katsamakas, 2006; Seamans, 2012).

A core element that is emphasized by this research is that managing multiple business models simultaneously represents a non-trivial strategic task. On the one hand offering multiple business models might offer firms some opportunity for synergy, especially if the models share some elements of similarity (Markides & Charitou, 2004). However, competing business models might also conflict with one another, reducing the attractiveness of a dual strategy (Markides & Charitou, 2004; Porter, 1980). For instance, by moving aggressively into private labels, retail companies might dilute their differentiation strategy (Markides & Charitou, 2004). This makes the choice difficult and also presents firms with strategic challenges that concern the implementation of such strategies. Similarly, moving between business models appears a possible option for firms. However, it often leads firms to uncertain transitional state business models with substantial declines in their profits (McNamara, Peck, & Sasson, 2013).

Even in the absence of radical technological change, business model innovation can create a substantial challenge for incumbents due to the fact that a new business model requires re-shuffling or recombining the various business activities that compose the model in a novel way. This might imply a complete revision of the patterns regulating the use and/or shared use of the resources and assets underlying those activities. On the one hand, this change might offer new opportunities for resource co-deployment or re-deployment. On the other hand, it also requires a complete rebalance and careful consideration of the benefits and costs associated with alternative resource and asset configurations.

In addition to raising issue of whether the incumbent's resource allocation is appropriate, business model innovation also raises other considerations in an industry. Most importantly from the perspective of our current question it is important to note that the entry of a new business model in an industry can generate at least two important dynamics that may affect the incumbent's response. First the entrant's incursion increases the uncertainty in the industry through at least two mechanisms (a) it raises questions about the relative efficacy and competitiveness of the two business models (in equilibrium either, neither or both models could thrive), and consequently, (b) it potentially changes the valuation of the incumbent's assets. Both of these raise issues that the incumbent has to engage with in fashioning their response. For instance, uncertainty about the relative efficacy of the business models is going to feature prominently in the incumbent's response. If the new model is significantly superior or inferior relative to the incumbent's model the incumbent's response may tilt in one way. If there is extreme uncertainty about which model is better the response may tilt another way. Similarly uncertainty and volatility in the value of the incumbent's assets may also influence the choices an incumbent makes.

Second, the arrival of a new business model may also influence the market dynamics. For instance the new model may target a new segment which hitherto was not consuming the product or not in significant quantities (e.g., good quality wine sold to non-users by simplifying the wine selection process). Alternately, the new model might entail some novel feature that, once identified and offered (e.g., the ability to return rented DVD's by mail rather than having to go to the store), is found particularly desirable by customers. These kinds of innovations could lead to an expansion of the market; alternately they may target an existing set of customers and simply cannibalize the existing sales. Clearly, such considerations are going to be relevant to the incumbent's decision. In our framework we will account for both these factors as we try to predict how incumbents will react.

Competing Business Models and Resource Deployment

The synergy and re-deployment literatures (Helfat & Eisenhardt, 2004; Karim & Mitchell, 2000; Sakhartov & Folta, 2014, 2015) can provide a very useful set of constructs to understand the strategic options available to incumbents in the context of the emergence of a new business model. For elaboration purposes we note that the literature on co-deployment has identified multiple sources of synergy such as operational, vertical integration, competitive and financial synergies as well as the costs that accompany such synergies (Ahuja & Novelli, 2015). Notable synergy related costs include coordination costs required to share resources across businesses (Hill & Hoskisson, 1987; Rawley, 2010; Zhou, 2011); attention costs (Levinthal & Wu, 2010; Penrose, 1959), contagion costs as problems (e.g., brand damage) from one business spill over to another business (Greenwood, Li, Prakash, & Deephouse, 2005); compromise costs that undercut the value addition of an asset in each specific use to make it usable across different uses (Porter, 1980; Zahavi & Lavie, 2013); vertical integration and administrative costs relating to the rigidities of an integrated or complex structure (Jones & Hill, 1988; Sutherland, 1980; Williamson, 1975); costs of adaptation of the currently institutionalized routines and practices (Kaplan & Henderson, 2005; Leonard-Barton, 1992; Rawley, 2010); conflict costs arising from internal competition between divisions (Hoskisson & Hitt, 1988).

Similarly, the re-deployment literature has also referred to both re-deployment benefits as well as adjustment or adaptation costs in re-deployment (Helfat & Eisenhardt, 2004). Re-deployment benefits arise from using an existing asset in a new venture wherein the prior access to the asset lowers the cost of obtaining its services in the new domain (Helfat & Eisenhardt, 2004; Karim & Mitchell, 2000; Sakhartov & Folta, 2014, 2015). Re-deployment benefits will usually arise in contexts where the market for the relevant assets is imperfect. Indeed if the assets could be sold for their full value correctly accounting for opportunity costs would imply that there are no re-deployment benefits. A re-deployment can, however, simultaneously create adjustment costs, which are the costs of transferring resources between businesses, including the time that it takes to re-deploy resources (Helfat & Eisenhardt, 2004; Helfat & Raubitschek,

2000; Kogut & Kulatilaka, 1994; Sakhartov & Folta, 2015). These can be direct costs of resource transfer, such as expenses of moving people and equipment between businesses, or indirect costs of resource transfer, such as disruption to existing businesses over these moves and time delays that may result in foregone revenues (Helfat & Eisenhardt, 2004).

In the context of multiple business models the constructs of co-deployment and re-deployment and their attendant costs and benefits potentially come into play at two levels. If we assume that the incumbent in question is a single-business firm then the co-deployment and re-deployment constructs arise in terms of sharing or re-deployment of assets across business models within a business. However, it is also possible that the incumbent is itself a multi-business corporation. In such an event in addition to the within-business co-deployment and re-deployment possibilities there is also the possibility of across business sharing or re-deployment of assets, raising the possibility of co-deployment and re-deployment benefits and costs at another level. For instance in confronting a point-to-point competitor in the airline industry (e.g.. Jet Blue, Southwest) an incumbent such as Delta may consider how to share assets between not just its main hub and spoke business (Delta) and point-to-point business (Delta-Song) but also its cargo business. Or Wal-Mart may need to consider resource allocation not just across its online (Wal-Mart.com) and offline businesses (Wal-Mart Stores) but also its warehouse club business (Sam's Club). The possibilities of co-deployment and re-deployment of assets across other businesses that are owned by the incumbent under attack, beyond the business that is being attacked, could also influence an incumbent's response in the business that it is being attacked in. In our analysis of the question of the incumbent's response we will consider the influence of both within-business and across business re-deployment and co-deployment benefits and costs.

However, relatively little work has targeted the question of what are the different strategies available to an incumbent as they face a challenger with a new business models and under what conditions are incumbents likely to pick a particular choice over another. It is to this task that we now turn.

THE INCUMBENT'S RESPONSE TO AN ENTRANT WITH A NEW BUSINESS MODEL

When examining the issue of how incumbents should respond to the entrants intrusion with a new business model, much work has focused on how the incumbent could run parallel business models (Casadesus-Masanell & Zhu, 2010; Markides & Charitou, 2004) or mix the two models in a third one (Casadesus-Masanell & Llanes, 2011; Casadesus-Masanell & Zhu, 2010). For instance, in 1998 British Airways launched a separate airline, GO, to compete against European low-cost airlines such as Ryanair (Casadesus-Masanell & Zhu, 2013; Rivkin, 2000). A second combination consists of combining the characteristics of the two business model in a "mixed" or "hybrid" business model (Bonaccorsi et al., 2006; Bonaccorsi & Rossi, 2003; Casadesus-Masanell & Zhu, 2010; Chesbrough & Appleyard, 2007). For instance customers could order online but pick up in from a physical store.

Yet, these are not the only strategies available to an incumbent. Given the existential importance of this question from the incumbent's perspective, and the complexity of maintaining combination models, it is important to understand more broadly a holistic set of competitive alternatives available to the incumbent in the face of an entrant's attack. Ghemawat (2001) enumerated possibly the first (and probably most comprehensive) such schema describing the incumbents' choices through terms such as Straddle, Switch, Recombine, Harvest, Fight, Non-Response. Casadesus-Masanell and colleagues have provided another schema describing Pure, Mixed and Dual strategies (Casadesus-Masanell & Llanes, 2011; Casadesus-Masanell & Zhu, 2010). Bonaccorsi et al. (2006) also present a typology of Pure and Hybrid strategies.

We build upon this past work, especially Ghemawat's typology and we suggest that thinking about the incumbent's choice as a co-deployment versus re-deployment decision could help in providing a nuanced view of the choices for the incumbent. If we look at the problem from the perspective of the incumbent, it faces two decisions that are not mutually exclusive. First, it can decide whether to adopt the new business model as it is, modify it and adopt it or reject it. Second, it can decide whether to retain the old business model, to modify it and retain it or reject it. These two dimensions (i.e., *Extent of Adoption of the New Business Model; Extent of Commitment to the Existing Business Model*) can be considered as continuous and, as a consequence, the strategic choices that emerge from combining them are in principle an infinite number. However, for analytic convenience and to retain correspondence with prior typologies, we identify discrete strategies that emerge from taking into consideration the intersections between certain levels of these choices.

Using alliteration as a mnemonic device we offer "s" labels for these seven strategies: Straddle, Status Quo, Synthesis, Strengthen, Switch, and Scoot/Start Over. Conceptualizing the problem in this fashion allows us to identify the incumbent's options more systematically and completely. Note that the two dimensions that define this matrix are also the two dimensions that could be used to define the constructs of re-deployment and co-deployment in a business model setting since co-deployment implies investment in the new business model without withdrawal of commitment from the old one and re-deployment implies investment in the new business model and withdrawal of commitment from the old one. Hence, the construct of re-deployment is going to be more relevant for the strategies at the bottom-left side of the matrix, while the construct of co-deployment is more relevant for the strategies in the top-right side of the matrix. This derivation of the strategies is also holistic in the sense that it enables us to integrate all the available typologies in prior literature. In Table 1 we match up the S-terminology with the corresponding differing terms used in the literature where they are available. In the next section we describe each strategy more completely and also offer propositions predicting their adoption by the incumbent.

CHOOSING BETWEEN RESPONSE STRATEGIES

The previous section highlighted a set of different strategies that incumbents could use to compete against an entrant with a new business model. Despite their relevance in improving our understanding of the problem, prior research provides only limited guidance on the set of conditions that might lead to one choice versus the other (see related pieces by Casadesus-Masanell & Zhu, 2010, 2013; Ghemawat, 2001; Charitou & Markides, 2003).

In this section of the paper we describe the strategies presented in Table 1 and identify some of the factors that could induce an incumbent to select that strategic choice. In principle there are likely to be many factors influencing the decision of choosing one response over another. However, given the scope of this study, and to theoretically bound our focus we will concentrate our attention on the key components that our prior discussion has unearthed. Our analysis of a new business model's effects on an industry suggests that in evaluating the incumbent's decision we need to consider the uncertainties it generates in terms of the relative efficacy of the two models and the value of the assets of the incumbent. Additionally, we also need to consider the effects of market dynamics that emerge from the new business model entering the industry, in as much as it leads to the discovery of new customers and segments or the cannibalization of the incumbent's existing customers.

Table 1. The Incumbent's Choices.

		Extent of Adoption of the New Business Model		
		Reject	Modify and adopt	Adopt as is
Extent of commitment to the existing business model	Retain as is	*Status Quo* (Co-deployment and re-deployment not meaningful) Pure model (Bonaccorsi et al., 2006; Casadesus-Masanell & Llanes, 2011; Casadesus-Masanell & Zhu, 2010); Not responding (Ghemawat, 2001); Harvesting (Ghemawat, 2001)	*Straddle* (Co-deployment *across old and new* business model) Dual business model (Casadesus-Masanell & Zhu, 2010; Markides & Charitou, 2004); Straddling (Ghemawat, 2001)	*Straddle* (Co-deployment *across old and new* business model) Dual business model (Casadesus-Masanell & Zhu, 2010; Markides & Charitou, 2004); Straddling (Ghemawat, 2001)
	Modify and retain	*Strengthen* Fighting (Ghemawat, 2001)	*Synthesize* (Partial Re-deployment – some assets re-deployed in conjunction with some new assets) Mixed business model (Casadesus-Masanell & Llanes, 2011; Casadesus-Masanell & Zhu, 2010); Hybrid business model (Bonaccorsi et al., 2006); Recombining (Ghemawat, 2001)	*Straddle* (Co-deployment *across old and new* business model) Dual business model (Casadesus-Masanell & Zhu, 2010; Markides & Charitou, 2004); Straddling (Ghemawat, 2001)
	Reject	*Scoot* (Re-deployment in a *different product market* or liquidation) *Start Over* (Re-deployment in the same *product market*)	*Switch* (Re-deployment *into the new* business model) Pure model (Bonaccorsi et al., 2006; Casadesus-Masanell & Llanes, 2011; Casadesus-Masanell & Zhu, 2010); Switching (Ghemawat, 2001)	*Switch* (Re-deployment *into the new* business model) Pure model (Bonaccorsi et al., 2006; Casadesus-Masanell & Llanes, 2011; Casadesus-Masanell & Zhu, 2010); Switching (Ghemawat, 2001)

Our review of the co-deployment and re-deployment literature suggests that two other factors would also be natural determinants of the decision – the benefits and costs of within business re-deployment and co-deployment and across-business co-deployment and re-deployment. Finally, a fifth key consideration is identified by our scope condition in that our model applies to incumbents. Given the focus on incumbents we need to recognize that their status as incumbents conveys certain endowments and constraints. Thus, to summarize, we build on five sets of factors that may influence an incumbent's response to an entrant with a new business model – (1) the uncertainty created by the entrants entry with regard to the relative efficacy of the two models and the value of the incumbent's assets, (2) the new business model's effect on market dynamics in terms of whether it leads to the discovery of a new customer segment and to an expansion of the market or that it targets an existing set of customers and simply cannibalizes the existing sales, (3) the possibilities and incidence of *within-business-across-business-model* co-deployment and re-deployment costs and benefits, (4) *across-business* co-deployment and re-deployment costs and benefits, and (5) the incumbents' prior commitments and expectations set because of its historic presence in the industry. We focus on these five set of factors to help us understand what drives the choice of a given S-strategy. In examining the above factors for each of the seven S-strategies we focus on a select subset of factors that we see as most clearly helping us make a prediction about that specific strategy. We describe the strategies and our predictions beginning from the strategy that is most conservative with respect to change from the incumbent's perspective and then move across to increasingly distant strategies. Table 2 summarizes the propositions and highlights these five factors.

Choosing the Status Quo Strategy

The Status quo strategy corresponds to the situation in which the incumbent (e.g., Blockbuster) retains the existing business model as it is and rejects the new business model. In other words, it chooses not to react to the entrant, but stays on its own prior course. The uncertainties generated by a new business model are likely to be central in the decision to go with status quo. When a new business model emerges there may be uncertainty in the perception of the potential customers regarding the competitive viability of the new model versus the incumbent one (Humphreys & Latour, 2013). In such a context an incumbent's adoption or even reaction to the

Table 2. Synthesis of Different Strategies, Factors Affecting Them and Propositions.

Strategy	Factors Affecting Choice	Proposition
Status quo	• Uncertainty about relative efficacy of business models, value of incumbents assets • Within-business-across business-model co-deployment and re-deployment costs • Across-business re-deployment costs	*P1: The probability of incumbents adopting a "Status Quo" strategy is higher, the higher the uncertainty about the viability of the new business model, the lower the marketability of the incumbent's assets outside the existing business, and the higher the co-deployment and re-deployment costs.*
Strengthen	• Uncertainty about relative efficacy of business models • Market – size effects of new business model • Incumbent prior experience and history • Within-business-across business-model co-deployment and re-deployment costs	*P2: The probability of incumbents adopting a "Strengthen" strategy is higher, the lower the overlap between the customer preferences in the segments targeted by the old and the new model, the closer the expected competitive performance of the two models the higher the gap between the incumbent's historic profitability and the projected profitability of the new model, and the higher the co-deployment and re-deployment costs.*
Straddle	• Market – size effects of new business model, • Within-business-across business-model co-deployment and re-deployment costs	*P3: The probability of incumbents adopting a "Straddle" strategy is higher, the greater the new business model expands the market by either converting non-customers to customers or causing an increase in the level of consumption of existing customers, the lower the "co-deployment costs" of running the two business models in parallel and the lower the "re-deployment costs" of moving resources from one business model to another*
Synthesis	• Market – size effects of new business model • Market – discovery of key customer preference • Within-business-across business-model re-deployment costs	*P4. The probability of incumbents adopting a "Synthesis" strategy is higher the lower the re-deployment costs, the smaller the market size increment from the new model, and the greater the extent to which the new business model domination of the old one depends on a significant novelty that enhances WTP significantly for some customer segment even if such novelty does not necessarily fit well with the incumbent's existing model and commitments.*

Table 2. (*Continued*)

Strategy	Factors Affecting Choice	Proposition
Switch	• Uncertainty about relative efficacy of business models, value of incumbents assets • Within-business-across business-model re-deployment costs • Across-business co-deployment benefits	*P5. The probability of incumbents adopting a "Switch" strategy is higher, the less the uncertainty about the efficacy of the new model over the old one, the lower the costs of re-deployment, the fewer the other related businesses of the company that use the same assets.*
Scoot/start over	• Uncertainty about relative efficacy of business models, value of incumbents assets • Across-business co-deployment benefits	*P6. The probability of incumbents adopting a "Scoot"/"Start Over" strategy is higher, the more generic the assets being used in the existing business or the greater the variance in the valuation of specific assets, and the greater the number of related businesses of the incumbent.*

new business model may be interpreted as legitimizing the new model (McKendrick & Carrolls, 2001; McKendrick, Jaffee, Carroll, & Khessina, 2003; Pólos, Hannan, & Carroll, 2002). Therefore, the incumbent may strategically choose not to react to the model (Berger, Ridgeway, Fisek, & Norman, 1998). The higher the uncertainty about the relative viability of the two models the more likely that the incumbent may prefer not to legitimize the model by making changes to its own strategy.

In addition, the tendency to remain with the status quo will be particularly high in the presence of high co-deployment costs from a competing business model such as conflict costs, and higher re-deployment or adaptation costs. Getting into the new business model may necessitate different routines, logics and skills. Such an organizational transformation will require not just a significant conceptual effort to develop and implement the new model (cf. Rivkin's failures of inspiration, 2006), but will also entail redistribution of organizational power to the parts of the organization that house the new business model from the parts that housed the old model. Such a power redistribution may not be attractive to management (Rajan, Servaes, Zingales, 2000; Rajan & Zingales, 1997; Stulz, 1990).

Finally, the revaluation of the firm's assets that is highlighted by the entry of new business model provides another mechanism to understand the emergence of a status quo strategy. Highly specific assets that have limited value in another business or business model may provide the firm with another reason to stay with the current business model. Since such assets would have limited outside value, staying in the current business model and sweating the assets (a "harvesting" strategy) till their value goes to zero may be a better alternative. Although in principle the costs on such assets are sunk and should not prevent the firm from switching to a new model if the new model is superior (and hence adopt a straddle strategy), evidence suggests that corporations are often excessively influenced by past commitments (Feldman, 2014; Folta, Johnson, & O'Brien, 2006; Staw, 1981).

> **P1.** The probability of incumbents adopting a "Status Quo" strategy is higher, the higher the uncertainty about the viability of the new business model, the lower the marketability of the incumbent's assets outside the existing business, and the higher the co-deployment and re-deployment costs.

Choosing the Strengthen Strategy

The *Strengthen* strategy is based on the incumbent rejecting the entrant's new business model but modifying its own to be more competitive with the new model. For instance, Blockbuster being able to renegotiate lower rents for its stores or increasing automation at the stores to lower costs would be illustrations wherein it would have strengthened its model in response to the Netflix incursion. Similarly, HP improving its reseller-based business model through actions such as enhanced inventory management to reduce working capital requirements or acquiring Compaq to increase procurement scale and lower costs to compete with Dell's customized-build and direct sales model would be another illustration of strengthening.

The decision to infuse resources into the existing model while ignoring the new one is likely to be most consistent with a context wherein there is low uncertainty about the viability of the new model but where there is some ambiguity about the relative performance of the two models (O'Brien, Folta, & Johnson, 2003). Specifically, if the uncertainty is reduced because it becomes clearer that the performance of the two models in serving the same set of customers is really similar even though the models are fundamentally different there may be incentives for the incumbent to strengthen the existing business model may serve as a mechanism to break the stalemate.

From the point of market dynamics if the new business model targets customer segments in the underlying market that have fundamentally different preferences (Sakhartov & Folta, 2014) there are incentives for incumbent to strengthen its own model. For instance, if the customers targeted by the existing model continue to be significant and have different preferences than the customers targeted by the new business model, the incumbent will likely be persuaded to invest in strengthening the model as such strengthening may be a way to "keep" the customers who have already expressed a preference for the incumbent's model and prevent the entrant from eventually coming after those customers.

High re-deployment costs for instance when the value of the incumbent assets is specific to the existing business model, would also favor a Strengthen strategy. For instance, this could be the case when the incumbent business model has a long and storied history of success so that the brand is strongly associated with that business model (e.g., Kodak and film processing). In this case, re-deploying those assets outside of the original business model would incur high re-deployment costs.

At the same time, the incumbent's prior commitments to the existing model may also lead to perceptual biases favoring the existing model relative to the old one (Ahuja & Lampert, 2001). If the incumbent's original model provided historically superior returns relative to the new business model (e.g., Kodak and film processing), the new model with lower expected returns may be considered unacceptable and may be unfavorably evaluated. Research suggests that readjusting expectations downward is more difficult (Oliver, 1977). Having experienced higher returns from the incumbent business model managers may seek to perpetuate them by strengthening the incumbent model rather than accept another model with lower returns.

Finally, a fourth argument for strengthening would emerge strongly if there were sharp conflicts in the activities required to execute the two business models simultaneously. In such an event the synthesize and straddle options are likely to be of limited value, enhancing the attractiveness of strengthening the model.

P2. The probability of incumbents adopting a "Strengthen" strategy is higher, the lower the overlap between the customer preferences in the segments targeted by the old and the new model, the closer the expected competitive performance of the two models, the higher the gap between the incumbent's historic profitability and the projected profitability of the new model, and the higher the co-deployment and re-deployment costs.

Choosing the Straddle Strategy

The *Straddle* strategy refers to the case in which the incumbent retains the current business model as it is but also –simultaneously – adopts the new one, in a dual strategy mode (Casadesus-Masanell & Zhu, 2010; Markides & Charitou, 2004). This would correspond to the hypothetical situation in which Blockbuster retained its existing rent-from-physical store business model but had simultaneously started a parallel rent-through-mail model. The hub and spoke airlines founding of low-cost subsidiaries could be another illustration of this strategy (British Airways and Go; Singapore Airlines and Silk Air, Rivkin, 2000). This is perhaps the most widely referred to strategy in the literature and also one of the common reactions that students and executives express when faced with the problem of an entrant with a new business model. In part the argument for this strategy is expressed as – "firms commonly diversify into related product categories and this is perhaps the case of an extremely closely related market so wouldn't it make sense to respond with this?" To explore the logic of this common argument we harken back to the underlying theory of related diversification that underlies this argument and establish why it may not be perfectly applicable in the dual business model setting even when it does apply to the related product setting more generally.

In her seminal work seeking to explain the growth and diversification of a firm Penrose (1959) identified the downward sloping demand curve as a natural limit to the firm's growth. In her argument the negatively sloped demand curve and its attendant even more steeply downward sloping marginal revenue curve would cause the single product firm to reach a natural limit to its size even if one assumed constant marginal costs as the downward sloping marginal curve intersected with the marginal cost curve.

However, as Penrose argued, such a demand constraint could be loosened if the firm were to expand into an additional product market. In this case, the notional "total demand" curve facing the firm would move outwards relaxing the constraint to the firm's growth. If, in addition, the firm had excess capacity in critical fixed "factors" then such growth could be quite profitable for the firm as (a) the additional volume of sales obtained from the "new" market would effectively further spread the costs of such fixed factors and (b) this expansion into adjacent markets would hurt pricing less than expanding volume in the existing market – where all high-willingness-to-pay customers were already served and where only cutting prices could expand demand (Penrose,1959). Thus, in the Penrose formulation, diversification into a second product was helpful in (a) better amortizing the costs of the fixed factors, that is, the fixed costs and (b) that it provided new demand and thus avoiding depressing pricing in the existing market as you sought to better exploit the fixed factors (Penrose, 1959).

Applying the above reasoning to the single-product-dual-business-model firm highlights some important differences between the diversified firm and single-product-multiple-business model contexts: most importantly, expansion into a second business model does not necessarily increase the addressable demand facing the firm. Unlike the Penrosian diversification-into-a-different-product-market case, there is a risk that that the second business model cannibalizes the first one as typically with a second business – model a new product-market is not necessarily added and the product sold is essentially the same. At the same time, when a firm launches a second business model, it will likely need to add some resources to operationalize it. The firm may already own such resources as it is using them in the first business model; alternately it needs to acquire them. Even if the firm already owns such assets there are likely to be significant re-deployment costs. Either way there are going to be potentially significant costs to be written off against any incremental revenue obtained through the new business model. Thus, unlike the Penrosian diversification case, there is a risk that that the second business model cannibalizes the first one as the product sold is essentially the same, while absorbing some of the firm resources in the process of business model operationalization. One factor that can overcome the above dynamic is the possibility that the new business model uncovers a new set of customers that hitherto were not consuming the product or causes existing customers to consume more of the product because it is made available in a different way. Such an event could then neutralize the above effect and even provide a revenue increase thus enhancing the possibility of a straddle.

On the cost side we note that if the resources to be used in operationalizing the second model are scale-free they can probably be shared across the two models creating synergy benefits (Bryce & Winter, 2009; Levinthal & Wu, 2010). However, it is likely that even scale-free resources, such as technology and brands, might imply additional types of co-deployment costs when they are used in additional applications (Ahuja & Novelli, 2015). First, they might imply adaptation costs to tailor them to the second model (e.g., modifying your warehousing procedures to accommodate online and offline models, even if you are using existing warehouse capacity; adapting your technological ordering system to interface with both physical and online customers; advertising, to indicate that you provide coordinated offline-online shopping, Kaplan & Henderson, 2005; Leonard-Barton, 1992;

Rawley, 2010). Second, such resources are likely to need coordination if they are to be shared across the two models bringing in coordination costs (Hill & Hoskisson, 1987; Rawley, 2010; Zhou, 2011). Third, such resources may be subjected to both conflict and compromise costs. If the resources in question are not scale-free they need to be re-deployed to serve the second model. In such a case there are likely to be various re-deployment costs as well (Helfat & Eisenhardt, 2004).

These arguments imply that, because in the case of dual business models the potential demand does not necessarily increase but the costs of synergies and re-deployment might do so, the conditions under which a straddle strategy generates value for a single-business firm might be more stringent than in the case of a multi-business firm expanding in multiple markets. Specifically, if the market size does not truly expand with the new business model or if there are significant co-deployment or re-deployment costs it may be difficult to justify a second business model and, hence, a straddle strategy. This leads us to suggest that:

> **P3.** The probability of incumbents adopting a "Straddle" strategy is higher, the greater the new business model expands the market by either converting non-customers to customers or causing an increase in the level of consumption of existing customers, the lower the "co-deployment costs" of running the two business models in parallel and the lower the "re-deployment costs" of moving resources from one business model to another

Choosing the Synthesis Strategy

An incumbent could also choose to modify its existing business model by incorporating components of the new business model and creating a mixed or hybrid version of the model (Ghemawat, 2001; Casadesus-Masanell & Llanes, 2011; Casadesus-Masanell & Zhu, 2010) an option we label "*Synthesize*" to capture the idea of mixing elements from two business models to create a new one. For instance, Blockbuster could permit its customers to order online but return to the physical store. Or it could eliminate late fees to make itself more attractive to customers. This strategy essentially leads to the emergence of business model innovation by recombination. For successful synthesis parts of the model have to be fused with parts of the new model. Such a re-deployment of the old model assets is much easier if there are low adaptation costs. Further, the motivation to seek a synthesis model would be greater if the new model is not really expanding the market, moving the incumbent away from a straddle strategy.

When there is limited conflict between the features of two business models and they can be seamlessly integrated one would naturally expect to see use of synthesis option. However, perhaps more interesting are circumstances in which there is a conflict between the two business models and yet the incumbent may choose synthesis (Casadesus-Masanell & Llanes, 2009). One such circumstance would be the case in which the new business model dominates the old one due to its incorporation of a central and meaningful innovation; one that is extremely attractive to customers. In the context of such a must-have feature in a business-model isomorphic legitimization pressures will force the incumbent to adopt such features (McKendrick & Carrolls, 2001). Since the feature is desired or regarded as critical the incumbent is forced to adopt it even though it may create an internal conflict in the incumbent's business model. Illustrations of such occurrences include standardized PC makers including customization in their value proposition, Blockbuster introducing no late fees and partial online-offline integration.

> **P4.** The probability of incumbents adopting a "Synthesis" strategy is higher the lower the re-deployment costs, the smaller the market size increment from the new model, and the greater the extent to which the new business model domination of the old one depends on a significant novelty that enhances WTP significantly for some customer segment even if such novelty does not necessarily fit well with the incumbent's existing model and commitments.

Choosing the Switch Strategy

The *Switch* strategy corresponds to the situation in which the incumbent decides to drop the existing business model and switch to the new one. This would correspond to the hypothetical situation in which Blockbuster decides to completely reject the rent-from-physical-store model and sells off all its stores and starts a new rental by mail model like Netflix, to compete against Netflix in the rent-from-mail arena.

Switching from one business model to another entails essentially the re-deployment of the firm's resources from the first business model to the second one (Helfat & Eisenhardt, 2004). A decision by a firm to switch to a completely different business model and drop the existing one would naturally make most sense if the new business model very visibly competitively dominates the old one in the sense that there remain no substantial set of customers for which the wedge between willingness to pay and cost for the incumbent model is greater than for the challenging model (Ghemawat & Rivkin, 2006; Penrose, 1959; Sakhartov & Folta, 2015).Thus reduction of uncertainty and establishing the superiority of the new models increases the probability and the speed of switching.

Such a switch is more likely to happen the fewer the constraints to the firm dropping its existing business model, that is, when the costs of re-deployment are low (Karim, 2012; Penrose, 1959). Further, if the firm is diversified into other product categories and is using its current resources to obtain synergies by sharing those resources across multiple product lines, paradoxically its degrees of freedom to switch may be limited. This conclusion draws from the basic idea that, in a related diversifier, resources are shared across businesses (Grant & Jammine, 1988; Palepu, 1985; Rumelt, 1974, 1982). If a given business faces a new business model that requires it to switch in a relatedly diversified firm such a switch would be more difficult to accomplish because the set of resources to be re-deployed were being shared across businesses and such a re-deployment may not be interests of the other businesses.

Thus, incumbents with many related businesses may have less freedom to "switch away" from an existing business model to a new one because the assets are currently being shared across multiple businesses and changing the business model in one business may have ripple effects in other businesses. In other words, prior pursuit of synergy may limit the firm's ability to re-deploy (Feldman, 2014; Folta et al., 2006). These arguments suggest:

> **P5.** The probability of incumbents adopting a "Switch" strategy is higher, the less the uncertainty about the efficacy of the new model over the old one, the lower the costs of re-deployment, the fewer the other related businesses of the company (higher across-business co-deployment benefits) that use the same assets.

Choosing the Scoot/Start over Strategy

Another possibility emerges when the incumbent decides to reject both models and either responds with a new business model different from the previous two (*Start over)* or to re-deploys the assets in a different business or possibly liquidates the business by selling to another firm (*Scoot*). For instance a firm unable to compete in the PC market develops a "thin client" approach wherein they provide computing services through larger server computers coupled with stripped down "dumber" terminals for individual users thus reducing the need for full-featured personal computers. The same type of response could also be envisaged in the opposite direction, where the firm focuses on one key subpart of the product and becomes a supplier for that and hence specializes on a sub-segment of the original market where its business model still retails a competitive advantage. GE and IBM have responded with such strategies when faced with competition from new business models that provided a commoditized version of their specialty services.

In a scoot/start over strategy the incumbent essentially exits from the focal market rapidly in the face of the new business model. Clearly, for such a call to be made, the incumbent should be quite clear that their model is competitively dominated (Ghemawat, 2001). However, scooting/starting over depends not only on the incumbent's assessment that their model will be dominated. An exit decision is facilitated if the assets can be re-deployed in some other business or through the creation of another business model (Anand & Singh, 1997; Helfat & Lieberman, 2002; Lee, Folta, & Lieberman, 2010; Sakhartov & Folta, 2014, 2015). Hence, the more generic the assets the more likely the incumbent is to scoot/start over. However, if the incumbent's assets are more specialized, for a scoot/start over strategy to be executed there would need to be buyers with different valuations at the other end of the trade (Barney, 1986; Bazerman & Samuelson, 1983).

The ability to devise a scoot/start over strategy is of course contingent upon the creativity of the focal firm as it responds to the new business model. However, it is likely that other firm characteristics may also influence its ability to develop a new model after dropping the existing one and rejecting the new one. If a firm is active in multiple related businesses several factors suggest that its motivation to find a new model, and likely its ability to do so, are going to be high. Presence in multiple related business implies that exit from one of those businesses is difficult to consider, as it will affect the synergies the corporation is based on. At the same time if the firm's business model in the focal business is being outcompeted, the focal business may not remain viable for long. The multiple businesses in turn could potentially also serve as a source for providing complementary services that may lead to a different type of business model (Chesbrough & Appleyard, 2007). The joint availability of resources and necessity of developing an alternate model should be supportive of developing scoot/ start over strategies.

> **P6.** The probability of incumbents adopting a "Scoot"/"Start Over" strategy is higher, the more generic the assets being used in the existing business (low across-business re-deployment costs) or the greater the variance in the valuation of specific assets, and the greater the number of related businesses (greater across-business synergies) of the incumbent.

DISCUSSION

Historically, the constructs of co-deployment and re-deployment have been considered relevant in the context of firms' decision of investing in different businesses (Helfat & Eisenhardt, 2004; Sakhartov & Folta, 2014). This paper contributes to research in this domain by exploring the boundaries of application of the constructs of co-deployment and re-deployment through its use in the context of the choice faced by incumbent firms when a competing business model emerges in the market.

Different from the phenomenon in which the emergence of a new business model is driven by the emergence of new technological innovation (Tripsas & Gavetti, 2000), we focus on the phenomenon in which new, competing, business models emerge in the markets in which the firm operates and we analyzed the possible strategic responses taking an incumbent's perspective. Specifically, we review and integrate existing literature on business models and identify seven strategies that incumbents can choose. If the incumbent firm decides to not adopt the new business model it can employ a status quo strategy (i.e., maintaining the existing business model), it can change the existing business model to make it stronger in the face of the competition created by the new model, or it can 'scoot' and liquidate or reconfigure existing resources and asset to use them in other contexts. Alternatively, the incumbent can adopt the new business model and run it in parallel with the existing one ("straddle"); it can modify the existing model synthesizing in it features of the new one, it can completely switch to the new model.

Note that adapting the ideas related to the co-employment and re-deployment of resources from the diversified firm to the single business-multi-business-model draws attention to how the underlying costs are likely to differ in their incidence across these settings. For instance, one could argue that conflict costs related to the co-employment of resources may well get worsened in the context of the straddling firm (i.e., implementing two business models in parallel) relative to a related diversifier, because the final product delivered across both business models of the straddling firm might be essentially identical; hence, the unit heads commanding the separate models may see themselves as in direct competition (Markides & Charitou, 2004). In contrast the compromise costs generated may be significantly lowered in many straddling cases (relative to the same costs to the in the context of relatedly diversified firms exploiting a synergy) due to the very same fact that the final products in the straddle setting are very close. In contrast, we could also imagine that the products being so close in the straddle setting may falsely convince managers that adaptation costs across the two models are very low (Kaplan & Henderson, 2005; Leonard-Barton, 1992; Rawley, 2010); in fact it may be the case that running an internet based business model may be very different from running a brick and mortar business model for the same product.

The bottom line to this argument is that the co-deployment and redeployment literatures provide a very useful set of constructs to apply to the business models literature in this setting; however, the incidence and level of the relevant costs and benefits may be different in the cases of related diversifiers versus single-business-multi-model firms. Reflecting upon the similarities and differences between related diversified firms and single-business multiple-business-model firms helps to uncover the circumstances under which firms may choose between various responses to react to new business models.

Clearly, further research will be required to identify a more complete set of conditions that will enhance our understanding of incumbent-entrant business model dynamics. Further, from an empirical standpoint, these hypotheses present a rich agenda for validation or refutation. A further task yet is to integrate this analysis of competitive responses to a new business model with the collaborative responses that are possible when a new business model emerges. Overall these possibilities suggest that applying established theories and constructs to the world of business models promises a fecund research agenda.

NOTE

1. The construct of business model has been defined in different ways by different authors. Amit and Zott (2001, p. 511), for instance, define business models as "the content, structure, and governance of transactions designed so as to create value

through the exploitation of business opportunities"; Casadesus-Masanell and Ricart (2010, p. 195) as "The logic of the firm – how it operates and creates value for its stakeholders," Baden-fuller and Haefliger as "a system that solves the problem of identifying who is (or are) the customer(s), engaging with their needs, delivering satisfaction, and monetizing the value." See Baden-Fuller and Morgan (2010) for a review.

ACKNOWLEDGMENT

The authors would like to thank the editors and reviewers for their very constructive and insightful comments through the review process. Elena Novelli also gratefully acknowledges the financial support of the ESRC Future Research Leaders Scheme (Grant ES/K001388/1). Gautam Ahuja would like to thank the University of Michigan for support.

REFERENCES

Adner, R. (2002). When are technologies disruptive? A demand-based view of the emergence of competition. *Strategic Management Journal*, *23*(8), 667–688.

Ahuja, G., & Lampert, C. (2001). Entrepreneurship in the large corporation: A longitudinal study of how established firms create breakthrough inventions. *Strategic Management Journal*, *22*(6-7), 521–543.

Ahuja, G., & Novelli, E. (2015). *Redirecting research efforts on the diversification-performance linkage: The search for synergy*. Working Paper.

Amit, R., & Zott, C. (2001). Value creation in e-business. *Strategic Management Journal*, *22*(6/7), 493.

Anand, J., & Singh, H. (1997). Asset re-deployment, acquisitions and corporate strategy in declining industries. *Strategic Management Journal*, *18*(S1), 99–118.

Baden-Fuller, C., & Haefliger, S. (2013). Business models and technological innovation. *Long Range Planning*, *46*(6), 419–426.

Baden-Fuller, C., & Morgan, M. S. (2010). Business models as models. *Long Range Planning*, *43*(2), 156–171.

Barney, J. B. (1986). Strategic factor markets: Expectations, luck, and business strategy. *Management Science*, *32*(10), 1231–1241.

Bazerman, M., & Samuelson, W. (1983). *The winner's curse: An empirical investigation. Aspiration levels in bargaining and economic decision making, lecture notes in economics and mathematical systems*, 213.

Berger, J., Ridgeway, C. L., Fisek, M. H., & Norman, R. Z. (1998). The legitimation and delegitimation of power and prestige orders. *American Sociological Review*, *63*(3), 379–405.

Bettis, R. A. (1981). Performance differences in related and unrelated diversified firms. *Strategic Management Journal*, *2*(4), 379–393.

Bettis, R. A., & Hall, W. K. (1982). Diversification strategy, accounting determined risk, and accounting determined return. *Academy of Management Journal*, *25*(2), 254–264.

Bonaccorsi, A., Giannangeli, S., & Rossi, C. (2006). Entry strategies under competing standards: Hybrid business models in the open source software industry. *Management Science*, *52*(7), 1085–1098.

Bonaccorsi, A., & Rossi, C. (2003). Why open source software can succeed. *Research Policy*, *32*(7), 1243–1258.

Bryce, D. J., & Winter, S. G. (2009). A general interindustry relatedness index. *Management Science*, *55*(9), 1570–1585.

Capron, L. (1999). *The long-term performance of horizontal acquisitions*. INSEAD.

Capron, L., Dussauge, P., & Mitchell, W. (1998). Resource re-deployment following horizontal acquisitions in Europe and North America, 1988–1992. *Strategic Management Journal*, *19*(7), 631–661.

Capron, L., & Mitchell, W. (1998). Bilateral resource re-deployment and capabilities improvement following horizontal acquisitions. *Industrial and Corporate Change*, *7*(3), 453–484.

Capron, L., Mitchell, W., & Swaminathan, A. (2001). Asset divestiture following horizontal acquisitions: A dynamic view. *Strategic Management Journal*, *22*(9), 817–844.

Carroll, G. R., Bigelow, L. S., Seidel, M. D. L., & Tsai, L. B. (1996). The fates of de novo and de alio producers in the American automobile industry 1885–1981. *Strategic Management Journal*, *17*(S1), 117–137.

Casadesus-Masanell, R., & Ghemawat, P. (2006). Dynamic mixed duopoly: A model motivated by Linux vs. Windows. *Management Science*, *52*(7), 1072–1084.

Casadesus-Masanell, R., & Hervas-Drane, A. (2010). Peer-to-peer file sharing and the market for digital information goods. *Journal of Economics & Management Strategy*, *19*(2), 333–373.

Casadesus-Masanell, R., & Llanes, G. (2011). Mixed source. *Management Science*, *57*(7), 1212–1230.

Casadesus-Masanell, R., & Ricart, J. E. (2010). From strategy to business models and onto tactics. *Long Range Planning*, *43*(2), 195–215.

Casadesus-Masanell, R., & Yoffie, D. B. (2007). Wintel: Cooperation and conflict. *Management Science*, *53*(4), 584–598.

Casadesus-Masanell, R., & Zhu, F. (2010). *Business model innovation and competitive imitation*. Harvard, MA: Harvard Business School.

Casadesus-Masanell, R., & Zhu, F. (2013). Business model innovation and competitive imitation: The case of sponsor-based business models. *Strategic Management Journal*, *34*(4), 464–482.

Cattani, G. (2006). Technological pre-adaptation, speciation, and emergence of new technologies: How Corning invented and developed fiber optics. *Industrial and Corporate Change*, *15*(2), 285–318.

Charitou, C. D., & Markides, C. C. (2003). Responses to disruptive strategic innovation. *MIT Sloan Management Review*, *44*(2), 55–63.

Chesbrough, H. W., & Appleyard, M. M. (2007). Open innovation and strategy.

Economides, N., & Katsamakas, E. (2006). Two-sided competition of proprietary vs. open source technology platforms and the implications for the software industry. *Management Science*, *52*(7), 1057–1071.

Feldman, E. R. (2014). Legacy divestitures: Motives and implications. *Organization Science*, *25*(3), 815–832.

Folta, T. B., Johnson, D. R., & O'Brien, J. (2006). Uncertainty, irreversibility, and the likelihood of entry: An empirical assessment of the option to defer. *Journal of Economic Behavior & Organization*, *61*(3), 432–452.
Ganco, M., & Agarwal, R. (2009). Performance differentials between diversifying entrants and entrepreneurial start-ups: A complexity approach. *Academy of Management Review*, *34*(2), 228–252.
Ghemawat, P. (Ed.). (2001). *Strategy and the business landscape: Core concepts*. Upper Saddle River, NJ: Prentice Hall.
Ghemawat, P., & Rivkin, J. W. (2006). *Creating competitive advantage*. Harvard, MA: Harvard Business School Publishing.
Grant, R. M., & Jammine, A. P. (1988). Performance differences between the Wrigley/Rumelt strategic categories. *Strategic Management Journal*, *9*(4), 333–346.
Greenwood, R., Li, S. X., Prakash, R., & Deephouse, D. L. (2005). Reputation, diversification, and organizational explanations of performance in professional service firms. *Organization Science*, *16*(6), 661–673.
Helfat, C. E., & Eisenhardt, K. M. (2004). Inter-temporal economies of scope, organizational modularity, and the dynamics of diversification. *Strategic Management Journal*, *25*(13), 1217–1232.
Helfat, C. E., & Lieberman, M. B. (2002). The birth of capabilities: Market entry and the importance of pre-history. *Industrial and Corporate Change*, *11*(4), 725–760.
Helfat, C. E., & Raubitschek, R. S. (2000). Product sequencing: Co-evolution of knowledge, capabilities and products. *Strategic Management Journal*, *21*(10–11), 961–980.
Henderson, R. M., & Clark, K. B. (1990). Architectural innovation: The reconfiguration of existing product technologies and the failure of established firms. *Administrative Science Quarterly*, *35*, 9–30.
Hill, C. W., & Hoskisson, R. E. (1987). Strategy and structure in the multiproduct firm. *Academy of Management Review*, *12*(2), 331–341.
Hoskisson, R. E., & Hitt, M. A. (1988). Strategic control systems and relative R&D investment in large multiproduct firms. *Strategic Management Journal*, *9*(6), 605–621.
Humphreys, A., & Latour, K. A. (2013). Framing the game: Assessing the impact of cultural representations on consumer perceptions of legitimacy. *Journal of Consumer Research*, *40*(4), 773–795.
Jones, G. R., & Hill, C. W. (1988). Transaction cost analysis of strategy-structure choice. *Strategic Management Journal*, *9*(2), 159–172.
Kaplan, S., & Henderson, R. (2005). Inertia and incentives: Bridging organizational economics and organizational theory. *Organization Science*, *16*(5), 509–521.
Karim, S. (2012). Exploring structural embeddedness of product market activities and resources within business units. *Strategic Organization*, *10*(4), 333–365.
Karim, S., & Mitchell, W. (2000). Path-dependent and path-breaking change: Reconfiguring business resources following acquisitions in the U.S. medical sector, 1978–1995. *Strategic Management Journal*, *21*, 1061–1081.
Klepper, S., & Simons, K. L. (2000). Dominance by birthright: Entry of prior radio producers and competitive ramifications in the US television receiver industry. *Strategic Management Journal*, *21*(10–11), 997–1016.
Kogut, B., & Kulatilaka, N. (1994). Operating flexibility, global manufacturing, and the option value of a multinational network. *Management Science*, *40*(1), 123–139.

Lanzolla, G., & Markides, C. (2015). *Does the strategy field need the business model concept?* London Business School Working Paper No. LBS SE WP 22.
Lee, G., Folta, T. B., & Lieberman, M. B. (May 20, 2010). *Relatedness and market exit.* INSEAD Working Paper No. 2010/39/ST. Fontainebleau: INSEAD.
Leonard-Barton, D. (1992). Core capabilities and core rigidities: A paradox in managing new product development. *Strategic Management Journal, 13*(S1), 111–125.
Levinthal, D. A., & Wu, B. (2010). Opportunity costs and non-scale free capabilities: Profit maximization, corporate scope, and profit margins. *Strategic Management Journal, 31*(7), 780–801.
Markides, C., & Charitou, C. D. (2004). Competing with dual business models: A contingency approach. *The Academy of Management Executive, 18*(3), 22–36.
McKendrick, D. G., & Carroll, G. R. (2001). On the genesis of organizational forms: Evidence from the market for disk arrays. *Organization Science, 12*(6), 661–682.
McKendrick, D. G., Jaffee, J., Carroll, G. R., & Khessina, O. M. (2003). In the bud? Disk array producers as a (possibly) emergent organizational form. *Administrative Science Quarterly, 48*(1), 60–93.
McNamara, P., Peck, S. I., & Sasson, A. (2013). Competing business models, value creation and appropriation in English football. *Long Range Planning, 46*(6), 475–487.
Mitchell, W. (1989). Whether and when? Probability and timing of incumbents' entry into emerging industrial subfields. *Administrative Science Quarterly, 34*, 208–230.
Mitchell, W. (1991). Dual clocks: Entry order influences on incumbent and newcomer market share and survival when specialized assets retain their value. *Strategic Management Journal, 12*(2), 85–100.
O'Brien, J. P., Folta, T. B., & Johnson, D. R. (2003). A real options perspective on entrepreneurial entry in the face of uncertainty. *Managerial and Decision Economics, 24*(8), 515–533.
Oliver, R. L. (1977). Effect of expectation and disconfirmation on postexposure product evaluations: An alternative interpretation. *Journal of Applied Psychology, 62*(4), 480.
Palepu, K. (1985). Diversification strategy, profit performance and the entropy measure. *Strategic Management Journal, 6*(3), 239–255.
Panzar, J. C., & Willig, R. D. (1981). Economies of scope. *The American Economic Review, 71*(2), 268–272.
Penrose, E. (1959). *The theory of the firm.* New York, NY: Wiley.
Pólos, L., Hannan, M. T., & Carroll, G. R. (2002). Foundations of a theory of social forms. *Industrial and Corporate Change, 11*(1), 85–115.
Porter, M. E. (1980). *Competitive strategy: Techniques for analyzing industries and competitors.* New York, NY: Free Press.
Rajan, R. G., & Zingales, L. (1997). Power in a theory of the firm *(No. w6274)*. National Bureau of Economic Research.
Rajan, R., Servaes, H., & Zingales, L. (2000). The cost of diversity: The diversification discount and inefficient investment. *The Journal of Finance, 55*(1), 35–80.
Rawley, E. (2010). Diversification, coordination costs, and organizational rigidity: Evidence from microdata. *Strategic Management Journal, 31*(8), 873–891.
Rivkin, J. W. (2000). Dogfight over Europe: Ryanair (C).
Rivkin, J. W. (2006). Delta Air Lines (A): The Low-Cost Carrier Threat and Delta Air Lines (B): The Launch of Song, Harvard Business School Teaching Note, 5-706-430.
Rosenbloom, R. S., & Christensen, C. M. (1994). Technological discontinuties, organizational capabilities, and strategic commitments. *Industrial and Corporate Change, 3*(3), 655–685.

Rumelt, R. (1974). *Strategy structure and economic performance: Division of research*. Boston, MA: Harvard Business School.

Rumelt, R. (1982). Diversification strategy and profitability. *Strategic Management Journal*, *3*(4), 359–369.

Sakhartov, A. V., & Folta, T. B. (2014). Resource relatedness, re-deployability, and firm value. *Strategic Management Journal*, *35*(12), 1781–1797.

Sakhartov, A. V., & Folta, T. B. (2015). Getting beyond relatedness as a driver of corporate value. *Strategic Management Journal*, *36*(13), 1939–1959.

Seamans, R. C. (2012). Fighting city hall: Entry deterrence and technology upgrades in cable TV markets. *Management Science*, *58*(3), 461–475.

Sosa, L. M. (2013). Decoupling market incumbency from organizational prehistory: Locating the real sources of competitive advantage in R&D for radical innovation. *Strategic Management Journal*, *34*(2), 245–255.

Staw, B. M. (1981). The escalation of commitment to a course of action. *Academy of Management Review*, *6*(4), 577–587.

Stulz, R. M. (1990). Managerial discretion and optimal financing policies. *Journal of Financial Economics*, *26*, 3–27.

Sutherland, J. W. (1980). A quasi-empirical mapping of optimal scale of enterprise. *Management Science*, *26*(10), 963–981.

Tripsas, M. (1997). Unraveling the process of creative destruction: Complementary assets and incumbent survival in the typesetter industry. *Strategic Management Journal*, *18*(s 1), 119–142.

Tripsas, M., & Gavetti, G. (2000). Capabilities, cognition, and inertia: Evidence from digital imaging. *Strategic Management Journal*, *21*(10–11), 1147–1161.

Tushman, M. L., & Anderson, P. (1986). Technological discontinuities and organizational environments. *Administrative Science Quarterly*, *31*, 439–465.

Williamson, O. E. (1975). *Markets and hierarchies* (pp. 26–30). New York, NY: The Free Press.

Zahavi, T., & Lavie, D. (2013). Intra-industry diversification and firm performance. *Strategic Management Journal*, *34*(8), 978–998.

Zhou, Y. M. (2011). Synergy, coordination costs, and diversification choices. *Strategic Management Journal*, *32*(6), 624–639.

RESOURCE CHARACTERISTICS AND REDEPLOYMENT STRATEGIES: TOWARD A THEORETICAL SYNTHESIS

Jaideep Anand, Hyunseob Kim and Shaohua Lu

ABSTRACT

Firms pursue a number of redeployment strategies in order to achieve growth and create value for their stakeholders. While the majority of previous research focuses on how firms create synergic value by sharing resources across multiple business units, we lack a systematic analysis of the determinants of different redeployment strategies. In this paper, we develop a theoretical framework that allows us to systematically investigate how intrinsic resource characteristics affect resource redeployment strategies. Our framework identifies four critical characteristics of resources, that is, fungibility, scale-free nature, decomposability, and tradability. We develop a number of predictions that provide guidance for researchers to identify the optimal resource

Resource Redeployment and Corporate Strategy
Advances in Strategic Management, Volume 35, 155–184

ISSN: 0742-3322/doi:10.1108/S0742-332220160000035007

redeployment strategy appropriate for resources with a certain set of characteristics.

Keywords: Resource redeployment strategy; fungibility; scale-free resources; decomposability; tradability; evolutionary theory

The ability to redeploy resources is essential to the growth of the firm (Penrose, 1959). The majority of previous research, with a few exceptions, has focused on how firms create synergy by deploying resources simultaneously (inter-temporal) across multiple businesses (e.g., Rumelt, 1974; Singh & Montgomery, 1987; Montgomery & Wernerfelt, 1988; Wernerfelt, 1988). Yet firms can pursue a number of strategies in order to achieve growth, including internal (intra-temporal and inter-temporal) resource redeployment and external resource redeployment. Strategy scholars have made profound advances in this area (e.g., Anand, 2004, 2005; Anand & Delios, 2002; Anand & Singh, 1997; Helfat, 2000; Helfat & Eisenhardt, 2004; Karim, 2006, 2009; Karim & Kaul, 2015; Lee, Folta, & Lieberman, 2010; Sakhartov & Folta, 2014, 2015). Nevertheless, previous studies have not been explicit enough in considering the resource characteristics that drive different types of resource redeployment strategies. For example, relatedness is seen as a determinant of reconfiguration strategy, but "relatedness" may aggregate several important, yet conceptually distinct, issues. In this paper, we aim to develop a theoretical framework that allows us to systematically investigate the resource-level determinants of different redeployment strategies. The principal question we seek to untangle is under what conditions specific resource redeployment strategies are most preferable.

Since Penrose's (1959) thought-provoking book on the growth of the firm, a vast literature has examined how firms choose different resource utilization and redeployment strategies in order to achieve growth. The broad literature can be categorized into two themes: resource redeployment strategies that seek "synergy" or intra-temporal scope economies (denoted thereafter "intra-temporal" redeployment strategies), and those that may generate value from inter-temporal scope economies (denoted thereafter "inter-temporal" redeployment strategies). The former refers to strategies in which firms create synergy by simultaneously sharing resources across multiple business units. The corporate diversification literature, in particular, casts light on the determinants and performance implications of the former (Barney, 1986; Montgomery & Hariharan, 1991; Penrose, 1959; Rumelt, 1974; Silverman, 1999; Singh & Montgomery, 1987; Villalonga, 2004; Wernerfelt, 1984). The latter describes that firms attain growth by withdrawing their resources from their original use and redeploying them to another business that yields higher returns (Anand, 2004, 2005; Anand & Singh, 1997; Helfat & Eisenhardt, 2004; Karim, 2006, 2009). Although the previous literature has enhanced our understanding of resource redeployment strategies, two limitations remain. First, scholarly efforts on "*intra-temporal*" and "*inter-temporal*" resource redeployment strategies appear in separate streams of study. Second, *internal* resource redeployment strategy has rarely been seen as an alternative to *external* redeployment strategy in which "firms carry out the transaction in the open market and resources are organized by another entrepreneur" (Coase, 1937, p. 394).

To address the limitations in the previous literature, we develop a framework to provide a synthesis of explanations of how intrinsic resource characteristics affect firms' resource redeployment strategies. We examine four characteristics of resources, that is, fungibility, scale-free resources, decomposability, and tradability, and develop a theoretical framework for answering the following questions: (1) would firms redeploy resources to another business or only extract residual value of resources in the existing business, (2) if firms redeploy their resources, would they choose intra-temporal or inter-temporal redeployment strategies, (3) would firms redeploy the resource as a whole or redeploy component assets to serve alternative businesses, and (4) would firms adopt an internal or external resource redeployment strategy? The theoretical framework predicts that firms would prefer inter-temporal redeployment if the resource is fungible, non-scale free, and non-tradable. Moreover, we consider the influence of individual and organizational motivations on firm resource redeployment strategies, including effects of aspiration levels, satisficing outcomes, and agency forces.

This paper has important theoretical and empirical implications for research on resource redeployment. It is the first attempt, to our knowledge, that integrates different streams of literature and systematically investigates how intrinsic resource characteristics affect resource redeployment strategies. Moreover, environmental changes in markets and technologies alter the value of resources in their original use, and require firms to redeploy their resources and sustain growth. Our work offers predictions on resource redeployment strategies that firms pursue in order to adapt to changing environments. In this sense, our framework can be seen as postulating both a positive and a normative view of redeployment strategy.

The remainder of the paper is organized as follows. We first provide the theoretical background and then proceed to the conceptual framework. We then develop our predictions about how resource characteristics affect resource redeployment strategies. The paper concludes with implications and future research opportunities.

THEORETICAL BACKGROUND

A Temporal View of Redeployment Strategies

A firm can pursue different types of resource redeployment strategies to achieve growth and create value for its stakeholders. The majority of previous scholarly efforts have been devoted to *intra-temporal* resource redeployment (e.g., Montgomery & Hariharan, 1991; Rumelt, 1974; Silverman, 1999; Singh & Montgomery, 1987; Villalonga, 2004). Centered in this stream of literature is the notion of "scope" and "relatedness."[1] Specifically, firms create synergetic value, or intra-temporal scope economies, when they share activities synchronically across multiple business domains, such as centralized finance, cross-selling, and umbrella branding.[2] Unused or underutilized resources, particularly managerial abilities, are seen as the driving force behind diversification strategy (Penrose, 1959; Wernerfelt, 1984). The synergy decreases as firms diversify further from their core business. Related diversification thus allows firms to more extensively exploit the economies of scope from valuable resources than unrelated diversification (Bettis, 1981; Markides & Williamson, 1994; Montgomery & Wernerfelt, 1988; Singh & Montgomery, 1987).

Alternatively, firms may resort to *inter-temporal* resource redeployment strategies in which they withdraw resources from one business and reallocate them to another business. As stated by Anand (1994),

> The resource-based theory proposes a primal-dual relationship between firm resources obtained from factor markets and the corresponding product markets ... Even though this theory is normally applied to the context of corporate diversification, it also has implications for corporate evolution and survival. If these resources are truly fungible across lines of business, then firms possessing these resources should not be constrained by the life of their lines of business. As one product or business line declines, firms should be able to shift the deployment of resources to growing businesses and survive in the long run .... (pp. 50–52)

Such an inter-temporal or diachronic redeployment strategy provides benefits related to the idea of "inter-temporal economies of scope" (Helfat & Eisenhardt, 2004). "Inter-temporal scope economies" are likewise an efficiency-based concept[3] in the sense that a firm achieves cost savings as it increases the variety of goods that it produces. Yet it highlights a temporal dimension of resource redeployment. Specifically, cost savings are achieved when firms diachronically reallocate their resources developed in their core business to a new business domain.

Opportunities for inter-temporal resource redeployment arise when a firm experiences a shock and consequently, some of its resources lose their value, while others retain their value due to their fungibility. Such a shock may be a negative demand shock, in which the firm loses its market but its technology and other resources may retain their value. Consequently, when the current business yields unfavorable returns because of shrinking demand and output, inter-temporal resource redeployment enables firms to redeploy their resources and serve alternative markets that yield more attractive returns (Anand, 2004, 2005; Anand & Singh, 1997; Helfat & Eisenhardt, 2004).

Alternatively, a shock may arise from a technological discontinuity. In the face of discontinuous technological changes incumbent firms redeploy their resources to overcome competitive turmoil and sustain an advantageous position (e.g., Anand, Oriani, & Vassolo, 2010; Hill & Rothaermel, 2003; Madsen & Walker, 2007). The literature on technological discontinuities reveals that firms that survive or thrive through such discontinuities, typically leverage their complementary assets (Anand et al., 2010; Rothaermel & Hill, 2005; Tripsas & Gavetti, 2000). While the technological discontinuity destroys or reduces the value or the firms' traditional technological resources, complementary assets can be redeployed over time to work with new technology, which may have been developed outside of the focal firm and acquired through a market transaction.

A Continuum of Theoretical Perspectives

Both *intra-temporal* and *inter-temporal* resource redeployment strategies rely on the idea that firms can adapt to different market settings by changing their bundle of resources as well as their redeployment. Yet a number of management theories provide different perspectives on the ability of a firm to change or redeploy its resources. Relative to other theoretical lenses, the resource-based perspective implies minimum restraints to resource redeployment (Penrose, 1959; Peteraf, 1993; Wernerfelt, 1984). Firms are expected to develop resources necessary for competing in a certain product market, and resources can be applied to new market settings to generate revenue and profits. This perspective offers two implications for a firm realigning itself to a changing environment. First, firms may adapt to new conditions by redeploying resources to serve alternative markets. The extent to which resources can be redeployed to new settings relies upon the underlying fungibility of the resources. Second, firms can adapt to new market settings by changing its bundle of resources via the factor markets. In sum, fungibility is an important resource characteristic that determines firm redeployment strategy (Anand, 1994, 2005; Helfat & Eisenhardt, 2004; Penrose, 1959).

Related work using the evolutionary theoretical framework, however, offers a different perspective on how firms redeploy their resources and adapt to new market settings. Resources are seen as "sticky" in the sense that they are developed as a result of path-dependent actions taken over time and are intertwined within the firm (Cohen & Levinthal, 1990; Nelson & Winter, 1982). Cohen and Levinthal (1990), for example, argue that the capacity of a firm to assimilate external knowledge is constrained by its prior state of knowledge, which they labeled as "absorptive capacity." More broadly, the evolutionary theory emphasizes the context-specific and industry-specific nature of the firm's routines and resources (Levinthal, 1991; Nelson & Winter, 1982). In addition, opportunities for learning and innovation are limited by a firm's previous experience and existing technology base (Dosi, 1982; Teece, 1987). These capacities and routines could also turn out to be a "competency trap" in the face of radical market and technological change (Levitt & March, 1988). Hence, firms have difficulties in redeploying their resources to adapt to new market settings.

Lastly, the population ecology literature offers an even more extreme perspective on organizational obstacles to resource redeployment (Hannan & Freeman, 1977, 1984). Hannan and Freeman (1984), for example, argue that most organizations have structural inertia and the strength of that inertia hinders firms from reconfiguring and redeploying their resources elsewhere. Even though firms may evolve under certain conditions, selection is a critical and frequent mechanism underlying the long-term change in the diversity of organizational forms. Those firms that become incompatible with the changing environment are eventually replaced by competition with new organizations that are better suited to external demands. Among the three streams of studies, population ecology scholars have the most rigid perspective on resource redeployment.

These different theoretical perspectives provide the rationale for firms' resource redeployment strategies. While the resource-based perspective enhances our understanding of successful internal redeployment, the evolutionary and population ecology perspectives offer explanations for why such a redeployment strategy may not always be possible, as well as provide arguments for the adoption of alternative resource redeployment strategies (Anand & Singh, 1997).

Redeployment Strategies: Role of Firms and Markets

Resource redeployment may be accomplished internally within the firm or through the interface of external markets (Anand, 2004). In the former, resource reallocation occurs within the internal control apparatus of a firm as highlighted by Penrose (1959). For instance, a defense contractor with technologies developed during the cold war can assist government agencies in database management or use sophisticated materials developed for defense purposes in surgical procedures (Anand & Singh, 1997). The alternative means to internal redeployment is external reconfiguration that involves redeployment of resources via open markets including outside contracting and asset divestiture (Anand & Singh, 1997; Silverman, 1999; Teece, 1982). The ability of a firm to reconfigure and reallocate its resources to alternative markets does not necessitate its internal resource redeployment. If markets function costlessly as described in neoclassical economic theory, resources are expected to be organized via the arm-length markets, and hence any form of internal resource redeployment is irrelevant (Coase, 1937). Anand (2004), for example, investigates the two different types of resource redeployment strategies, that is, internal redeployment in which firms acquire resources, and external redeployment in which firms sell and consolidate resources through the market, and points out that resource tradability is an important determinant of firms' resource redeployment strategies. We will further develop the idea of tradability and its implications in the next section.

In sum, the vast body of previous literature has enhanced our understanding of different resource redeployment strategies. Yet we still know little about under what conditions different redeployment strategies are more preferable, or more specifically, how intrinsic resource characteristics affect firm's resource redeployment strategies. In the next section, we introduce the conceptual framework of resource redeployment that is developed based on the four building blocks of resource characteristics.

CONCEPTUAL FRAMEWORK

Drawing upon intellectual heritage from various streams of literature on resource redeployment, we develop a coherent conceptual framework for the conditions under which each type of resource redeployment strategies creates value. It allows researchers to compare different redeployment strategies and conduct a thorough examination of the determinants of resource redeployment strategies. The framework consists of four principal characteristics of resources that are critical to predicting resource redeployment strategies, that is, fungibility, decomposability, scale-free resources, and tradability. It is important to point out here that we presume non-sub additivity of resource redeployment. Non-sub additivity refers to non-negative portfolio value when firms redeploy their resources to new areas (Vassolo, Anand, & Folta, 2004). In other words, we eliminate situations where overlapping or substitute resources exist in the new areas, or firms own a group of competing investments. We will elaborate on each resource characteristic. An overview of the framework is shown in Fig. 1.

Fungibility

Fungibility is the first and foremost condition needed to identify if a certain resource redeployment strategy is suitable. It is the basis for the explanation of resource redeployment. As stated by Penrose (1959), the stock of a firm's resources and the degree to which they are fungible across product markets are critical to the growth of the firm.

Fungibility denotes that resources are "capable of being substituted in place of one another."[4] The opposite of fungibility is resource specificity, defined as the degree to which a resource can be redeployed to alternative uses without sacrifice of productive value[5] (Williamson, 1991, p. 281). Fungible resources can be reallocated to serve alternative markets. Non-fungible resources, on the contrary, hinder firms from redeploying their resources because they involve durable investments and need to be cultivated within the firm over time.

Resources vary in the extent of their fungibility. Monetary assets, for instance, are the most fungible resource in the sense that money that is raised for one purpose can easily be used for another purpose. General human capital resources can be leveraged to a new business domain because they are not specialized in particular products that the firm is currently producing. Highly specialized human capital resources, on the

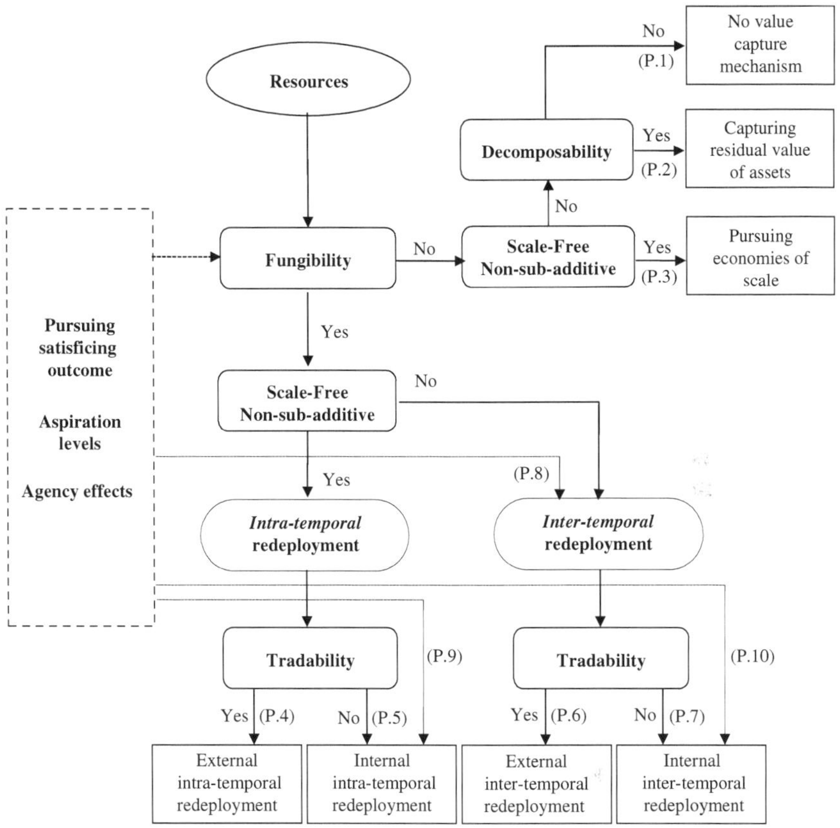

Fig. 1. A Theoretical Synthesis Framework of Resource Redeployment.

contrary, cannot be easily allocated for another purpose, and would lose all their value otherwise.

Scale-Free Resource

A second resource characteristic is a scale-free property. Resources are scale-free when "the value of resources is assumed to not be reduced as a result of the sheer magnitude of firm operations over which it is applied" (Levinthal & Wu, 2010, p. 781). The scale-free resource property is analogous to the rivalry feature of public good,[6] in that the cost of providing the good to a marginal (additional) individual is zero (Arrow, 1962). The most well-known scale-free resources are intangible assets including brand name and the knowledge of the firm. A patent, for example, can be easily applied to new businesses without incurring an additional cost.

The scale-free feature of resources has important implications for resource redeployment strategy. To the extent that a resource is scale-free,[7] it is not subject to opportunity cost and can be simultaneously deployed across multiple markets. Scale-free resources are thus associated with resource redeployment strategies in which firms simultaneously share resources across multiple business units. For non-scale free resources, their use at any point in time precludes uses in other settings. A set of versatile manufacturing facilities is a non-scale free resource. They can only be utilized for a certain production task, and when fully utilized they need to be withdrawn from the original business before redeployed to alternative business units. Thus, non-scale free resources relate to inter-temporal resource redeployment strategies.

Decomposability

A third resource characteristic is *decomposability*. Drawing insights from the idea of complexity and modularity/partitioning in product development and design literature (Baldwin & Clark, 1997; Simon, 1973; Von Hippel, 1990), we develop the concept of decomposability. Similar to the primal-dual relationship between strategic factor markets, in which firms buy and sell resources necessary to implement a certain product strategy, and the corresponding product markets (Wernerfelt, 1984), modularity in product development mirrors the decomposability of resources. Modularity is defined as "building a complex product or process from smaller subsystems that can be designed independently yet function together as a whole" (Baldwin & Clark, 1997, p. 84).[8] Decomposability, on the contrary, denotes the extent to which the interactions of subsystems are negligible.

To better illustrate the attribute of decomposability in this paper, we distinguish resources from assets while considering resource and capability as exchangeable. Specifically, Barney (1991) defines resources as "all assets, capabilities, organizational processes, firm attributes, information, knowledge, etc. controlled by a firm that enable the firm to conceive of and implement strategies that improve its efficiency and effectiveness" (1991, p. 101). Yet a resource is defined here as a set of assets that are combined to improve a firm's efficiency and effectiveness. The value of resources is rarely independently determined, but critically relies on a firm's heterogeneous resource combination. Physical assets alone can rarely become a source of competitive advantage; they create value when combined with other assets including organization routines and administrative skills (Chi, 1994; Reed & DeFillippi, 1990). Complementary resources refer to supplementary assets that are used in conjunction with the focal resource to deliver value (Teece, 1986). Complementarity creates opportunities for recombination and redeployments of resources. Thus, while decomposed resources can be more easily fungible to another market, the value of resources can be damaged when they are divided into a smaller combination or individual assets.

We consider two elements concerning resource decomposability, that is, the specification of component assets and the across-boundary interactions. Interactions describe the likelihood that one component asset is affected by others. Given that component assets are clearly identified, the value of a resource depends upon the intensity of interactions among those component assets. A loosely coupled resource can be easily divided into separate component assets without sacrifice much of value. On the contrary, component assets that are tightly bundled interact with each other extensively, and as a consequence, decomposition is expected to lose much of the value created from across-boundary interactions. Decomposability is particularly important for non-fungible resources in predicting firms' redeployment strategies.[9]

Tradability

A fourth characteristic of resources is *tradability*. Tradability indicates that the whole or part of the resources can be sold or bought in corresponding factor markets (Barney, 1986; Capron, Dussauge, & Mitchell, 1998; Dierickx & Cool, 1989). Some resources are simply not traded on factor markets (Dierickx & Cool, 1989). Resources with ambiguous property rights or "ownership externality" cannot be sold easily on factor markets (Bator, 1958). In addition, information impactedness causes market failure when traded in factor markets. The "information dilemma" describes that the holder cannot sell it without revealing its content; once the information is revealed, however, imitation quickly ensues (Arrow, 1962). The attribute of tradability shifts attention to conditions under which resources can be exploited externally via the arm-length factor markets.

Even though resources are potentially tradable, firms may not choose to redeploy their resources through market interfaces because of the cost of the transaction via arm-length markets. The most notable cost associated with market-based resource redeployment is associated with identifying the relevant price (Coase, 1937). Holding the bargaining power of buyers and suppliers as given, the price of a resource is a reflection of the resource's economic value (Brandenburger & Stuart, 1996). The value, however, may not be recognized by potential buyers in factor markets. Strategy scholars have offered a variety of explanations for the undervalued resources. The first element associated with the resource-based cost of the transaction is tacitness. As stated by Polanyi (1966), "the aim of a skillful performance is achieved by the observance of a set of rules which are not known as such to the person following them" (Polanyi, 1966, p. 49). If individuals appear to know more than they can explain, outsiders hardly comprehend the value of resources.

Another explanation for undervalued resources is that they are embedded in a complex system. Complexity comprises two major factors, that is, the number of elements in a system and the degree of interaction among those elements (Simon, 1962). Strategic choices are characterized by numerous factors intertwined with one another. As a consequence, the extent complexity can go beyond managers' ability to manage (Barney, 1991; Milgrom & Roberts, 1990). As Lippman and Rumelt (1982) point out, "it may never be possible to produce a finite unambiguous list of the factors of production responsible for the success of such firms." Rivkin (2000), for example, applies Kaufman's NK model to strategy formulation problems. He illustrates that interdependence turns strategy decision problems into technically intractable NP-complete problems, and that when the pieces of strategy are substantial and the time spent on each calculation step is not trivial, no step-by-step procedure can be devised to solve the problem in reasonable time. Therefore, complexity can deter the perception of potential buyers about the value of resources.

In addition to the underestimation of the value of resources by potential buyers, the cost of trading resources via open markets may deter firms from adopting inter-firm redeployment. Potential opportunistic behaviors adverse selection, moral hazard, cheating, and economic hold-up, can increase the cost of using the contractual approach to resource redeployment (Arrows, 1964; Capron et al., 1998; Chi, 1994; Rumelt, 1987; Teece, 1986; Williamson, 1985). It is particularly severe for scale-free resources under weak property right protection (Bator, 1958; Teece, 1986). Hence, to reap the benefits generated by scale-free resources with low tradability, firms that own the resource need to redeploy them by diversification rather than external redeployment via the factor markets.

In sum, the four characteristics of resources, that is, fungibility, scale-free resources, decomposability, and tradability, serve as four building blocks of the conceptual framework we develop in this paper. The framework synthesizes insights from different streams of literature and forms a coherent, comprehensive reasoning map that enables us to examine systematically the conditions under which a certain redeployment strategy may be appropriate. In the following section, we develop a number of propositions concerning how the intrinsic resource characteristics affect firms' resource redeployment strategies.

RESOURCE CHARACTERISTICS AND REDEPLOYMENT STRATEGIES

In this section, we draw predictions derived from the conceptual framework of the conditions under which a certain resource redeployment strategy is most likely to take place. These predictions are derived based on the intrinsic characteristics of resources that a firm owns. The analysis provides guidance for researchers to identify the optimal resource redeployment strategies that are appropriate for resources with a certain set of characteristics. As shown in Fig. 1, we start with fungibility, and proceed to other characteristics, that is, scale-free resources, decomposability, and tradability.[10]

Non-Fungible, Non-Scale Free, and Non-Decomposable Resources

The first proposition concerns firm resources that are non-fungible, non-scale free, and non-decomposable. Non-fungible resources cannot be redeployed without sacrifice of their value. If a resource does not meet the fungibility criteria, firms have no incentive to look for new opportunities of redeploying the resource outside its current business. Non-scale free resources are subject to opportunity cost, and therefore restrict firms from sharing the resources among multiple business units. If the non-scale free, non-fungible resource is tightly coupled, most of the value is embedded in the links between component assets. As a consequence, the resources lose almost all the value after decomposed into component assets. For non-fungible, non-scale free, and indecomposable resources, there would be no value capture mechanism for non-fungible, non-scale free, and indecomposable resources. We thus derive the following proposition:

> **Proposition 1.** When firm resources that are non-fungible, non-scale free, and non-decomposable lose their value in their current deployment, the value of these resources cannot be recovered by redeployment.

Non-Fungible, Non-Scale Free, and Decomposable Resources

For non-fungible, non-scale free resources, similar to the analysis above, firms that possess these resources lose all value if they relocate them to a new market setting. Nevertheless, the resource attribute of decomposability opens up new opportunities to recoup the value of resources. Specifically, if the non-fungible, non-scale free resource is a loosely coupled system, resource value mainly resides in component assets. In other words, the resources can be decomposed into individual assets without much sacrifice of the value. The optimal strategy for the firm that possesses non-fungible, non-scale free, and decomposable resources is thus to dispose of component assets and redeem residual value. We formally express the proposition as follows:

> **Proposition 2.** When firm resources that are non-fungible, non-scale free, and decomposable lose their value in their current deployment, the optimal strategy is external reconfiguration by disposing off component assets and capturing residual value.

Non-Fungible and Scale-Free Resources

The prediction of the optimal redeployment strategy for non-fungible and scale-free resources is straightforward. Non-fungible resources hinder firms from utilizing the resources across multiple markets or inter-temporarily redeploying the resources to alternative markets. Nevertheless, resources that are scale-free are not subject to opportunity cost, and thus allow firms to harvest the residual value in the current business. Not being subject to opportunity costs also implies that the redeployment is not within a "winner-take-all" type market. Firms can thus make the best use of their resources by, for example, developing more offerings in the existing market without concerns of "sub-additivity" among different investments. Hence, the optimal strategy for non-fungible, scale-free resources is to stay in the current business and maximize the economies of scale of the resources. The proposition is formally described as follows:

> **Proposition 3.** When the resources are non-fungible and scale-free/non-sub additive, the optimal strategy is to pursue economies of scale to the extent possible, within the existing business.

Fungible, Scale-Free, and (Non-) Tradable Resources

The combination of fungibility and tradability has significant implications for resource redeployment strategy. First, fungibility indicates that a resource can be applied to different market settings. Yet, it is merely a necessary, not a sufficient condition for predicting firms' specific resource redeployment strategies, in particular the strategic choices between redeployment accomplished internally within the firm and externally. Underestimation of the value of resources by potential buyers, for instance, strengthens a firm's incentive for adopting internal resource redeployment strategies. However, if the resources are tradable with their value fully appreciated on factor markets, an external strategy may be preferable for redeployment of its resources. In addition, because scale-free resources are not subject to opportunity cost, they allow firms to share the resources across multiple business units without withdrawing from the current business.

Combining the three characteristics of resources, we expect to derive the following predictions. For fungible, scale-free, and tradable resources, external intra-temporal resource redeployment enables firms to maximize their returns. If the fungible, scale-free resources are non-tradable, a suitable redeployment strategy would be internal intra-temporal resource redeployment. If an invention is granted exclusive rights under rigid patent protection regime, for instance, the inventor can maximize its returns by licensing the invention to as many users as possible. Yet the inventor might prefer leveraging its invention to a new business domain if the property right protection is weak. The propositions are formally expressed as follows:

> **Proposition 4.** When firm resources are fungible, scale-free, and tradable, the optimal strategy to capture their value is by redeploying their resources with external intra-temporal reconfiguration.

Proposition 5. When firm resources are fungible, scale-free, non-sub-additive and non-tradable, the optimal strategy to capture their value is their internal intra-temporal redeployment.

Fungible, Non-Scale Free, and (Non-)Tradable Resources

Similar to the analysis of fungible, scale-free, tradable resources, the resource attribute of tradability provides guidance on comparing internal and external redeployment strategies. Fungibility, likewise, suggests potential opportunity of redeploying resources in another area. For resources that are non-scale free, their value reduces as a result of the magnitude of operations over which they are applied, which precludes their use in other market settings at any point in time. For this reason, firms that own fungible, non-scale free resources need to withdraw the resources from the original business unit before deploy them to serve an alternative market. In other words, fungible, non-scale free resources relate to inter-temporal resource redeployment strategies.

The feature of resource tradability offers additional insights on redeployment strategy. Specifically, if the value of the resources can be fully appreciated by potential buyers and the factor market is costless, external redeployment is the proper redeployment strategy. However, if the value of the resources is underestimated by potential buyers, or the cost of trading the resources is high, firms that own the fungible, non-scale free resources would choose to redeploy internally the resources to serve an alternative business unit. We thus derive the following propositions:

Proposition 6. When firm resources that are fungible, non-scale free, and tradable lose their value in their current deployment, the optimal strategy to capture the residual value of resources is external markets.

Proposition 7. When firm resources that are fungible, non-scale free, and non-tradable lose their value in their current deployment, the optimal strategy to capture the residual value of resources is internal inter-temporal redeployment.

In this section, we develop a number of predictions about how the intrinsic resource characteristics affect firms' resource redeployment strategies. As shown in the conceptual framework (Fig. 1), we identify four characteristics of resources that are critical for developing the predictions, that is, fungibility, scale-free resources, decomposability, and tradability.

Fungibility is the fundamental assumption for all types of redeployment strategy. Thus for non-fungible resources, as we demonstrate in the analysis and proposition development, firms can redeem the value of resources in the current business unit. Specifically, the optimal strategy for non-fungible, scale-free resources is to pursue the economies of scale. For non-fungible, non-scale free resources, the strategies for redeeming the value of resources are limited; yet, the attribute of decomposability allows firms to exploit the residual value of component assets. For fungible resources that allow firms to adopt different types of redeployment strategies, we further examine the tradability and scale-free resource attributes. The analysis leads to a number of intriguing predictions. For fungible, scale-free resources firms choose external intra-temporal redeployment strategies if the resources are also tradable, and internal intra-temporal redeployment if the resources are non-tradable. Each of the resource characteristics plays an important role in predicting resource redeployment strategies. In the next section, we will move on to discuss additional forces that may affect the resource redeployment strategies.

BEHAVIORAL AND AGENCY EFFECTS ON ADOPTION OF RESOURCE REDEPLOYMENT STRATEGIES

In the previous sections, we examine four critical resource characteristics and explain how these characteristics affect resource redeployment strategies. However, behavioral and agency forces may have complementary effects on resource redeployment. The Behavioral Theory of the Firm suggests that firms try to achieve the "satisficing," not "optimal" outcome in reality due to the bounded rationality and existing organizational constraints on resource redeployment (Cyert & March, 1963). On the other hand, Agency Theory proposes the pursuit of value-creating may not be the exclusive motivation of redeployment, but rather a pursuit of other managerial goals, such as revenue maximization (Jensen, 1986; Jensen & Meckling, 1976). Even though intra-temporal resource redeployment is a most promising and optimal strategy, a potential drawback would be that the firm may not pursue it because of managerial and organizational constraints on proper value expectation. On the contrary, external or internal inter-temporal resource redeployment can be executed merely based on a manager's preference without proper performance expectation.

Satisficing Outcomes and Aspiration Levels

According to the Behavioral Theory of the Firm, managers are boundedly rational. They must rely on a simplified representation of the world in order to identify and process information and make managerial decisions (Cyert & March, 1963; Simon, 1955). These simplified representations also influence how managers frame problems and how they search for solutions (Tripsas & Gavetti, 2000). Amit and Schoemaker (1993), for example, show that behavioral decision-making biases and organizational implementation challenges could be critical impediments to the transferability of a firm's resources and capabilities.

Boundedly rational managers may not always be able to adopt optimal resource redeployment strategies. Specifically, if they choose to "satisfice" rather than optimize, the search for a resource redeployment strategy may not be triggered if the performance is above the threshold aspiration level (Cyert & March, 1963). Consequently, some firms may not redeploy their fungible, scale-free resources in the absence of poor performance. Only when the performance falls below the aspiration level that the search for a redeployment strategy is triggered. Even when our framework suggests that intra-temporal resource redeployment is the optimal strategy for the fungible and scale-free resources to maximize value, it may take significantly poor performance to galvanize the firm and its managers to actually take actions to implement it. Accordingly, the Behavioral Theory of the Firm suggests that firms may overlook the opportunity of intra-temporal resource redeployment, and only the incentives from performance below their aspiration levels precipitate the firm's efforts for inter-temporal resource redeployment (Anand, 1994; Anand & Singh, 1997).

Proposition 8. Other things being equal, firms are not likely to adopt intra-temporal redeployment strategy with scale-free resources when performance exceeds the aspiration level. However, they are more likely to adopt inter-temporal redeployment strategy when performance falls below the aspiration level.

Agency Motives

Agency Theory focuses on the divergence of interests of shareholders and managers (Jensen & Meckling, 1976), which could result in the pursuit of goals that do not maximize the shareholders' wealth. In the absence of significant ownership stakes, managers can pursue growth-oriented strategies that do not maximize the value of the firm. There are several reasons why managers may have such preferences. First, they can reduce their risk without necessarily benefiting the shareholders because the shareholders can diversify their investments. Second, this might increase the value of managers' individual human capital. For example, top management compensation is often tied to the size of the firm and their span of control (Rosen, 1982). Third, such ventures might relieve the boredom of management, and provide the challenges and satisfaction of building empires (Hayward & Hambrick, 1997), against the unpleasantness of consolidation. Therefore, managers are more likely to pursue intra-temporal resource redeployment for the growth of the firm.

In the absence of explicit incentives, managers are also likely to be reluctant to pursue external inter-temporal redeployment. Under conditions of imperfect internal and external control, managers have a tendency to delay the process of capacity rationalization (Jensen, 1986). Managers might be biased toward internal inter-temporal redeployment for fungible non-scale free resources even when they are not appropriate because managers tend to seek growth. This decision may be rational at the individual level but are not justifiable in terms of economic gains to the firm. Internal inter-temporal redeployment may be undertaken to pursue managerial goals that do not converge with a firm's profit maximization objective while having a bias about fungibility and tradability of resources. In this situation, managers may overestimate fungibility while underestimating tradability of resources.

In declining or mature businesses, such agency problems can be particularly severe (Dial & Murphy, 1995). Even in the decline phase of the industry, managers would still like to enlarge the firm or reduce risk through growth-oriented strategies because those approaches represent a feasible path toward growth in such environments. Previous literature in corporate finance and strategy indicates that agency issues drive non-value creating internal intra-temporal resource redeployment (Amihud & Lev, 1981; Daily, Dalton, & Cannella, 2003; Eisenhardt, 1989; Lane, Cannella, & Lubatkin, 1998). Anand (2004, 2005) also suggests that such forces will be higher when the industry experiences an ongoing decline (relative to growth), in firms that have a greater dependence on declining industries, and firms with less effective control by shareholders or with more significant misalignment between the interests of shareholders and top management. The environment of such businesses is generally not appropriate to pursue individual goals and also does not provide any natural value creating investment options for managers. Therefore, in declining conditions that encourage inter-temporal redeployment, agency forces may drive non-value maximizing internal inter-temporal redeployment (Anand, 1994, 2004, 2005). Consequently, managers would have a strong preference toward adopting internal intra-temporal redeployment or internal inter-temporal redeployment strategies.

Proposition 9. Other things being equal, firms are more likely to adopt internal intra-temporal resource redeployment when agency assumes greater importance.

Proposition 10. Other things being equal, firms are more likely to adopt internal inter-temporal resource redeployment when agency assumes greater importance.

DISCUSSION AND CONCLUSION

In this paper, we endeavored to untangle how intrinsic resource characteristics affect resource redeployment strategies. The principal questions we aim to answer include: Under what conditions do firms adopt *intra-temporal* or *inter-temporal* resource redeployment, would they pursue *internally* or *externally*, and when does it create value? To address these questions, we identify four important resource characteristics that are critical to predict resource redeployment strategies, that is, fungibility, scale-free resources, decomposability, and tradability, and develop a coherent theoretical framework that allows us to systematically examine the determinants of different redeployment strategies. Each resource characteristic affects the direction of resource redeployment. Specifically, consistent with conventional wisdom on *intra-temporal* resource redeployment, fungibility is the first and most important step toward understanding firms' decisions on resource redeployment, although an excess capacity of resources is nonessential to *inter-temporal* resource redeployment, as it is in the analysis of *intra-temporal* resource redeployment. Specifically, according to our framework, inter-temporal redeployment is most likely to occur in a firm when its resources are fungible, non-scale free, and non-tradable.

In addition, we consider the influence of behavioral and agency forces on resource redeployment strategies. We cannot fully comprehend firms' resource redeployment without careful attention to alternative strategies based on critical elements of resources. We complement the framework of resource redeployment strategies based on the intrinsic resource characteristics with behavioral and agency forces that can affect each process of resource redeployment. Our framework generates a number of predictions. Different predictions from resource-based views, evolutionary theory, and population ecology on the possibility and ability of the firm to pursue redeployment may result from a partial understanding of resource characteristics. Our framework indicates that firms cannot recoup the value of resources if they are non-fungible, non-scale free, and non-decomposable. This is consistent with predictions of population ecology on resource redeployment. For fungible, scale-free resources the optimal strategy is pursuing external intra-temporal redeployment strategies if the resources are also tradable, and internal intra-temporal redeployment if the resources are non-tradable. These predictions reiterate the resource-based perspective on redeployment. Yet, firms are more likely to adopt internal resource redeployment when agency forces assume greater importance.

This paper has important theoretical implications for resource redeployment research. It is the first attempt, to our knowledge, which systematically investigates the determinants of resource redeployment by integrating distinct streams of literature. The question that previous works have addressed is whether firms redeploy resources *internally* or *not*; on the contrary, the question we are endeavored to address in this study is whether firms redeploy or not; and if they redeploy, whether firms adopt *intra-temporal* or *inter-temporal*, *internal* or *external* resource redeployment. We argue in this study that optimal value creation strategies can vary with critical elements of resources. In addition, individual and organizational behavioral forces may interfere in firms' perceived value of the resource, which leads to non-value creating resource redeployment.

Moreover, the majority of previous studies on resource redeployment have focused on internal resource redeployment, that is, redeploying resources within the internal control apparatus of a firm (Helfat & Eisenhardt, 2004; Karim, 2006, 2009; Sakhartov & Folta, 2014, 2015). What has been broadly overlooked is the external resource redeployment strategies. As Helfat and Eisenhardt (2004) suggest, timely market exit from a declining market is important for firms to take advantage of new opportunities (Helfat & Eisenhardt, 2004; Penrose, 1959; Sull, 1999). However, resource redeployment does not necessarily take place within the boundary of the firm. If a bundle of resources can be traded via the arm-length markets with their value fully appreciated by potential buyers, external intra-temporal and inter-temporal resource redeployment could be a proper redeployment strategy. Internal intra-temporal and inter-temporal redeployment should be considered only if the redeployed resource could bring competitive advantage to the firm in the other market.

Recent theoretical and empirical studies call for studies on elements other than relatedness that determine redeployment strategies, such as specific inducements, the cost for exit and entering a new market, and market uncertainty (Lee et al., 2010; Sakhartov & Folta, 2014, 2015). In addition, as some prior works have already suggested, scale-free resources may have the direct or indirect cost of redeployment (Levinthal & Wu, 2010; Rubin, 1973). Vassolo et al. (2004), for example, demonstrate that the redeployment of scale-free resources may cause redundancies in outcomes, which they refer to as "sub-additivity." Thus, more careful investigation of redeployment cost is needed for future research. Moreover, as we can see in Proposition 2, while decomposed resources can be more easily fungible to another market, the value of resources can be damaged when they are divided into smaller combinations or even individual assets. In line with these works, a more comprehensive examination with our framework would be needed for the variation of resource value and cost of resource redeployment.

This paper also has implications for how firms cope with a discontinuous technological change. Opportunities for redeployment critically rest upon the overlap and uniqueness between resources needed to compete in a new market and the resources possessed by the firm. Rothaermel and Hill (2005) show that an incumbent firm's financial strength has a stronger positive impact on incumbent firm performance if the new technology needs generic complementary assets; but an incumbent firm's R&D capability has a stronger positive impact on incumbent firm performance if the new technology needs specialized complementary assets. Anand et al. (2010) also demonstrate that technological and complementary capabilities potentially affect firms' entry into emerging technologies and entry mode. Even when markets for partnering and corporate control allow firms to obtain new technologies, the advantage of these externally sourced resources is constrained by the value of the internal complementary capabilities (Anand et al., 2010). "Appropriability advantages" based on resource fungibility enable incumbent firms to redeploy their resources and survive disruptive changes despite their technological disadvantages in the new product markets.

There are many potential theoretical and empirical extensions to this research. For example, the value of redeployment of firm resources to new uses and markets may not be known ex-ante. This value can also be judged based on experience given the causal ambiguity and uncertain imitability of resources. When competing firms are unsure of the value of their resources redeployed into new domains, it changes the nature of competition among them and raises the prospects of strategic interaction. This has significant implications for the resource-based perspective (Anand & Lu, 2013), and the methodological tools that can be developed to analyze such redeployment-based entry (Nandialath & Anand, 2009).

Another interesting issue related to internal redeployment strategies concerns the organizational constraints in redeploying and replicating resources to new sub-units within the firm. Given the complex and embedded nature of firm resources, routines, and capabilities, there are non-trivial constraints in transferring these to new applications and organizational units. Some recent research helps unpack these constraints and proposes solutions based on field observations and theoretical analysis (Zhao & Anand, 2009, 2013). In this research, the focus is on the structures and processes that are used to replicate and redeploy capabilities from a source unit to a recipient unit within the firm.

Regarding implications for future empirical studies, this paper builds theoretical foundations for studies that empirically examine firms' redeployment strategies and their resource-level determinations. Future research could try to make more direct comparisons between intra-temporal and inter-temporal, as well as between internal and external resource redeployment. The previous empirical evidence shows that firms are better off shrinking with the declining market or not attempting to grow new businesses in mature markets (Anand, 2005). It would be useful to examine the effect of fungibility, scale-free, decomposability, and tradability by using our integrative theoretical framework.

We have to acknowledge several limitations of this paper. First, we see resource-level determinants of redeployment strategies presented as discrete. In reality, however, they are continuous with varying magnitudes along a scale. We thus expect a mixed redeployment strategy rather than pure redeployment strategy presented in this study. Specifically, firms might develop a probability distribution to choose among a set of pure redeployment strategies. More efforts are thus needed to develop a precise statement about conditions under which a certain pure redeployment strategy is most preferable. Nevertheless, our paper enhances our understanding of each pure redeployment strategy. In addition, some resource features are easier to measure than others. The extent of fungibility depends upon how easily a resource can be adapted to alternative uses. The accuracy of a fungibility measure would be impaired if there is a lack of consensus on the scope of substitute areas. In addition, a firm might adopt both intra- and inter-temporal resource redeployment strategies simultaneously. Moreover, individual and organizational perspectives should also be considered in the future research. As we discussed earlier, both the Behavioral Theory of the Firm and Agency Theory provide their own theoretical explanations about resource redeployment strategies. Both these arguments may be complementary, but the critical feature of the agency explanation is that redeployment to new applications is not profitable or value-enhancing for the firm. Future studies may be able to focus explicitly on both perspectives and examine each effect.

To conclude, this study investigates resource-level determinants of redeployment strategies. Drawing insights from various streams of literature on resource redeployment, we identify four intrinsic resource characteristics and develop a coherent conceptual framework. It allows researchers to thoroughly examine the conditions under which a certain type resource redeployment strategy is preferable. According to our framework, inter-temporal redeployment is likely to take place when resources are fungible, non-scale free, and non-tradable. This study analyzes the determinants of resource redeployment at a finer level of disaggregation, and lays a solid theoretical foundation for future empirical studies.

NOTES

1. It is also noteworthy that "relatedness" is a not a conceptually explicit term since it measures the overall impact of several theoretical drivers. Consequently, there is some benefit to unpacking the components of this overall effect in order to achieve a superior conceptual understanding.

2. Mathematically, "economies of scope" can be expressed as, $TC(Q\_x, Q\_y) < TC(Q\_x, 0) + TC(0, Q\_y)$, where $TC(Q\_x, Q\_y)$ denotes the total cost of producing Q_x units of product x and Q_y units of product y.

3. As a comparison, we mathematically describe the "inter-temporal economies of scope" as follows, $TC(0, Q_y) \leq TC(Q_x, 0)$, s.t. $Q_y = g(f^{-1}(Q_x))$. The constraint describes that a firm reallocates its resources from producing product x to product y. Specifically, $Q_y = g(\cdot)$ denotes the production function of product y; it is a function of the firm's resources and capabilities. $f^{-1}(Q_x)$ is an inverse production function of product x, representing the collection of resources that the focal firm employs to produce x. The objective function indicates that the alternative market opportunity generates returns that are at least as appealing as the existing business; otherwise, firms have no incentive to redeploy their resources to an alternative business.

4. Merriam-Webster Online Dictionary and Thesaurus. Merriam-Webster, Incorporated.

5. An alternative perspective on resource/asset specificity is developed in the transaction cost economics (TCE) literature (Grossman & Hart, 1986; Klein, Crawford, & Alchian, 1978; Williamson, 1979). It includes physical asset specificity, site specificity, human asset specificity, dedicated assets, and temporal specificity (Masten, Meehan, & Snyder, 1991; Williamson, 1985). A widely cited example of non-fungible resources in this literature is Fisher Body Corp building highly specific stamping machines for General Motors as the production process began to shift to mental closed body construction in 1919 (Klein et al., 1978). This perspective emphasizes specificity from a firm perspective rather than from a redeployment perspective.

6. A good is classified into four categories along two dimensions, that is, excludability and rivalry. A public good is non-excludable and non-rival.

7. Since nothing is truly scale-free, we use the term "scale-free" and "non-scale free" in a relative sense.

8. The early form of modularity is established in architecture by Alexander (1964) as a solution to building a complex product or process. He proposes that a subsystem structure overcomes the growing complexity of design problems. Simon (1973) developed a similar idea of factorizing the decision-making information system. The relevant studies on modularity in Strategy can be traced back to streams of literature on partitioning and architectural innovation (Abernathy & Clark, 1985; Henderson & Clark, 1990; Von Hippel, 1990). Von Hippel (1990), for example, examines the efficiency implications of task specifications and interaction, and proposes that reduced interdependence leads to innovation process efficiency. Henderson and Clark (1990) demonstrate the implications for innovation and competitive dynamics of changes in the interactions between subsystems or components.

9. As shown in Fig. 1, we consider decomposability as a necessary condition merely for non-fungible resources. Because non-fungible resources are inapplicable to redeployment strategies, decomposability is crucial for firms to maximize the value or fully capture the residual value of such resources. For fungible resources, decomposability is inessential to resource redeployment. Yet, it might moderate the effect of tradability on firms' redeployment strategies. Nevertheless, to remain simplicity and parsimony of our theoretical framework, we would not expand in this paper on the moderating effect of decomposability for fungible resources.

10. We want to emphasize here that not all combinations of these four resource characteristics can be developed into propositions because the four intrinsic characteristics of resources are nonparallel. The examination of one characteristic might be conditional upon others. Fungibility, for example, is a prerequisite for examining tradability. For non-fungible resources, we discuss the characteristics of decomposability.

ACKNOWLEDGMENTS

We are very grateful to the editors of the special issue, Tim Folta, Connie Helfat, and Samina Karim, for their insightful feedback on earlier drafts of this paper. We are also grateful to the anonymous reviewers and attendees at the special issue conference in Strasbourg, France for their comments, as well as to BETA for the funding. The first author would also like to thank Dan Levinthal and Harbir Singh for many helpful conversations over the years.

REFERENCES

Abernathy, W. J., & Clark, K. B. (1985). Innovation: Mapping the winds of creative destruction. *Research Policy*, *14*(1), 3–22.

Alexander, C. (1964). *Notes on the synthesis of form*. Cambridge, MA: Harvard University Press.

Amihud, Y., & Lev, B. (1981). Risk reduction as a managerial motive for conglomerate mergers. *The Bell Journal of Economics*, *12*(2), 605–617.

Amit, R., & Schoemaker, P. J. H. (1993). Strategic assets and organizational rent. *Strategic Management Journal*, *14*(1), 33–46.

Anand, J. (1994). *Responding to a declining product market: A study of defense contractors using resource based, evolutionary and agency perspectives* (Doctoral dissertation). Retrieved from ProQuest Dissertations and Theses. Accession Order No. AAT 9520995.

Anand, J. (2004). Redeployment of corporate resources: A study of acquisition strategies in the US defense industries, 1978–1996. *Managerial and Decision Economics*, *25*(6–7), 383–400.

Anand, J. (2005). M&A strategies in mature and declining industries: Theoretical perspectives and implications. *Advances in Mergers and Acquisitions*, *4*, 163–179.

Anand, J., & Delios, A. (2002). Absolute and relative resources as determinants of international acquisitions. *Strategic Management Journal*, *23*(2), 119–134.

Anand, J., & Lu, S. (2013). Beyond strategic factor market: Competitive advantage under imperfect information. Paper presented at the Academy of Management, Orlando.

Anand, J., Oriani, R., & Vassolo, R. S. (2010). Alliance activity as a dynamic capability in the face of a discontinuous technological change. *Organization Science*, *21*(6), 1213–1232.

Anand, J., & Singh, H. (1997). Asset redeployment, acquisitions and corporate strategy in declining industries. *Strategic Management Journal*, *18*, 99–118.

Arrow, K. J. (1962). Economic welfare and the allocation of resources for invention. In *The rate and direction of inventive activity: Economic and social factors* (pp. 609–626). Princeton, NJ: Princeton University Press.

Arrow, K. J. (1964). The role of securities in the optimal allocation of risk-bearing. *The Review of Economic Studies*, *31*(2), 91–96.

Baldwin, C. Y., & Clark, K. B. (1997). Managing in an age of modularity. *Harvard Business Review*, *75*(5), 84–93.

Barney, J. B. (1986). Strategic factor markets: Expectations, luck, and business strategy. *Management Science*, *32*(10), 1231–1241.

Barney, J. B. (1991). Firm resources and sustained competitive advantage. *Journal of Management*, *17*(1), 99–120.

Bator, F. M. (1958). The anatomy of market failure. *The Quarterly Journal of Economics*, *72*(3), 351–379.

Bettis, R. A. (1981). Performance differences in related and unrelated diversified firms. *Strategic Management Journal*, *2*(4), 379–393.
Brandenburger, A. M., & Stuart, H. W. (1996). Value-based business strategy. *Journal of Economics Management Strategy*, *5*(1), 5–24.
Capron, L., Dussauge, P., & Mitchell, W. (1998). Resource redeployment following horizontal acquisitions in Europe and North America, 1988–1992. *Strategic Management Journal*, *19*(7), 631–661.
Chi, T. (1994). Trading in strategic resources: Necessary conditions, transaction cost problems, and choice of exchange structure. *Strategic Management Journal*, *15*(4), 271–290.
Coase, R. H. (1937). The nature of the firm. *Economica*, *4*(16), 386–405.
Cohen, W. M., & Levinthal, D. A. (1990). Absorptive capacity: A new perspective on learning and innovation. *Administrative Science Quarterly*, *35*(1), 128–152.
Cyert, R. M., & March, J. G. (1963). *A behavioral theory of the firm*. Englewood Cliffs, NJ: Prentice Hall.
Daily, C. M., Dalton, D. R., & Cannella, A. A. (2003). Corporate governance: Decades of dialogue and data. *Academy of Management Review*, *28*(3), 371–382.
Dial, J., & Murphy, K. J. (1995). Incentives, downsizing and value creation at general dynamics. *Journal of Financial Economics*, *37*(3), 261–314.
Dierickx, I., & Cool, K. (1989). Asset stock accumulation and the sustainability of competitive advantage: Reply. *Management Science*, *35*(12), 1514.
Dosi, G. (1982). Technological paradigms and technological trajectories. *Research Policy*, *11*(3), 147–162.
Eisenhardt, K. M. (1989). Agency theory: An assessment and review. *Academy of Management Review*, *14*(1), 57–74.
Grossman, S. J., & Hart, O. D. (1986). The costs and benefits of ownership: A theory of vertical and lateral integration. *Journal of Political Economy*, *94*(4), 691.
Hannan, M. T., & Freeman, J. (1977). The population ecology of organizations. *American Journal of Sociology*, *82*(5), 929.
Hannan, M. T., & Freeman, J. (1984). Structural inertia and organizational change. *American Sociological Review*, *49*(2), 149–164.
Hayward, M. L. A., & Hambrick, D. C. (1997). Explaining the premiums paid for large acquisitions: Evidence of CEO hubris. *Administrative Science Quarterly*, *42*(1), 103–127.
Helfat, C. E. (2000). Guest editor's introduction to the special issue: The evolution of firm capabilities. *Strategic Management Journal*, *959*, 955–959.
Helfat, C. E., & Eisenhardt, K. M. (2004). Inter-temporal economies of scope, organizational modularity, and the dynamics of diversification. *Strategic Management Journal*, *25*(13), 1217–1232.
Henderson, R. M., & Clark, K. B. (1990). Architectural innovation: The reconfiguration of existing product technologies and the failure of established firms. *Administrative Science Quarterly*, *35*(1), 9–30.
Hill, C. W. L., & Rothaermel, F. T. (2003). The performance of incumbent firms in the face of radical technological innovation. *Academy of Management Review*, *28*(2), 257–274.
Jensen, M. C. (1986). Agency costs of free cash flow, corporate finance, and takeovers. *The American Economic Review*, *76*(2), 323–329.
Jensen, M. C., & Meckling, W. H. (1976). Theory of the firm: Managerial behavior, agency costs and ownership structure. *Journal of Financial Economics*, *3*(4), 305–360.

Karim, S. (2006). Modularity in organizational structure: The reconfiguration of internally developed and acquired business units. *Strategic Management Journal, 27*(9), 799–823.

Karim, S. (2009). Business unit reorganization and innovation in new product markets. *Management Science, 55*(7), 1237–1254.

Karim, S., & Kaul, A. (2015). Structural recombination and innovation: Unlocking intraorganizational knowledge synergy through structural change. *Organization Science, 26*(2), 439–455.

Klein, B., Crawford, R. G., & Alchian, A. A. (1978). Vertical integration, appropriable rents, and the competitive contracting process. *Journal of Law and Economics, 21*(2), 297–326.

Lane, P. J., Cannella, A. A., & Lubatkin, M. H. (1998). Agency problems as antecedents to unrelated mergers and diversification: Amihud and Lev reconsidered. *Strategic Management Journal, 19*(6), 555–578.

Lee, G. K., Folta, T. B., & Lieberman, M. B. (2010). Relatedness and market exit. *Academy of Management Proceedings, 2010*(1), 1–6.

Levinthal, D. A. (1991). Organizational adaptation and environmental selection-interrelated processes of change. *Organization Science, 2*(1), 140–145.

Levinthal, D. A., & Wu, B. (2010). Opportunity costs and non-scale free capabilities: Profit maximization, corporate scope, and profit margins. *Strategic Management Journal, 31*(7), 780–801.

Levitt, B., & March, J. G. (1988). Organizational learning. *Annual Review of Sociology, 14*, 319–340.

Lippman, S., & Rumelt, R. (1982). Uncertain Imitability: An Analysis of Interfirm Differences in Efficiency under Competition. *The Bell Journal of Economics, 13*(2), 418–438.

Madsen, T. L., & Walker, G. (2007). Incumbent and entrant rivalry in a deregulated industry. *Organization Science, 18*(4), 667–687.

Markides, C. C., & Williamson, P. J. (1994). Related diversification, core competences and corporate performance. *Strategic Management Journal, 15*, 149–165.

Masten, S. E., Meehan, J. W., & Snyder, E. A. (1991). The costs of organization. *Journal of Law, Economics, and Organization, 7*(1), 1–25.

Milgrom, P., & Roberts, J. (1990). Rationalizability, learning, and equilibrium in games with strategic complementarities. *Econometrica, 58*(6), 1255–1277.

Montgomery, C. A., & Hariharan, S. (1991). Diversified expansion by large established firms. *Journal of Economic Behavior & Organization, 15*(1), 71–89.

Montgomery, C. A., & Wernerfelt, B. (1988). Diversification, Ricardian rents, and Tobin's q. *Rand Journal of Economics, 19*(4), 623–632.

Nandialath, A. M., & Anand, J. (2009). Is strategic interaction important in models of entry? Implications for sustainability of competitive advantage. Paper presented at the Academy of Management meetings, Chicago, August.

Nelson, R. R., & Winter, S. G. (1982). *An evolutionary theory of economic change*. Boston, MA: Harvard University Press.

Penrose, E. T. (1959). *The theory of the growth of the firm*. New York, NY: Wiley.

Peteraf, M. A. (1993). The cornerstones of competitive advantage: A resource-based view. *Strategic Management Journal, 14*(3), 179–191.

Polanyi, M. (1966). The logic of tacit inference. *Philosophy, 41*(155), 1–18.

Reed, R., & DeFillippi, R. J. (1990). Causal ambiguity, barriers to imitation, and sustainable competitive advantage. *Academy of Management Review, 15*(1), 88–102.

Rivkin, J. W. (2000). Imitation of complex strategies. *Management Science*, *46*(6), 824–844.

Rosen, S. (1982). Authority, control, and the distribution of earnings. *The Bell Journal of Economics*, *13*(2), 311–323.

Rothaermel, F. T., & Hill, C. W. L. (2005). Technological discontinuities and complementary assets: A longitudinal study of industry and firm performance. *Organization Science*, *16*(1), 52–70.

Rubin, P. (1973). The expansion of firms. *Journal of Political Economy*, *81*(4), 936–949.

Rumelt, R. P. (1974). *Structure and economic performance*. Boston, MA: Harvard University Press.

Rumelt, R. P. (1987). Theory, strategy, and entrepreneurship. In D. J. Teece (Ed.), *The competitive challenge: Strategies for industrial innovation and renewal* (pp. 137–158). Cambridge, MA: Ballinger.

Sakhartov, A. V., & Folta, T. B. (2014). Resource relatedness, redeployability, and firm value. *Strategic Management Journal*, *35*(12), 1781–1797.

Sakhartov, A. V., & Folta, T. B. (2015). Getting beyond relatedness as a driver of corporate value. *Strategic Management Journal*, *36*(13), 1939–1959.

Silverman, B. S. (1999). Technological resources and the direction of corporate diversification: Toward an integration of the resource-based view and transaction cost economics. *Management Science*, *45*(8), 1109–1124.

Simon, H. A. (1955). A behavioral model of rational choice. *The Quarterly Journal of Economics*, *69*(1), 99–118.

Simon, H. A. (1962). The architecture of complexity. *Proceedings of the American Philosophical Society*, *106*(6), 467–482.

Simon, H. A. (1973). Applying to information technology design organization. *Public Administration Review*, *33*(3), 268–278.

Singh, H., & Montgomery, C. A. (1987). Corporate acquisition strategy and economic performance. *Strategic Management Journal*, *8*(4), 377–386.

Sull, D. N. (1999). The dynamics of standing still: Firestone tire & rubber and the radial revolution. *Business History Review*, *73*(3), 430–464.

Teece, D. J. (1982). Towards an economic theory of the multiproduct firm. *Journal of Economic Behavior and Organization*, *3*(1), 39–63.

Teece, D. J. (1986). Profiting from technological innovation: Implications for integration, collaboration, licensing and public policy. *Research Policy*, *15*(6), 285–305.

Teece, D. J. (1987). Technological change and the nature of the firm. In D. J. Teece (Ed.), *The competitive challenge*. New York, NY: Harper & Row.

Tripsas, M., & Gavetti, G. (2000). Capabilities, cognition, and inertia: Evidence from digital imaging. *Strategic Management Journal*, *21*(10–11), 1147–1161.

Vassolo, R. S., Anand, J., & Folta, T. B. (2004). Non-additivity in portfolios of exploration activities: A real options-based analysis of equity alliances in biotechnology. *Strategic Management Journal*, *25*(11), 1045–1061.

Villalonga, B. (2004). Diversification discount or premium? New evidence from the business information tracking series. *Journal of Finance*, *59*(2), 479–506.

Von Hippel, E. (1990). Task partitioning: An innovation process variable. *Research Policy*, *19*(5), 407–418.

Wernerfelt, B. (1984). A resource-based view of the firm. *Strategic Management Journal*, *5*(2), 171–180.

Wernerfelt, B. (1988). Umbrella branding as a signal of new product quality: An example of signalling by posting a bond. *The Rand Journal of Economics*, *19*(3), 458–466.

Williamson, O. E. (1979). Transaction-cost economics: The governance of contractual relations. *The Journal of Law and Economics*, *22*(2), 233.

Williamson, O. E. (1985). *The economic institutions of capitalism*. New York, NY: Free Press.

Williamson, O. E. (1991). Comparative economic organization: The analysis of discrete structural alternatives. *Administrative Science Quarterly*, *36*(2), 269–296.

Zhao, Z., & Anand, J. (2009). The role of collective teaching and collective absorptive capacity in transferring firm capabilities: Evidence from the Chinese automotive industry. *Strategic Management Journal*, *30*(9), 959–983.

Zhao, Z., & Anand, J. (2013). Beyond boundary spanners: The 'collective bridge' as an efficient inter-unit structure for transferring collective knowledge. *Strategic Management Journal*, *34*(13), 1513–1530.

WHAT GOES ON BENEATH THE SURFACE OF RECONFIGURATION? THE IMPACT OF REDEPLOYMENT VIA ACTIVITY ADDITION AND SUBTRACTION ON FIRM SCOPE AND TURNOVER

Joel Blit, Christopher C. Liu and Will Mitchell

ABSTRACT

Strategy research has long understood that reconfiguration of the scope of the activities a firm engages in over time is critical to its long-run success, while under-emphasizing differences in redeployment strategy that underlie apparently similar scope and changes in scope. In this paper, we build on the idea that a firm's number of activities (scope) and change in activities (turnover) arise from two fundamental rates of redeployment: the rate at which activities are added and the rate at which activities are subtracted. In net, the turnover rate reflects how actively a firm reconfigures its resource base by redeploying resources via addition and subtraction of activities. We develop a model that links addition and

Resource Redeployment and Corporate Strategy
Advances in Strategic Management, Volume 35, 185–216

ISSN: 0742-3322/doi:10.1108/S0742-332220160000035008

subtraction with the composition of a firm's activities and then provide an empirical illustration using data from the U.S. Patents and Trademarks Office. As an example of one extension, the model can be generalized to incorporate elements of absorptive capacity. The analysis contributes to our understanding of how firms reconfigure their activities and provide managers with a clearer understanding of tools that guide redeployment of existing resources.

Keywords: Firm activity scope; firm activity turnover; activity redeployment; absorptive capacity; firm patent activity

INTRODUCTION

Strategy research has long been interested in understanding the activities that firms undertake, both in terms of how many activities that a firm engages in at a point in time and the degree to which it reconfigures itself by adding and subtracting activities over time (Collis & Montgomery, 1998). By activities, we mean the routines and other processes that a firm undertakes as it seeks to create goods and services (Cyert & March, 1963; Makadok, 2001; Nelson & Winter, 1982). Since at least Coase (1937) and Penrose (1959), the concept of the scope of the firm has been central to strategic management; scope reflects the number of activities that firms undertake (Barney, 1991; Chatain & Zemsky, 2007; Wernerfelt, 1984). In parallel, a large literature has examined strategies that firms use to turn over their activities (e.g., Burton, Obel, & DeSanctis, 2011; Galunic & Rodan, 1998; Helfat, 1997; Karim, 2006; Karim & Capron, 2015; Teece, Pisano, & Shuen, 1997); studies have considered adding via the redeployment of internal resources (Hambrick & Macmillan, 1985; Pacheco-de-Almeida & Zemsky, 2007; Sakhartov & Folta, 2014), business acquisitions (Capron, 1999), and alliances (Mahmood, Zhu, & Zajac, 2011), as well as subtracting via employee departures (Karim & Williams, 2012; Klepper, 2007), divestitures (Capron, Mitchell, & Swaminathan, 2001), and shut downs (Duhaime & Grant, 1984; Greve, 1995). This work on scope and turnover of activities has provided important insights into how firms reconfigure themselves through internal redeployment as well as the shedding of resources over time.

The literature is beginning to pay attention to the temporal patterns of reconfiguration (e.g., Helfat & Eisenhardt, 2004). Few studies, though, have integrated the themes of scope and turnover (see Karim & Capron, 2015), to investigate the joint evolution of a firm's scope of activities at one time, together with resource redeployment via the rate of adding and subtracting activities over time. As a result, there are substantial gaps in our understanding of the forces that shape the revealed scope of a firm's activities. Why are some firms involved in a limited set of activities in some period, while others engage in a multitude? How often do these activities change? And, in considering these questions, what might we learn about the external factors and internal managerial levers that shape a firm's portfolio of activities? A more complete understanding of the redeployment processes that underlie business reconfiguration will aid scholars and managers alike.

In this paper, we develop a model that seeks to explain firm scope at a point in time, together with the rate of turnover of a firm's activities that may occur from one period to the next. The model suggests that the addition of new activities and subtraction of existing activities generate two complementary characteristics of a firm. The net balance of addition and subtraction rates determines whether a firm's activity scope will increase (if addition dominates), decrease (if subtraction dominates), or be stable (if addition and subtraction balance). In parallel, the aggregate of addition and subtraction of activities from one period to the next, which we refer to as turnover, determines how actively a firm is reconfiguring its activities and redeploying existing resources. The presence of these complementary characteristics illustrates the idea that firms with identical scope at a given time can have dramatically different rates of activity turnover. A key contribution of the paper is to highlight the innate interconnection between firm activity scope and turnover and, in turn, help unpack the nature of resource redeployment.

Our model of activity scope and turnover contributes to redeployment research in four ways. First, we suggest that assessing both firm scope and activity turnover is necessary for a more general typology of redeployment. Second, we focus attention on two elemental redeployment rates that drive scope and turnover: firms' rates of activity addition and subtraction. Third, we outline external factors and internal managerial levers that can change the magnitudes of these rates and, as a consequence, aspects of the activities that are core to issues in resource redeployment. Fourth, we illustrate the flexibility of our model by incorporating the concept of absorptive capacity.

This paper unfolds as follows. In the next section, we present our conceptual framework, linking activity addition and subtraction rates to the firm characteristics of scope and turnover. We then provide a basic illustrative model of our conceptual framework. Next, we map the model implications onto firm-level patent data from the consumer electronics and pharmaceutical industries to demonstrate the salience of the model. We then extend the model to incorporate assumptions concerning absorptive capacity. We end with a broader discussion of the implications of the argument.

BACKGROUND: ADDITION, SUBTRACTION, TURNOVER, AND SCOPE

The goal of this conceptual framework is to outline our model of a firm's activity composition. As we noted earlier, by activities we mean the routines and other processes that a firm undertakes as it seeks to create goods and services. Examples of activities include processes involved in innovation, production, sales, and other business endeavors. Activities tend to become embodied in tangible outputs such as products and patents.

A natural point of entry in the consideration of a firm's activity composition is firm scope. We define firm scope as the number of discrete activities that a firm is undertaking. Given the importance of firm activities, firm scope is a foundational component for central theories in strategy such as transaction cost (Teece, 1986; Williamson, 1979), resource-based (Penrose, 1959; Wernerfelt, 1984), and dynamic capabilities (Teece et al., 1997) theories, as well as literatures as diverse as alliance and acquisition management (Villalonga & McGahan, 2005), resource allocation (Bower, 1986; Burgelman, 1991), and organizational ecology (Hannan & Freeman, 1977).

To explain firm scope, we focus on two forces that will shape the characteristics of a firm's activity composition: (a) the rate at which firms add new activities and (b) the rate at which firms subtract existing activities. Taken together, addition and subtraction rates determine whether firm scope will expand, contract, or be stable.

Net Addition and Subtraction Rates Determine the Change in Firm Scope

Adding and subtracting activities are key elements of firm strategy. A large body of research has focused on a firm's addition of new activities, whether by redeploying resources between internal efforts or redeploying resources from external agents into internal uses. For example, firms may seek new capabilities through mergers and acquisitions (e.g., Capron, Dussauge, & Mitchell, 1998; Mowery, Oxley, & Silverman, 1996), use location choices to capitalize upon knowledge spillovers and agglomeration (e.g., Alcacer & Chung, 2014; Baum & Mezias, 1992; Chakrabarti & Mitchell, 2013; Greve, 2009; Shaver & Flyer, 2000; Stuart & Podolny, 1996), or to develop absorptive capacity internally (Cohen & Levinthal, 1990; Lenox & King, 2004).

Juxtaposed against the literature on expansive forces of the firm is the notion that firm activities may be eliminated, whether by shutting down existing efforts or redeploying internal resources to external agents, resulting in a decrease in firm scope. The most prominent mechanism for the active reduction in firm scope is the divestiture of business activities (Capron et al., 2001; Duhaime & Grant, 1984). Firms may also actively abandon their strategies (Greve, 1995) or actively strive to forget (Bettis & Prahalad, 1995; de Holan & Phillips, 2004; Thompson, 2007). Complementing the active shedding of business activities, a firm's internal processes of resource redeployment may also affect the loss rate of incumbent activities. In the process of resource allocation within the firm, resource scarcity in some business lines, manifest through a shift in managerial attention or insufficient internal working capital, may induce employees to leave (Klepper, 2007). Because knowledge is commonly embodied in labor, employee departures often correlate with the exit of firm resources. Moreover, employees' individual stocks of knowledge tend to decay over time, which can reduce business activity (Jain, 2013). Hence, there are many ways by which firms add and subtract activities as they seek to provide profitable goods and services.

By definition, adding new activities increases firm scope and subtracting existing activities decreases firm scope. We define the addition rate as the rate at which firms acquire new activities in some period; the subtraction rate is the rate at which firms shut down or divest existing activities. In turn, the net value of these two rates determines the change in firm scope.

This intuitive basic idea underlies important differences in the observed scope of firms' activities. Consider a stylized example where a firm that desires to expand – whether to capitalize on underutilized economies of scope, seek new markets, or for other reasons – adds a new activity every month. If the firm's goal is to expand its scope, managers need to consider the monthly addition rate *relative* to the firm's subtraction rate. If the firm is subtracting many activities a month, even a torrid rate of arrival might result in contraction in firm scope. Hence, the relative rates of these two forces determine the change in firm scope.

Aggregate Addition and Subtraction Rates Determine the Turnover Rate

Just as the net *difference* in addition and subtraction rates determines a firm's scope of activities, the *sum* of these rates determines a second key characteristic of a firm's activities, which is its turnover rate. We define turnover rate as the sum of new activities added and existing activities subtracted from one period to the next. The concept of turnover is relevant in the literature on product renewal, which argues that firms often benefit by replacing older products over time (e.g., Burgelman, 1996; Danneels, 2002; Dougherty, 1992). Thus, we propose that a firm's activities have two complementary characteristics, scope and turnover, both of which are the result of the combined addition and subtraction rates.

Most generally, the turnover rate reflects how actively a firm reconfigures the scope of its resource base by redeploying resources via addition and subtraction of activities. If a firm does not add many new activities and subtracts few existing activities, the composition of its activities will change slowly. By contrast, a high rate of addition and/or a high rate of subtraction will induce significant change in the firm's activities as reflected in a high turnover rate.

This means that two firms with the same scope (i.e., same number of activities) can have very different turnover rates, reflecting intrinsically different resource redeployment strategies. At one extreme, an inertial firm may engage in the same activities year after year; at the other extreme, a dynamic firm with the same number of activities in any given period may have wholesale change over time. Fig. 1 illustrates the distinction between scope and turnover by mapping the characteristics of a firm's activity composition along addition and subtraction rate axes.

Begin by considering activity scope. If the firm's addition rate is greater than the subtraction rate, the firm will be situated in the bottom-right quadrangle of Fig. 1, where scope will increase. If subtraction rate dominates, the firm will be situated in the upper-left quadrangle, where scope will decrease. If the rates are relatively equal, the firm will be situated near the diagonal, with stable scope.

Now consider activity turnover. Because a firm's turnover rate depends on the summed magnitude of the addition and subtraction rates, the farther away the focal firm is from the origin in Fig. 1, the greater the rate at which a firm's activities are reconfigured. Thus, even if two firms have stable scope and hence lie on the diagonal, the two firms may vary dramatically in their turnover rates. By characterizing a firm's activity characteristics along addition and subtraction rate dimensions, this logic provides a

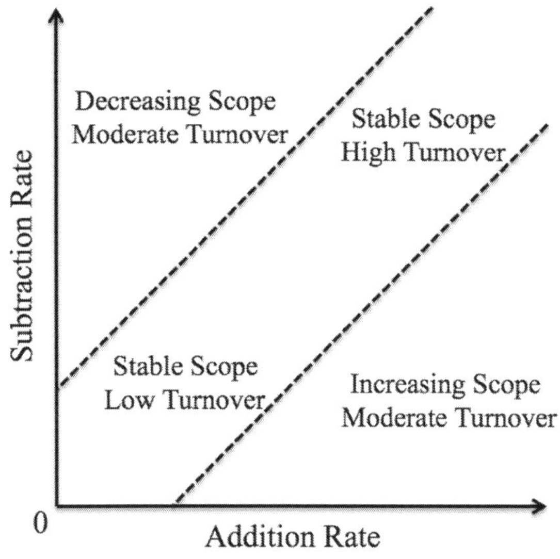

Fig. 1. The Mapping of Scope and Turnover onto Addition and Subtraction Axes. *Notes*: This figure illustrates the difference between firm scope and firm turnover by mapping the characteristics of a firm's activity composition along addition and subtraction rate axes. If the addition rate is greater than the subtraction rate, the firm will be situated to the bottom-right and firm scope will increase. If the addition rate is less than the subtraction rate, the firm will be situated to the upper-left and firm scope will decrease. For firms that have relatively equal addition and subtraction rates, the firm will have stable scope and lie along the diagonal. Firm turnover, which is the aggregate of addition and subtraction rates, will increase as firms are situated farther from the origin. Firms with high rates of turnover (i.e., reconfiguration) will be situated to the upper-right of the diagram.

more complete view of the potentially changing activities that comprise a firm's resource base.

What is not yet clear are the conditions that would lead to a steady-state equilibrium, where a firm has both stable scope and a constant turnover rate. The following model helps to illustrate this condition, as well as to derive comparative statics that demonstrate how changes in addition and subtraction rates affect scope and turnover. After introducing and discussing an equilibrium model, the subsequent section will turn to conditions that shift a firm toward new potential equilibria reflecting new scope and turnover rate.

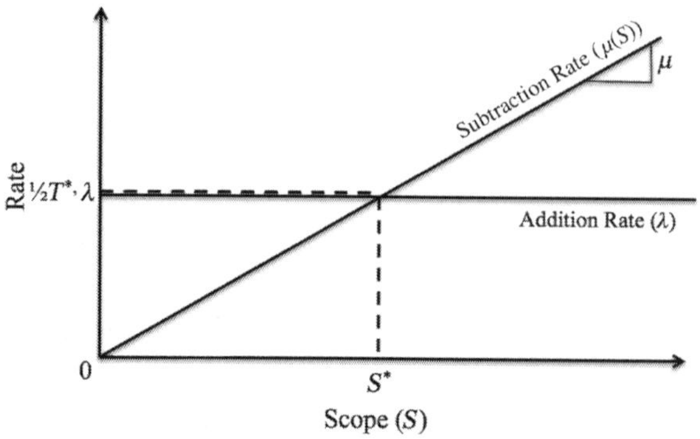

Fig. 2. A Firm's Steady State Equilibrium Point. *Notes*: This figure illustrates the model's derivations. Assumption A3 suggests that there is an unlimited number of potential activities, resulting in a constant addition rate. By contrast, the subtraction rate increases with firm scope (S), which is shown on the X-axis. The intersection of the addition and subtraction rate determines the steady state equilibrium point, which also defines S^* and T^*. Note that our model does not assume that firms are in steady state equilibrium but, rather, that without a change in the addition or subtraction rate, a firm's activity characteristics will move toward the equilibrium point. In this graph we depict $T^*/2$, to normalize it to λ (see Eq. (6)).

To be clear, our model does not assume or require that a firm ever reach equilibrium. Rather, the idea of a predicted equilibrium point is useful because it specifies tendencies in the direction and rate of change in a firm's turnover rate and scope (i.e., movement toward the equilibrium point in Fig. 2, which we introduce in the discussion of the model below). In turn, changes in the external environment and/or firm strategies may redirect the firm toward a new scope and a new turnover rate. The model provides a means to understand this process and to potentially help guide managers in their reconfiguration efforts.

MODEL

To make our arguments more concrete, we present a parsimonious formal model for a firm's activity scope and turnover. In the first iteration, the goal of this model is to outline several simplifying assumptions and then consider the implications of relaxing the assumptions in the basic model. This modeling lends precision to our theory: it highlights the conditions that are necessary and sufficient for our ideas to hold. In a later section, we use the scaffold of our model to introduce a possible refinement of the model that incorporates absorptive capacity. Thus, the second portion of our modeling exercise illustrates the myriad possibilities that our model enables.

Model Set Up

We define the instantaneous activity arrival rate λ (the rate at which the firm acquires activities) and the instantaneous activity loss rate μ (the rate at which the firm shuts down or divests a given existing activity). The rate at which the firm subtracts activities is then μ multiplied by the number of total activities in the firm. We define activity scope, $S(t)$, as the number of distinct activities present in the firm at time t.

The basic model makes three simplifying assumptions; in a later section, we discuss the implications of relaxing each of the three assumptions:

A1. All activities are equally likely by the firm to be added, while all existing activities have an identical subtraction rate μ.

A2. Activity addition is independent across activities (i.e., the addition of activity X does not affect the likelihood of activity Y being added); similarly, activity divestiture is independent across activities.

A3. An unlimited number of potential activities are available.

With an unlimited number of potential activities (A3), any single added activity is new from the point of view of the firm, and therefore the firm's activity addition rate is the same as the arrival rate. The law of motion for the scope of the firm is given by the difference between the firm's addition and subtraction rates:

$$\frac{\mathrm{d}S}{\mathrm{d}t} = \lambda - \mu S \qquad (1)$$

This is a first-order linear differential equation with solution

$$S(t) = \frac{\lambda}{\mu} + C\mathrm{e}^{-\mu t} \qquad (2)$$

where C is some constant that is determined by, for example, the initial scope of the firm; the effect of C vanishes as t increases. Equation (2) describes the evolution of S over time.

We define a firm's activity turnover, $T(t)$, as the aggregate number of distinct activities in a firm that are added and subtracted at time t (the sum of the addition and subtraction rates).

$$T(t) = (\lambda + \mu S) \tag{3}$$

Combining this equation with Eq. (2), we obtain an expression for turnover:

$$T(t) = 2\left(\lambda + C' e^{-\mu t}\right) \tag{4}$$

where C' is also some constant. Eq. (4) describes the evolution of T over time.

Steady State

Having derived expressions for $S(t)$ and $T(t)$, we can now compute the steady state equilibrium values S^* and T^*. For a given λ and μ, $S(t)$ and $T(t)$ will converge to

$$S^* = \frac{\lambda}{\mu} \tag{5}$$

and

$$T^* = 2\lambda \tag{6}$$

Fig. 2 depicts the steady state equilibrium point, in which both the number of activities (S^*) on the x-axis is stable and the turnover rate (T^*) on the y-axis is constant. In this figure, the equilibrium point is the intersection of the addition and subtraction rate curves. To the left of the equilibrium point, the addition rate ($\lambda(S) = \lambda$) exceeds the subtraction rate ($\mu(S) = \mu S$), so that scope will increase. By contrast, to the right of the equilibrium point, the subtraction rate exceeds the addition rate, so that scope will decrease.

What causes a firm to converge toward a potential equilibrium point? Consider a new firm with no initial activities (i.e., scope = 0). The firm experiences an arrival rate λ, which might be given by the characteristics of its founding location (e.g., the presence of sources of activities such as established firms and/or universities). Over time, as the addition rate (which under A3 is equal to the arrival rate λ) drives the expansion of scope, the firm accumulates activities to subtract; where the subtraction rate is given by factors such as locational characteristics. The key point is that the addition rate is constant for any scope, while the firm subtraction rate ($\mu * S$) increases proportionately with scope (see Eq. (1)). As a result, there will exist an intersection point where addition and subtraction rates are equal. This is the potential equilibrium point, denoted by S^* and T^* in Fig. 2, toward which the firm will converge.

By contrast, firms can find themselves to the right of a potential equilibrium point if the arrival rate (λ) declines and/or the loss rate (μ) increases. Such a drop in the arrival rate might arise through exogenous shocks such as the disappearance of potential sources of new activities due to the exit of established firms or closure of university labs. An increase in loss rates could be due to exogenous changes in market taste that lead to shedding of prior activities. A reduction in arrival and/or increase in loss might also arise through active managerial intent; for example, moving into a tax haven with more limited technical resources might reduce arrival rates, while moving into a desirable market with several competitors might increase loss rates if competitors hire away key employees.

Such cases, where there are changes in the arrival or loss rates, will result in a new potential equilibrium point. As a result, whether or not a firm was at equilibrium before the change, the trajectory of the firm's scope and turnover will change. As an example, when a firm's arrival rate declines, it will have a scope greater than the new S^*, subtraction rates exceed addition rates, and the firm's scope will decrease. As the firm's number of activities declines, subtraction rates will also decline, causing the firm to shift toward the new equilibrium point, S^*, to the left of the firm's position at the time of the change. In a similar manner, the turnover rate may shift toward a new T^* when the arrival rate changes.

Assessing Assumptions A1–A3 in the Basic Model

Before formally examining the effect of changes in arrival and loss rates, it is useful to consider the strictness of the simplifying assumptions, A1–A3, in deriving S^* and T^*. Relaxing assumption A1 – whether by allowing some activities to arrive more frequently than others or allowing existing activities to have different loss rates – leads to similar implications though with slightly different patterns. Those activities with the highest arrival rates are most likely to be added first, so that the addition rate curve in Fig. 2 will be concave rather than straight. If existing activities have different loss rates, the ones with the highest rate are most likely to be lost first, leaving more persistent activities. As a result, the subtraction rate curve in Fig. 2 will also be concave rather than a straight line.

A2, concerning the independence of arrival and loss rates, provides a stronger challenge. If we relax this assumption, individual activity arrival and loss rates may depend upon one another. For example, the arrival of activity X (e.g., smartphones) could lead to a propensity for activity Y (e.g., tablets) to arrive. Alternatively, the arrival of one activity (e.g., smartphone innovation) might inhibit a second activity (e.g., netbook innovation). Intuitively, interdependencies may result in the arrival and loss rate curves in Fig. 2 to be non-monotonic. If these non-monotonicities are large enough, there may be multiple equilibria and a firm may become "trapped" in a local minimum, S' and T'. Nonetheless, we would expect firm behavior around a local minimum point, such as S' and T', to be consistent with our predictions. Graphically, we would expect rate curves around the local minimum to be similar to those shown in Fig. 3.

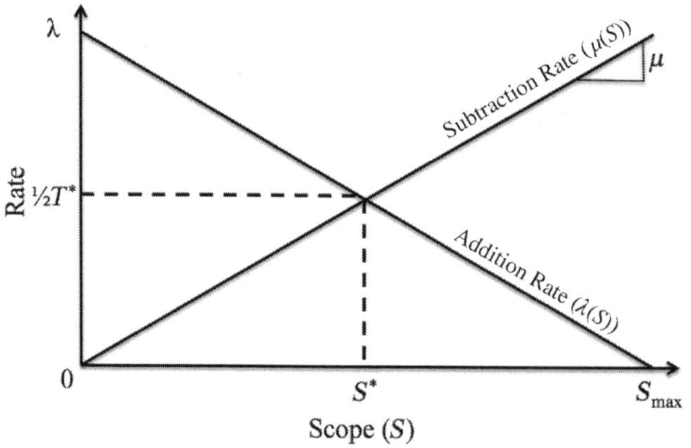

Fig. 3. A Firm's Steady State Equilibrium Point with Limited Activities. *Notes*: This figure illustrates the effect of relaxing assumption A3 and allowing only a limited number of activities. In this case, as firm scope (S) increases, fewer activities will be available to be added to the firm, resulting in a downward sloping addition rate. The implications are unchanged from our baseline model.

Lastly, consider assumption A3. Rather than an unlimited number of potential activities, what happens if we allow only a limited number? A limited number of potential activities could occur through either a limited pool of potential additions (e.g., if the firm is isolated from external sources of activities) or simply because there are a limited number of ways to accomplish a certain thing. In this case, when the firm has zero activities the rate of addition is still equal to the rate of arrival (λ), but as a firm's number of incumbent activities (S) increases, fewer of the arrivals are novel additions that expand S. As a result, the addition rate will be downward sloping, rather than flat, as shown in Fig. 3. With a declining addition rate, coupled with an increasing subtraction rate, the firm will still converge on a potential equilibrium point, again defined by S^* and T^*.

Comparative Statics

We next use comparative statics to demonstrate the implications of changes to the activity arrival and loss rates. In doing so, we examine how the steady state equilibrium activity scope (S^*) and turnover rate (T^*) vary with changes in the activity arrival rate λ and activity loss rate μ. Specifically, we take the partial derivatives of S^* and T^* with respect to λ and μ (from Eqs. (5) and (6)).

Change in activity arrival rate: Taking the partial derivatives with respect to λ, we have:

$$\partial S^*/\partial\lambda = 1/\mu > 0 \tag{7}$$

$$\partial T^*/\partial\lambda = 2 > 0 \tag{8}$$

This first set of comparative statistics (Eqs. (7) and (8)) implies that an increase in the arrival rate, λ, results in a new equilibrium point $S^{*\prime}$ that has greater firm scope as well as a higher turnover rate $T^{*\prime}$ than the previous equilibrium point. In Fig. 2, an increase in λ shifts the potential equilibrium point to the upper right.

Change in loss rate: Now taking the partial derivatives of S^* and T^* with respect to the loss rate, μ, we obtain:

$$\partial S^*/\partial\mu = -\lambda/\mu^2 < 0 \tag{9}$$

$$\partial T^*/\partial\mu = 0 \tag{10}$$

This second set of comparative statics (Eqs. (9) and (10)) implies that an increase in the loss rate results in a new equilibrium point that has decreased firm scope but the same turnover. The intuition for the latter finding is that as the activity loss rate (μ) increases, firm scope, S^*, will decrease in the same proportion, keeping the firm subtraction rate (μS^*) constant (we will still have that $\mu S^* = \lambda$). In Fig. 2, an increase in μ makes the subtraction curve steeper, shifting the potential equilibrium point to the left (smaller S^*) but leaving turnover unchanged.

Implications of the Model so Far

Up to this point, the model provides three initial insights for understanding resource redeployment: (1) the juxtaposition of firm scope and turnover at a point in time, (2) predictable trajectories of scope and turnover over time, and (3) the link between these redeployment dimensions and activity arrival and loss rates. We illustrate these implications using USPTO data on firm patenting (Lai, D'Amour, & Fleming, 2009).

Implication 1 – Scope and turnover at a point in time: The model draws attention to fundamental forces driving firm activity scope and turnover: resource redeployment via activity addition and subtraction rates, which are important both in their net effect (determining scope) and their aggregate effect (determining turnover). There are important differences in these effects: addition increases both scope and turnover, while subtraction decreases scope but increases turnover. Thus, addition and subtraction diminish each other in determining scope, but augment each other in shaping turnover, which reflects how actively the firm is reconfiguring its activities (Fig. 1). This duality of resource redeployment provides a more complete image of the firm's activity composition than simply focusing on scope at a point in time. Firms with similar scope may have very different underlying turnover rates. Quite simply, if one compares firms only in terms of scope, it is easy to overlook differences in underlying turnover and in their related reconfiguration strategies.

Until this point, we have spoken about firm activities in the general sense, as the routines and other processes that a firm undertakes. Although there are many scholarly perspectives on how specific firm activities are chosen, there is general acceptance that one of the duties of the strategic manager is to choose which activities the firm should and should not engage in. To provide one window into the internal activities of the firm, we turn to a firm's patenting activity, as recorded in the USPTO. We believe that examining a firm's patenting activities is highly relevant: (a) patenting is the embodiment of appropriable assets in the knowledge economy, (b) there is a rich taxonomy organizing patents into distinct classes and subclasses, and (c) shifting of patenting activity from one class to another may be a trace of the activity reconfiguration process within a firm. Hence, a rich body of research uses patent data to study business activity.

The following examples illustrate implication 1. We focus on firms from the pharmaceutical and consumer electronics industries, using the number of patent classes in which these firms patent as a measure of their number of activities. Patent classes are relevant indicators of activities – though certainly not fully encompassing – because they indicate where a firm applies effort in attempting to create goods and services. We define redeployment via additions as new patenting activity (patenting in a three-digit patent class that the firm did not patent in during the prior year). Conversely, we define redeployment via subtractions as the absence in a given year of patenting in patent classes in which the firm patented in the previous year. Table 1 provides more information on how we measure additions and subtractions, as well as scope and turnover.

Panel A in Table 1 reports patent class activity for five pharmaceutical firms – Takeda, Astra, Pfizer, Glaxo, and Sanofi – in 1995. We chose these five firms because they had similar scope that year, each reporting activity in 14–16 discrete patent classes. Despite the similar scope, the firms differed strikingly in their activity turnover.

Digging into the illustration, the firms differ in the patterns of additions and subtractions that generated the turnover. Both Takeda and Astra had high turnover, but Takeda's turnover was via high subtractions while Astra's turnover was via high additions. Pfizer and Glaxo also had high turnover but their additions and subtractions were more balanced. Sanofi, with similar scope to other firms in the sample, had low turnover due to limited additions and subtractions. Thus, simply examining the scope of activities of the five firms in 1995 would mask major differences in key aspects of their underlying reconfigurations.

Now consider turnover rates and scope in the consumer electronics industry in 2004. The three firms in Panel B of Table 1 – Apple, RIM, and Nokia – had similar turnover patterns that year. However, they had very different scope of technological activities, as well as different patterns of additions and subtractions. Compared to its peers, Apple had lower scope, achieving high turnover via a mix of additions and subtractions. RIM had a somewhat higher scope of activities, with high additions driving high

Table 1. Scope and Turnover for Consumer Electronics and Biopharmaceuticals Firms.

Firm-Year	Scope	Turnover	Additions	Subtractions	Addition-Subtraction	Description
Panel A. Biopharmaceuticals						
Takeda (1995)	16	16	4	12	−8	High turnover, via high subtraction
Astra (1995)	16	13	11	2	9	High turnover, via high addition
Pfizer (1995)	15	12	4	8	−4	High turnover, via mix of addition and subtraction
Glaxo (1995)	14	13	7	6	1	High turnover, via mix of addition and subtraction
Sanofi (1995)	14	6	4	2	2	Low turnover (limited addition and subtraction
Panel B. Consumer electronics						
Apple (2004)	29	12	12	16	−4	High turnover, via mix of addition and subtraction
RIM (2004)	35	19	19	7	12	High turnover, via high addition
Nokia (2004)	52	9	9	18	−9	High turnover, via high subtraction

Notes: To illustrate the importance of considering both firm scope and firm turnover, we use data on the patenting activities of firms in the biopharmaceutical (Panel A) and consumer electronics (Panel B) industries. We define firm scope as the number of distinct (primary) patent classes in which a firm applied for a patent within a given year. Additions are new patent classes (i.e., present in year *t*1 but absent in year *t*0) and subtraction is the absence of prior patent classes (i.e., absent in year *t*1, but present in year *t*0). Turnover is the sum of additions and subtractions. Panel A illustrates that firms with similar scope can have very different turnover, additions, and subtractions. Moreover, high turnover can occur through high addition, high subtraction, or both. Panel B illustrates that firms with relatively similar levels of turnover can vary greatly in firm scope.

turnover. Nokia, meanwhile, had the highest scope of all three firms: it had activity in 54 discrete patent classes that year. In contrast to RIM, Nokia's high turnover reflected high subtractions. Again, then, the examples in Table 1 highlight the need to examine scope and turnover in conjunction, as well as underlying additions and subtractions, in order to gain a more complete understanding of the resource redeployment that underlies firm reconfiguration.

Implication 2 – Predictable trajectory under stable conditions: A second implication of the model is that, given a firm's arrival and loss rates, the firm's activity characteristics converge toward a predicted equilibrium point (Fig. 2). Thus, the disparity between a firm's *current* scope and turnover and the *predicted* scope and turnover will shape the rate and direction (i.e., increase or decrease) of change in the firm's activity composition. Scope and turnover will first quickly converge toward the equilibrium value and later converge more slowly. That is, as firms approach their predicted equilibrium point, their scope (S) and turnover rates (T) will stabilize. It is important to note that firms will converge arbitrarily close to their predicted equilibrium point but will never actually reach it in finite time. Moreover, any change in the arrival or loss rate will set them on a new trajectory, as the next implication addresses.

Implication 3 – Changes in arrival and loss rates lead to changes in scope and turnover: In the comparative statics section of our model development, we illustrate how changes in the arrival and/or loss rate shift the predicted equilibrium point of a firm. As a consequence, following on implication 2 above, these shifts can alter, or even reverse, the direction of a firm's scope and turnover rate (in the case of the arrival rate). In this manner, our model suggests that a firm's activity composition is woven by the warp and weft of arrival and loss rates; as these rates change, so do the activity composition characteristics of scope and turnover that the rates underpin.

Recognizing the intimate relationship between arrival and loss rates pushes one to consider factors that shape these rates. To list a few possible elements, one can parse factors into external drivers, firm characteristics, and managerial levers. Potential external drivers include regional knowledge spillovers and employee poaching by competitors. Potential firm characteristics include size and employee departure rates that arise from demographic characteristics. Potential managerial levers include R&D budgeting, alliances, acquisitions and divestitures, creation of knowledge repositories, and organizational design such as skunkworks or forums (Chown & Liu, 2015); in turn, managerial levers need to be tuned to relevant aspects of the environment and firm characteristics. Thus, our model offers a flexible framework of resource redeployment that accommodates both passive and active factors that can shape both convergence and change in firm scope and turnover rates.

To illustrate implications 2 and 3, we further develop the examples from the pharmaceutical and consumer electronics industries to consider turnover rates and scope over time. We first turn attention to Apple, RIM, and Nokia in the consumer electronics industry (Fig. 4a). For Apple, we observe reasonably stable turnover throughout the observation period, although this was dominated by addition in the early 1990s, subtraction in the late 1990s, and balance between the two thereafter. As a consequence, Apple's patent class scope has remained relatively stable through recent history. By contrast, Nokia had a significant number of additions, with its scope of activities tripling over the course of a decade, from 1990 through 2002. After 2002, although Nokia maintained stable turnover, subtractions dominated with a concomitant decrease in scope. For RIM, both scope and turnover increased steadily throughout our observation period. Hence, these three firms illustrate markedly different patterns, whether arising through planned or emergent strategy, for companies situated in the same consumer electronics space.

Fig. 4b depicts firm activity compositions in the pharmaceutical industry, reporting varied patterns of reconfiguration. For our observation period, Takeda, Sanofi, and Pfizer have relatively stable scope and turnover. By contrast, in the early 1990s, Glaxo increased its scope dramatically (largely via acquisitions) and has been stable ever since. Lastly, following a prolonged period of stability in the 1980s, Astra had a change in strategy in the mid-1990s. The company expanded the scope of its activities dramatically in the latter part of that decade through a strategic alliance with Merck, which increased access to external knowledge and therefore increased the addition of new activities.

MODEL EXTENSION: ABSORPTIVE CAPACITY

Model Extension

To illustrate the flexibility of the model, we develop an extension to address a firm's absorptive capacity. So far, the model has assumed that the arrival rate is independent of firm scope (Eq. (1)). However, Cohen and Levinthal's (1990) concept of absorptive capacity suggests that firms differ in their ability to receive and assimilate activities, based on the internal characteristics of their knowledge base (in our model an activity arrives if it is both received and assimilated). They argue that "diversity of knowledge plays an important role" (Cohen & Levinthal, 1990, p. 131) in the ability to recognize, assimilate, and apply new capabilities, where we use the term activity as

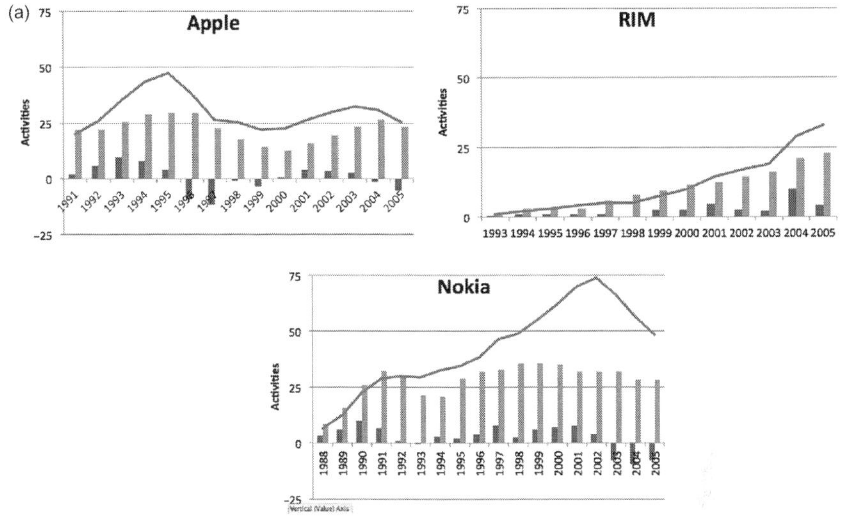

Fig. 4. Scope and Turnover Changes over Time. (a) Consumer Electronics Firms. (b) Pharmaceutical Firms. *Notes*: (a) To illustrate changes in firm scope and firm turnover over an extended period of time, we first focused on the patenting activities of three firms in the consumer electronics industry. Firm scope, the number of distinct (primary) patent classes in which a firm applied for a patent within a given year, is shown by the solid line. Firm turnover, the composite of additions (new patent classes not in prior year) and subtractions (absent patent classes present in prior year) is shown in light bars. The net of additions and subtractions, or the year-to-year change in firm scope, is shown in dark bars. (b) This figure illustrates changes in firm scope and firm turnover over an extended period of time for five biopharmaceutical firms. Firm scope, the number of distinct (primary) patent classes in which a firm applied for a patent within a given year, is shown by the solid line. Firm turnover, the composite of additions (new patent classes not in prior year) and subtractions (absent patent classes present in prior year) is shown in light bars. The net of additions and subtractions, or the year-to-year change in firm scope, is shown in dark bars.

analogous to their term capability. In turn, Cockburn and Henderson (1998) suggest that active engagement with some activities enables a firm to absorb others, and this may refract into the internal intensive structures of firms (Liu & Stuart, 2014). Conversely, scholars such as Levitt and March (1988) and Leonard-Barton (1992) have discussed cases in which current

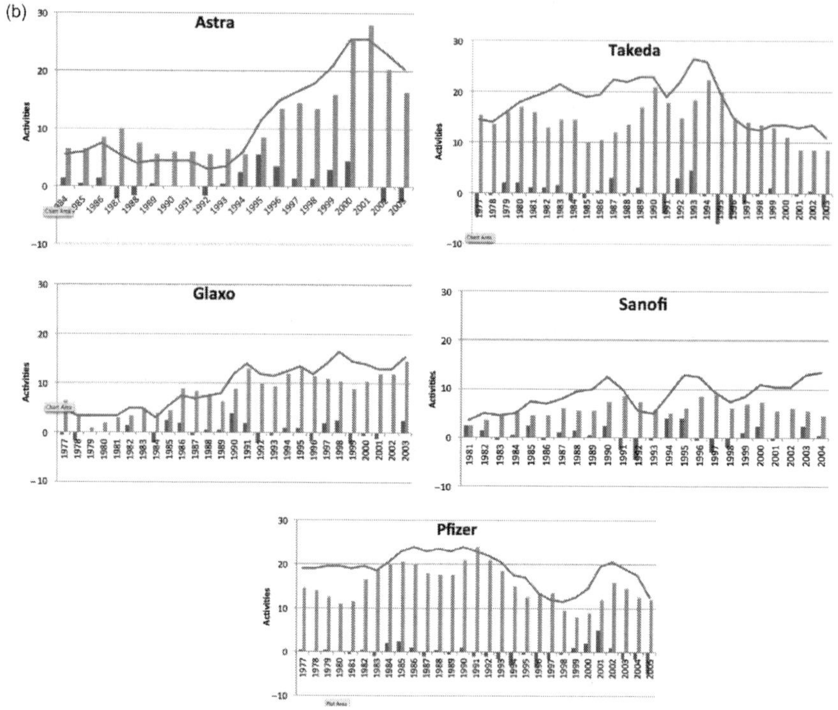

Fig. 4. (*Continued*)

activities constrain the ability of a firm to add new activities. The extension of the model accommodates either view, depending on whether the firm's arrival rate is a positive or negative function of the firm's existing number of activities (i.e., scope).

We model absorptive capacity (in the form of a firm's arrival rate) by adopting the following more general form for the addition rate of activities, which now, in addition to the firm's constant rate λ, is also affected by the firm's existing scope S:

$$Addition(S) = \lambda + \alpha S \tag{11}$$

where $\lambda \geq 0$ and α are constants. λ models the fact that the baseline (constant) arrival rate may differ across firms; α models whether scope positively or negatively impacts the arrival rate of activities as well as the degree to which it does. We can think of α as a modeling parameter, that is, the extent to which we want to model the fact that absorptive capacity depends on scope and in what direction. In parallel, we can think of α as a parameter that captures additional firm heterogeneity, namely the extent to which each firm's arrival rate depends on its scope; this might occur if a firm is organized in such a way that the arrival rate is more dependent on scope or if a firm is in a location where scope has a bigger impact. The expression derived in the previous section is then a special case where absorptive capacity is potentially different across firms, but constant (λ), rather than being affected by scope (S).

Under these conditions, the law of motion for the scope of the firm is then given by the difference between the addition rate ($\lambda + \alpha S$) and the subtraction rate (μS):

$$\frac{\mathrm{d}S}{\mathrm{d}t} = \lambda + \alpha S - \mu S \tag{12}$$

This is a first-order linear differential equation with solution:

$$S(t) = \frac{\lambda}{(\mu - \alpha)} + C\mathrm{e}^{-(\mu-\alpha)^t} \tag{13}$$

where C is a constant that is pinned down, for example, by the initial conditions of the firm.

Turnover is now

$$T(t) = \lambda + (\alpha + \mu)S \tag{14}$$

Combining this equation with Eq. (13), we obtain

$$T(t) = \frac{2\lambda\mu}{\mu - \alpha} + C'\mathrm{e}^{-(\mu-\alpha)t} \tag{15}$$

where C' is some constant.

Having derived an expression for $S(t)$ and $T(t)$, we can now compute the steady state equilibrium values S^* and T^* when the model incorporates the more complex modeling of absorptive capacity. There are two qualitatively distinct cases:

Case 1. *Convergence:* $\mu > \alpha$

$S(t)$ and $T(t)$ will converge to

$$S^* = \frac{\lambda}{\mu - \alpha} \quad (16)$$

and

$$T^* = \frac{2\lambda\mu}{\mu - \alpha} \quad (17)$$

Case 2. *No distinct steady state:* $\mu \leq \alpha$

$S(t)$ and $T(t)$ will increase without bound over time because the addition rate will always be larger than the subtraction rate. Therefore, there is no steady state.

Fig. 5 illustrates the steady state for the two types of cases. When $\mu > \alpha$ (case 1), scope and turnover converge to a steady state (Fig. 5a); by contrast, there is no convergence when $\mu \leq \alpha$ (case 2). In Fig. 5b we have the case where $\mu = \alpha$; the addition and subtraction curves are parallel and meet only at infinity. In the case of $\mu < \alpha$, the dashed line in Fig. 5b highlights how the addition curve lies above the subtraction curve and has higher slope, so that the divergence between the two increases with S; again, the addition and subtraction curves do not intersect.

Thus far, we have focused on the case with $\alpha \geq 0$, but the case where $\alpha < 0$ also could arise. For instance, this would occur in firms that face a "not-invented-here" syndrome in the form of core rigidities (Leonard-Barton, 1992; Levitt & March, 1988). Rather than an addition curve with a positive slope (Fig. 5a), the addition curve will have a negative slope, with the steepness of the slope determined by α. This special case relaxes assumption 3 in Fig. 3 and, as with the earlier discussion of relaxing that assumption, having $\alpha < 0$ yields consistent implications with our baseline model.

Implications of Absorptive Capacity Extension

The extended model has two implications for redeployment research. First, whether α is positive or negative, the larger the absolute magnitude of α (i.e., the more the firm's addition rate is affected by S), the steeper the

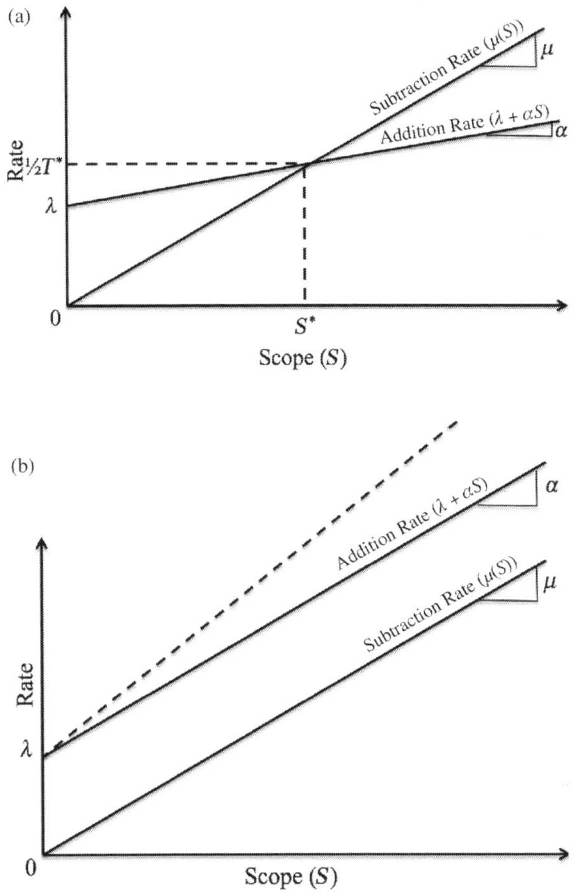

Fig. 5. Convergence and Non-Convergence in Model with Absorptive Capacity. (a) Steady State S^* and T^* when $\mu > \alpha$ (Case 1). (b) No Steady State when $\mu = \alpha$ (Case 2a). *Notes*: (a) This figure illustrates the model extension, incorporating elements of absorptive capacity. If the arrival rate depends upon scope, but $\mu > \alpha$, then a potential equilibrium point will be reached and our model implications are largely unchanged. (b) This figure graphically illustrates the results if $\mu = \alpha$, where no potential equilibrium point is possible. The condition where $\alpha > \mu$, which also yields no equilibrium point, is shown in the dashed line.

addition rate. In practice, this means that a firm with greater positive α (greater sensitivity to scope) will ratchet up to a higher level of scope and turnover, reaching a potential equilibrium point defining S^* and T^* farther from the origin (e.g., Fig. 5a). By contrast, a firm with a greater negative α will ratchet down to lower S^* and T^*, lying closer to the origin.

Second, the model lays out the necessary conditions for stability in a firm's scope and turnover rate and, in turn, suggests points of emphasis for redeployment strategy in practice. The model illustrates two ways in which firms may be unstable. If α is particularly large, greater than or equal to the subtraction rate, the firm might never reach an equilibrium point (e.g., Fig. 5b); similarly, if activity loss rates (μ) are particularly low, the firm's scope and turnover rate also may increase without limit. To the extent that managers desire stability in a firm's activity composition, they can adjust these two parameters. They can attempt to adjust α by seeking ways to link a firm's existing activities (S) to potential new activities, possibly through organizational changes that emphasize opportunities for addition. In parallel, they can seek to affect the activity loss rate μ, such as by adjusting incentives to retain diverse people and information. Hence, the parameter α links firm scope to addition rates with an upper limit ($\alpha < \mu$) for the firm to achieve stable activity composition.

DISCUSSION

This paper has put forward a framework to explain the reconfiguration of firms' activities. We suggest that a firm's activity composition lies at the intersection of redeploying resources as reflected in activity addition and subtraction rates. As a consequence, we highlight two complementary characteristics of a firm's activity composition: its scope (the net of addition and subtraction rates) and its turnover (the sum of addition and subtraction rates). We then illustrated an empirical operationalization of our theory using USPTO patent filings by firms in the consumer electronics and biopharmaceuticals industry. Lastly, a model extension allowed the arrival rate to vary with firm scope. In so doing, we demonstrated the flexibility of our model to incorporate aspects of the literature on absorptive capacity and the not-invented-here syndrome.

Importantly, our model offers a more complete view of a firm's redeployment activity than simply comparing firms' scope at a point in time or even over time; it is possible for firms with identical scope to have drastically different rates of underlying activity redeployment. Fig. 1 illustrates this masking. Two firms may have identical, stable scope over time; that is, the same number of activities year after year. However, it is possible that one of them has very high addition and subtraction rates and is situated in the upper-right sector of the graph. By contrast, a seemingly identical firm, if one looks only at the dimension of scope, could be situated in the lower-left sector of the graph with low addition and subtraction rates, and hence low turnover. This representation is reinforced by our empirical illustration in the consumer electronics industry (Fig. 4). If a researcher were to simply examine firm scope and net turnover, she would miss dynamics of activity redeployment that drive the reconfiguration of the firm's resources.

Managerial Implications

Our logic provides implications for strategic managers. First, the model suggests that changes in the fundamental, underlying addition or subtraction rates are essential if the manager is to enact lasting changes in the activity composition of the firm. For example, consider a manager who desires to increase the scope of the firm. This manager may bring in a new set of activities into the focal firm, thus increasing the firm's scope. In Fig. 2, this shifts the firm's scope (S) and turnover rate (T) to the right. However, without a change in the addition and subtraction rate curves (neither λ nor μ has changed), the firm is now in disequilibrium: the loss rate is now higher and, over time, the firm's breadth of activities will revert back to S^*. Within the model, shifts in a firm's activity composition, without changes to the underlying forces, (ultimately) result in reversion to the equilibrium state. While this point may appear arithmetically intuitive, the separation of control over different activities that is common in firms of any complexity can lead to such unanticipated results.

Second, a central contribution of the model is to segregate addition and subtraction rates. As suggested above, changes in the addition and subtraction rates correspond to changes in the activity composition of the firm. Thus, the model provides two complementary levers for the strategic manager to enact these changes. What might drive redeployment via addition and subtraction rates? We suggest that the rates may be driven by a mix of environmental factors, endogenous structuring processes, and managerial actions.

Third, any discussion of the managerial implications of scope and turnover needs to touch upon potential links to firm performance. For example, a firm's reconfiguration activity has been linked to its innovative capabilities (Henderson & Cockburn, 1994), learning (Khanna, Gulati, & Nohria, 1998), and ongoing performance (Galunic & Rodan, 1998; Helfat & Eisenhardt, 2004; Levinthal & Wu, 2010; Rumelt, 1974, 1982; Sakhartov & Folta, 2014). While we emphasize that the goal of our model is descriptive, not normative, we highlight two potential implications for performance.

First, firms in different environments might benefit from different scope and turnover rates, while such firm-environment fits are likely to change over time. Consider the case of Polaroid (Tripsas & Gavetti, 2000). After reaping profits for decades in an environment that rewarded the stable allocation of resources with low scope and turnover, a dramatic change in the external technical and competitive environment found the firm unable to adapt its capabilities. When the external environment is stable, a narrow, focused set of activities (i.e., small S and T) may tend to be beneficial. However, when environments change sharply, a diversified activity portfolio (e.g., Intel's pivot from memory to microprocessors), as well as rapid activity turnover, may be desirable (Brown & Eisenhardt, 1998; Sull, Tedlow, & Rosenbloom, 1997).

Although speculative, it is possible that some element of stability in firm scope, whether such scope is broad or narrow, is beneficial. Consider the counterfactual: a firm that swings wildly between a large number of activities and a narrow number of activities, year-over-year. It is unlikely that benefits of renewed activities would fully counter-act inefficiencies that arise through constantly hiring, reallocating, and shedding employees. Although drawing conclusions from a small number of firms requires caution, the notion that stable scope is beneficial is supported by our analysis of consumer electronics firms in Fig. 4, particularly with respect to the recent declining performance of both RIM and Nokia.

A second perspective would suggest that moderate levels of both scope and turnover might be beneficial. Continuing with the earlier example, Polaroid may have benefited from partitioning the firm into different subsections. Rather than a focus on its "cash cow," Polaroid might well have benefited by dedicating a limited set of resources to a secondary unit as a hedge against future volatility. For this second set of activities, an ongoing stream of redeployment and turnover, allowing entrepreneurial managers to constantly seek new ventures, may have facilitated a more favorable outcome for the company.

Most generally, we believe that a strength of this paper is to provide both clarity and levers to enable managers to tune the firms' scope and turnover characteristics to current needs for resource redeployment and business reconfiguration. Strengthening this linkage between firm activity characteristics and firm performance is an exciting opportunity for future research.

Limits and Directions for Future Research

This paper has limits that suggest directions for future research. First is an issue of boundary conditions. A central goal of this paper has been to develop a model to explain how redeployment of activities shapes a firm's knowledge base; addressing this goal has required a trade-off between parsimony and verisimilitude. Our model is a starting point for more complex iterations. We have shown that our model is largely robust to a relaxation of our core assumptions. Moreover, the model is flexible enough to allow several alternative specifications, such as assuming that absorptive capacity causes the arrival rate to depend on scope.

Second, our model has only considered a single firm, in isolation from the influence of others. Nonetheless, although largely outside the scope of this paper, we believe that our model also speaks to interrelationships between firms. It is logical to consider entities beyond the focal firm as sources of activities, leading to a higher addition rate. Alternatively, external firms may also act as competitors, serving to lure away the focal firm's strategic human capital and accelerating the firm's subtraction rate. Moreover, if the unit of analysis shifts from a firm to the business unit, one could apply a similar logic inside the firm, with activities from one unit cross-fertilizing another (e.g., corporate strategy) or crowding out (e.g., the exploitation/exploration paradox). We believe that this image of a firm as an archipelago of business units, situated in the greater constellation of entities may be a useful future avenue of study.

Third, we have defined activity scope, $S(t)$, as the number of distinct activities present in the firm at time t and have treated firm size as independent of turnover. Our implicit assumption concerning this definition of scope is that any one added activity has the potential to seed future growth, while any one subtracted activity has the potential to eliminate future trajectories of activities. Nonetheless, an alternative definition of firm scope would take into account the distribution of resources allocated to each activity in the firm. For example, for a firm that is engaged in multiple different activities, one could envision a Herfindahl-type measure that captures how evenly or unevenly sales are distributed between the activities.

In parallel, large firms with plentiful resource may dedicate more resources to each type of activity. This issue, the magnitude of resources allocated to each activity, will likely affect the subtraction rate of that activity. With greater redundancy in knowledge, departures of key employees are less likely to cause gaps in the firm's knowledge stocks. Moreover, larger firms may move more slowly to reallocate resources away from unattractive product lines. For these reasons, we suspect that the subtraction rate for larger firms will be lower than smaller firms. However speculative this line of reasoning is, linking different firm characteristics (e.g., industry, size, age) to the focal firm's addition and subtraction rates is an interesting future line of research.

Fourth, the focus of this paper has been on conceptual development rather than empirical testing. Our examples serve only to illustrate how aspects of our model might map onto characteristics of firm activities and perhaps to suggest a setting where one might empirically explore the model. In theory, a causal test is straightforward. One would require exogenous shocks to either a firm's arrival or loss rate, with the pre- and post-shock examinations of firm scope and turnover. Although identifying a set of exogenous shocks to either the arrival or loss rate without an effect on its complement will be challenging, we believe that these studies would be a useful addition to the current avenue of inquiry.

Several other issues merit attention. It would be useful to address the causes of addition and subtraction of activities in more detail, including factors that influence discrete additions and subtractions, as well as the degree to which addition and subtraction may arise from a firm's goals for overall scope. It would be useful to assess profitability, both in terms of how different patterns of addition and subtraction affect profitability and how profitability might affect addition and subtraction choices. One could also extend the investigation of interdependencies among arrival and loss beyond the discussion that we outlined above and in Table 2.

We hope that this paper highlights the importance of looking not just at firm scope, but also at the firm's rate of turnover for a more complete view of how resource redeployment shapes the composition of a firm's activities. In highlighting the role of redeployment via addition and subtraction rates of a firm's set of activities, we provide a richer perspective on the fundamental levers that drive reconfiguration of a firm's resource base.

ACKNOWLEDGMENTS

The authors give thanks to Alex Oettl for sharing USPTO data with us. We also thank participants at the Academy of Management, the Maryland

Entrepreneurship Conference, and the Conference on Corporate Strategy and Resource Redeployment. Lastly, we thank the editors and reviewers for helpful comments. Joel Blit and Chris Liu thank the INET/CIGI foundation for project funding.

REFERENCES

Alcacer, J., & Chung, W. (2014). Location strategies for agglomeration economies. *Strategic Management Journal, 35*, 1749–1761.

Barney, J. (1991). Firm resources and sustained competitive advantage. *Journal of Management Firm Resources and Sustained Competitive Advantage, 17*(1), 99–120.

Baum, J. A. C., & Mezias, S. J. (1992). Localized competition and organizational mortality in the Manhattan hotel industry, 1898–1990. *Administrative Science Quarterly, 37*, 580–604.

Bettis, R. A., & Prahalad, C. K. (1995). The dominant logic: Retrospective and extension. *Strategic Management Journal, 16*, 5–14.

Bower, J. L. (1986). *Managing the resource allocation process: A study of corporate planning and investment*. Cambridge, MA: Harvard Business Press.

Brown, S. L., & Eisenhardt, K. M. (1998). *Competing on the edge: Strategy as structured chaos*. Boston, MA: Harvard Business Press.

Burgelman, R. A. (1991). Intraorganizational ecology of strategy making and organizational adaptation: Theory and field research. *Organization Science, 2*(3), 239–262.

Burgelman, R. A. (1996). A process model of strategic business exit: Implications for an evolutionary perspective on strategy. *Strategic Management Journal, 17*(S1), 193–214.

Burton, R. M., Obel, B., & DeSanctis, G. (2011). *Organizational design: A step-by-step approach*. Cambridge: Cambridge University Press.

Capron, L. (1999). The long-term performance of horizontal acquisitions. *Strategic Management Journal, 20*(11), 987–1018.

Capron, L., Dussauge, P., & Mitchell, W. (1998). Resource redeployment following horizontal acquisitions in Europe and North America, 1988–1992. *Strategic Management Journal, 19*(7), 631–661.

Capron, L., Mitchell, W., & Swaminathan, A. (2001). Asset divestiture following horizontal acquisitions: A dynamic view. *Strategic Management Journal, 22*(9), 817–844.

Chakrabarti, A., & Mitchell, W. (2013). The persistent effect of geographic distance in acquisition target selection. *Organization Science, 24*(6), 1805–1826.

Chatain, O., & Zemsky, P. (2007). The horizontal scope of the firm: Organizational tradeoffs vs. buyer-supplier relationships. *Management Science, 53*(4), 550–565.

Chown, J. D., & Liu, C. C. (2015). Geography and power in an organizational forum: Evidence from the U.S. Senate Chamber. *Strategic Management Journal, 36*(2), 177–196.

Coase, R. H. (1937). The nature of the firm. *Economica, 4*(16), 386–405.

Cockburn, I. M., & Henderson, R. M. (1998). Absorptive capacity, coauthoring behavior, and the organization of research in drug discovery. *The Journal of Industrial Economics, 46*(2), 157–182.

Cohen, W. M., & Levinthal, D. A. (1990). Absorptive capacity: A new perspective on learning and innovation. *Administrative Science Quarterly*, *35*(1), 128–152.

Collis, D. J., & Montgomery, C. A. (1998). *Corporate strategy: A resource-based approach*. Boston, MA: Irwin.

Cyert, R. M., & March, J. G. (1963). *A behavioral theory of the firm*. Englewood Cliffs, NJ: Blackwell Publishing.

Danneels, E. (2002). The dynamics of product innovation and firm competences. *Strategic Management Journal*, *23*(12), 1095–1121.

de Holan, P. M., & Phillips, N. (2004). Remembrance of things past? The dynamics of organizational forgetting. *Management Science*, *50*(11): 1603–1613.

Dougherty, D. (1992). A practice-centered model of organizational renewal through product innovation. *Strategic Management Journal*, *13*(S1), 77–92.

Duhaime, I. M., & Grant, J. H. (1984). Factors influencing divestment decision-making: Evidence from a field study. *Strategic Management Journal*, *5*(4), 301–318.

Galunic, C., & Rodan, S. (1998). Resource recombination in the firm: Knowledge structures and the potential for Schumpeterian innovation. *Strategic Management Journal*, *19*(2), 1193–1201.

Greve, H. R. (1995). Jumping ship: The diffusion of strategy abandonment. *Administrative Science Quarterly*, *40*, 444–473.

Greve, H. R. (2009). Bigger and safer: The diffusion of competitive advantage. *Strategic Management Journal*, *30*, 1–23.

Hambrick, D. D., & Macmillan, I. C. (1985). Efficiency of product R&D in business units: The role of strategic context. *Academy of Management Journal*, *28*(3), 527–547.

Hannan, M. T., & Freeman, J. H. (1977). The population ecology of organizations. *American Journal of Sociology*, *82*(5), 929–964.

Helfat, C. E. (1997). Know-how and asset complementary and dynamic capability accumulation: The case of R&D. *Strategic Management Journal*, *18*(5), 339–360.

Helfat, C. E., & Eisenhardt, K. M. (2004). Inter-temporal economies of scope, organizational modularity, and the dynamics of diversification. *Strategic Management Journal*, *25*(13), 1217–1232.

Henderson, R. M., & Cockburn, I. M. (1994). Measuring competence? Exploring firm effects in pharmaceutical research. *Strategic Management Journal*, *15*, 63–84.

Jain, A. (2013). Learning by doing and the locus of innovative capability in biotechnology research. *Organization Science*, *24*, 1683–1700.

Karim, S. (2006). Modularity in organizational structure: The reconfiguration of internally developed and acquired business units. *Strategic Management Journal*, *27*(9), 799–823.

Karim, S., & Capron, L. (2015). *Adding, redeploying, recombining, and divesting resources and business units. Editors' introduction to virtual special issue of strategic management society journal publications on reconfiguration*. Retrieved from http://onlinelibrary.wiley.com/journal/10.1002/%28ISSN%291097-0266/homepage/reconfiguration_vsi_introduction.htm

Karim, S., & Williams, C. (2012). Structural knowledge: How executive experience with structural composition affects intrafirm mobility and unit reconfiguration. *Strategic Management Journal*, *33*(6), 681–709.

Khanna, T., Gulati, R., & Nohria, N. (1998). The dynamics of learning alliances: Competition, cooperation, and relative scope. *Strategic Management Journal*, *19*(3), 193–210.

Klepper, S. (2007). Disagreements, spinoffs, and the evolution of Detroit as the capital of the US automobile industry. *Management Science*, *53*(4), 616–631.

Lai, R., D'Amour, A., & Fleming, L. (2009). *The careers and co-authorship networks of U.S. patent-holders since 1975*. Harvard Institute for Quantitative Social Science [Distributor] Version 3. Retrieved from http://hdl.handle.net/1902.1/12367%20UNF:5:daJuoNgCZlcYY8RqU+/j2Q==%20Harvard%20Business%20School. Accessed on October 20, 2014.

Lenox, M., & King, A. (2004). Prospects for developing absorptive capacity through internal information provision. *Strategic Management Journal*, *25*, 331–345.

Leonard-Barton, D. (1992). Core capabilities and core rigidities: A paradox in managing new product development. *Strategic Management Journal*, *13*(S1), 111–125.

Levinthal, D. A., & Wu, B. (2010). Opportunity costs and non-scale free capabilities: Profit maximization, corporate scope, and profit margins. *Strategic Management Journal*, *31*(7), 780–801.

Levitt, B., & March, J. G. (1988). Organizational learning. *Annual Review of Sociology*, *14*, 319–340.

Liu, C. C., & Stuart, T. (2014). Positions and rewards: The allocation of rewards within a science-based entrepreneurial firm. *Research Policy*, *43*(7), 1134–1143.

Mahmood, I. P., Zhu, H., & Zajac, E. J. (2011). Where can capabilities come from? Network ties and capability acquisition in business groups. *Strategic Management Journal*, *32*(8), 820–848.

Makadok, R. (2001). Toward a synthesis of the resource-based and dynamic-capability views of rent creation. *Strategic Management Journal*, *22*(5), 387–401.

Mowery, D. C., Oxley, J. E., & Silverman, B. S. (1996). Strategic alliances and interfirm knowledge transfer. *Strategic Management Journal*, *17*, 77–91.

Nelson, R. R., & Winter, S. G. (1982). *An evolutionary theory of economic change*. Cambridge, MA: Harvard University Press.

Pacheco-de-Almeida, G., & Zemsky, P. (2007). The timing of resource development and sustainable competitive advantage. *Management Science*, *53*(4), 651–666.

Penrose, E. T. (1959). *The theory of the growth of the firm*. London: Basil Blackwell.

Rumelt, R. P. (1974). *Strategy, structure, and economic performance*. Boston, MA: Harvard Business School.

Rumelt, R. P. (1982). Diversification strategy and profitability. *Strategic Management Journal*, *3*(4), 359–369.

Sakhartov, A., & Folta, T. (2014). Resource relatedness, redeployability, and firm value. *Strategic Management Journal*, *35*(12), 1781–1797.

Shaver, J. M., & Flyer, F. (2000). Agglomeration economics, firm heterogeneity, and foreign direct investment in the United States. *Strategic Management Journal*, *21*, 1175–1193.

Stuart, T. E., & Podolny, J. M. (1996). Local search and the evolution of technological capabilities. *Strategic Management Journal*, *17*, 21–38.

Sull, D. N., Tedlow, R. S., & Rosenbloom, R. S. (1997). Managerial commitments and technological change in the US tire industry. *Industrial and Corporate Change*, *6*(2), 461–500.

Teece, D. J. (1986). Profiting from technological innovation: Implications for integration, collaboration, licensing and public policy. *Research Policy*, *15*(6), 285–305.

Teece, D. J., Pisano, G., & Shuen, A. (1997). Dynamic capabilities and strategic management. *Strategic Management Journal*, *18*(7), 509–533.

Thompson, P. (2007). How much did the liberty shipbuilders forget? *Management Science, 53*(6), 908–918.

Tripsas, M., & Gavetti, G. (2000). Capabilities, cognition, and inertia: Evidence from digital imaging. *Strategic Management Journal, 21*(10–11), 1147–1161.

Villalonga, B., & McGahan, A. M. (2005). The choice among acquisitions, alliances, and divestitures. *Strategic Management Journal, 26*(13), 1183–1208.

Wernerfelt, B. (1984). A resource-based view of the firm. *Strategic Management Journal, 5*(2), 171–180.

Williamson, O. E. (1979). Transaction-cost economics: The governance of contractual relations. *Journal of Law and Economics, 22*(2), 233–261.

RESOURCE RECONFIGURATION AND TRANSACTIONS ACROSS FIRM BOUNDARIES: THE ROLES OF FIRM CAPABILITIES AND MARKET FACTORS

Patia J. McGrath and Harbir Singh

ABSTRACT

Firms operate in a market for their corporate assets, wherein important assets being bought and sold are business units. This market is therefore a primary mechanism for firm reconfiguration, and offers the opportunity for firms to gain performance advantage as they prepare for and engage in their boundary-changing moves. This paper focuses on resource reconfiguration between firms, and examines internally and externally driven sources of performance heterogeneity in firms' use of the market for firm reconfiguration. Viewing between-firm resource reconfiguration through three theoretical lenses surfaces several potential avenues for firm differentiation. For one, the necessity of firms' possessing capabilities to execute both sides of the external resource reconfiguration transaction – acquisition and divestiture capabilities – is revealed. For another, the

Resource Redeployment and Corporate Strategy
Advances in Strategic Management, Volume 35, 217–251

ISSN: 0742-3322/doi:10.1108/S0742-332220160000035013

institutional prerequisites that are needed in the operating environment for a firm to build a sustainable resource reconfiguration strategy are brought to the fore, and are well illustrated by the private equity industry. Lastly, the potential benefits of using the transactional view of firm scope to animate the study of external resource reconfiguration are raised. Taken together, these elements lead to a research agenda around resource reconfiguration across firm boundaries.

Keywords: External reconfiguration; firm scope; firm capabilities; capability development; divestiture

INTRODUCTION

Why Is Resource Reconfiguration between Firms Important to Study?

More than ever, firms operate in an extremely dynamic environment that is characterized by a high velocity of change. Firms' reconfiguration of their resources is an integral part of this dynamism, serving as both antecedent and consequence of the change landscape. Resource reconfiguration may take place within firm boundaries, such as in the case of transferring resources from one product line to another (Helfat & Eisenhardt, 2004; Penrose, 1959; Sakhartov & Folta, 2014). Resource reconfiguration may also occur across firm boundaries (Anand & Singh, 1997; Capron & Mitchell, 1998; Karim & Mitchell, 2000), such as when a firm divests a business unit that is then acquired by another entity. This external reconfiguration necessarily causes change in the scope of both the divesting firm and also the receiving firm. The extent and intensity of such firm reconfiguration is reflected by the large number of scope-changing transactions that are executed in the market for corporate assets today. Announced merger and acquisition (M&A) activity worldwide has doubled in dollar terms since 2002, corresponding to a 50-percent increase in deal volume (Thomson ONE). Of this deal activity, scope reduction via divestiture is a major component, consistently accounting for approximately one-third of total M&A volume overall (Fig. 1).

Furthermore, resources may be divested and acquired across firm boundaries in both the domestic and the international contexts, with the latter showing substantive increases in the past two decades. Indeed, when

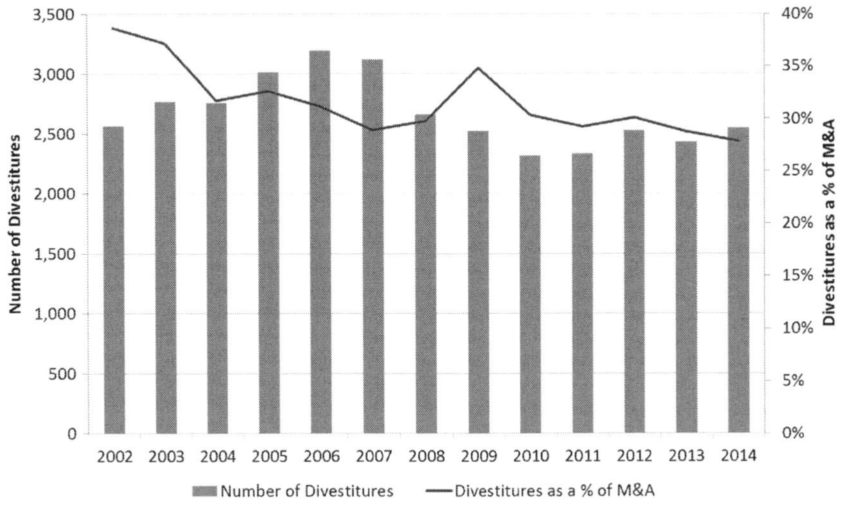

Fig. 1. Divestitures as a Percentage of the US M&A Market. *Source*: Thomson ONE.

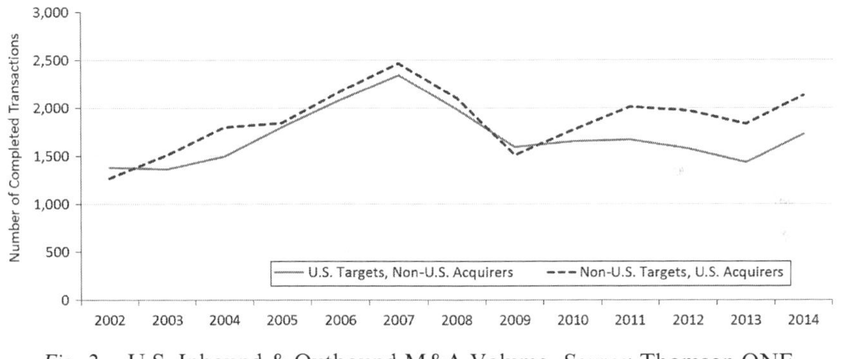

Fig. 2. U.S. Inbound & Outbound M&A Volume. *Source*: Thomson ONE.

considering acquirers headquartered in the United States, the number of completed cross-border acquisitions has risen by two-thirds since 2002, with more than 2,000 transactions in 2014 (Fig. 2). These trends suggest that the market for corporate assets is robust and global, and that the degree to which firm assets may be readily transferred across firm boundaries (e.g., the "external reconfigurability" of these assets) is an increasingly valuable resource characteristic.

There are numerous factors that can influence a firm's decision to divest its assets. Disappointing financial performance – be it of the parent firm or the target business unit – can be a major impetus for divestiture (Duhaime & Grant, 1984; Montgomery & Thomas, 1988; Ravenscraft & Scherer, 1991). Strategic rationales, such as when firms divest to refocus or to shed non-core assets, are also key drivers of divestiture (Chang & Singh, 1999; Markides, 1992; Montgomery, Thomas, & Kamath, 1984). Divestiture may also be triggered when a firm determines that certain of its assets could be put to more efficient or higher value use elsewhere outside of the firm (Berry, 2010; Kaul, 2012; Montgomery & Wernerfelt, 1988); the divestiture thus frees up managerial and operational resources that may then be applied to other opportunities within the firm. In the same vein, a firm may engage in divestiture as a means of financing growth opportunities.

The firm's decision to divest is also driven by externally oriented factors. In response to the financial markets and its players, firms may divest in an effort to present the firm in an easy-to-analyze way (Feldman, 2015; Zuckerman, 2000). Regulators, such as the Federal Trade Commission, can require firms to divest assets as a condition of their approval of mergers and acquisitions in order to preserve competition. Firms may proactively divest their assets when preparing to engage in a merger or acquisition to preempt these mandated divestitures. Activist shareholders may also influence firm divestment; as such, activist shareholders are notable contributors to the vitality of the market for corporate control of these assets. Indeed, shareholder activism in this market has been playing an increasingly larger role in instigating firm reconfiguration. This is an emerging, but strengthening, trend, with activist campaigns increasing from just over 200 in 2010 (with a 60 percent success rate) to 343 in 2014 (with a 73 percent success rate) (Benoit, 2015). Recent campaigns have resulted in the announcement of numerous high profile divestitures, such as the spin-off of PayPal from eBay and the separation of Hewlett-Packard's enterprise software business from its computer and printing manufacturing operations.

One view of firms' engagement with activist investors' demands is that the CEOs of these firms have become excessively short-term in their outlooks – a view which is shared by many major shareholders, including the leader of BlackRock, one of the world's largest asset management firms (Sorkin, 2015). Alternatively, the fact that shareholder activists are gaining ground in their demands for firm restructuring and divestiture specifically may be interpreted as indicating that firms are not realizing the full value of their assets. Viewed in this way, activist investors help to unlock shareholder value by triggering firm reconfiguration through their campaigns.

Activist pressures can reverberate beyond their immediate targets. Firms observing these tussles on the sidelines may subsequently adopt a more proactive approach to their own firm's divestiture programs in an effort to avoid attracting the attention of and tangling with their own potential activist investors.

One outcome of activist investors' role in driving divestiture is its impact on the market for corporate control. This market is vibrant, as reflected in its numerous acquisitions and divestitures worldwide, and in the attraction of stakeholders like activist investors who help to fuel its momentum. The market for corporate control is also vast, since assets of all shapes and sizes – from entire firms to business units to the parts and pieces of these larger assets – feed the supply of assets entering this market. This dynamism and scale translates into resource reconfiguration across firm boundaries being a timely and important topic in its own right, and thereby creates a sense of urgency around advancing our understanding of this aspect of firm reconfiguration.

On this front, however, much work remains. In particular, the divestiture aspect of firm reconfiguration has historically been an under-researched topic. Indeed, although firms both buy and sell assets, including business units, as part of their corporate strategies, there has not been comparable interest between the two. One reason for this discordance in research streams may simply stem from scholars following the cues of managerial interests. Managerial appetites for firm growth have long been voracious, and scholars may be responding to this emphasis on scope expansion. Another reason may originate from the challenges associated with studying divestiture. There is a general reluctance by executives to publicize or openly discuss their divestiture plans or activities, since it is typically (albeit often unfairly) associated with strategic mistakes (Dranikoff, Koller, & Schneider, 2002). This managerial reticence to address divestiture can be harmful – be it due to concerns about being cast as a poor manager, being caught in an escalation of commitment to a unit, etc. – as it can cause managers to retain units that are impairing the firm's performance (Boot, 1992). Furthermore, the regulatory disclosure requirements around divestiture and the business units of focus are far less stringent than those of acquisition, making data collection for divestiture studies comparatively much more difficult. Taken together, these issues have created a research environment that has been weighted toward the study of acquisitions and alliances rather than on their divestiture counterparts in between-firm resource reconfiguration.

Although the number of divestiture studies has been limited, extant work provides a strong platform upon which to continue to build our understanding of the phenomenon. Table 1 presents a chronological view of representative papers in divestiture research, and thereby serves to illustrate a high-level view of the evolution of the study of divestiture to date.

The diversity of the papers and research contributions reflected in Table 1, along with the enormity of the research opportunities that lie ahead, suggest that there is a need for a shared working language to animate firm reconfiguration research going forward. Identifying and formalizing key concepts of most interest and value, along with establishing a consistent vocabulary to describe them, will help to unify and thereby accelerate the impact of the research efforts that are to follow. Table 1 also helps to highlight several issues that merit further scholarly attention, such as whether and how firms develop divestiture capabilities, and the need to further our understanding of resource reconfiguration via the market. In the next section, we start to address these topics by beginning with presenting one approach to a common language around resource reconfiguration.

Creating a Common Language for Resource Reconfiguration

A shared vocabulary around resource reconfiguration must first begin with a shared definition of resources. A general definition of resources includes the assets (tangible or intangible), knowledge, and capabilities that the firm owns outright or that the firm controls at arm's length (cf., Amit & Schoemaker, 1993; Helfat et al., 2007). These resources may be organized and distributed across the firm's business units. Accordingly, business units are themselves resources. Business units can be defined as economically distinct business areas of the parent company, typically characterized in terms of the product markets in which parent competes (Hill & Jones, 1995). In this paper, business units are our primary resource of interest.

The second consideration is to establish what is meant by reconfiguration. Broadly stated, there are two primary types of resource reconfiguration: internal resource reconfiguration, which takes place entirely within the firm itself; and external resource reconfiguration, which takes place across firm boundaries.[1] As illustrated in Fig. 3, the first type, internal resource reconfiguration includes a process whereby resources that were serving one area of the firm (here, those of Business Unit A in Firm 1) and have now been redeployed to serve another area of the firm (here, Business Unit B in Firm 1) (Capron, Dussauge, & Mitchell, 1998; Helfat & Eisenhardt, 2004; Penrose, 1959; Sakhartov & Folta, 2014). As such, the process of internal resource redeployment is markedly different from that of synergy, wherein

Table 1. Illustrating the Evolution of Divestiture Research through Representative Studies.

Study	Empirical Setting and Sample	Empirical Approach	Divestiture Insights
Nees (1981)	14 cross-industry divestitures, with parent firms located in U.S. and Europe.	Qualitative analysis: combination of field research and analysis and previously completed case studies.	The division manager of the divesting unit plays five key roles. The divestiture process benefits when division managers are informed and allowed to participate in the divestment process.
Duhaime and Grant (1984)	59 divested units in 40 Fortune 500 firms, which represented five industry groups.	Semi-structured interviews with executives. Qualitative analysis and non-parametric statistical methods.	Identified three key factors that drive corporate-level divestment decisions: business unit strength, unit interdependency, and the parent firm financial strength relative to industry competitors.
Montgomery et al. (1984)	78 divestitures completed by Fortune 500 firms.	Content analysis of regulatory reports used to capture the motive for the divestiture. Cumulative abnormal returns used to capture market response.	Divestitures are value creating when they are part of integrated, strategic plans. Divestitures are value destroying when they are routine, nonstrategic divestitures of unwanted units.
Ravenscraft and Scherer (1991)	FTC Line of Business data; compared 285 business lines that were divested versus 2,157 retained in 450 firms.	Hazard function analysis used to determine what characteristics determine the probability that a line of business would be divested during the time period of focus.	Primary divestiture driver is low business unit profitability. Units from previous acquisitions were more likely to be divested than the firms' original units. Unit acquirers were able to improve performance, but not enough to realize a return.
Markides (1992)	45 firm refocusing announcements gathered from the business press.	Event study approach used to examine the impact of the restructuring announcement on shareholder value.	Refocusing announcements are associated with positive and significant cumulative abnormal returns.
Bergh (1995)	112 horizontal sell-offs by Fortune 500 firms.	Hierarchical multiple regression (examine size of unit sold) and logistic regression (for relatedness of unit sold)	Firms sold unrelated and small units (which facilitated firm refocusing) when owner influence was high. Firms sold more related

Table 1. *(Continued)*

Study	Empirical Setting and Sample	Empirical Approach	Divestiture Insights
			and larger units (setting the stage to reap benefits of competitive resource allocation systems in the diversified firm), when owner influence was low.
Chang (1996)	Longitudinal dataset of 772 US public manufacturing companies identified from the TRINET database.	Used logit regression to examine a firm's decision to enter a new business. Used Cox proportional hazard models for firm exit decisions.	Treating entry and exit together as a unit of analysis, rather than discretely, reveals that firms are constantly changing their boundaries through an ongoing search and selection process. The firm's knowledge base plays a critical role in catalyzing these scope-changing actions.
Chang and Singh (1999)	Longitudinal dataset of 772 US public manufacturing companies identified from the TRINET database.	Used logit regression to analyze the mode (acquisition or internal development) by which firms entered a new business. Used Cox proportional hazard models to analyze the mode (sell-off or closure) by which firms exited these businesses.	By linking the firm's mode of entry and mode of exit for the same business, show the firm's choice of entry mode for a business impacts its choice of exit mode for that business. Similarity in the resource profiles between the focal business and the parent's other lines of business, as well as the age and accumulation of idiosyncratic assets in the focal business also influence the exit mode choice.
Capron et al. (2001)	253 horizontal acquisitions in the U.S. and Europe across a variety of industries.	Survey used to collect the study's data. Structural modeling approach (AMOS) used to examine the causes of post-acquisition asset divestiture.	Offers evidence for a positive interpretation of post-acquisition divestiture. Rather than acquisition failure, the (partial) asset divestitures are a logical result of the merging firms' reconfiguration.

Moliterno and Wiersema (2007)	Major league baseball franchises over 15 years; pitchers were divested.	Cross-sectional time series regression analysis, with team/year as the unit of observation.	Firms can develop a resource divestment capability, which entails both the firm's being motivated to divest and its decision-making as to which resources to divest.
Bergh et al. (2008)	204 U.S. public firms, with 82 spin-offs and 122 sell-offs. For sample, used largest restructuring announcements over an 8-year period.	Hierarchical logistic regression, with a binary variable to represent the restructuring choice and cumulative abnormal returns used to measure the firm's stock market value.	Information asymmetries associated with the restructured assets and the firm's diversification strategy drive managers' decision between sell-off and spin-off of the assets. Managers choose on the basis of which option best mitigates the information asymmetry while maximizing financial value.
Moschieri (2011)	Six divestitures from six multinational diversified firms.	Qualitative case study analysis used to consider whether and how several factors concerning the implementation and structuring of a divestiture may impact the unit's performance.	Several factors (and their combinations) concerning the divestiture process impact the unit's post-divestiture success, with unit managers' "sense of opportunity" for the unit playing a major role.
Semadeni and Cannella (2011)	142 firms spun-off from U.S. publicly listed companies over a 12-year period.	Hierarchical generalized least squares regression used to study how the relationship between the parent and spun-off child firm affects the stock market performance of the child firm.	Ownership and governance links between the parent and spun-off child firms impact the spin-off's performance. Maintaining some ties with the parent can be beneficial to the spun-off firm, but having too many links impairs the spin-off's performance.
Feldman (2014)	Cross-industry sample of 300 firms from FTC Statistical Report on M&A. Sample included 56 legacy divestitures.	Event study to study market reaction to legacy divestitures; Heckman selection models to examine relationship between the legacy divestiture and firm's subsequent operating performance.	Divestiture of a firm's legacy business impairs the firm's post-divestiture operating performance. CEOs with shorter tenures are more likely to undertake legacy divestitures.

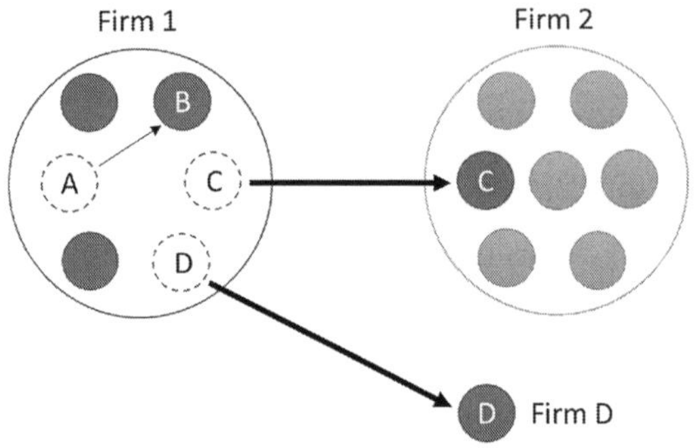

Fig. 3. Resource Reconfiguration Schematic.

firms are sharing resources simultaneously among different business units in the firm. In the case of synergy, the shared resources are unconstrained by capacity limitations and are thus "scale free" resources. In contrast, internal resource redeployment often concerns "non-scale free" resources that do have capacity constraints. Internal resource redeployment accordingly entails a complete withdrawal of the resources from one use in the firm to another (Bryce & Winter, 2009; Levinthal & Wu, 2010; Sakhartov & Folta, 2014).

The second type of resource reconfiguration, external resource reconfiguration, concerns resources that are separated from and transferred outside of the disposing firm (Anand, 2004). There are two primary types of divestiture that firms use to reduce their scope: sell-offs and spin-offs. In Fig. 3, a sell-off is illustrated as the sale and transfer of Business Unit C from Firm 1 to Firm 2, and a spin-off is shown as Firm 1's separation and transformation of Business Unit D into an independent entity (Firm D). Both scale free and non-scale free resources are candidates for resource reconfiguration across firm boundaries. Indeed, a business unit selected for divestiture typically includes a combination of both types of resources, such as, for example, the brand or knowledge held within the target unit (scale free resources) and its employees or manufacturing equipment (non-scale free resources).

Internal and external reconfigurations are by no means mutually exclusive. Firms can engage in both types concurrently, and both can play a crucial role in shaping the firm's strategic direction and enabling its growth. While the appropriate mix and timing depends upon many factors, including the firm's circumstances and capabilities, firms that have enjoyed long term superior performance, such as Johnson & Johnson, have been observed to use a combination of both types (Karim & Mitchell, 2000). In this paper, we focus on the externally oriented type of these two reconfiguration mechanisms, resource reconfiguration across firm boundaries.

When investigating resource reconfiguration between firms, there are numerous distinct, but inextricably connected, issues that may be examined. One is the *external reconfigurability*[2] of the resources (Bryce & Winter, 2009; Sakhartov & Folta, 2014, 2015). Stated in terms of Fig. 3, this issue concerns those characteristics of Business Unit C that facilitate and enable its transfer from Firm 1 to Firm 2. Thus, external reconfigurability encompasses such topics as the degree of tradability of the resource in the secondary market, the scope of the resource's flexibility of application to different purposes (Anand & Singh, 1997), the ease of separability of the resource from the firm (Bergh, 1995, 1997; Duhaime & Grant, 1984; Semadeni & Cannella, 2011), and the amount of combinatorial value that the resource holds with other sets of resources beyond the firm's own (Kogut & Zander, 1992). It bears highlighting that the issue of a resource's external reconfigurability is intertwined with the firm's decision to divest and the market for corporate control. The nature and degree of asset specificity impacts the number of potential bidders for the asset. In turn, without potential bidders, divestiture then becomes an unattractive (or unavailable) option for the firm.

Other key research questions consider the *process* of between-firm resource reconfiguration. These include, for example, the examination of the external factors that trigger the process of resource reconfiguration across firm boundaries. As per Fig. 3, external factors that drive Firm 1 to divest Business Unit C may stem from Firm 2 itself, or even the broader market in which Firm 1 and Firm 2 participate (Anand, 2004; Eisenhardt & Brown, 1998). Another aspect of interest is the execution of the between-firm reconfiguration process itself. Here, researchers examine the process mechanics of Business Unit C's divestiture by Firm 1 and its acquisition by Firm 2, and consider the factors that shape how the process unfolds and impact its eventual performance outcome (Bergh & Lim, 2008; Capron, Mitchell, & Swaminathan, 2001; Chang, 1996; Moliterno & Wiersema, 2007). All of these issues are germane to this paper.[3]

Clearly, resource reconfiguration is a multifaceted topic. Distinguishing between reconfiguration that occurs within and across firm boundaries reveals different avenues of research opportunity. Furthermore, in recognizing that resource reconfiguration across firm boundaries itself encompasses two areas for study – the external reconfigurability of the resources and the process of external reconfiguration itself – the opportunities to advance our understanding of this topic expand even further. In this paper, we consider both in the between-firm context.

Setting a Research Agenda for Between-Firm Resource Reconfiguration

Our major objective in this paper is to set forth a research agenda for studying resource reconfiguration across firm boundaries. To do so, we begin by examining resource reconfiguration through the resource-based, market-based, and capability-based views. This facilitates a rich consideration of what internal factors serve to enhance the external reconfigurability of firm resources, what market-based factors work to create an operational environment that is suitable for (and drives) resource reconfiguration between firms, and what opportunities exist for firms to learn to build and deploy capabilities that provide the potential for performance advantage in the context of between-firm resource reconfiguration. This examination, in turn, leads to the identification of several major, but under-examined, research topics that are central to the study of external resource reconfiguration. These are:

(a) The existence and determinants of firm-level capabilities for external resource reconfiguration
(b) The interplay between the market for corporate control and resource reconfiguration across firm boundaries
(c) The identification of the theoretical views of the firm that hold particular promise as an effective means by which to study the multifaceted nature of external resource reconfiguration.

After specifying the key questions associated with these research areas, we next take first steps toward answering them. In so doing, we uncover the potential value that development of divestiture capabilities holds for firms eager to differentiate their execution of their external resource reconfiguration strategies. We also surface the central role that private equity has played (and continues to play) in growing and institutionalizing the secondary market for corporate assets. Furthermore, we propose that the transactional view of firm scope offers an effective lens through which to examine resource reconfiguration between firms and to identify sources of performance advantage in firms' use of the market for firm reconfiguration. Taken together, these issues not only work to serve as the pillars of a research agenda for between-firm resource reconfiguration, but they also offer several managerial implications that are of immediate practical significance.

THREE PERSPECTIVES OF BETWEEN-FIRM RESOURCE RECONFIGURATION

In this section, three theoretical lenses are used to examine between-firm resource reconfiguration. Collectively, these three perspectives treat resource reconfiguration from the vantage points of inside the firm, outside of the firm, and the intersection of the two. Each view surfaces unique insights into reconfiguration, in terms of both the external reconfigurability of assets and the process of between-firm reconfiguration. When combined, these three perspectives further serve to raise intriguing, but as of yet unanswered, research questions about resource reconfiguration across firm boundaries.

Resource Reconfigurability and the Resource-Based View

The resource-based view of the firm (Barney, 1991; Penrose, 1959; Peteraf, 1993; Wernerfelt, 1984) offers an especially powerful means by which to examine the concept of resource reconfigurability. Here, we are treating resource reconfigurability as being a characteristic of the resource itself. Reconfigurability can be a highly valuable attribute, and the resource-based view serves to help reveal this value in both the within-firm and the between-firm resource reconfiguration cases.

The resource-based view of the firm proposes that the fundamental driver of scope expansion is the appropriation of Ricardian rents from underutilized specific resources (Montgomery & Wernerfelt, 1988). This stimulus for scope change is unrelenting due to the indivisibility of resources, as the firm will always have some resources that are sub-optimally utilized. There will be diminishing returns as the firm is forced to deploy its underutilized assets in increasingly less related applications that are further from its core (Markides, 1992). As such, under the resource-based view, a firm's diversifying move into an adjacent area is explained as resulting from the firm's hunting for resources and capabilities that improve the rent-earning capability of its underutilized assets (Helfat & Peteraf, 2003; Helfat & Raubitschek, 2000). As a consequence of these scope changes, the firm's strategic focus may shift through time, dynamically changing as new opportunities arise. Resource reconfiguration is therefore a perpetual process.

In the resource-based view, the firm's strategic focus dictates the optimal use of the firm's resources. Assets that best fit with the firm's core competencies, and thus reinforce and enhance the firm's focus, are reconfigured within the firm toward this purpose. The less that resources, such as business units, align with the parent firm's focus, the fewer opportunities there will be for value creation with that resource inside the firm. The resource therefore has more potential for value generation outside of the firm, making it a candidate for between-firm reconfiguration (Berry, 2010; Kaul, 2012). This potential for value generation across firm boundaries – for the potential worth of between-firm, external reconfigurability – merits highlighting. Too often, unretained resources are assumed to be impaired, poorly performing resources. Examples that run counter to this blanket assumption abound. Consider GE's recent decision to divest its high-performing GE Capital unit. GE Capital's strong performance was not in question; rather, its misalignment with GE's new industrial focus was the stimulus behind GE's external reconfiguration decision.

The determination of which assets should be reconfigured internally versus externally, however, is not necessarily a one-dimensional one. Resources – particularly when those resources are business units – may be imagined as jockeying between each other in the race for deciding which should stay and which should go. Certainly, the extent of the resource's strategic fit (or lack of fit) with the firm's core competencies is a primary factor that contributes to between-firm resource reconfigurability. But it is not the only one. Two resources may have equivalent strategic fit, but there is need internally for only one of them. Other factors that lead to a resource's external reconfigurability then come into play.

These factors include any features of the resource that make it easily separable from its parent firm, as well as any attributes that help make the resource transferable to the acquiring firm. Regarding the former, the origin of the resource in the firm is a major driver of separability. Business units originating from acquisition do not "take root" as firmly as those that were home-grown by the firm, facilitating their separability (Chang & Singh, 1999). Thus, there is a connection between the origins of the firm's assets and how these assets are subsequently reconfigured: all else being equal, resources obtained through acquisition are stronger candidates for reconfiguration across firm boundaries than their internally developed siblings. As for the latter factor, transferability, it is shaped extensively by the organizational structure of the parent. Resources that are unintegrated (or less integrated) into the firm are less likely to be used in an intertwined fashion throughout the firm. Such unintegrated business units would function quite independently, and the rest of the firm would not depend on the unit for the successful execution of its other operations. Less integration thus sets the stage for a smooth transfer to the acquirer, making unintegrated units particularly appealing candidates for between-firm reconfiguration.

Each of these factors – separability, transferability, and especially the fit (or misfit) of the resource with the firm's strategic focus – contributes to the external reconfigurability of the resource. The resource-based view is well-suited for identifying and evaluating the impact of these characteristics. Yet, this discussion of the firm and its resources has been necessarily inwardly focused. In the next section, we turn to the external environment of the firm, and consider what aspects of the market for corporate control fuel firms' engagement with the act of reconfiguration itself.

Reconfiguration across Firm Boundaries and the View of the Market for Corporate Control

In the market for corporate control, potential acquirers hungrily scan the industry landscape in search of vulnerable targets. Poor performance of business unit resources (and by extension, the parent firm) is a first visible signal to would-be acquirers that conditions may be ripe for a takeover (Jensen & Ruback, 1983; Manne, 1965). The market for corporate control is an acquirer's game, with the bold, hostile acquisitions of the aggressors starkly juxtaposed by the defensive, forced-hand divestitures of the targets.

One powerful aspect of this perspective is it underscores how the impetus for firm reconfiguration across firm boundaries may stem from external sources. In so doing, scholarly attention is typically directed toward acquisition (rather than toward the divestiture side of the transaction). This perspective also illustrates how firms that are unable or unwilling to take advantage of the external reconfigurability of their assets will find themselves being scrutinized by firms who do recognize the potential for external reconfiguration. In this view, resource reconfiguration across firm boundaries typically manifests as being a reactive move performed in response to these external pressures.

Market Characteristics that Shape the Environment for Resource Reconfiguration across Firm Boundaries

The market for corporate control encourages deep consideration of the numerous contextual factors that catalyze external resource reconfiguration.

The presence of a robust secondary market for assets is one such contextual element needed for external resource reconfiguration to occur. At a minimum, development of such a secondary market requires three things: assets for sale, potential acquirers for those assets, and sufficient capital to complete the transactions. Institutionalization of these mechanisms shapes and enriches this market. Moreover, globalization, with its ease of engaging in and managing cross-border transactions, further expands the secondary market.

The market for corporate control also illuminates the important role of motivated, savvy potential acquirers. These acquirers expand the market by identifying resources for acquisition that might not have otherwise been put on the market by the selling firm. The activist investors described in this paper's introduction are often part of this pool, and, along with other potential acquirers like traditional corporate firms, participate in the bidding process for the assets (or business units) that are in play. The competition among bidders not only ensures a vibrant market, but offers insight into how different firms are valuing the resources undergoing reconfiguration. Thus, the market for corporate control is also a mechanism for asset valuation.

There are several factors that contribute to the external valuation of a resource and, likewise, the types of resources might pique the interest of potential acquirers. For one, potential acquirers are often searching for poorly performing, or undervalued, parent firms. In this case, value may be unlocked if some of the firm's resources are reconfigured externally. This is the situation that IBM is currently facing, wherein some investors are advocating that external reconfiguration of some of IBM's assets will revitalize the firm. For another, acquirers may be intrigued with business units that are strongly outperforming their parents. The market's persistent calls for Barnes & Noble to spin-off its Nook unit is a recent example of this situation. Interestingly, such investor interest is not lost on firms – and firms may consequently use it to their advantage as a defensive mechanism. In this case, the parent firm may deliberately divest a well-performing business unit in order to make itself a less attractive candidate for takeover, or less of a target for activist interest. This is nicely illustrated by Darden Restaurants' controversial sale of Red Lobster.

The market for corporate control additionally underscores how other external stakeholders influence the environment for resource reconfiguration across firm boundaries. Regulatory agencies, such as the Federal Trade Commission and the Department of Justice, are a primary stakeholder (Montgomery et al., 1984). Stringent regulators' concerns about preserving industry competition post-merger or post-acquisition will require the divestiture of assets as a condition of merger approval. As a consequence, this forces business units into the market – and these business units would likely never have been voluntarily placed there. One example of this phenomenon is the mandated divestiture of Advantage Rent-A-Car by Hertz upon its acquisition of Dollar Thrifty. Another is found in the merger between two supermarket chains, Albertsons and Safeway, wherein the two firms sold a combined 146 stores to competitor Haggen in order to secure Federal Trade Commission approval of the transaction. Thus, the market for corporate control reveals that not only acquirers, but also other stakeholders, impact between-firm resource reconfiguration.

Market-Driven Motives for Reconfiguration across Firm Boundaries

Strategy scholars have typically taken a neutral stance toward the market for corporate control. Neither the characteristics described above, nor the underpinning market motives for reconfiguration, have been their focus. Yet, these market motives matter – and their examination can help unlock several key insights about resource reconfiguration between firms.

Some scholars have used an agency perspective to decipher the drivers of resource reconfiguration across firm boundaries (Jensen & Ruback, 1983). In this interpretation, the market plays a disciplining role to ensure that optimal value is extracted from the firm's resources. The rise of activist investors described earlier is a real-time manifestation of the drive to correct agency problems that are seen as being present in firms. The M&A activity that results from their campaigns, viewed from an agency lens, illustrates their collective efforts to solve the agency problem.

Another perspective sees the market as a clearinghouse that ensures optimal asset ownership (Castanias & Helfat, 1992; Manne, 1965). Potential acquirers will only bid for the assets for which they have the confidence that they can derive value. The highest bid reflects the highest amount of acquirer confidence – and the asset in play is matched with the most effective owner accordingly.[4] This interpretation of the market for corporate control is especially relevant toward explaining the robust growth of the private equity industry. A private equity firm that bids on a business does so since its executives believe that they can improve the operations of the firm better than others. Moreover, this "best owner wins" perspective helps to explain the structure of assets being bought and sold. Private equity firms are very deliberate in their analyses of potential targets and assessments of the operational efficiencies they can glean. Private equity firms are thus selective – and accordingly bid only on the parts of the businesses for which they feel they are best suited to own. Intermediaries and advisors can help to identify these partial assets, as well as help create the conditions for a fast sale. Thus, optimal value extraction can drive pieces and parts of businesses out into the private market that might not have reached the open one.

Overall, in the realm of resource reconfiguration across firm boundaries, how much of the activity is driven by correcting agency problems versus using the market to find a better owner for the assets of the firm is still an open question. But, nevertheless, these perspectives reveal ramifications for between-firm resource reconfiguration that might otherwise be overlooked if the market for corporate control is not considered by scholars.

Resource Reconfiguration across Firm Boundaries and the Capabilities-Based View

When examining resource reconfiguration, a fundamental consideration is whether and how firms may learn to reconfigure resources across firm boundaries. The capabilities-based view of the firm (Grant, 1996; Helfat et al., 2007; Helfat & Peteraf, 2003; Teece, Pisano, & Shuen, 1997; Winter, 2003) is an ideal springboard from which to explore the potential for the development of firm-level external reconfiguration capability. In so doing, this perspective recognizes the linkage between the firm and the market for assets, and thus bridges the internal resource and external market views of reconfiguration.

Firms are faced with a relentless stream of activities that are required for present and future success; capability development is catalyzed by firms needing to manage these activities successfully. Many of these activities are predictable and practiced; they collectively form the familiar beat of the firm's operating rhythms. Others are occasional but influential; they profoundly change the tempo and tone of the firm's functions and processes. The higher the firm's ability to perform these value-creating activities – hence, the greater its capabilities – the better it is positioned to achieve sustained competitive advantage (Amit & Schoemaker, 1993; Barney, 1991; Helfat et al., 2007; Nelson & Winter, 1982; Peteraf, 1993; Winter, 1995). While some organizational capabilities concern the current operations of the firm, and are therefore directed toward ensuring the firm's prosperity in the predictable present (Winter, 2003), others concern the firm's capacity to "purposefully create, extend, or modify its resource base" in order to successfully navigate changes it may face across time (Helfat et al., 2007). One class of organizational capabilities that fall into the latter category are scope expansion capabilities, as they are actuated with deliberate intent to increase the range and depth of resources and capabilities to which the firm has access (Zollo & Winter, 2002).

The capabilities-based view helps to unpack the specifics of what it means for firms to learn to reconfigure their assets in an externally oriented way, and why this learning is valuable. In this regard, the capabilities perspective offers a rich precedent in the context of scope expansion. It has been clearly demonstrated that firms can hone acquisition and alliance capabilities (both of which may be classified as scope expansion capabilities), and that these capabilities have value to the firms possessing them (Anand & Khanna, 2000; Kale & Singh, 2007; Nadolska & Barkema, 2007; Sarkar, Aulakh, & Madhok, 2009; Zollo & Singh, 2004). The idea that firms could similarly foster divestiture capabilities is an intuitive extension to their development of scope expansion capabilities.

So, just what would firms be learning to do when building external reconfiguration capabilities? What parts of the between-firm reconfiguration process offer the greatest learning – and performance differentiating – opportunities? For one, firms would be learning what attributes make assets reconfigurable across its boundaries. For another, firms would be learning to navigate the between-firm resource reconfiguration process. In this regard, the potential for divestiture capabilities becomes paramount. A firm's capability to separate from and transfer its resources to the chosen acquirer is as important as the acquisition capability that originally brought the resources to the firm (Chang & Singh, 1999). Thus, external reconfiguration capabilities not only encompass activities that the firm performs within its own boundaries, but also how the firm interfaces with the market environment beyond them. These issues will be further explored in the sections that follow.

Research Questions Motivated by the Three Views of Resource Reconfiguration

The three perspectives of resource reconfiguration described above are summarized in Table 2 across several dimensions. Taken together, the resource, market, and capabilities views surface several intriguing research questions concerning resource reconfiguration across firm boundaries.

Table 2. Three Perspectives of Between-Firm Resource Reconfiguration.

Dimension	Resource-Based View	Market for Corporate Control	Capabilities-Based View
Unit of analysis	Firm	Industry/Market	Firm
Element of interest	Resource	Firm	Reconfiguration capability
Orientation	Internal	External/Market	Knowledge/experience
Major drivers of external resource reconfiguration	Proactive: ○ Scope economies ○ Scale ○ Market access	Reactive: ○ Valuation ○ Competition among bidders	Proactive: ○ Firm learning ○ Codified knowledge
Major barriers to external resource reconfiguration	Interdependencies between resources	• Asset tradability • Demand	Transactional competencies
Notable area of research impact	External reconfigurability as a resource characteristic	External context of resource reconfiguration	Firm-level external resource reconfiguration capability

These include:

(1) What constitutes external resource reconfiguration capabilities, and how do they evolve?
(2) How can firms harness the opportunities in the secondary market for assets to achieve performance advantage?
(3) What theoretical lenses are best suited to advance the study of between-firm resource reconfiguration?

We take first steps toward answering these questions in the discussion that follows.

DISCUSSION

In this section, we start the exploration of the unanswered research questions posed above, and use them as a platform to propose a research agenda for between-firm resource reconfiguration. There are three research areas that together form the foundation of our proposed agenda: external resource reconfiguration capability, private equity as an alternative mode of external reconfiguration, and the use of the transactional lens as a means to study resource reconfiguration across firm boundaries.

Exploring Research Question 1: Firm-Level External Resource Reconfiguration Capability

Scope expansion and scope reduction are integral parts of the between-firm resource reconfiguration process. For firms to excel at this process, firms need to excel at both acquisition and divestiture. Thus, acquisition capabilities and divestiture capabilities are equally important pillars of performance success – so much so that the combination of the two underpins the firm's "external resource reconfiguration capability."[5]

Scope expansion has traditionally captured the attention of scholars and managers, with the development of acquisition capabilities as a means to achieve performance advantage being of particular interest (Haleblian & Finkelstein, 1999; Haspeslagh & Jemison, 1991; Hayward, 2002; Puranam, Singh, & Chaudhuri, 2009; Zollo & Singh, 2004). Scope reduction and the primary avenue by which to achieve it, divestiture, have been understudied in comparison. This is despite divestiture's fundamental role in corporate development and its higher returns relative to those from acquisition. Extant research on divestiture has largely focused on the divestiture decision itself, with particular emphasis on the reasons underpinning the divestiture and target selection (Berry, 2010; Capron et al., 1998, 2001; Duhaime & Grant, 1984; Feldman, 2014; Montgomery & Thomas, 1988; Ravenscraft & Scherer, 1991). Rigorous understanding of the divestiture process remains incomplete, with only a handful of efforts making gains toward penetrating this black box (Bergh, Johnson, & Dewitt, 2008; Bergh & Lim, 2008; Gopinath & Becker, 2000; Moschieri, 2011; Nees, 1981; Semadeni & Cannella, 2011). Yet, divestiture holds the potential for being as valuable a source of firm capability and performance heterogeneity as is acquisition capability. Indeed, without divestiture capability, even a firm with best-in-class acquisition capability will see its performance advantage dissipate – a successful externally oriented reconfiguration strategy requires firms to be adept at both.

However, although acquisition and divestiture are often thought of as two sides of the same coin, they are also fundamentally different from each other. When building acquisition capabilities, firms are learning how to grow; when building divestiture capabilities, firms are learning how to shrink. This raises the intriguing issue of how firms are able to develop and hone these complementary, yet potentially contradictory, capabilities. Indeed, developing capabilities that are oppositional in their objectives is one challenge; utilizing them is wholly another.

External Resource Reconfiguration Capability Development and Use

Regarding the first challenge of capability development, there are several factors that suggest that firms may resolve the possible tug-of-war between acquisition and divestiture capability building by deferring to scope expansion at the expense of scope reduction – and thus firms may "learn to grow" but not transfer their capability toward learning "how to shrink." Foremost, growth typically precedes scope reduction in a firm's evolution. Scope expansion capabilities begin to take root before even the need for divestiture surfaces. Positive growth outcomes reinforce the firm's proclivity to continue the activity – and hone the corresponding capability (Haleblian, Kim, & Rajagoplan, 2006; Levinthal & March, 1993; Levitt & March, 1988). Firms' increasing commitments to widening and deepening their repertoire of scope expansion capabilities would be a natural next step. Since scope reduction capability has some fundamental differences from scope expansion capability, it would take deliberate, taxing effort to foster divestiture capability in the face of entrenched scope expansion capabilities. Firms have limited resources, and thus must make tradeoffs in their capability development choices (Porter, 1996; Winter, 2003). As firms continue to invest in the direction of expansion, deviation from learning along the growth-oriented trajectory will become less likely – for better or worse (Dyer, Kale, & Singh, 2004).

Yet, in spite of their differences, the processes of scope expansion and reduction do have commonalities as well. These shared features could serve as a platform for learning transfer across the two activities for their comparable components, and therefore help to accelerate divestiture capability development. Indeed, extant research has shown that firms may learn to transfer their experience in one mode of corporate development activity to benefit their performance in another – such as from alliances to acquisitions (Bingham, Heimeriks, Schijven, & Gates, 2015; Nadolska & Barkema, 2007; Zaheer, Hernandez, & Banerjee, 2010; Zollo & Reuer, 2010). To what extent firms may be able to similarly leverage their acquisition capabilities to benefit their divestiture capability development is an intriguing question. The overlapping components between the two processes are largely found in the transactional portion – the mechanics of designing and executing the transaction itself. The dynamics of deal making includes a range of activities, such as the identification of the combination, price negotiation, and defending the deal to the investment community. Similarities become weaker (to the point of possible conflict) the further away the activities are from the locus of deal making. For example, the integration of a business unit after acquisition is quite different from disentangling operations between a parent and a unit upon divestiture. Indeed, while a deep integration of a particular unit may have been the optimal organizational design choice for ongoing operations, divestiture of such embedded units can significantly impair the parent's performance (Feldman, 2014). Should firms try to apply learning between activities that are more different than similar, such transfer would be subject to potential pitfalls of inappropriate generalization or faulty analogy across the transaction types (Gavetti, Levinthal, & Rivkin, 2005; Haleblian & Finkelstein, 1999; Nadolska & Barkema, 2007).

As for how to address the second challenge of capability utilization between acquisition and divestiture, possible approaches may be gleaned from other parts of the firm's operations, where tensions akin to the expansion-reduction relationship are being managed. To wit, in the firm's capability portfolio, conflicts may arise through firms' pursuit of both explorative and exploitative activities (March, 1991). In this arena, one way firms have been observed to manage the balance between conflicting activities is through a "punctuated equilibrium" approach (Burgelman, 2002). Here, the firm continuously cycles between activities, engaging in one after a period of engaging in the other. Other approaches encourage the firm to treat the activities orthogonally, and thus encourage simultaneous execution (Gibson & Birkinshaw, 2004; O'Reilly & Tushman, 2008). For example, a structural approach to building such ambidexterity may be taken, wherein different groups or areas within the firm would each focus on one of the activities (Benner & Tushman, 2003). Another avenue is for firms to leverage the capabilities of process intermediaries, rather than build the capability of focus themselves. Thus, firms may opt to focus on building their own acquisition capabilities, or dedicate attention to building capabilities for only certain parts of the acquisition and divestiture processes, and "rent" the remaining capabilities from external parties. In the case of the divestiture process, for example, investment bankers could be a good source for transaction execution capability, while consultants could be well positioned to address the unwinding of the unit from the parent, both operationally and organizationally.

The possibility of renting capabilities from intermediaries surfaces the question of where external resource reconfiguration capabilities are accumulated in the firm. Clearly, if they are rented, then the capabilities are developed by another party outside of the firm's walls. Yet, even in the case where the firm is building its own external resource reconfiguration capabilities, it is not immediately clear that all parts of each capability will be accumulated in the same place. To illustrate, consider the execution of the mechanics of the deal process. As transactions are often managed from corporate headquarters, members of the top management team or a business development group are best positioned to be accumulating the deal making experience and honing capabilities for it (Nadolska & Barkema, 2014). Yet, the top management team is unlikely to be deeply involved in integrating (in acquisition) or unwinding (in divestiture) business units and the parent. Functional managers, such as those in IT or HR, and operating managers in the business units, however, are necessarily involved in these activities, and are accumulating the requisite experience accordingly. Clearly, identifying where external resource reconfiguration capabilities are developed in the firm is a multifaceted issue, and it merits additional research.

In summary, building and leveraging acquisition and divestiture capabilities are not easy tasks. Yet, these dual capabilities are inveterate parts of resource reconfiguration across firm boundaries, and firms that can develop and deploy them are well positioned to realize performance advantage. As will be discussed in the next section, there are several market institutions that can facilitate this process for firms, and one organizational form in particular – private equity firms – has learned to reap the benefits.

Exploring Research Question 2: External Reconfiguration Choices and the Role of the Market

In addition to the readiness of the firm's own capabilities, the success of an external reconfiguration strategy also depends on the firm's operating environment. Firms have choice among several modes of reconfiguration; different modes expose the firm to different aspects of its external environment. When resources are transferred across firm boundaries, they may be sold to a conventional firm (a firm-to-firm divestiture), spun-off into the market, or sold to a private equity firm. (These modes are similarly available should the focal firm be a private equity firm.) As different as each of these modes are, there are likewise differences in their ramifications for the external environment. Institutionalization of certain conditions in the marketplace can go far toward ensuring the ongoing viability of an externally oriented resource reconfiguration strategy. Three conditions are notably critical environmental factors. First, there needs to be availability of assets for sale. Second, there needs to be availability of acquirers for those assets. Third, there needs to be availability of capital (so that the acquisitions may be completed). External reconfiguration via the avenue of private equity propels the firm into a highly institutionalized marketplace that has been fine-tuned for facilitating resource reconfiguration across firm boundaries.

Institutionalizing the Market for Assets: Private Equity

The continuing rise of private equity firms as a formidable player across the corporate landscape is a direct result of the co-occurrence of capabilities and market institutions needed for resource reconfiguration across firm boundaries. Indeed, with $1.2 trillion in freshly committed capital and $456 billion in total exit value in 2014 globally, private equity's success in harnessing market institutions to realize their reconfiguration strategies demands close examination (MacArthur, 2015).

To date, consideration of private equity firms has been sparse in the strategic management literature (Montgomery & Baker, 1994), and has predominantly addressed the leveraged buyout aspect of the sector (Palepu, 1990; Wright, Hoskisson, Busenitz, & Dial, 2000). However, measured comparison between private equity and the conventional "strategic corporate" firms, especially when animated by the transactional view, can provide a valuable platform from which to identify factors that promote (or impair) external resource reconfiguration and firm performance. That private equity firms represent extremes of both strategy and structure – while still engaging in similar transactions as corporate firms (if not identical ones, as private equity and corporate firms are often found bidding against each other) – serves only to enrich such comparisons.

For example, in contrast to the "buy to hold" approach of strategic corporate firms, private equity firms are uniquely centered on the premise that they "buy to sell" their portfolio companies, usually within a five- to eight-year timeframe (Barber & Goold, 2007). This relatively short, fixed time horizon has interesting implications for how private equity firms manage their acquired units. For example, in contrast to the annual operating review rhythms (interspersed with perhaps quarterly sessions) found in strategic corporate firms, private equity firms review their units on a near-constant basis and are thus able to react quickly at the first sign of a performance problem (Beroutsos, Freeman, & Kehoe, 2007). Frequent reviews are facilitated by use of exceptionally clear and consistent operational goals and performance metrics, in spite of the diversity of the private equity firm's holdings. Since the private equity executive who oversaw or was involved in the due diligence of the unit's acquisition is most likely the executive who then oversees the overhaul and management of the unit, the performance indicators and targets used are very tightly connected to the value creation plan for the unit. In strategic corporate firms, "baton passing" is instead the norm, with the executive involved in the acquisition transaction seldom responsible for the management of the unit.

Moreover, private equity firm success is predicated solely upon the successful divestiture (or "exit") of their portfolio companies in the short term (Rogers, Holland, & Haas, 2002). While this requirement forestalls the use of structural integration (and thus the benefits of any corresponding capabilities), it does instead encourage a synthesized view of transactions. Private equity firms treat acquisition and divestiture as being the two halves of a single transaction; they do not acquire without having a sharp line of sight into the unit's divestiture end-game. In contrast, strategic corporate firms, by treating acquisition and divesture as separate transactions, see two distinct opportunities (or hurdles) for capability-building – and set the stage for possible tensions in their development. Private equity firms, in adopting the "one transaction" perspective, look to build a very different type of firm-level capability – one which optimizes the execution of the firm's scope changes (including both scope expansion and reduction) in a holistic, end-to-end manner. Consideration of firms' acquisition and divestiture transactions in tandem serves to underscore the differences between these two approaches to external reconfiguration.

Furthermore, this distinction underscores how private equity firms evaluate their asset purchases and also identify potential buyers. When making a purchase, the private equity firm most values the external resource reconfigurability of the business unit, as it is a prerequisite for performance – the private equity firm makes the majority of its money only upon the "exit," or divestiture, of the unit. Since the business unit will become one of numerous unintegrated portfolio companies, achieving new synergies or realizing within-firm resource reconfiguration opportunities in the private equity firm is not an objective. Of course, in looking ahead to the eventual sale of the unit, the private equity firm does need to consider how potential buyers would value the unit. The external resource reconfigurability of the unit would again be a priority should the eventual buyer be another private equity firm, whereas a strategic corporate firm would more heavily stress any synergies or internal reconfiguration opportunities that the unit could catalyze within the firm. This distinction highlights how these two types of organizations value an asset's external reconfigurability differently.

Strategic corporate firms and private equity firms reflect two ends of an organizational spectrum. But firms may choose to operate in a position along that spectrum, leveraging different aspects from each approach. Conglomerates like Johnson & Johnson, GE, and Beatrice are cases in point (Baker, 1992; Karim & Mitchell, 2000). Certainly, some concepts may be harder to borrow than others. Firms that aim to reap synergies (and build capabilities to do so) may be hard pressed to adopt a shorter-term "buy to sell" approach. Not only are internal systems (such as human resource and rewards systems) and employee expectations set in place for a longer term view, but the acquisition-finding process is likely designed to find longer term plays. Additionally, external factors, such as the tax implications of a corporate firm selling a business unit, may hamper the implementation of a "buy to sell" approach. But there are pieces that may be more easily borrowed. Setting clear metrics for business units, where the metrics are meaningfully connected to the performance outcomes, is one such avenue. More frequent reviews, "owned" by managers who have a deep understanding of the business operations, is another.

Taken together, these options reflect the absence of a "one size fits all" approach. Different approaches, especially in the area of resource reconfiguration, are appropriate for different firm objectives – and have different implications accordingly. These implications can be negative and controversial. Private equity firms have been accused of short-termism (stemming from their "quick flip" model of reconfiguration) (Kaplan & Strömberg, 2009); strategic corporates have been accused of instigating and exacerbating goal and incentive misalignment between owners and managers (originating from the fundamental issue of how and by whom resources should be controlled and deployed) (Jensen & Meckling, 1976). Thus, as firms consider different models of resource reconfiguration, they must be cognizant of not only the challenges associated with developing new capabilities for the process – especially in the face of having honed existing ones – but also the potential ramifications, positive and negative, of their choices.

Exploring Research Question 3: Resource Reconfiguration Viewed through a Transactional Lens

Although the transactional view of firm scope is not a new lens, it has been underutilized – especially in the arena of resource reconfiguration. The transactional perspective focuses on the boundary-changing moves of a firm – each of which may expand or reduce a firm's scope – and evaluates the benefits and costs of these scope changes correspondingly. In so doing, this lens encourages consideration of the "how" underpinning these boundary changes – how firms execute these boundary moves, how firms learn to engage in them, how firms manage the tensions and opportunities that arise when dealing with both scope expansion and contraction. As such, crucial aspects of resource reconfiguration across firm boundaries are more readily identifiable and observable with the transactional lens than is possible with alternative views.[6]

A central factor in this perspective of firm scope change is the means by which firms engage in these transactional moves. For expansion, acquisitions are a primary inorganic alternative, but such options as licensing, alliances, joint ventures, and even organic internal development processes may be used by firms to execute their scope widening choices. For scope reduction, divestiture is a typical approach, although shuttering operations is, of course, another option. Applying a transactional lens underscores how the combination of a firm's acquisitions and divestitures shapes the firm's evolution, and suggests the potential for a firm to apply its experience and learning in one activity to the other. Furthermore, by capturing the linkage between seller and buyer, the transactional lens not only surfaces the important role of resource reconfiguration across firm boundaries, but it also underscores how the external reconfigurability of the assets is an essential catalyst in the formation of the seller-buyer link. Thus, here too, the transactional lens emphasizes the dual importance of both acquisition and divestiture in a firm's growth trajectory and sustained performance, and, accordingly, the potential for firm performance advantage in learning how to execute both well in their reconfiguration strategies. The transactional view of firm scope is therefore an especially valuable lens through which to consider the capability component of externally oriented asset reconfiguration.

Such capability-building opportunities must be proactively pursued by the firm and nurtured internally. While the transactional view of firm scope change capably captures this internal dynamic, it further encourages consideration of the firm's external environment and how it may shape the potential for resource reconfiguration across firm boundaries. While such opportunities are typically realized (or lost) from a more reactive position, private equity firms, as described above, have done resoundingly well by taking a proactive stance to shaping the external context. In this regard, the transactional view helps to bridge the internally oriented resource element and the externally oriented market element of between-firm resource reconfiguration.

CONCLUSION

Resource reconfiguration across firm boundaries is a domain that merits further research. There has been a great deal of prior research on acquisitions and growth, along with some on divestiture. By focusing specifically on between-firm resource reconfiguration, we can shed light on three distinct areas. First, firms are proactively and extensively changing their scope – this is clearly reflected in the significant amount of acquisition, sell-off, and spin-off activity that abounds in the global markets. Second, there is the resurgence of activist investors, whose relentless focus on unlocking asset value serves as an impetus for resource reconfiguration across firm boundaries. In this domain, the assumption that divestiture may unlock value is an important one to examine. Third, there is the dramatic growth of the private equity industry. Private equity firms have powerfully helped to institutionalize the market factors that are requirements for a well-functioning and robust environment for resource reconfiguration across firm boundaries.

The resource-based view, the view of the market for corporate control, and the capabilities-based view served as a foundational departure points from which to begin a reconsideration of between-firm resource reconfiguration. The resource-based view highlighted the impact of interdependencies of resources, and how they may be exploited (or avoided) to activate a firm's resource reconfiguration plan. The market for corporate control illuminated the external factors that drive resource reconfiguration across firm boundaries, including the actors that motivate firms to utilize their assets optimally or otherwise return value to shareholders through their divestiture. The capability perspective highlighted how the firm's external resource reconfiguration capability is only as strong as its ability to initiate and navigate the divestiture process. Thus, this triad of perspectives surfaced the critical roles of a resource's external reconfigurability, the factors that combine to create the market for these resources, and firm-level external resource reconfiguration capabilities.

For managers, the implications are substantial. While developing and investing in external resource reconfiguration capability will take deliberate effort, it holds promise as a source of performance heterogeneity. But to do so, managers must turn their attention away from scope expansion to consider divestiture and use the full array of mechanisms to adapt the scope of the firm to market opportunities. Furthermore, there are potentially important lessons that firms may learn from private equity firms, and their approach to external reconfiguration. Foremost is the consideration of business entry and exit, or acquisition and divestiture, as a singular transaction. Moreover, firms can certainly learn to benefit from the institutionalization of the market factors needed for between-firm resource reconfiguration.

The research implications are very promising. Our proposed research agenda is centered on the pillars of external resource reconfiguration capability, the drivers and factors that create the external market for resource reconfiguration, and our advocacy of the use of the transactional lens to examine resource reconfiguration across firm boundaries. These research areas surface a plethora of questions: What are the determinants of external resource reconfiguration capability? How do firms participate in the divestiture market? What should be the balance between a firm's acquisition and divestiture activity? Questions such as these will set the stage for the next phase of external resource reconfiguration research.

NOTES

1. In the extant literature, the term "resource redeployment" has been used to refer to the transfer of firm resources in both the internal (within-firm) and external (between-firm) reconfiguration cases. In keeping with the vernacular of this volume, we will use "external reconfiguration" or "between-firm reconfiguration" to refer to what readers might be familiar with as resource redeployment across firm boundaries.

2. We use the phrase "external reconfigurability" to refer to the resource characteristic that some readers may be familiar with as the "redeployability" of a resource across firm boundaries.

3. In this paper, we do not address how the acquiring firm receiving the divested resource subsequently chooses to leverage the resource (i.e., how Firm 2 integrates and leverages Business Unit C in Fig. 3). While the integration choices of the acquirer are likely good clues as to what made the resource attractive to the acquirer in the first place, the mechanics, tradeoffs, and execution of the post-acquisition integration process form an important literature in their own right (e.g., see Haspeslagh & Jemison, 1991; Puranam et al., 2009). In this paper we are concerned with the earlier reconfiguration of the resources that necessarily predicates their integration after acquisition.

4. Of course, should the acquirer have been overconfident and thus overbid, the winning bidder might not be the firm that could use those resources the most productively, but rather the firm that most overvalued the resources – an example of "the winner's curse" in action.

5. Our focus in this paper is resource reconfiguration capability in the between-firm or "external" reconfiguration context.

6. Note that, despite a similarity in nomenclature, the transactional view of firm scope should not be confused with transaction cost economics. While the transactional view of firm scope is concerned with the boundary-changing moves of the firm, transaction cost economics is concerned with explaining where those boundaries lie.

REFERENCES

Amit, R., & Schoemaker, P. (1993). Strategic assets and organizational rent. *Strategic Management Journal, 14*(1), 33–46.

Anand, B. N., & Khanna, T. (2000). Do firms learn to create value? The case of alliances. *Strategic Management Journal, 21*(3), 295–315.

Anand, J. (2004). Redeployment of corporate resources: A study of acquisition strategies in the US defense industries, 1978–1996. *Managerial and Decision Economics, 25*(6–7), 383–400.

Anand, J., & Singh, H. (1997). Asset redeployment, acquisitions and corporate strategy in declining industries. *Strategic Management Journal, 18*(S1), 99–118.

Baker, G. P. (1992). Beatrice: A study in the creation and destruction of value. *Journal of Finance, 47*(3), 1081–1119.

Barber, F., & Goold, M. (2007). The strategic secret of private equity. *Harvard Business Review, 85*(9), 53–61.

Barney, J. (1991). Firm resources and sustained competitive advantage. *Journal of Management, 17*(1), 99–120.

Benner, M. J., & Tushman, M. L. (2003). Exploitation, exploration, and process management: The productivity dilemma revisited. *Academy of Management Review, 28*(2), 238–256.

Benoit, D. (2015). Activists are on a roll, with more to come. *The Wall Street Journal*, January 1.

Bergh, D. D. (1995). Size and relatedness of units sold: An agency theory and resource-based perspective. *Strategic Management Journal, 16*(3), 221–239.

Bergh, D. D. (1997). Predicting divestiture of unrelated acquisitions: An integrative model of ex ante conditions. *Strategic Management Journal, 18*(9), 715–731.

Bergh, D. D., Johnson, R. A., & Dewitt, R. L. (2008). Restructuring through spin-off or sell-off: Transforming information asymmetries into financial gain. *Strategic Management Journal, 29*(2), 133–148.

Bergh, D. D., & Lim, E. N. K. (2008). Learning how to restructure: Absorptive capacity and improvisational views of restructuring actions and performance. *Strategic Management Journal, 29*(6), 593–616.

Beroutsos, A., Freeman, A., & Kehoe, C. F. (2007). What public companies can learn from private equity. *McKinsey on Finance, 22*(Winter), 1–6.

Berry, H. (2010). Why do firms divest? *Organization Science, 21*(2), 380–396.

Bingham, C. B., Heimeriks, K. H., Schijven, M., & Gates, S. (2015). Concurrent learning: How firms develop multiple dynamic capabilities in parallel. *Strategic Management Journal, 36*(12), 1802–1825.

Boot, A. W. (1992). Why hang on to losers? Divestitures and takeovers. *The Journal of Finance, 47*(4), 1401–1423.

Bryce, D. J., & Winter, S. G. (2009). A general interindustry relatedness index. *Management Science, 55*(9), 1570–1585.

Burgelman, R. A. (2002). Strategy as vector and the inertia of coevolutionary lock-in. *Administrative Science Quarterly, 47*(2), 325–357.

Capron, L., Dussauge, P., & Mitchell, W. (1998). Resource redeployment following horizontal acquisitions in Europe and North America, 1988–1992. *Strategic Management Journal, 19*(7), 631–661.

Capron, L., & Mitchell, W. (1998). Bilateral resource redeployment following horizontal acquisitions: A multi-dimensional study of business reconfiguration. *Industrial and Corporate Change*, *7*(3), 453–484.

Capron, L., Mitchell, W., & Swaminathan, A. (2001). Asset divestiture following horizontal acquisitions: A dynamic view. *Strategic Management Journal*, *22*(9), 817–844.

Castanias, R. P., & Helfat, C. E. (1992). Managerial and windfall rents in the market for corporate control. *Journal of Economic Behavior & Organization*, *18*(2), 153–184.

Chang, S., & Singh, H. (1999). The impact of modes of entry and resource fit on modes of exit by multibusiness firms. *Strategic Management Journal*, *20*(11), 1019–1035.

Chang, S. J. (1996). An evolutionary perspective on diversification and corporate restructuring: Entry, exit, and economic performance during 1981–89. *Strategic Management Journal*, *17*(8), 587–611.

Dranikoff, L., Koller, T., & Schneider, A. (2002). Divestiture: Strategy's missing link. *Harvard Business Review*, *80*(5), 74–85.

Duhaime, I. M., & Grant, J. H. (1984). Factors influencing divestment decision-making: Evidence from a field study. *Strategic Management Journal*, *5*(4), 301–318.

Dyer, J. H., Kale, P., & Singh, H. (2004). When to ally and when to acquire. *Harvard Business Review*, *82*(7–8), 109–115.

Eisenhardt, K. M., & Brown, S. L. (1998). Patching: Restitching business portfolios in dynamic markets. *Harvard Business Review*, *77*(3), 72–82.

Feldman, E. R. (2014). Legacy divestitures: Motives and implications. *Organization Science*, *25*(3), 815–832.

Feldman, E. R. (2015). Corporate spinoffs and analysts' coverage decisions: The implications for diversified firms. *Strategic Management Journal*, *37*(7), 1196–1219.

Gavetti, G., Levinthal, D. A., & Rivkin, J. W. (2005). Strategy making in novel and complex worlds: The power of analogy. *Strategic Management Journal*, *26*(8), 691–712.

Gibson, C., & Birkinshaw, J. (2004). The antecedents, consequences, and mediating role of organizational ambidexterity. *Academy of Management Journal*, *47*(2), 209–226.

Gopinath, C., & Becker, T. (2000). Communication, procedural justice, and employee attitudes: Relationships under conditions of divestiture. *Journal of Management*, *26*(1), 63–83.

Grant, R. M. (1996). Toward a knowledge-based theory of the firm. *Strategic Management Journal*, *17*(S2), 109–122.

Haleblian, J. J., & Finkelstein, S. (1999). The influence of organizational acquisition experience on acquisition performance: A behavioral learning perspective. *Administrative Science Quarterly*, *44*(1), 29–56.

Haleblian, J. J., Kim, J., & Rajagoplan, N. (2006). The influence of acquisition experience and performance on acquisition behavior: Evidence from the US commercial banking industry. *Academy of Management Journal*, *49*(2), 357–370.

Haspeslagh, P. C., & Jemison, D. B. (1991). *Managing acquisitions: Creating value through corporate renewal*. New York, NY: Free Press.

Hayward, M. L. (2002). When do firms learn from their acquisition experience? Evidence from 1990 to 1995. *Strategic Management Journal*, *23*(1), 21–39.

Helfat, C. E., & Eisenhardt, K. M. (2004). Inter-temporal economies of scope, organizational modularity, and the dynamics of diversification. *Strategic Management Journal*, *25*(13), 1217–1232.

Helfat, C. E., Finkelstein, S., Mitchell, W., Peteraf, M., Singh, H., Teece, D., & Winter, S. (2007). *Dynamic capabilities: Understanding strategic change in organizations*. Malden, MA: Blackwell.

Helfat, C. E., & Peteraf, M. A. (2003). The dynamic resource-based view: Capability lifecycles. *Strategic Management Journal*, *24*(10), 997–1010.

Helfat, C. E., & Raubitschek, R. S. (2000). Product sequencing: Co-evolution of knowledge, capabilities and products. *Strategic Management Journal*, *21*(10–11), 961–979.

Hill, C., & Jones, G. (1995). *Strategic management: An integrated approach* (3rd ed.). Boston, MA: Houghton Mifflin Company.

Jensen, M. C., & Meckling, W. H. (1976). Theory of the firm: Managerial behavior, agency costs and ownership structure. *Journal of Financial Economics*, *3*(4), 305–360.

Jensen, M. C., & Ruback, R. S. (1983). The market for corporate control: The scientific evidence. *Journal of Financial Economics*, *11*(1), 5–50.

Kale, P., & Singh, H. (2007). Building firm capabilities through learning: The role of the alliance learning process in alliance capability and firm-level alliance success. *Strategic Management Journal*, *28*(10), 981–1000.

Kaplan, S. N., & Strömberg, P. (2009). Leveraged buyouts and private equity. *Journal of Economic Perspectives*, *23*(1), 121–146.

Karim, S., & Mitchell, W. (2000). Path-dependent and path-breaking change: Reconfiguring business resources following acquisitions in the US medical sector, 1978–1995. *Strategic Management Journal*, *21*(10–11), 1061–1081.

Kaul, A. (2012). Technology and corporate scope: Firm and rival innovation as antecedents of corporate transactions. *Strategic Management Journal*, *33*(4), 347–367.

Kogut, B., & Zander, U. (1992). Knowledge of the firm, combinative capabilities, and the replication of technology. *Organization Science*, *3*(3), 383–397.

Levinthal, D., & March, J. G. (1993). The myopia of learning. *Strategic Management Journal*, *14*(S2), 95–112.

Levinthal, D. A., & Wu, B. (2010). Opportunity costs and non-scale free capabilities: Profit maximization, corporate scope, and profit margins. *Strategic Management Journal*, *31*(7), 780–801.

Levitt, B., & March, J. G. (1988). Organizational learning. *Annual Review of Sociology*, *14*, 319–340.

MacArthur, H. (2015). *Global private equity report 2015*. Boston, MA: Bain & Company Publication.

Manne, H. G. (1965). Mergers and the market for corporate control. *The Journal of Political Economy*, *73*(2), 110–120.

March, J. G. (1991). Exploration and exploitation in organizational learning. *Organization Science*, *2*(1), 71–87.

Markides, C. (1992). Consequences of corporate refocusing: Ex ante evidence. *Academy of Management Journal*, *35*(2), 398–412.

Moliterno, T. P., & Wiersema, M. F. (2007). Firm performance, rent appropriation, and the strategic resource divestment capability. *Strategic Management Journal*, *28*(11), 1065–1087.

Montgomery, C. A., & Baker, G. (1994). *Conglomerates and LBO associations: A comparison of organizational forms*. Working Paper. Harvard Business School, Boston, MA.

Montgomery, C. A., & Thomas, A. R. (1988). Divestment: Motives and gains. *Strategic Management Journal*, *9*(1), 93–97.

Montgomery, C. A., Thomas, A. R., & Kamath, R. (1984). Divestiture, market valuation, and strategy. *Academy of Management Journal, 27*(4), 830–840.

Montgomery, C. A., & Wernerfelt, B. (1988). Diversification, Ricardian rents and Tobin's q. *Rand Journal of Economics, 19*(4), 623–632.

Moschieri, C. (2011). The implementation and structuring of divestitures: The unit's perspective. *Strategic Management Journal, 32*(4), 368–401.

Nadolska, A., & Barkema, H. G. (2007). Learning to internationalize: The pace and success of foreign acquisitions. *Journal of International Business Studies, 38*(7), 1170–1186.

Nadolska, A., & Barkema, H. G. (2014). Good learners: How top management teams affect the success and frequency of acquisitions. *Strategic Management Journal, 35*(10), 1483–1507.

Nees, D. (1981). Increase your divestment effectiveness. *Strategic Management Journal, 2*(2), 119–130.

Nelson, R., & Winter, S. (1982). *An evolutionary theory of economic change*. Cambridge, MA: Harvard University Press.

O'Reilly, C. A., & Tushman, M. L. (2008). Ambidexterity as a dynamic capability: Resolving the innovator's dilemma. *Research in Organizational Behavior, 28*, 185–206.

Palepu, K. G. (1990). Consequences of leveraged buyouts. *Journal of Financial Economics, 27*(1), 247–262.

Penrose, E. T. (1959). *The theory of the growth of the firm*. New York, NY: Wiley.

Peteraf, M. (1993). The cornerstones of competitive advantage: A resource-based view. *Strategic Management Journal, 14*(3), 179–191.

Porter, M. E. (1996). What is strategy? *Harvard Business Review, 74*(6), 61–78.

Puranam, P., Singh, H., & Chaudhuri, S. (2009). Integrating acquired capabilities: When structural integration is (un)necessary. *Organization Science, 20*(2), 313–328.

Ravenscraft, D. J., & Scherer, F. M. (1991). Divisional sell-off: A hazard function analysis. *Managerial and Decision Economics, 12*(6), 429–438.

Rogers, P., Holland, T., & Haas, D. (2002). Value acceleration: Lessons from private-equity masters. *Harvard Business Review, 80*(6), 94–103.

Sakhartov, A. V., & Folta, T. B. (2014). Resource relatedness, redeployability, and firm value. *Strategic Management Journal, 35*(12), 1781–1797.

Sakhartov, A. V., & Folta, T. B. (2015). Getting beyond relatedness as a driver of corporate value. *Strategic Management Journal, 36*(13), 1939–1959.

Sarkar, M. B., Aulakh, P. S., & Madhok, A. (2009). Process capabilities and value generation in alliance portfolios. *Organization Science, 20*(3), 583–600.

Semadeni, M., & Cannella, A. (2011). Examining the performance effects of post spin-off links to parent firms: Should the apron strings be cut? *Strategic Management Journal, 32*(10), 1083–1098.

Sorkin, A. R. (2015). BlackRock's Chief, Laurence Fink, urges other C.E.O.s to stop being so nice to investors. *The New York Times*, April 13.

Teece, D., Pisano, G., & Shuen, A. (1997). Dynamic capabilities and strategic management. *Strategic Management Journal, 18*(7), 509–533.

Wernerfelt, B. (1984). A resource-based view of the firm. *Strategic Management Journal, 5*(2), 171–180.

Winter, S. G. (1995). Four Rs of profitability: Rents, resources, routines, and replication. In C. Montgomery (Ed.), *Resource-based and evolutionary theories of the firm* (pp. 147–158). Boston, MA: Kluwer.

Winter, S. G. (2003). Understanding dynamic capabilities. *Strategic Management Journal*, *24*(10), 991–995.

Wright, M., Hoskisson, R. E., Busenitz, L. W., & Dial, J. (2000). Entrepreneurial growth through privatization: The upside of management buyouts. *Academy of Management Review*, *25*(3), 591–601.

Zaheer, A., Hernandez, E., & Banerjee, S. (2010). Prior alliances with targets and acquisition performance in knowledge-intensive industries. *Organization Science*, *21*(5), 1072–1091.

Zollo, M., & Reuer, J. J. (2010). Experience spillovers across corporate development activities. *Organization Science*, *21*(6), 1195–1212.

Zollo, M., & Singh, H. (2004). Deliberate learning in corporate acquisitions: Post-acquisition strategies and integration capability in US bank mergers. *Strategic Management Journal*, *25*(13), 1233–1256.

Zollo, M., & Winter, S. G. (2002). Deliberate learning and the evolution of dynamic capabilities. *Organization Science*, *13*(3), 339–351.

Zuckerman, E. W. (2000). Focusing the corporate product: Securities analysts and de-diversification. *Administrative Science Quarterly*, *45*(3), 591–619.

THE HARE AND THE FAST TORTOISE: DYNAMIC RESOURCE RECONFIGURATION AND THE PURSUIT OF NEW GROWTH OPPORTUNITIES BY YAHOO AND GOOGLE (1995–2007)

Violina P. Rindova, Luis L. Martins and Adrian Yeow

ABSTRACT

Strategic management research has shown growing interest in understanding the dynamic resource reconfiguration processes through which firms grow, evolve, and sustain profitability. The goal of our study is to understand how dynamic resource reconfigurations enable firms to pursue growth opportunities. We use the methods of inductive theory building from case studies to elaborate current theoretical understanding about how firms draw on both internal and external resources in the pursuit of growth. We examine the patterns of resource reconfigurations through which Yahoo and Google powered their early growth strategies in their

Resource Redeployment and Corporate Strategy
Advances in Strategic Management, Volume 35, 253–284

ISSN: 0742-3322/doi:10.1108/S0742-332220160000035009

first 10 years of existence. We analyze a total of 192 new product launches in 43 markets by the two firms to capture how they reconfigured resources dynamically. Our analysis reveals that both firms developed highly dynamic strategies exhibiting both surprising similarities and differences. These similarities and differences provided the basis for our theoretical insights about the development of what we term "dynamic resource platforms," comprising of (a) dynamic resource shifts; (b) targeted resource orchestration; and (c) complementary processes balancing dynamism and capability development. These ideas contribute novel theoretical insights to current strategic management research on dynamic capabilities and on resource reconfiguration and redeployment.

Keywords: Resource reconfiguration; dynamic capabilities; opportunity creation; growth; Yahoo; Google

The need to reconfigure resources in order to pursue new growth opportunities for value creation is widely acknowledged in strategy research (Karim & Mitchell, 2000). Scholars studying corporate diversification (Helfat, 1997; Montgomery & Wernerfelt, 1988; Silverman, 1999), international expansion (Bingham, 2009), and dynamic capabilities (Daneels, 2007; Teece, 2007) have all examined how firms leverage and extend their resource bases to compete in new contexts and environmental situations. Therefore, the question of how firms reconfigure resources to create value, pursue growth, and evolve is a central question in strategic management research.

Within this broad interest in resource reconfiguration processes, a subset of scholars has focused on the challenges associated with dynamic resource reconfigurations in rapidly changing environments (Helfat & Eisenhardt, 2004) that have been variously characterized as "dynamic" (Teece, Pisano, & Shuen, 1997), "hypercompetitive" (D'Aveni, 1995), and "high-velocity" (Bingham & Eisenhardt, 2008; Eisenhardt & Martin, 2000). In such environments "consumer needs, technological opportunities, and competitor activity are constantly in a state of flux" (Teece, 2007, p. 1322). As a result, opportunities are fleeting and uncertain, requiring firms to extend, build, and redeploy resources and capabilities at a rapid clip. The construct of dynamic capability (Teece, 2007, 2012; Teece et al., 1997) has been advanced to explain the mechanisms that enable firms to reconfigure resources and capabilities rapidly. Teece (2007) elaborates the construct by discussing a variety of firm-level processes that can be used for sensing and seizing opportunities, and reconfiguring resources, thereby outlining the micro-foundations of dynamic capabilities. The distinction between sensing and seizing is particularly important, as each is seen as resting on different activities for "identification, development, co-development, and assessment of technological opportunities in relationship to customer needs (sensing)" versus "mobilization of resources to address needs and opportunities, and to capture value from doing so (seizing)" (Teece, 2014, p. 332). Reconfiguration is viewed as "the third leg of the dynamic capabilities triad [that] involves sustaining growth and profitability, by enhancing, combining and reconfiguring the firm's organizational assets" (Helfat & Peteraf, 2015, p. 842).

In this paper we depart from this view and argue that reconfiguration is a core process for making varying resource commitments along all stages of opportunity pursuit: sensing, seizing, as well as sustaining market presence when markets are deemed significant. Further, we adopt Karim and Capron's (2015) tripartite distinction between internal, external, and hybrid modes of reconfiguration, which they explain as follows: "Internal modes of reconfiguration include internal resource sourcing, redeployment and recombination. External modes include acquisitions and divestitures, while alliances, spin outs and corporate venturing are hybrid modes" (p. 4). We adopt the term "internal deployment" for all three internal modes of reconfiguration they identify because deployment of internal resources in general, is seen as a constraint on "the development of truly innovative resources" (Capron & Mitchell, 2009, p. 296). Thus, although internal reconfigurations can involve either sharing and recombining, or redeployment, with the latter emphasizing that resources are withdrawn from one use and reallocated to another and the former emphasizing resource sharing and/or changing how they are combined with others, all internal reconfigurations involve processes of delinking internal resources from their current deployment and relinking them in new combinations (Daneels, 2007). As a result, they are seen as more constraining than external resources, which are seen as "mechanisms for change, reconfiguration, recombination, and potential innovation" (Karim & Mitchell, 2000, p. 1074).

We analyze how internal, external, and hybrid reconfigurations are combined in the different stages of opportunity pursuit in order to understand how firms balance dynamism and capability development in their pursuit of opportunities. In addressing this question, we take an action-based perspective, which emphasizes that market actions, such as new product launches, are the means through which opportunities are discovered and created (Smith & DiGregorio, 2002; Young, Smith, & Grimm, 1996). Opportunities are sensed through actions that elicit user responses and reveal possible demand (Rindova & Fombrun, 1999), and seized through subsequent actions that refine and broaden the offerings to capitalize on emerging demand. Finally, frequent and ongoing new product introductions are required to sustain presence and gain competitive advantage (Rindova & Kotha, 2001; Young et al., 1996).

The action-based perspective calls for attention to the need for rapid resource reconfigurations in all stages of opportunity pursuit. It emphasizes the links between resource reconfigurations and new product introductions, leading us to focus on the specific reconfigurations underlying those, as well as their patterns at different stages of opportunity pursuit. Thus, we are not concerned with the magnitude of reconfiguration (e.g., levels of investment), but with the patterning of internal, external, and hybrid reconfigurations for opportunity sensing and seizing, and sustaining presence in a market. Our focus is motivated by our efforts to address a key theoretical puzzle about dynamic capabilities regarding how firms balance dynamism and capability development in a manner that ensures both dynamic actions and capable performance.

To address this puzzle, we draw on research on resource sourcing that has shown that internal and external resources enable firms to pursue different strategic objectives, as well as on research that considers how they dynamically affect the scope of firm activities (Villalonga & McGahan, 2005). In considering internal, external, and hybrid resource reconfigurations, we specifically attend to how the relative flexibility of access and commitment to resource ownership associated with these resource reconfigurations supports the three stages of opportunity pursuit. The theoretical ideas guiding this study are illustrated in Fig. 1.

We use the methods of inductive theory building from case studies to elaborate current theoretical understanding about how firms draw on both internal and external resources to enact dynamic growth strategies. We examine the patterns of resource reconfigurations through which Yahoo and Google powered their early growth strategies in their first 10 years of existence. We track the resource reconfiguration approaches that the focal firms used in each new product launch they announced in their first 10 years. We use new product launches to track the actions through which firms pursue new opportunities as new product introductions are key

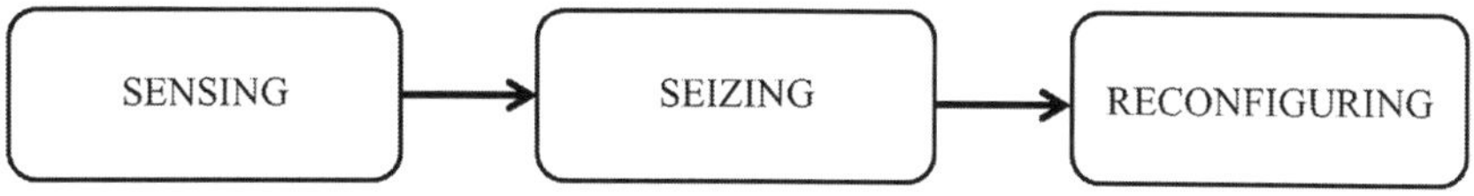

Model of Dynamic Capabilities (Teece, 2007; Helfat & Peteraf, 2015)

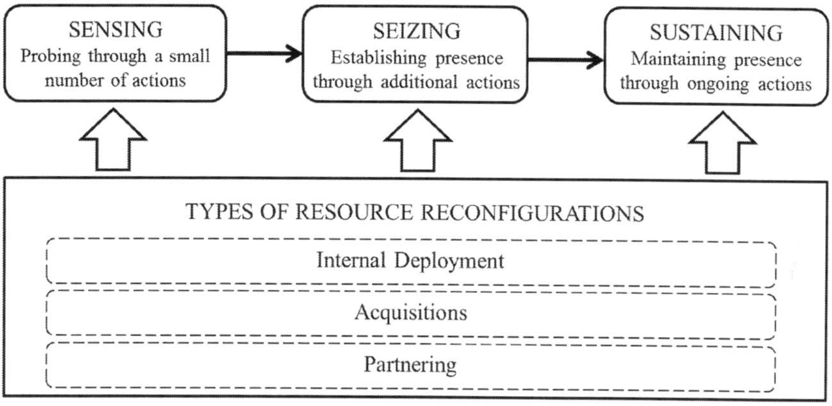

An actions-based model of opportunity pursuit

Fig. 1. Guiding Theoretical Framework.

indicators of opportunity recognition (Shepherd, McMullen, & Jennings, 2007). Further, new product launches both indicate the development of capabilities (Helfat & Raubitschek, 2000) and manifest "firm's abilities to deploy knowledge about technologies and customers that underpin the development of a product" (Lee, 2008, p. 1276). Finally, the design of our study enables us to examine independently (i) the patterns of opportunity pursuit through new product launches in new markets, as well as (ii) large-scale orchestration processes through which firms reconfigure internal and external resources (Teece et al., 1997).

Our analyses revealed that both firms developed highly dynamic strategies, exhibiting both surprising similarities and differences. The observed similarities and differences prompted the reference to the hare and the tortoise in our title – the characters from Aesop's fable that have come to exemplify two fundamentally different approaches to running a race, along with the idea that a fast start does not guarantee a successful end. In the race between Yahoo and Google, like the hare, Yahoo's strategies exhibited very high levels dynamism in both number of opportunities sensed and effective use of partner resources to rapidly sense and seize many of them; like the tortoise, despite sensing opportunities in fewer markets, Google maintained a steadfast approach to growth that relied heavily on internal deployment. Despite its reliance on this less flexible approach to resource reconfiguration, it seized opportunities and sustained presence in the same number of markets as Yahoo did, leading to the reference to "the fast tortoise" in the title.

Collectively, our observations revealed a complex and dynamic picture of how two iconic high-growth firms used different resource reconfiguration approaches to pursue a large number of opportunities at a very rapid pace. We refer to these different resource reconfiguration patterns as "dynamic resource platforms" and theorize them as comprising of (a) dynamic resource shifts; (b) targeted resource orchestration; and (c) complementary processes balancing dynamism and capability development. These ideas extend current understanding of the mechanisms through which firms generate both dynamism and capability in the pursuit of new growth opportunities, thereby contributing to research on dynamic capabilities and entrepreneurial growth.

METHODS

The design of the study followed the methods for inductive theory building from multiple case studies (Eisenhardt, 1989) involving use of diverse data sources to establish case facts, structured and open-ended coding to uncover patterns in the data, and iterative comparative analysis to develop observations and new theoretical insights.

Research Setting

Yahoo and Google were theoretically sampled as extreme revelatory cases (Yin, 1994) of two firms that developed highly dynamic strategies, and came to dominate their core Internet search market at different points in time, while also expanding rapidly in a variety of new markets. As such they provide an opportunity to observe rapid resource reconfiguration to pursue opportunities in multiple markets. In addition, the two firms exhibited a number of similarities in location of business, access to venture capital funding, and founders' human capital, that increased the comparability of the cases on factors that have been shown to affect new firm growth (Eisenhardt & Schoonhoven, 1990). This aspect of the research design enabled us to develop novel theoretical insight about how differences in their resource reconfigurations affected their growth paths.

Yahoo began its existence as an Internet search firm in 1995. In its early years it competed with several other early entrants, including Excite, Lycos, and InfoSeek. This initial cohort of Internet search firms competed intensely with an expanding array of offerings and quickly morphed into Internet portals (Rindova & Kotha, 2001). In spite of the intense competition, Yahoo became the dominant Internet search engine by 1999. During the dot-com bust in 2000, most of its competitors were acquired or went bankrupt. Yahoo survived as the top Internet search firm at the time (Angel, 2002).

Google entered the search market in 1998 as part of a second wave of Internet search entries, including AskJeeves, DirectHit, Goto.com (Overture) and Inktomi. Google entered with its highly responsive and relevant search engine based on a patented search algorithm. Like Yahoo's, Google's Internet search service soon became very popular due to its speed, ease of use, and highly relevant search results. In 2000, Yahoo chose Google as its Internet search service partner. Google expanded its products and services into paid search advertising and other related search services. The relationship between the two shifted from a partnership to direct rivalry as Google emerged as the market leader in search around 2005.

The dynamic relationship and market overlap between Yahoo and Google provided a common context for the study of their growth strategies. To mitigate the effects of the difference in their timing of entry, we focused our comparative analysis on their new product launches in their respective first decade of existence: 1995–2004 for Yahoo, and 1998–2007 for Google. Thus, the study spans the period from 1995 to 2007 overall, during which Yahoo and Google competed in the same set of markets for seven years.

Given the complexity of the two firms' strategies, and our theoretical interest in understanding the role of the various resource reconfiguration approaches in the pursuit of new growth opportunities through new product launches, we focused our data collection and analysis on announcements of two types of actions: (a) new product launches and (b) partnering and acquisitions, as discussed below.

Data Collection

New Product Launches

We used as a primary source of information about the two firm's new product launches, 830 press releases by the two companies. As recommended by Yin (1994), we supplemented these data with additional archival sources including 1,389 media articles (e.g., *Fortune*, *The Economist*, *The Wall Street Journal*), five books, 16 cases, 13 SEC filings, as well the historical websites of industry analyst organizations (e.g., Searchenginewatch.org). We also accessed the companies' historical websites (1995–2007) through the Wayback Machine at http://web.archive.org – a digital archive of the World Wide Web.

Resource Reconfiguration Approaches

We obtained information about the resources deployed in each new product launch from the same set of press releases described above, as well as databases such as SDC Platinum transaction database and Onesource.com. The archival sources described above were also used to triangulate information about the resource reconfiguration approaches of the two firms.

Data Analysis

Data Coding

First, we coded each press release announcing a product launch to identify the resources used in its development, and the market in which it was launched. When the press releases did not provide sufficient information, we used the companies' SEC filings, and other archival data. Further, when the resources used were sourced through a partnership or an acquisition, we triangulated the information with the partnership or acquisition announcement in the SDC Platinum Database and Onesource.com. To identify the market in which a product was launched, we triangulated information from press releases and firm SEC 10-K filings. While there were some changes across time in the names of product markets, using a variety of sources enabled us to compare across sources and reconcile markets that had slight changes to their names. For example, Yahoo announced its entry into the search market with a press release in 1995, and this information was validated by its 1996 SEC 10-K filing, listing search under the "Products and Media Properties." This listing was used from 1996 to 2001, after which the search service was listed as a separate category "Search" between 2002 and 2005. For Google, which went public in 2004, we coded its initial market launches based on press releases, industry publications, and comparisons with Yahoo's listing of market categories. Through these procedures we coded its launches into search, mobile search, advertising, browser tools, and enterprise services markets between 1998 and 2002. Google's subsequent SEC 10-K fillings between 2004 and 2007 specified its markets consistent with our coding, with web search, mobile search, advertising, browser tools, and enterprise services listed under "Products and Services." Using these data sources we coded the product launch, the market in which it was launched, and the sources of resources mentioned as underlying the product offering. Through this process we identified 93 new products resulting in 104 product launches (as some new products were launched in multiple markets) in 29 markets for Yahoo and 88 new products and launches in 14 markets for Google. Table 1 provides examples of our coding for product launches in the search market for Yahoo and Google.

Second, following past research on resource reconfigurations (Karim & Capron, 2015), we coded the resources used as derived from three core categories: internal, acquisitions, and partnering. For example, we coded Yahoo's press release in 1995 regarding its agreement with Reuters to provide co-branded reference and news headlines content as a new product launch in the "Content" market involving the partner-provided "online content" resource. Yahoo's subsequent press release regarding its agreement with Granite Corporation to produce customized portal sites for various regional markets in the United States was coded as another product launch in the content market using the partner-provided "local content" resource. Whenever possible, we coded internal reconfigurations in the three subcategories identified by Karim and Capron (2015), as illustrated in Table 2, but due to limited data and lack of observed relevant differences, we aggregated them into a single "internal deployment" category for the analyses presented here.

Third, we treated the first product launch in a market as opportunity sensing, and the subsequent product launches in the same market as opportunity seizing.[1] Both of these approaches were highlighted by Penrose (1959) as central to the pursuit of growth. Further, we observed that each firm sought to sustain presence in three markets (the number is the same for Yahoo and Google), as evidenced by the introduction of 10 or more products in 10 years. These markets, which accounted for 40% of Yahoo's new product launches and 55% of Google's, provided the basis for analysis of resource reconfigurations for sustaining presence.

Table 1. Examples of Yahoo and Google's Product Launches in the Search Market.

Product Name	Launch	Description	Resources Involved	Reconfiguration Approach
Yahoo				
Yahoo! directory	March 1995	Yahoo developed a search Directory	Employed surfers	Internal deployment
Yahoo! search	March 1995	Yahoo introduced keyword search results	Licensed and incorporated full-text web search technology from Open Text	Partnering
Yahoo! local	October 1996	Yahoo introduced local business listing search, map and driving	Licensed and incorporated map and driving technologies from Vicinity Corporation	Partnering
Yahoo! classifieds	February 1997	Yahoo developed its own classified listing service to expand its directory listing service	Classifieds listing technology with search directory	Internal Deployment
Yahoo! search	June 2000	Yahoo added text search	Licensed search technology from Google	Partnering
Yahoo! sponsor	November 2001	Launched pay-for-performance search results	Yahoo combined Overture's pay-for-performance search results with its directory search results	Partnering
Yahoo! search	April 2003	Yahoo launched its own web text search engine (index)	Integrated the keyword text search engines from acquired companies, including Inktomi, Overture, FAST, and Altavista.	Acquisition
Yahoo! search	April 2003	Yahoo developed search engine technology (multimedia index)	Yahoo developed multimedia search indices to extend its web search engine capabilities	Internal deployment
Yahoo! Assistant for web browser	January 2004	Toolbar browser software	Yahoo acquired 3721 Network Software and integrated its keyword text search engine into its browser toolbar	Acquisition
Yahoo! paid search	March 2004	Yahoo developed a paid inclusion service allowing advertisers to include their businesses in the search index	Advertising system (Paid inclusion); Search engine technology	Internal deployment

Google				
Google web search	September 1999	Google launches its web search	Created the Pagerank algorithm to provide search results, built the search index infrastructure, and web interface	Internal deployment
Google web search	July 2000	Launches wireless search for personal data assistants (PDAs)	Wireless browser technology obtained through a partnership with Neomar	Partnering
Google image search	July 2001	Launches image search	Incorporated publicly available online image content with its web search index and interface.	Internal deployment
Froogle	December 2002	Launches a shopping search tool	Incorporated merchant feeds and merchant web pages into its web search index	Internal deployment
AdSense	March 2003	Launches contextual ad product	Acquired Applied Semantics and integrated its semantic text processing and online advertising technology into its search technology platform Semantic text processing technology	Acquisition
Gmail search	April 2004	Launches web-based email integrated with search and advertising	Developed web-based email integrated with its search engine and contextual advertising platform	Internal deployment
Google desktop search	October 2004	Launches desktop search	Acquired Phatbits' widget technology and integrated it with its desktop search	Acquisition
Google scholar	October 2004	Google includes scholarly articles within its web search index and interface	Licensed access from publishing organizations	Partnering
iGoogle	May 2005	Launches a personalized search interface based on personalized and contextual search	Acquired Outride and Kaltix and integrated their personalized and contextual search technologies with its search platform	Acquisition
Google auto-complete function	March 2008	Improves search offering by linking terms to keyword entered by users	Acquired Orion and integrated its patented search technology into its search service.	Acquisition

Table 2. Examples of Types of Internal Deployment: Redeployment, Recombining, and Sharing.

Product Name	Launch	Description	Resources Involved	Reconfiguration Approach
Yahoo! small business	April 2002	Yahoo Small Business developed using resources from the discontinued Corporate Yahoo! Offering	E-Commerce website, Webmail, Web hosting	Redeployment
Yahoo! shopping	October 2001	Yahoo Shopping for used goods developed by combining technologies from Auctions and Everywhere Shopping	E-commerce website, payment systems, mobile technology	Recombining
Yahoo! my shopping service	July 2000	Yahoo introduced personalized shopping service using its personalization technology from My Yahoo!	Personalization technology	Sharing
Google				
Google desktop application	October 2004	Google Desktop used toolbar widget technology from the discontinued toolbar application	Widget engine technology, desktop search application	Redeployment
Google audio search	October 2004	Google search engine technology was combined with online audio content	Search engine technology, online audio content	Recombining
Google AdSense	April 2005	AdSense contextual advertising shared Google's AdWords advertising platform	Contextual advertising in RSS and domain feeds, advertising network	Sharing

Extracting Patterns and Theory Development

Following the methodological guidance for inductive theory building (Miles & Huberman, 1994; Yin, 1994), we used a variety of analytic techniques for qualitative data analysis to uncover the patterns in the data. We examined the data through multiple comparisons, including within firm analysis (aggregate patterns throughout a firm's 10-year history), between-firm analysis based on both "evolutionary time" (e.g., Year 1, Year 2, first five years of existence) and chronological time (e.g., 1998, 1999, 2000), as well as within- and between-firm patterns across the three stages of opportunity pursuit. We mapped the patterns of opportunity pursuit for the two firms, noting surprising similarities and differences. A subsequent round of comparisons of resource reconfigurations by stage of opportunity pursuit led to the identification of distinct firm-specific patterns of use of reconfiguration approaches. Following Teece et al. (1997), we conceptualized these firm-specific patterns as "resource orchestration processes."

Traveling between existing theory, data, and emerging insights, we articulated novel theoretical ideas about the development of dynamic resource platforms and the balancing of dynamism and capability development through the use of different resource reconfiguration approaches. Consistent with the methods of inductive theory building, we validated our insights by presenting our ideas to colleagues, as well as executives operating in high-velocity environments. These presentations provided questions and feedback that we used to engage in iterative data analysis and theory development.

FINDINGS

How do two highly dynamic firms, Yahoo and Google, pursue new growth opportunities in the first 10 years of their existence? In this section we present our observations about the key patterns in their new product launches and resource reconfigurations around two core findings: (1) Growth paths that reflect interfirm differences in opportunity sensing and modes of opportunity identification (e.g., discovery versus creation) and (2) dynamic resource platforms involving: (a) dynamic shifts in resource stocks; (b) targeted resource orchestration; and (c) complementary processes for balancing dynamism and capability development. Fig. 2 illustrates these ideas, showing the growth paths that firms take as outcomes of the resource reconfiguration approaches strategically organized in dynamic resource platforms.

Growth Paths: Interfirm Differences in Product Launches and Opportunity Pursuit

Yahoo and Google exhibited interesting similarities and differences in their growth paths revealed in the levels of sensing, seizing, and sustaining they engaged in. During their first 10 years of existence, Yahoo made 104 product launches into 29 markets, while Google made 88 product launches into 14 markets. These similarities in high levels of new product launches

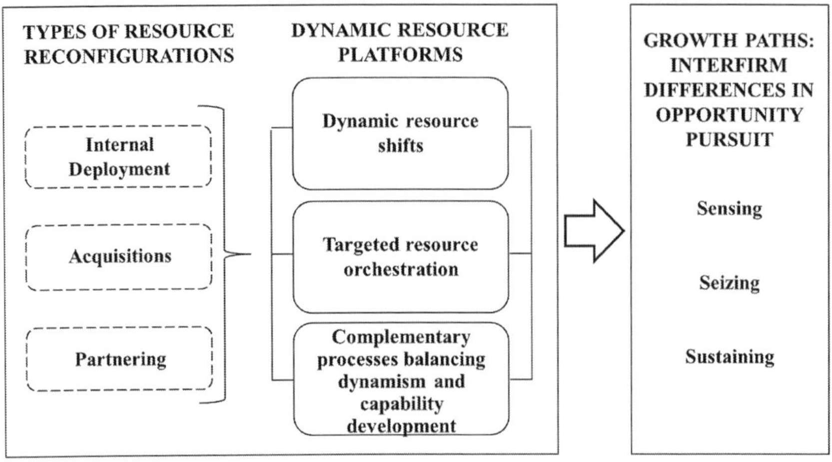

Fig. 2. A Model Linking Dynamic Resource Platforms to Growth Paths.

(10.4 per year for Yahoo and 8.8 per year for Google) are expected within our sampling logic focused on high-growth firms competing in dynamic, rapidly evolving markets.

The interesting similarities between the two firms extend beyond the dynamic quality of their product-market strategies. As Table 3 illustrates, the two firms exhibited notable differences in sensing, but surprising similarities in seizing and sustaining. In terms of sensing, Yahoo launched new products in twice as many markets as Google did, and in four times more markets in the first five years of its existence (20 markets) than Google did in its first five years (five markets). Yet, the two firms seized opportunities in the same number of markets through a similar number of product launches; they also sought to sustain presence in the same number of markets through a similar number of product launches. Overall, a simple look at the two firms' product-market strategies reveals surprising similarity in their patterns of opportunity pursuit, except for the number of opportunities sensed.

We note that since prior research has not distinguished between sensing and seizing in the pursuit of opportunities, it would have overemphasized the differences between the two firms, while overlooking the similarities and their implications for understanding opportunity pursuit. Distinguishing between sensing and seizing led us to observe the surprising similarities

Table 3. Comparing Growth Paths: Product Launches, Stages of Opportunity Pursuit, and Resource Reconfigurations.

	Yahoo	Google
Total number of product launches	104	88
Market opportunities sensed	29	14
Market opportunities seized	11	11
Number of product launches for seizing opportunities	36	29
Markets with sustained presence	3	3
Number of product launches for sustaining market presence	39	45
Number of resource reconfigurations		
– Internal deployment	20 (19%)	26 (30%)
– Acquisitions	17 (16%)	35 (40%)
– Partnering	67 (64%)	27 (31%)

between the two firms, as detailed in Table 3. These observations suggest that sensing, seizing, and sustaining are indeed distinct aspects of opportunity pursuit and that we need to systematically examine how firms commit resources to these different stages, as discussed next.

Sensing and Mode of Opportunity Identification: Discovery versus Creation

Probing into the differences in the levels of sensing between our focal firms we observe a pattern consistent with expectations set by prior research on the effects of different resources on firm growth. Specifically, prior research finds that specialized resources, such as technological resources, limit the scope of growth opportunities for a firm (Silverman, 1999), whereas broad and fungible resources are associated with a larger scope of growth (Daneels, 2007). Yahoo's entry into the search market through a human-centered directory enabled it to develop a strong consumer-focused brand. By 1998, the year when Google entered the search market, Yahoo's brand recognition was at the same level as that of all of the rest of its competitors combined (Nakache, 1998). Their brand is a broad fungible resource that Yahoo used to facilitate the pursuit of opportunities in content provision, ecommerce, and a number of other markets. Google entered the commoditized search market with a proprietary results-ranking algorithm, targeted primarily at the enterprise market (Battelle, 2005). It continued to invest in other specialized technological resources, including index development, that is, building and expanding the core databases that stored Internet web-page data, as well as the index that enabled the search engine to rapidly parse through the database to retrieve relevant information. Yahoo and Google therefore entered the search market with different resources that may have given them different options for future opportunity pursuits.

Examined the resource reconfiguration approaches that the two firms used for opportunity sensing, however, revealed further important differences in their strategies. Underlying Yahoo's broad sensing strategy are not only more general resources, such as its brand, but also a distinct pattern of resource reconfiguration involving a high percentage of product launches based on partnering. This strategy is consistent with a view of sensing opportunities through low-cost probes based on resource- and risk-sharing through partnering (Baum, Calabrese, & Silverman, 2000). Using partnering, which is less resource intensive than other alternatives, as a resource reconfiguration approach for sensing allowed Yahoo to cast a wide net to discover opportunities across a broad range of markets.

In contrast, Google is constrained in sensing not only by its more specialized resources, but also by a strategy for reconfiguring resources that relies heavily on internal deployment – 50% (compared to 17% for Yahoo). Google's strategy differs from Yahoo's in making more intense resource commitments to sensing through internal deployment. Such a strategy is consistent with seeking to shape, rather than adapt to, uncertainty (Courtney, 2001) and to create, rather than discover, opportunities (Alvarez & Barney, 2007). One can argue that its entry in its initial market, the commoditized search space, where in 1998 the early entrants such as Yahoo, Lycos, and Excite, had shifted their attention away from search functionality and toward portal services (Gavetti & Rivkin, 2007; Rindova & Kotha, 2001) had an imprinting effect on Google, showing it how distinctive resources and capabilities, such as its patented search algorithm, superior capability in indexing, and index size, serve to outcompete rivals such as Inktomi. In 2000, Google and Inktomi had a similar number of full-text pages indexed (560M and 500M, respectively). By 2002, Google had 2.1 B pages indexed while Inktomi was no longer in the running. Thus, although Google entered the search market relatively late, it did so through strong capabilities that helped it reshape the basis of competition in the industry. Similarly, in mobile search, Google entered first through internal deployment, when the market was difficult to envision because the devices and network were not at the right stage of development. The leaders in mobile devices – Palm and Handspring – offered personal digital assistant

(PDA) devices that were not connected to the Internet. As Wireless Application Protocol (WAP) came into the picture, mobile phones began to access parts of the Internet, but were limited to websites that had been converted to mobile through a WAP server. As users and companies come to recognize the possibility of using search technologies from mobile phones, Google's WAP search and SMS search became the dominant alternatives.

In each of these cases, along with others in our data, Google used capability development to change the value for consumers in a given market – an existing one – search, or one yet to emerge – mobile search. In both cases, they entered by using internal deployment – internally developed technologies, – which enabled them to reshape the existing search market and to create the market for mobile search. By using internal deployment heavily as a resource reconfiguration approach to sensing, Google places itself in a position to create rather than discover opportunities. Opportunity discovery is associated with the analysis of exogenously arising market imperfections caused by "changes in technology, consumer preferences, or some other attributes of the context within which an industry or market exists" (Kirzner, 1973, p. 10), cited in Alvarez and Barney (2007, p. 13). The emphasis on exogenous shocks as a source of opportunities leads to an emphasis on search based on broad environmental scanning, as observed in the case of Yahoo. In contrast, opportunity creation is understood as an enactment process based on the actions of entrepreneurs exploring ways to produce new products or services (Alvarez & Barney, 2007; Rindova & Fombrun, 2001). Market actions create opportunities both through social construction (Rindova & Fombrun, 1999) and market learning (Dougherty, 1992).

The distinction between opportunity discovery and creation calls for further theoretical elaboration, as current theory does not explain what enables entrepreneurs to operate in these modes. Our analysis of Yahoo's and Google's processes of opportunity pursuit offers some intriguing insights about how the resource reconfigurations they rely on may enable different modes of opportunity pursuit. We note that both Yahoo and Google take actions to "sense" new market opportunities in highly uncertain environments, but Google's actions are based on internally developed technologies and capabilities, enabling it to significantly define and shape the technologies and the consumer benefits they generate (Brown & Eisenhardt, 1997).

This observation suggests that the current view of opportunity creation may be incomplete, as it underplays the possession of capabilities as a means to create unanticipated and significant changes in market demand. Whereas Google certainly learned from the market, by investing in internal capability development it was able to offer fundamentally novel functionalities that led to changes in the market. Thus, its market actions can be seen not only as ways of testing what the market demands, but also as means of reshaping what consumers want and expect. These observations suggest an important link between investing in capability development and opportunity creation.

Seizing and Sustaining through Dynamic Resource Platforms

Dynamic Resource Shifts through External Resource Sourcing

Given that the pattern of opportunity pursuit that we observe does not conform to the expectations about how our focal firms' scope of growth should be constrained by the differences in their core initial resources, we systematically examined how they reconfigured their resources to pursue opportunities (Helfat et al., 2007). Consistent with research on external resource sourcing (Capron & Mitchell, 2009; Karim & Mitchell, 2000, 2004), we found that the focal firms dynamically adjusted the resources they employed in new product development by accessing external resources through acquisitions and partnering. For example, Yahoo's foray into the e-commerce market began by partnering with VISA to develop an online shopping guide, quickly followed by a series of partnerships with e-commerce vendors. It then acquired Viaweb – an online store hosting system – and followed with internal development of e-commerce technologies. In pursuing key early partnerships, such as the one with VISA, Yahoo redeployed many of its surfers into business development roles, giving itself an advantage in the discovery of partnering opportunities.

Google relied on partnering to a lesser extent, but it also sourced external resources to adjust its resource stocks dynamically. In expanding its search index, Google first tapped into publicly available data on the web, such as product data from vendor websites for its Froogle service and news data from web news sources for Google News. In order to incorporate books, scholarly articles, and other licensed content, however, it partnered with content owners through licensing agreements. Overall, both firms undertook a considerable number of acquisitions (17 for Yahoo and 35 for Google), and partnering agreements (67 for Yahoo and 27 for Google), thereby routinely extending the resources they used in new product development beyond their current resource bases. A more fine-grained analysis of their resource reconfigurations for different stages of opportunity pursuit revealed further nuance about how these iconic high-growth firms used resource reconfiguration to pursue opportunities.

Targeted Resource Orchestration

Research on resource sourcing has argued that sourcing appropriately across internal and external options is key to performance (Capron & Mitchell, 2009). Building on this insight, we compared the resource reconfiguration approaches underlying the product launches of our focal firms across the three stages of opportunity pursuit. We found that underlying the striking *similarities* in the pattern of product launches – e.g., both firms sought to sustain presence in three markets, in which each launched more than 10 products, – were equally striking differences in the resource reconfiguration approaches used. Figs. 3(a)–(c) summarize our observations about the resource reconfigurations of the two firms for each stage of opportunity pursuit.

As Figs. 3(a)–(c) illustrate, Yahoo senses opportunities primarily through external resources from partnering (66%), whereas Google does so through significant internal deployment (50%). For seizing, Yahoo's amps up its reliance on partnering to 74%, while reducing internal deployment to 6%. Interestingly, Google's resource reconfigurations for seizing also exhibit an increase in use of external resources with acquisitions being involved in 48% of new product launches (up from 36% for sensing) and partnering involved in 22% (up from 14%). Correspondingly, Google's internal deployment for seizing drops to 30% from 50%. The difference in the pattern of resource configurations between the two firms is notable in their product launches to sustain presence in core markets. Yahoo nearly doubles the percentage of products based on internal deployment (from 17% for sensing to 28% for sustaining), whereas Google halves the percentage of products developed through internal deployment (from 50% for sensing to 24% for sustaining), while nearly tripling the percentage of products developed through partnering (from 14% for sensing to 40% for sustaining).

These observations indicate that each firm *systematically* varied how it combined resource reconfiguration approaches across the three stages of opportunity pursuit. These systematic differences can be conceptualized as targeted resource orchestration. Teece (2007) points to the importance of the orchestration metaphor for understanding how firms combine resources in a changing, yet patterned fashion to compete in dynamic markets. He explains: "The management functions identified are analogous to that of an orchestra conductor, although in the business context the "instruments" (assets) are themselves constantly being created, renovated, and/or replaced. Moreover, completely new instruments appear with some frequency, and old ones need to be abandoned. While flexibility is certainly an

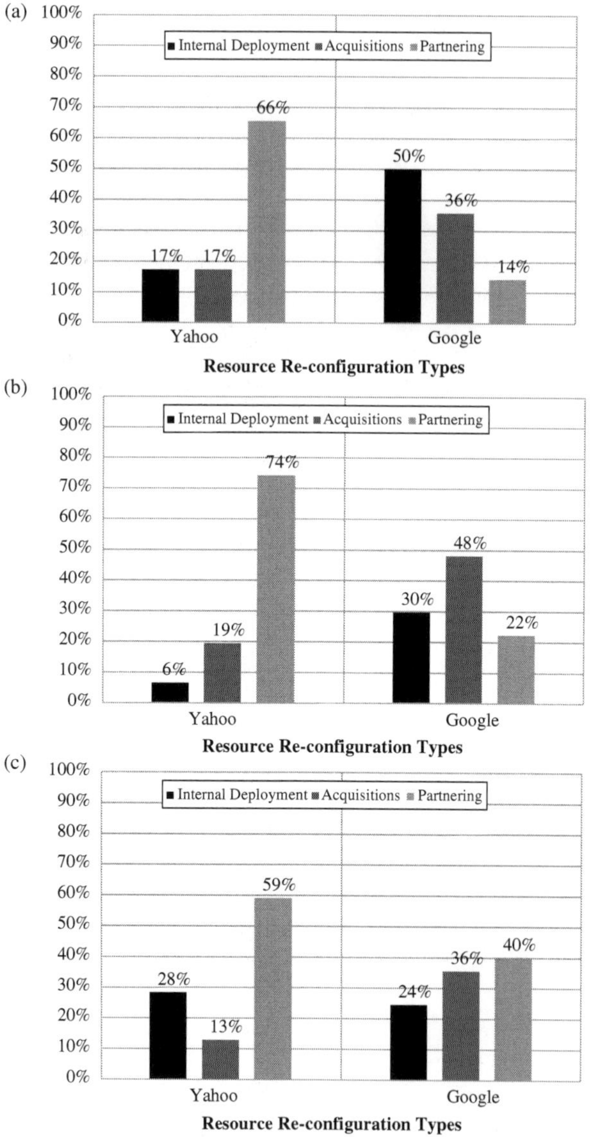

Fig. 3. (a) Yahoo and Google's Resource Reconfiguration Approaches for Sensing; (b) Yahoo and Google's Resource Reconfiguration Approaches for Seizing; (c) Yahoo and Google's Resource Reconfiguration Approaches for Sustaining.

element of orchestration, the latter concept implies much more" (Teece, 2007, p. 1320, footnote 2).

Our analysis begins to unpack the notion of resource orchestration by identifying several key aspects of the process. First, we show that a key aspect of resource orchestration is the shift in relative emphasis on internal and external resources across the different stages of opportunity pursuit. This insight also extends Capron and Mitchell's (2009) idea of appropriate resource sourcing by showing that orchestration processes vary both by firm and the related selection capability, and with the changing strategic objectives related to opportunity pursuit.

A second important insight that emerges from our analysis is that how firms combine resource reconfiguration approaches depends on why they combine them. Each of our focal firms exhibited distinct orchestration of internal deployment, acquisitions, and partnering for sensing, seizing, and sustaining. Thus, although the reconfiguration approaches used are generic, the orchestration processes for different stages of opportunity pursuit are firm-specific. Third, whereas internal deployment, acquisitions, and partnering involve a set of complex routines, their orchestration for different stages of opportunity pursuit appears to follow simple rules (Eisenhardt & Martin, 2000; Eisenhardt & Sull, 2001), as evidenced by the contrast between Yahoo's consistency in sensing with external resources, but also increasing investment in internal deployment for sustaining presence in its core markets; and Google's consistency on sensing through internal deployment, but also increasing use of external resources for seizing and sustaining. These observations can inform current debates in research on dynamic capabilities about the extent to which dynamic capabilities are firm-specific (Teece et al., 1997) or generic (Eisenhardt & Martin, 2000), as well as whether they involve simple or complex routines, or a combination thereof in "dynamic bundles" (Peteraf, DiStefano, & Verona, 2013, p. 1405).

The idea of targeted resource orchestration also calls for widening the analytical lens in the study of resource reconfigurations. Much of prior research in the area has given detailed consideration to the antecedents and consequences of specific reconfiguration approaches, including internal deployment versus acquisitions (Karim & Mitchell, 2004), types of partnering (e.g., equity alliances versus licensing), or acquisitions for what firms know versus what they do (Puranam & Srikanth, 2007). Researchers have also emphasized how the possession of specific knowledge and resources leads to differences in preferences for external resource sourcing. For example, firms are thought to partner differently based on the extent to which they are willing to reveal knowledge about their distinct capabilities to their partners (Dutta & Weiss, 1997). Our analyses suggest that firms may use resource reconfigurations as a portfolio that they vary for different stages of opportunity pursuit. Further, varying the portfolio of reconfigurations used may enable them to balance dynamism and capability development, as discussed next.

Complementarity in Targeted Resource Orchestration to Balance Dynamism and Capability Development

The firm-specific differences in the use of resource reconfiguration approaches shown in Figs. 3(a)–(c) suggest that the focal firms created dynamic complementarities through firm-specific resource orchestration processes to balance dynamism and capability development in the pursuit of opportunities in a given market. Specifically, Yahoo senses through extensive use of external resources (66% through partnering) which enables rapid reconfiguration; it, however, increases its investments in capability development for sustaining presence, increasing the percentage of product launches based on internal deployment (28%). In contrast, Google senses through heavy reliance on internal deployment (50%), and increases the use of external resources for sustaining (e.g., 40% partnering for sustaining vs. 14% partnering for sensing).

These observed patterns suggest that Yahoo senses by reducing risk and tapping resources it presently does not have, but increases its investment in development of core capabilities in the markets where it presumably finds the opportunities to be more attractive. For example, to pursue the e-commerce opportunity discussed earlier, Yahoo partnered with VISA for its relationships with early e-commerce vendors (1997), and invested in internal development for launching Yahoo Store (1998) and Yahoo Wallet (1999). We note that Yahoo's high levels of partnering may indicate a distinct partnering capability in its own right (Gulati, 1995). Such partnering capability involves the development of integrative knowledge, whereas our analysis focuses on core capabilities required for new product development (Helfat & Raubitschek, 2000).

Google, in contrast, tends to sense opportunities using innovative internally developed technologies to introduce novel offerings in a market. It then expands the scope and value of its offering by engaging in partnering and acquisitions for rapid addition of needed resources. For example, it launched its Internet advertising service by adding attractive new features, such as unique auction-based and self-service systems for advertising bids, both of which were internally developed. It increased the scope of the offering by dynamically adding external resources through technology acquisitions and alliances with companies like AOL and XM satellite radio, which enabled it to syndicate advertising beyond its web search page to other online properties and even digital radio.

Collectively, our observations about the interfirm differences in resource reconfigurations reveal three important dynamics: dynamic resource shifts, targeted resource orchestration, and complementary processes for balancing dynamism and capability development. We refer to these interrelated dynamics as "dynamic resource platforms." Organizational platforms are structures that "both carry organizational resources and capabilities and enable the rapid recombination of these to rapidly and flexibly adapt to shifting demands and address emerging opportunities" (Thomas, Autio, & Gann, 2014, p. 210). We extend the work in the area focusing on lower-order and higher order-capabilities by emphasizing resource orchestration processes and the complementarities among them.

Our theoretical ideas resonate with Ciborra's (1996, p. 114) view of platforms as "a bundle of trajectories, punctuated by solutions," as well as with the notion of dynamic bundles (Peteraf et al., 2013). Dynamic resource platforms comprise of dynamic bundles of resources and routines for their reconfiguration by accessing, linking, delinking, or releasing them (Daneels, 2007; Eisenhardt & Martin, 2000; Peteraf et al., 2013). In addition, however, dynamic resource platforms are characterized by a dynamic architecture derived from large-scale, strategically designed orchestration processes that generate distinct firm-specific patterns of resource use and market actions. These large-scale processes fit with Ciborra's (1996, p. 114) idea that a platform should be conceptualized as "a 'string,' that is, the sequence of forms it is able to display, and the temporal links between them." Understanding the processes that define organizational platforms is important in order to understand their capacity to "contribute toward a reorientation of the firm's competitive scope and focus through capability buildup, combination, reorientation, and deployment" (Thomas et al., 2014, p. 202). In our study, both Yahoo and Google organized dynamic resource platforms to rapidly sense, seize, and sustain presence in a large number of growth opportunities. While their dynamic resource platforms shared the three attributes we outlined in this section – dynamic resource shifts, targeted resource orchestration, and complementary processes balancing dynamism and capability development – their specific pattern of actions and forms differed, as did the outcomes they obtained on their growth paths.

DISCUSSION

The question of how firms reconfigure resources to pursue growth opportunities has attracted research attention from several theoretical perspectives, including dynamic capabilities, strategic growth and renewal, and corporate diversification. We extend current thinking in this area through inductive theory building based on the analysis of the dynamic resource reconfigurations that Yahoo and Google used to pursue new growth opportunities in their respective first 10 years of existence. We adopt an actions-based view of opportunity pursuit, by examining firm market actions as means for sensing and seizing opportunities, as well as sustaining presence in markets. Our actions-based approach to opportunity pursuit builds on entrepreneurship research on new market and opportunity creation (Rindova, Petkova, & Kotha, 2007; Santos & Eisenhardt, 2009), which treats market actions such as new product launches as the means to both explore and shape opportunities. We use this perspective to connect entrepreneurship research to the work in strategy on the sources of dynamism in firm strategies for growth and renewal.

Whereas entrepreneurship research has emphasized entrepreneurial actions, it has given less attention to the differential use of resources and capabilities in supporting market actions. Conversely, strategy research has paid close attention to the possession as well as reconfiguration of resources and capabilities for the pursuit of profitability and growth (Wernerfelt, 1984), but has not linked tightly reconfiguration processes to firm actions (see Helfat & Raubitschek, 2000 for an exception). As a result, strategy research has tended to study the relative advantages of specific reconfiguration approaches under different conditions, but has paid limited attention to their dynamic utilization in various combinations for the pursuit of growth. This gap in the literature informed the design of our study, which tracks what resource reconfiguration approaches firms used for their product launches targeted at specific market opportunities.

Our analysis further distinguished between sensing, seizing, and sustaining as stages of opportunity pursuit in order to capture the differences in extent of resource commitments evidenced in the number of products launched. Through this approach we both disaggregated the analysis of opportunity pursuit and examined resource reconfiguration and actions in concert. The resultant complex and dynamic picture of how two iconic high-growth firms used different resource reconfiguration approaches to pursue a large number of opportunities at a very rapid pace enabled us to develop novel theoretical insights on three key dilemmas about effective resource reconfiguration: (1) how firms tap into a diverse and changing pool of resources, (2) how they deploy them, given the trade-offs associated with each type of resource reconfiguration, and (3) how they use multiple reconfiguration approaches in a portfolio manner to balance dynamism and capability development. The consistency in choices regarding these three dilemmas supplies a dynamic architecture of dynamic resource platforms.

Dynamic Capabilities and Dynamic Resource Platforms

The construct of dynamic capabilities has attracted a great deal of research attention. In a recent review article, Peteraf et al. (2013) note that more than 1,000 articles have been published on the topic over the last decade. However, according to their analysis, research in the area is characterized by two distinct, and according to the authors' analysis, incompatible conceptualizations of what dynamic capabilities are and what their consequences may be. One view is based on Teece et al.'s seminal article (1997), which defined dynamic capabilities as the abilities of firms to integrate, build and reconfigure internal and external competences to sustain competitive advantage in rapidly changing environments. Another view reflects Eisenhardt and Martin's (2000) reconceptualization of the construct as specific strategic and organizational processes (e.g., product development) that create value for firms in dynamic markets by manipulating resources into new value-creating strategies. Peteraf et al. (2013) stress that these distinct conceptualization present an impediment to the development of a cumulative body of knowledge on DC. They propose that researchers should seek possible paths for integrating the two perspectives by examining more closely the actual processes through which dynamic capabilities are enacted.

Our findings respond to this call, as our detailed analysis of the specific resource reconfiguration approaches that Yahoo and Google used to pursue a large number of opportunities across a variety of markets enabled us to specify some of the mechanisms that underlie their dynamic strategies. We propose the construct of dynamic resource platforms as an integrative construct that encompasses both complex resource orchestration processes and simple rules that provide an organizing logic – a dynamic architecture – for them. It builds on several constructs present in the dynamic capabilities literature, such as orchestration (Teece, 2007), dynamic bundles (Peteraf et al., 2013), and reconfiguration (Helfat et al., 2007), but goes beyond them.

A distinguishing attribute of the construct of dynamic resource platforms relative to other constructs used to describe dynamic resource reconfigurations is that it foregrounds the dynamic architecture that gives internal coherence and integrative logic to what otherwise appear to be heterogeneous choices about various aspects of firms strategies, including product markets, inter-organizational relations, and resource allocation. The key elements of the dynamic architecture are (1) shifts in resource stocks (2) that are based on resource reconfigurations orchestrated strategically for different stages of opportunity pursuit, and (3) balance dynamism and capability. For example, Yahoo's dynamic resource platform integrates its broad sensing in a wide range of product markets with low-cost probing to discover opportunities, with a shift to internal deployment to build capability in core markets in later stages of opportunity pursuit. Google's dynamic resource platform integrates targeted sensing in a narrower set of markets through "capable" entry to shape or create opportunities, adding flexibility through external resources in later stages of opportunity pursuit.

We recognize that we derived the construct of dynamic resource platforms from the analysis of the actions of two very high-growth firms operating in rapidly evolving, growing markets. This raises the question about the extent to which our ideas generalize to the resource reconfiguration processes of other types of firms operating in different types of environments. We note that what is generalizable from our case study is not the specific empirical patterns of how the focal firms used different reconfiguration approaches, but the theoretical insights about the attributes of dynamic resource platforms.

To develop better understanding of when and how firms develop dynamic resource platforms, future research needs to attend simultaneously to the heterogeneous elements that constitute them, and to the simple rules and managerial logics that give them coherence. To the extent that platforms exhibit patterns of orchestration and coherence, researchers need to understand the managerial and organizational conditions that enable diversity and change to be coupled with coherence and integration. As "unity in diversity" is considered one of the principles of good design, researchers can examine the organizational design arrangements that manifest this principle. The development of platforms further depends on big-picture, longitudinal understanding of the trajectories of resource and capability development inside firms and in their ecosystems.

Many of the reconfiguration processes involved in dynamic resource platforms already exist in organizations and are often thought of as distinct dynamic capabilities, such as dynamic R&D or marketing

(Eisenhardt & Martin, 2000). The advantage of locating dynamic capabilities in such organizational routines is that they can more readily be mapped in organizational systems of activities and charts of authority, analyzed and benchmarked against competitors, and evaluated based on relatively tractable outputs. Dynamic resource platforms – as we observed and conceptualized them – lack such advantages of concreteness and demarcation. However, they have advantages of large-scale orchestration and process complementarity that can power high levels of growth across multiple and heterogeneous opportunities.

The challenge for organizational scholars and practicing managers may be to better understand and design the organizational arrangements that enable them. Our analyses suggest that strategically managing the processes that reconfigure resources and the relations among them, rather than the resources themselves, generates the dynamic architecture we associate with dynamic resource platforms. As we noted earlier, a key aspect of orchestration is the use of a multiplicity of instruments, in varying combinations, to express different musical qualities (Teece, 2007). In a similar vein, we argue that dynamic resource platforms harbor multiplicity, and channel it strategically, to enable levels of growth and opportunity pursuit that conventional capability development and resource sourcing strategies may not be sufficient to support. We hope that these ideas will stimulate research and practice using more integrative analysis of the sources of dynamism and capability development in the pursuit of growth.

Dynamic Resource Platforms and Entrepreneurial Growth

A great deal of entrepreneurship research has focused on understanding opportunity recognition, considering the process of opportunity pursuit to follow known and well understood start-up steps. Less attention has been given to the processes through which entrepreneurial firms develop and access unique and valuable resources, and the actions in which they deploy them to explore and shape opportunities. Thus, even current debates about the differences between the discovery and creation modes of opportunity identification continue to emphasize how entrepreneurs think differently about markets and opportunities (Alvarez & Barney, 2007) and not how they take different actions to probe, understand, and shape markets, as well as the resources they need to mobilize to take such actions. Similarly, the analysis of the resources entrepreneurs leverage emphasizes the human capital of entrepreneurs and their teams, their networks, and investors, but stops short of studying the resource sourcing and reconfiguration strategies of entrepreneurial firms. The current research focus on how entrepreneurs overcome the resource constraints they face in the early start-up stages has limited our understanding of start-up resource reconfiguration strategies. Finally, entrepreneurship research has viewed opportunity pursuit primarily in the context of the initial start-up opportunity and has not addressed the evolving strategies of opportunity pursuit for growth.

Focusing on two high-growth firms in their first 10 years of existence, in this paper we identify resource reconfiguration as a key mechanism behind the pursuit of new growth opportunities by entrepreneurial firms. We further uncover two different patterns of use of resource reconfiguration for sensing and seizing opportunities, as well as sustaining presence in core markets. We find that whereas both firms pursued a large number of opportunities, and launched a comparable number of new products, they used resource reconfigurations differently. Further, whereas both firms developed what we term dynamic growth platforms, the dynamic architectures that they created for them were quite different.

As the ante pone of our paper's title highlights, both dynamic resource platforms imbued the two firms with dynamism that enabled them to run highly competitive races in their multiple rapidly evolving markets, which they either entered or created. As in Aesop's fable, Yahoo may have given itself a head start by sensing a very large number of opportunities early on – twice as many as Google overall, and four times as many in its first five years of existence. Google started more slowly, but escalated its sensing by launching products in almost double the number of new markets in its second five years (nine markets), as it did in its first five years (five markets). However, in a departure from Aesop's fable, both firms sustained high levels of reconfiguration as evidenced by 17 acquisitions and 67 partnerships by Yahoo and 35 acquisitions and 25 partnerships by Google, over their first 10 years; and both firms used these different resource reconfiguration approaches to simultaneously generate dynamism and capability.

These observations have important implications for studying the reconfiguration strategies of entrepreneurial firms. In particular, we note that in contrast to the research in the area that tends to focus either on specific alliances or acquisitions and their performance consequences, or on a type of resource reconfiguration approach and the effect of prior experience with it on its subsequent use, we find that our focal firms took a portfolio approach using multiple reconfiguration approaches in combination. Our observations are consistent with prior arguments that the levels of alliances and acquisitions firms engage in is, in part, a function of their resource endowments. However, we also note that this line of analysis tells an incomplete story, and it omits the important question of how firms with different initial endowments ensure needed dynamism and capability development to survive dynamic, hypercompetitive races. Our findings offer a complementary perspective in understanding the resource reconfiguration strategies of high-tech firms competing in dynamic environments that can guide research in the area toward examining both value creation and value capture in the context of high growth.

CONCLUSION

The issue of resource reconfiguration and redeployment for opportunity pursuit is central to the dynamic view of strategy. Research on how firms reconfigure resources has focused on three core approaches to resource reconfiguration – internal (including recombination and redeployment), external (acquisitions), and hybrid (partnering) – but has eschewed a portfolio view looking at combinations of these approaches across markets and over time. Examining the patterns of dynamic resource reconfigurations of two iconic high-growth firms, we discovered that they took a portfolio approach to their resource reconfiguration strategies and organized them in dynamic resource platforms. Our analysis suggests that dynamic resource platforms may enable firms to simultaneously generate high levels of dynamism and capability development that afford them the capacity to pursue (to varying extents) a large number of diverse growth opportunities.

NOTE

1. In a sensitivity analysis looking at the second and third product launches in a given market, we observed that the patterns of resource reconfigurations for those were more similar to the patterns associated with opportunity seizing.

ACKNOWLEDGMENT

The authors gratefully acknowledge the support from the Herb Kelleher Center for Entrepreneurship, Growth and Renewal at the McCombs School of Business at the University of Texas at Austin.

REFERENCES

Alvarez, S. A., & Barney, J. B. (2007). Discovery and creation: Alternative theories of entrepreneurial action. *Strategic Entrepreneurship Journal, 1*(1–2), 11–26.

Angel, K. (2002). *Inside Yahoo!: Reinvention and the road ahead.* New York, NY: Wiley.

Battelle, J. (2005). *The search: How google and its rivals rewrote the rules of business and transformed our culture.* New York, NY: Penguin Group.

Baum, J., Calabrese, T., & Silverman, B. (2000). Don't go it alone: Alliance network composition and startups' performance in Canadian biotechnology. *Strategic Management Journal, 21*(3), 267–294.

Bingham, C. B. (2009). Oscillating improvisation: How entrepreneurial firms create success in foreign market entries over time. *Strategic Entrepreneurship Journal, 3*(4), 321–345.

Bingham, C. B., & Eisenhardt, K. (2008). Position, leverage and opportunity: A typology of strategic logics linking resources with competitive advantage. *Managerial and Decision Economics, 29*(2–3), 241–256.

Brown, S. L., & Eisenhardt, K. M. (1997). The art of continuous change: Linking complexity theory and time-paced evolution in relentlessly shifting organizations. *Administrative Science Quarterly, 42*(1), 1–34.

Capron, L., & Mitchell, W. (2009). Selection capability: How capability gaps and internal social frictions affect internal and external strategic renewal. *Organization Science, 20*(2), 294–312.

Ciborra, C. U. (1996). The platform organization: Recombining strategies, structures, and surprises. *Organization Science, 7*(2), 103–118.

Courtney, H. (2001). *20/20 foresight: Crafting strategy in an uncertain world.* Boston, MA: Harvard Business School Publishing.

Daneels, E. (2007). The process of technological competence leveraging. *Strategic Management Journal, 28*(5), 511–533.

D'Aveni, R. A. (1995). Coping with hypercompetition: Utilizing the new 7S's framework. *Academy of Management Executive, 9*(3), 45–57.

Dougherty, D. (1992). A practice-centered model of organizational renewal through product innovation. *Strategic Management Journal, 13*(S1), 77–92.

Dutta, S., & Weiss, A. (1997). The relationship between a firm's level of technological innovativeness and its pattern of partnership agreements. *Management Science, 43*(3), 343–356.

Eisenhardt, K. M. (1989). Building theories from case study research. *Academy of Management Review, 14*(4), 532–550.

Eisenhardt, K. M., & Martin, J. A. (2000). Dynamic capabilities: What are they? *Strategic Management Journal, 21*(10–11), 1105–1121.

Eisenhardt, K. M., & Schoonhoven, C. (1990). Organizational growth: Linking founding team, strategy, environment, and growth among US semiconductor ventures, 1978–1988. *Administrative Science Quarterly, 35*, 504–529.

Eisenhardt, K. M., & Sull, D. N. (2001). Strategy as simple rules. *Harvard Business Review, 79*(1), 107–116.

Gavetti, G., & Rivkin, J. W. (2007). On the origin of strategy: Action and cognition over time. *Organization Science, 18*(3), 420–439.

Gulati, R. (1995). Social structure and alliance formation patterns: A longitudinal analysis. *Administrative Science Quarterly, 40*(4), 619–652.

Helfat, C. E. (1997). Know-how and asset complementarity and dynamic capability accumulation: The case of. *Strategic Management Journal*, *18*(5), 339–360.

Helfat, C. E., & Eisenhardt, K. M. (2004). Inter-temporal economies of scope, organizational modularity, and the dynamics of diversification. *Strategic Management Journal*, *25*(13), 1217–1232.

Helfat, C. E., Finkelstein, S., Mitchell, W., Peteraf, M. A., Singh, H., Teece, D. J., & Winter, S. G. (2007). *Dynamic capabilities: Understanding strategic change in organizations*. Hoboken, NY: Blackwell Publishing.

Helfat, C. E., & Peteraf, M. A. (2015). Managerial cognitive capabilities and the microfoundations of dynamic capabilities. *Strategic Management Journal*, *36*, 831–850.

Helfat, C. E., & Raubitschek, R. S. (2000). Product sequencing co-evolution of knowledge, capabilities and products. *Strategic Management Journal*, *21*(10–11), 961–980.

Karim, S., & Capron, L. (2015). Reconfiguration: Adding, redeploying, recombining and divesting resources and business units. *Strategic Management Society Virtual Special Issue Introduction*. Retrieved from http://onlinelibrary.wiley.com/journal/10.1002/(ISSN)1097-0266/homepage/reconfiguration_vsi_introduction.htm

Karim, S., & Mitchell, W. (2000). Path-dependent and path-breaking change: Reconfiguring business resources following acquisitions in the U.S. medical sector, 1978–1995. *Strategic Management Journal*, *21*(10/11), 1061–1081.

Karim, S., & Mitchell, W. (2004). Innovating through acquisition and internal development. *Long Range Planning*, *37*, 525–547.

Kirzner, I. (1973). *Competition and entrepeneurship*. Chicago, IL: University of Chicago Press.

Lee, G. K. (2008). Relevance of organizational capabilities and its dynamics: What to learn from entrants' product portfolios about the determinants of entry timing. *Strategic Management Journal*, *29*(12), 1257–1280.

Miles, M. B., & Huberman, A. M. (1994). *Qualitative data analysis: An expanded sourcebook*. Thousand Oaks, CA: Sage.

Montgomery, C., & Wernerfelt, B. (1988). Diversification, Ricardian rents, and Tobin's q. *RAND Journal of Economics*, *19*(4), 623–632.

Nakache, P. (1998). Secrets of the new brand builders AOL, Yahoo, palm computing. *Fortune*.

Penrose, E. (1959). *The theory of the firm*. New York: Wiley.

Peteraf, M. A., DiStefano, G., & Verona, G. (2013). The elephant in the room of dynamic capabilities: Bringing two diverging conversations together. *Strategic Management Journal*, *34*(12), 1389–1410.

Puranam, P., & Srikanth, K. (2007). What they know vs. what they do: How acquirers leverage technology acquisitions. *Strategic Management Journal*, *28*(8), 805–825.

Rindova, V., & Fombrun, C. J. (1999). Constructing competitive advantage: The role of firm-constituent interactions. *Strategic Management Journal*, *20*(8), 691–710.

Rindova, V., & Fombrun, C. J. (2001). The growth of the specialty coffee niche in the U.S. coffee industry. In K. Bird-Schoonhoven & E. Romanelli (Eds.), *The entrepreneurship dynamic*. Stanford, CA: Stanford University Press.

Rindova, V., & Kotha, S. (2001). Continuous morphing: Competing through dynamic capabilities, form, and function. *Academy of Management Journal*, *44*(6), 1263–1280.

Rindova, V. P., Petkova, A. P., & Kotha, S. (2007). Standing out: How new firms in emerging markets build reputation. *Strategic Organization*, *5*(1), 31–70.

Santos, F. M., & Eisenhardt, K. M. (2009). Constructing markets and shaping boundaries: Entrepreneurial power in nascent fields. *Academy of Management Journal*, *52*(4), 643–671.

Shepherd, D., McMullen, J. S., & Jennings, P. D. (2007). The formation of opportunity beliefs: Overcoming ignorance and reducing doubt. *Strategic Entrepreneurship Journal*, *1*(1–2), 75–95.

Silverman, B. S. (1999). Technological resources and the direction of corporate diversification: Toward an integration of the resource-based view and transaction cost economics. *Managerial Science*, *45*(8), 1109–1124.

Smith, K. G., & DiGregorio, D. (2002). Bisociation, discovery and the role of entrepreneurial action. In M. Hitt, R. D. Ireland, & D. Sexton (Eds.), *Strategic entrepreneurship: Creating a new mindset* (pp. 129–149). Malden, MA: Blackwell Publishers.

Teece, D. J. (2007). Explicating dynamic capabilities: The nature and microfoundations of (sustainable) enterprise performance. *Strategic Management Journal*, *28*(13), 1319–1350.

Teece, D. J. (2012). Dynamic capabilities: Routines versus entrepreneurial action. *Journal of Management Studies*, *49*(8), 1395–1401.

Teece, D. J. (2014). A dynamic capabilities-based entrepreneurial theory of the multinational enterprise. *Journal of International Business Studies*, *45*(1), 8–37.

Teece, D. J., Pisano, G., & Shuen, A. (1997). Dynamic capabilities and strategic management. *Strategic Management Journal*, *18*(7), 509–533.

Thomas, L. D. W., Autio, E., & Gann, D. M. (2014). Architectural leverage: Putting platforms into context. *Academy of Management Perspectives*, *28*(2), 198–219.

Villalonga, B., & McGahan, A. M. (2005). The choice among acquisitions, alliances, and divestitures. *Strategic Management Journal*, *26*(13), 1183–1208.

Wernerfelt, B. (1984). A resource-based view of the firm. *Strategic Management Journal*, *5*(2), 171–180.

Yin, R. (1994). The abridged version of case study research. In L. Bickman & D. J. Rog (Eds.), *Handbook of applied social research* (pp. 229–260). Thousand Oaks, CA: Sage.

Young, G., Smith, K. G., & Grimm, C. M. (1996). "Austrian" and industrial organization perspectives on firm-level competitive activity and performance. *Organization Science*, *7*(3), 243–254.

LINKING TECHNOLOGIES TO APPLICATIONS – INSIGHTS FROM ONLINE MARKETS FOR TECHNOLOGY

Gary Dushnitsky and Thomas Klueter

ABSTRACT

An important precondition for resource redeployment is that firms are aware of the commercial applications for which their resources can be used. We take an inventing-firm perspective and ask: how many new commercial applications will a firm associate with an existing technological invention? We note that both technological and organizational characteristics determine the number of distinct applications firms consider feasible for a given technological invention. In particular, we suggest that inherently fungible technologies, that is, technologies that have a broad impact on other technological fields (highly general technologies), will be associated with a larger set of commercial applications. We also suggest that linking applications to an inherently general technology can be challenging when the technology is already embedded in organizational (commercial) routines. Proprietary data from an online marketplace allow us to investigate the applications firms consider feasible for their

Resource Redeployment and Corporate Strategy
Advances in Strategic Management, Volume 35, 285–317

ISSN: 0742-3322/doi:10.1108/S0742-332220160000035010

technological inventions. In line with extant work, a firm assigns a greater number of applications to more general technologies. As expected, however, this relationship is shaped by how the technology is embedded within the organization. Our results have implications for redeployment as firms may face challenges in the initial step of redeployment when fungible resources need to be linked to emerging market opportunities.

Keywords: Corporate entrepreneurship; licensing; open innovation; patent marketplace; markets for technology; technology-application matches

INTRODUCTION

An important stream of research examines how firms grow by continuously deploying their resources to emerging and growing market opportunities (Penrose, 1959; Wernerfelt, 1984). Specific attention has been paid to the exploitation of intertemporal economies of scope, that is, redeploying resources from one market to another (Anand & Singh, 1997; Helfat & Eisenhardt, 2004; Penrose, 1959; Sakhartov & Folta, 2014). Inherent to these perspectives is that firm resources can be deployed in multiple market applications as "the final products produced by a firm at any given time merely represent one of several ways in which the organization could be using its internal resources" (Basalla, 1988, p. 45; Penrose, 1959; Teece, 1982). Hence, an important precondition for resource redeployment is to make effective linkages between firm resources and possible market applications.

Linking inventive resources (i.e., technologies such as a substance with resistance to high heat)[1] to commercial applications (e.g., kitchenware in the form of frying pans) lies at the heart of the entrepreneurial process of innovation (Basalla, 1988; Gruber, MacMillan, & Thompson, 2008; Schumpeter, 1934). From this perspective, the linking of inventive resources and commercial applications is a delicate matching process and requires evaluating technical possibilities as well as commercial opportunities (Danneels, 2007; Freeman & Soete, 1997; Shane, 2000). This can be challenging as some applications for an existing technology may be known to the firm while others are not or are only revealed over time (Basalla, 1988). Hence, to deploy their technological resources, firms must be aware of the commercial applications for which their resources can ultimately be used (Danneels, 2007). As a result, firms may possess a substantial reservoir of what researchers have characterized as "dormant" or underused technological resources as they are not aware of some of the commercial applications to which they can deploy those resources (Penrose, 1959; Rivette & Kline, 2000). In a similar vein, redeployment (i.e., the withdrawal of resources from one business to another) may never occur if firms are unaware of alternative applications of existing technologies. Therefore, understanding what applications firms consider feasible for a given technology and why, in some cases, linking technologies to applications is challenging is of fundamental importance to both scholars in entrepreneurship and those studying redeployment.[2]

In this paper, we take the perspective of incumbent firms that want to grow by deploying their inventions in a broad range of markets. We examine how both technological and organizational characteristics determine the number of distinct applications firms consider feasible for a given technological invention. Our first argument is driven by technology considerations. Following prior literature, we expect that firms are first and foremost guided by a technology's fungibility, that is, the potential of a technology to be used in multiple applications (Danneels, 2007; Levinthal & Wu, 2010; Teece, 1982). We suggest that a technology's generality, that is, the extent to which a technology influences a wide range of technical fields, may be an important indicator for a technology's inherent fungibility (Gambardella & Giarratana, 2013; Gruber et al., 2008; Maine & Garnsey, 2006). We then argue that technologies with high generality are particularly attractive to be deployed and redeployed in a broad range of applications as they can generate revenues across a range of commercial applications.

Our second argument draws on organizational considerations, utilizing studies which have suggested that linking applications to inherently fungible technologies can be challenging (Levinthal & Wu, 2010; Maine & Garnsey, 2006; Shane, 2000). We argue that such challenges stem from prior deployment of a technology in organizational routines and, hence, predefined heuristic maps as to how technologies and commercial applications are linked within an organization (Chesbrough & Rosenbloom, 2002; Danneels, 2007; Grégoire & Shepherd, 2012). Accordingly, we suggest that firms face a "dilemma": once deployed in organizational routines, it may be harder to unpack the possible range of applications for an inherently fungible technology. Hence, firms may be not effective in linking technologies and applications and, as a result, in their redeployment of technologies to emerging market opportunities.

We examine our hypotheses using a proprietary novel dataset that allows us to capture technology-application linkages as reported by incumbent firms. In particular, we examine 199 technologies listed by firms on an online market for technology. Researchers have suggested that markets for technology may be an important setting in which firms systematically attempt to deploy their technologies in a broad range of applications (Arora & Gambardella, 2010; Nelson, 1990). In such a market, technologies discovered by one firm (the technology owner) may be utilized and commercialized by another firm (the technology buyer/partner). This setting enables us to take the perspective of a technology-owning firm and observe how the number of applications considered feasible is influenced by both technological (fungibility) and organizational (prior commercial commercialization and routines) characteristics.

We find that firms engaged in the market for technology do indeed assign commercial applications based on the inherent potential of a technology to be used in multiple application domains (i.e., a technology's generality). As expected, however, this relationship is shaped by how the technology is embedded within the organization. Namely, prior deployment through commercial routines of a given technology leads to challenges in linking technologies to applications as firms only consider a limited number of applications, even though the technology has a high technological generality. This suggests important challenges for firms attempting to deploy inherently fungible technologies in a broad range of commercial applications.

Overall, the study contributes to our understanding of the linkages between technologies and market applications and illustrates that both technological and organizational factors shape the number of applications firms consider feasible for their technologies. Beyond demonstrating the unique role of fungible resources (associated with more applications), we also extend the research describing the challenges of technology-application matching process. This has important implications for redeployment as, absent an effective match of technologies to applications, subsequent redeployment may not be possible. We reveal that when a technology is already deployed in commercial routines, subsequent redeployment may be much more difficult as firms may face challenges in making novel connections between their technologies and applications.

THEORY AND HYPOTHESES DEVELOPMENT

Linking Technological Inventions and Commercial Applications

Redeployment is characterized by the continuous allocation of resource to growing businesses, which may, ultimately, allow firms to expand and survive in the long run (Penrose, 1959; Teece, 1982). Inherent to the idea of redeployment is that not all applications are known at a single point in time and that firms exploit intertemporal economies of scope by shifting resources from one (often declining) application to another (often growing) application (Anand & Singh, 1997; Helfat & Eisenhardt, 2004; Sakhartov & Folta, 2014).

The continuous deployment of resources to applications mirrors the innovation process described by Schumpeter (1934), who distinguished inventive resources (e.g., a technology) from innovations. Technological inventions are the result of knowledge creation and constitute the technical resources that a firm can draw upon to solve problems (Ahuja & Morris Lampert, 2001). Innovation refers to the application of such inventions to productive use by deploying them in commercial applications (Kline & Rosenberg, 1986, p. 162; Schumpeter, 1934). Both technological resources and application are necessary conditions for profitable innovation; failure to execute either would likely lead to inferior performance. Researchers distinguishing a firm's technological resources and its applications have long argued that technological resources lie upstream of commercial applications (Penrose, 1959; Prahalad & Hamel, 1990; Wernerfelt, 1984). Technologies are, hence, more than the elements embedded in commercial products (Danneels, 2007). Penrose (1959, p. 25), for example, observed early that "*exactly the same resource when used for different purposes or in different ways and in combination with different types or amounts of other resources provides different service.*" As an example, DuPont's Teflon (Polytetrafluoroethylene) has distinct technological properties as it is hydrophobic, heat resistant, and provides a low coefficient of friction. Today, Teflon's market applications span a broad range of industries, including automobiles (for paint), housing, cookware and photovoltaic energy products and Dupont has substantially shifted resources from prior to new applications with growing economic potential over time (DuPont, 2011).

The above example also suggests that technology-application linkages can change over time as the "*the first uses [of an invention] are not always the ones for which the invention will become best known*" (Basalla, 1988, p. 141). This gives rise to intertemporal economies of scope, in which firms redeploy resources by shifting their emphasis from one application to another (Helfat & Eisenhardt, 2004). As an example, many technological inventions in the pharmaceutical industry are redeployed over time as treatments are deployed to alternative usages. For example, originally approved for the treatment of enlarged prostate in 1992 as Proscar, Merck later deployed the technology in the hair loss market (as Propecia) and the commercial success of the latter application outpaced the original one. In many cases, new applications in the pharmaceutical industry are also found for previously failed and abandoned drugs. For example, in the 1960s, Ziovudine was developed by Burroughs Wellcome[3] for the treatment of cancer, but later, resources were withdrawn from this application and reallocated toward the HIV/AIDS market, in which the therapy became the first treatment in 1987 (brand name: Retrovir). Today, pharmaceutical firms have established systematic processes for a form of redeployment (called repositioning), including dedicated units with the mandate to better link existing technologies (drugs) to applications (indications) (Ashburn & Thor, 2004; Hartmann & Hassan, 2006).[4]

Those examples reveal the importance of firms linking technologies to commercial opportunities in their attempts to grow through redeployment. Moreover, they reveal an important precondition for redeployment: firms cannot redeploy their technologies unless they are aware of the applications to which they can be redeployed. Next, we take the perspective of an incumbent whose intention is to grow by leveraging their existing resources toward a broad range of applications to create value. We theorize about the range of possible applications they believe to be feasible for a focal technology, considering both technological and organizational factors.

Technological Generality and Commercial Applications

Important to the process of redeployment is that some technological inventions more than others are fungible as they are amenable to multiple applications (Levinthal & Wu, 2010; Penrose, 1959; Teece, 1982). This suggests that some technological inventions are characterized by an inherently greater potential to be deployed in a broad range of commercial applications, which should influence the number of applications firms would consider for such technologies.

Researchers have long identified that technological inventions differ in the extent to which they influence subsequent technological inventions and that an important technological characteristic of an invention is its technological generality, that is, the extent to which the invention influences a diverse set of technology domains (Gambardella & Giarratana, 2013; Hall, Jaffe, & Trajtenberg, 2001). Technological inventions do not occur in isolation but rather are a result of an evolutionary process, which can be conceptualized as the recombination of existing inventions to form new solutions (Murray & O'Mahony, 2007; Nelson & Winter, 1982). An existing invention may have the potential to influence other technological inventions in multiple ways. First, technologies that build on the focal invention may be from a narrow range of technology domains; therefore, the usefulness of the invention may be limited to that distinct technological domain (Fleming & Sorenson, 2004). Such technologies, in general, facilitate specialization and incremental improvements within a given technological field. Alternatively, an invention may spur technologies across a broad set of technological domains. The extent to which a technological invention influences subsequent inventions in a variety of technological fields has been labeled as its breadth of impact (Argyres & Silverman, 2004) or technological generality (Gambardella & Giarratana, 2013; Hall et al., 2001). Given these characteristics, a technology that influences a broader set of technological fields may suggest fungibility, that is, the potential of the technology to be applied in a broader set of commercial applications (Gruber et al., 2008).

Once a firm decides to deploy a technology, it must consider the commercial applications in which the technology can be of value. Understanding that technologies differ along a key characteristic, namely, the level of their technological generality, should be an important factor in explaining the number of commercial applications to which a firm will associate its technology. Assuming that firms will attempt to maximize the anticipated returns from commercializing their technology, we expect that they are motivated to associate that technology with an exhaustive set of possible commercial applications. This is reinforced by the fact that commercializing an invention in different commercial applications will not lead to rent dissipation (Fosfuri, 2006). Hence, to maximize value creation, firms would consider more applications as feasible for highly general technologies.

Also, firms are not only aware of the inherent potential of the invention to influence technological subfields but are also cognizant of the way in which their invention is subsequently used, be it internally, by external partners or by competitors (Yang, Phelps, & Steensma, 2010). For highly general technologies, firms receive cues from a variety of technological fields and actors. This may lead them to become more aware of the inherent potential of the technology, again suggesting fungibility for that technology, and associate such technologies with a broad range of applications.

Overall, we expect that firms would associate a more general technology in a larger number of market applications. Surprisingly, empirical evidence regarding the fungibility of resources and commercial applications in general and, specifically, the relationship between technological generality and commercial applications is scarce. An exception is Gruber et al. (2008) who examined the number of alternative market opportunities entrepreneurs consider prior to the first market entry. However, the authors did not find evidence that technological generality drove the number of commercial applications considered. Following our arguments, we predict:

Hypothesis 1. The greater the level of an invention's technological generality, the greater the number of commercial applications a firm will associate it with.

Challenges Linking Technologies and Applications

Researchers in entrepreneurship have long suggested that the process of linking technological resources and market opportunities is far from trivial and can be as challenging, costly and time-consuming as the original discovery of a technology (Chesbrough & Rosenbloom, 2002; Maine & Garnsey, 2006; Shane, 2000). In a similar vein, researchers have suggested that technologies remain "dormant" and underused within organizations as they face challenges in successfully deploying their technologies to applications (Danneels, 2007; Rivette & Kline, 2000).

Penrose's (1959, p. 76) classic work emphasized that resources are often not fully used as "*at any given time, the known productive services inherent in a resource do not exhaust the full potential of the resource.*" Such challenges are particularly salient to inherently fungibility technologies for which the number of potential applications is large. This suggests that many technologies in firms may, indeed be "underused" and that linking technologies to applications may not be trivial (Rivette & Kline, 2000). Extant research indicates that to effectively match a technology to its applications, firms need to understand the underlying characteristics and functionality of that technology in its own right (Grégoire & Shepherd, 2012). As such, firms need to de-link the technology from its existing competencies, applications and organizational context to identify potential technology-application combinations (Danneels, 2002).

Another challenge linking technologies to applications is related to different applications requiring diverse complementary assets and business models, which the firm currently does not have at its disposal (Hill & Rothaermel, 2003; Tripsas & Gavetti, 2000). Using a new business model, for example, likely requires different routines and commercial logics (Chesbrough & Rosenbloom, 2002). In a similar vein, firms may also require new personnel and a redistribution of power to pursue new applications, which may be not attractive to existing managers.

Related to the above challenges, researchers have observed the tendency of firms to remain in the status quo. For example, knowledge resources tend to remain sticky within specific business units and difficult to leverage across a broad range of such units within a firm (Chatterjee, Lubatkin, Schweiger, & Weber, 1992). In the context of new knowledge creation, researchers have observed a "familiarity trap" as firms continue to focus on familiar technologies that they have used in the past (Ahuja & Morris Lampert, 2001; Rosenkopf & Nerkar, 2001). Such tendencies may also apply to the process by which firms move an invention toward applications and decide to which commercial markets their technology can be linked. Hence, linking technologies to applications may require firms to purposefully experiment and make "long" jumps to identify for what applications their technology can be ultimately useful (Freeman & Soete, 1997; Maine & Garnsey, 2006).

Overall, the above suggest that for technologies, despite their being inherently fungible, firms may also face challenges in considering an exhaustive set of applications. We next examine when such challenges most likely materialize by taking into account how the technology is embedded within organizational routines.

Prior Commercialization, Organizational Routines and Highly General Technologies

Given that firms are guided by organizational routines, they may search for commercial applications in the area of the firm's current expertise and emphasize specializing in existing application domains (Gruber et al., 2008; Shane, 2000). Such organizational routines may also shape the number of applications they consider feasible for inherently fungible technologies.

Extant research in the context of knowledge creation emphasizes the increasing returns gained by experience and positive feedback, which leads firms to a path of refinement and specialization (Ahuja & Morris Lampert, 2001). In a similar vein, firms may focus on a specific set of applications for a technology that has already been successfully embedded in commercial routines within the organization and which has already been effectively deployed in commercial markets (Danneels, 2007; Shane, 2000). While, in principle, prior commercialization ensures that firms are aware of at least one existing application for a technology, the presence of commercial routines may not allow them to consider an exhaustive set of applications for inherently fungible technologies, that is, those with strong potential to be deployed in a broad range of applications.

First, organizational routines in commercialization lead to the codification and translation of a technology for a particular application (Zollo, Reuer, & Singh, 2002). Prior work has indicated that commercial applications co-evolve with a firm's experience in markets and industries shaping routines (Shane, 2000; Venkataraman, 1997). The presence of such routines may influence (and potentially limit) a firm's perspective as to other linkages between the technology and new applications (Danneels, 2007; Winter, 2000). In particular, these routines may make it more difficult to de-link the technology from its existing commercial routines; that, in turn, increases the difficulty of uncovering applications that go beyond the neighborhood of their current expertise (March & Simon, 1958). As an example, firms invest in dedicated and application-specific complementary assets (e.g., a sales team), which may make firms tightly connected to existing, but less open toward alternative application paths (Danneels, 2002). While this is not critical for a technology having only one possible application, it may limit the possible technology-applications combinations which firms consider feasible for an inherent fungible technology (i.e., with high generality). In a similar vein, prior commercialization within the firm leads to dedicated personnel that push the technology for its existing application path. However, such personnel may not make connections to alternative applications that require too drastic shifts, for example, in business models or new skills (Chesbrough & Rosenbloom, 2002). Hence, dedicated personnel associated with commercial routines may also limit the number of applications considered for a technology with an inherent potential to be applied in a broad range of applications.

Second, prior commercialization may reduce a firm's propensity to experiment, that is, to redefine their heuristics as to how technologies and application are interconnected (Itami & Roehl, 1991). Once a successful application is found, firms may limit their efforts to identify alternative applications as they specialize in the existing application domains. This is supported by research on performance feedback, which highlights that firms engage in less search once they have experienced success (Audia, Locke, & Smith, 2000). Another potential source of rigidity and a lack of propensity to experiment may be existing customers. Christensen and Rosenbloom (1995) indicated early that firms may become locked into technology-application paths by previous commercial success. For inherently general technologies, existing customers can be problematic, as firms may prefer continuing on existing application paths demanded by their current customers, but are unable to uncover applications which go beyond their established customer base.

It follows that challenges in effectively linking technologies for highly general technologies may arise following prior commercialization. In particular, identifying those applications that are unrelated and distant from the existing applications may become more difficult once a technology is already deployed in commercial routines. This has important implications for redeployment as, once deployed within the organization, firms may face challenges in linking the technology to alternative applications (compared to technologies that have been embedded in organizational routines to a lesser extent).

We propose:

> **Hypothesis 2.** Prior commercialization of a technology within an organization negatively moderates the effect of technological generality on the number of commercial applications a firm will associate it with.

METHODS AND ANALYSIS

Context – Online Market for Technology

To identify which applications firms consider feasible for their technologies, we need to go beyond observing where firms ultimately deploy their resources and capture what applications firms are aware of, independent of the technologies' actual deployment. Put differently, our research question necessitates observation of all technologies available for deployment and of all applications firms associate with these technologies. To resolve this issue, we propose a novel research setting: online markets for technology to study technology-application linkages.

Specifically, we consider the marketplace, www.Yet2.com (hereafter Yet2), for patents in which inventors and potential partners interact and trade these inventions. Prior work has recognized Yet2 as an important intermediary (Gambardella, Giuri, & Luzzi, 2007; Leone & Reichstein, 2012; Palomeras, 2007). The marketplace operates as an online platform that allows "technology listers" to post their inventions for a fee, while potential partners can register free of charge, search the listed inventions and engage in an exchange. Charging the technology listers a fee is a common practice among online markets for technology and ensures that only high-quality technology owners will list their inventions in the marketplace (Dushnitsky & Klueter, 2011).[5]

We observe that the use of online markets such as Yet2 is not limited to entrepreneurs and nascent firms; they are also utilized by established incumbents (e.g., DuPont and Honeywell). The technology listers engage in the online marketplace to deploy their technologies, for example, through licensing, partnering or outright sale of those technologies. On the other (potential partners') side, barriers to entry are low since participants can search technology listings on Yet2 free of charge. Two years after its launch, Yet2 had over 15,000 registered users; roughly 100,000 users were registered with Yet2 in 2008 (Yet2.com, 2009).

Yet2 closely resembles a two-sided marketplace for technology, where inventors list their technologies unconditionally of the application (i.e., the needs of a potential partner do not dictate which inventions are listed). Most importantly, Yet2 allows us to capture a broad range of technologies that firms want to deploy to a broad range of applications independent of realized deployment. When first listing a technology on the marketplace, technology owners use pre-specified technology listings of Yet2 (called Tech Packs) to provide all information.[6] The listings give a brief functional overview of the technology and its underlying intellectual property in the form of patents. Firms listing a technology also assign potential applications for each technology. Hence, by studying online markets like Yet2, we can directly capture the applications firms consider feasible for their technological inventions. In sum, studying online markets for technology allows us to go beyond observing the actual deployment of resources to applications. Instead, we can study a broad range of technologies which firms intend to deploy in a broad range of applications and can systematically observe the applications to which focal technologies are ultimately assigned by the technology lister.[7]

Sample

We examined all technology listings that were posted on the Yet2 marketplace between 2003 and 2008.[8] To be included in our sample, a technology listing had to originate from a publicly listed organization (e.g., Honeywell, Dupont), and include at least one patent filed. We found 256 technology listings fulfilling these criteria with complete data. Given our independent variables, we also required the inventions listed to have received citations to measure their technological generality; this further reduced the sample to 199.[9]

Variables

Dependent Variable

When a technology owner initially submits an invention, she/he assigns it to its application categories. In 2008, Yet2 included 27 major application categories (listed in Table 1) that captured distinct industries. The quote below explains the role of application categories in Yet2:

> Categories are important! They help searchers find your technology – even when searchers don't know precisely what they are looking for, and they help Yet2 promote your technology appropriately. Think about categories outside the normal application of the technology: radar for machine tool alignment or color-changing paint to measure airflow. (Yet2 website)

By capturing the application categories utilized by the firm at the point of listing, we could identify which commercial applications firms consider feasible for a focal listed technology. For each technology listing on Yet2, we captured the number of unique applications to which the firms considered it as feasible to be applied. When listing a technology, the technology owners indicate in which of the 27 Yet2 application categories the technology may be useful. The 27 categories represent a comprehensive set of industry categories, from automotives to medical equipment. Namely, each of the categories represents a broad domain of commercial application.

Table 1. Yet2 Broad Application Categories.

Aerospace	Geology
Agriculture	Health, wellness, personal care
Automotive	Instrumentation
Biological sciences	IP professionals
Chemistry[a]	Manufacturing
Communications	Materials
Education	Mechanical
Electronic data processing	Medical
Electronics	Optics
Energy	Physics computer applications
Environmental	Public administration
Finance	Techniques
Foods	Transportation
Fuels	

[a]Contains, for example, refrigerants, cleaning agents.

Thus, observing that a technology is assigned to more than one application domain implies that the technology has a truly diverse application potential. The variable *Commercial Applications* is the count of the number of unique categories to which the focal invention has been assigned by the technology owner. We observe heterogeneity in the number of applications across and within firms and listing multiple applications for a single technology is very common. In 70% of all cases, firms assign their technology to more than one application category (see the distribution of *Commercial Applications* in Fig. 1).[10]

Independent Variables

We followed prior research and employed a measure of technological generality proposed by Hall et al. as a proxy for fungibility of a technology across a broad range of applications (Argyres & Silverman, 2004; Hall & Trajtenberg, 2004; Hall et al., 2001). It is based on US patent classes and equals 1 minus the Herfindahl index of the forward citations to the patent. In detail, generality is defined as (Hall et al., 2001, p. 45):

$$G_i = 1 - \sum_{j-1}^{J} \left(\frac{N_{ij}}{N_i} \right)^2$$

where N_i denotes the number of forward citations to a patent, and N_{ij} is the number received from patents in class j. A higher value of G_i indicates

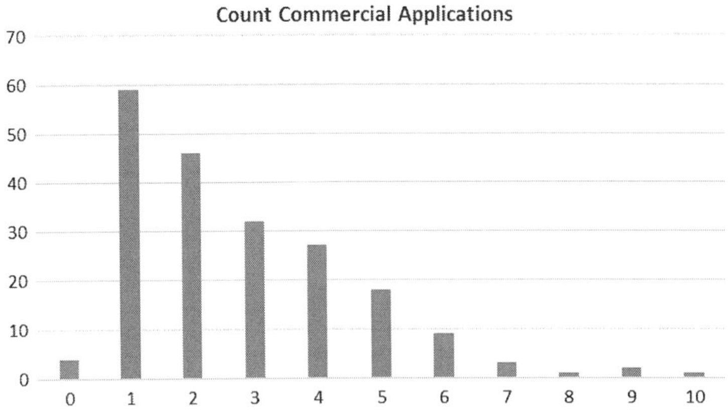

Fig. 1. Distribution Dependent Variable – Count of Applications.

that the focal patent is cited across a broad range of patent classes, revealing that the technology has greater technological generality. Given that, for technologies with a small number of citations, G_i is a biased estimate of the true measure, we followed Hall and Trajtenberg (2004) and applied the following correction to derive an unbiased estimate $\bar{y}$:[11]

$$\bar{y} = \frac{N_i}{N_i - 1} * G_i$$

We measured *Generality* based on all forward citations up to a year prior to the listing of the technology.[12] Put differently, for technology listings in 2007, we used the *Generality* in the year 2006.

Next, we developed a measure of prior commercialization of a focal technology. Recall that Hypotheses 2 theorizes about the moderating effect of technological characteristics and the relationship of the technology with the organizational context. In their technology listing, firms in Yet2 indicate if they have already commercially deployed a listed technology internally, which proxies the presence of existing organizational commercial routines for a focal technology. We set the variable *Prior Commercialization* to one if firms indicated in their listing that the technology was already commercialized internally. The variable was set at zero if we could not find evidence that the firm has already built in-house commercial routines for the specific technology.

Controls

We controlled for a host of invention and firm characteristics that may affect the number of applications identified for a focal technology. For invention characteristics, we used the USPTO database to construct several variables. Extant research has shown that the age and scope, that is, how well the invention is protected, affect the likelihood of commercialization (Nerkar & Shane, 2007). Accordingly, we used the variable *Technology Age*, which was calculated as the difference between the listing year and the patent's application year. *Claims* counts the number of claims for a listed invention, which is an indication of how well the invention is protected and *Technology Breadth* captures the number of international patent classes with which a technology listing is associated.[13] We further controlled for the underlying value of an invention by including the number of forward citations that an invention has received (Griliches, 1990; Harhoff, Narin, Scherer, & Vopel, 1999).[14] The variable *Technology Importance* is the number of citations to a given technology up to the year prior to the technology listing year. An additional control, *Inventors*, counts the number of inventors for the patent of an invention as recorded by USPTO. We also controlled how the technology fits into the existing patenting behavior of the firm by calculating how many of the patents in the prior 3 years were in the different main IPC category of the focal patent. The variable *non-Core Technology* is the percentage of all patents in IPCs which are not classified in the IPC of the focal patent.

From the technology listing, we controlled if firms are willing to commit their own personnel to support potential partners to capture the *Organizational Support* for the technology listing, which may lead firms to search for a broader range of applications. We also controlled if the applications mentioned are not the simple result of firms filing a very long and wordy technology listing by controlling for *Listing Length* by counting number of words used in the technology listing. Also, we controlled if the technology listing contained multiple patents to control for Complex Technologies as such listings by nature may cater to multiple applications. The concentration of sales in markets could drive the number of applications firms consider for their technologies. Hence, using Compustat segment data, we calculated a Herfindahl index of sales for the various business segments (four-digit NAICS) reported in Compustat in the year prior to the technology listing. Concentration of sales was measured as:

$$Sales\ \ Concentration = \sum_{i=1}^{N} S_i^2$$

where s_i is the share of industry sales of firm i and N is the number of industries in which the firm has generated sales. *Sales Concentration* is a value bound between zero and one and larger values indicate that most sales for a firm are concentrated in a few industries. Finally, on the organizational level, we controlled for *Firm Size* (total sales from Compustat) in the year prior to the technology listing on Yet2.

Empirical Specification

As application categories assigned by technology owners are integer counts that take only positive values, we employed a negative binomial specification. Models with dependent count variables may be misspecified using OLS regression, and Poisson regressions are restrictive as they require the mean and variance of the dependent variable to be equal (Long & Freese, 2006). The distribution of observations y_i of application categories follows the following Poisson distribution:

$$\Pr(y_i|x_i, \delta_i) = \frac{e^{-\mu_i}\mu_i^{y_i}}{y_i!}$$

In this model, δ_i corrects for the overdispersion and μ represents the mean count of application categories (Cameron & Trivedi, 1998). It is estimated by

$$\mu_i = \exp(x_i\beta)$$

wherein x_i contains our independent variables, including technological characteristics, financial resources and complementary assets. We also corrected the standard error by using robust errors. We controlled firm-fixed effects by entering firm dummies into all regression.[15]

Analysis

Table 2 reports the correlation matrix and descriptive statistics. In our sample, the average number of applications associated with a technology is 2.8. Also noteworthy are the technology age and citation counts, which indicate that the technologies listed on the market are, on average, over 6 years old and highly cited. Our key independent variables show little correlation, thus allowing us to interact them in the empirical analysis.

Table 3 reports the empirical results. Model 1 reports the baseline specification, including all control variables. Interestingly, the main effect of age demonstrates that the younger the technology, the more commercial applications are considered in the market for that technology. For *Prior Commercialization*, firms already have some proven and familiar applications, which is positively related to the number of applications assigned to a technology.[16] *Firm size* has a negative effect on the number of commercial applications. We also find robust evidence that the availability of

Organizational Support has a strong positive effect on the number of commercial applications considered feasible for a technology.

Model 2 adds technological *Generality*, which is our proxy for the technology's inherent fungibility, that is, the potential of the technology to be applied in a broad range of domains. The regression results support Hypothesis 1: the larger the number of applications considered by a firm, the greater the invention's technological generality. The marginal effect for *Generality* is positive as well ($p < 0.05$) and is meaningful: a standard deviation around the mean indicates an increase in generality, holding all other variables fixed at their mean, increasing the number of applications by 21%.

Next, we investigate how the effect of *Generality* on the *Count of Applications* may be moderated in the presence of commercial routines for the technology within the organization (*Prior Commercialization*). In Model 3, we interact *Generality* with the *Prior Commercialization* indicator. The result is consistent with Hypothesis 2: the interaction reveals a negative and significant effect. This suggests that once a technology has been internally deployed in commercial routines, the listing firm assigns a smaller number of applications for technologies, although the technology is inherently fungible (i.e., would have the potential to be applied broadly).

These results are meaningful: the marginal effect for *Generality* is positive and significant ($p < 0.01$) when *Prior Commercialization* is *0*. However, once Prior Commercialization is 1, the marginal effect of *Generality* becomes negative (insignificant at $p < 0.12$). To demonstrate, we visualized the interaction by plotting the effect of *Generality* on *Commercial Applications* for technologies with and without commercial routines in Fig. 2. For technologies absent commercial routines (i.e., *Prior Commercialization* is 0) we observe, as expected, a higher number of applications with higher levels of generality. However, this relationship does not hold in the presence of commercial routines for a focal technology. As one would expect in such cases, an inherently general technology is considered feasible for fewer applications. This suggests that firms may face issues in identifying a broad range of applications once a technology is already deployed in commercial routines.[17]

We collected further qualitative evidence on this effect to rule out the possibility that the pattern we observe stems from firms deliberately not reporting an application in which the technology has already been commercialized to avoid rent dissipating effects (Fosfuri, 2006). Counter to this concern, we observe a positive direct effect of *Prior Commercialization*, which suggests that firms do not underreport applications if they have

Table 2. Summary Statistics and Correlation Matrix.

		1	2	3	4	5	6	7	8	9	10	11	12	13	14
1	Commercial applications	1.00													
2	Technology age	0.03	1.00												
3	Number of inventors	−0.01	−0.20	1.00											
4	Number of claims	−0.06	−0.14	0.13	1.00										
5	Technology breadth	−0.03	−0.01	0.04	0.22	1.00									
6	Technology importance	0.03	0.25	0.08	0.24	0.00	1.00								
7	Non-core technology	0.04	−0.13	−0.01	0.07	−0.09	0.05	1.00							
8	Firm size	0.02	−0.08	0.08	−0.15	−0.07	−0.09	0.03	1.00						
9	Complex solution	0.02	0.04	0.02	−0.10	−0.11	−0.16	−0.19	−0.07	1.00					
10	Organizational support	0.21	−0.09	−0.01	0.11	−0.01	0.09	0.17	−0.12	0.06	1.00				
11	Listing length	0.15	0.10	0.11	0.12	0.03	0.22	0.01	0.04	0.23	0.38	1.00			
12	Sales concentration	0.19	0.12	−0.14	−0.06	−0.02	−0.05	−0.34	−0.01	0.22	−0.20	0.00	1.00		
13	Prior commercialization	0.14	0.23	−0.10	0.06	0.00	0.07	0.13	−0.09	0.22	0.21	0.26	0.12	1.00	
14	Generality	0.09	0.15	0.21	0.05	0.09	0.09	−0.04	−0.24	−0.08	−0.06	0.08	0.07	0.09	1.00
	Mean	2.82	6.47	2.42	15.71	5.84	8.41	0.97	2856.30	0.51	0.34	1002.41	0.53	0.23	0.68
	SD	1.97	4.19	1.29	10.74	3.78	7.76	0.03	1305.66	0.50	0.47	507.14	0.11	0.42	0.29
	Min	0.00	0.00	1.00	1.00	1.00	1.33	0.89	491.53	0.00	0.00	352.00	0.39	0.00	0.00
	Max	10.00	21.00	6.00	68.00	27.00	38.00	1.00	8546.99	1.00	1.00	2214.00	1.00	1.00	1.00

$n = 199$.

Table 3. Regression Results: Dependent Variable – Count of Commercial Applications.

Firm and Listing Year Effects	(1)	(2)	(3)	(4)	(5)	(6)	(7)	(8)	(9)
Technology age	–0.017	–0.017	–0.016	–0.018	–0.017	–0.014	–0.013	–0.025	–0.019
	+(0.009)	+(0.010)	+(0.009)	+(0.011)	+(0.010)	(0.009)	(0.009)	+(0.014)	+(0.012)
Number of inventors	–0.013	–0.030	–0.033	–0.012	–0.013	–0.052 +	–0.062*	–0.063	–0.053
	(0.037)	(0.038)	(0.037)	(0.037)	(0.033)	(0.031)	(0.030)	(0.055)	(0.053)
Number of claims	–0.006	–0.006	–0.005	–0.006	–0.006	–0.005	–0.004	–0.009	–0.006
	(0.004)	(0.004)	(0.004)	(0.004)	(0.004)	(0.004)	(0.003)	(0.006)	(0.005)
Technology breadth	0.000	0.001	0.002	–0.001	–0.002	0.004	0.003	–0.011	–0.006
	(0.013)	(0.013)	(0.013)	(0.010)	(0.010)	(0.011)	(0.010)	(0.014)	(0.014)
Technology importance	0.002	0.002	0.003	0.001	0.005	0.007	0.0155**	0.003	0.006
	(0.005)	(0.005)	(0.005)	(0.005)	(0.005)	(0.005)	(0.005)	(0.008)	(0.008)
Non-core technology	0.858	0.780	0.909	0.809	0.516	0.603	0.755	1.234	1.334
	(1.486)	(1.458)	(1.429)	(1.496)	(1.345)	(1.280)	(1.273)	(2.134)	(2.035)
Firm size	–0.002*	–0.002*	–0.002 +	–0.005**	–0.005**	–0.002*	–0.002*	–0.000	0.000
	(0.001)	(0.001)	(0.001)	(0.001)	(0.001)	(0.001)	(0.001)	(0.001)	(0.000)
Complex solution	–0.006	0.023	0.052	0.094	0.163	0.015	0.005	0.068	0.092
	(0.084)	(0.087)	(0.084)	(0.087)	+ (0.083)	(0.073)	(0.073)	(0.121)	(0.119)
Organizational support	0.344**	0.361**	0.348**	0.259*	0.263**	0.269**	0.257**	0.515**	0.606**
	(0.096)	(0.094)	(0.084)	(0.101)	(0.093)	(0.092)	(0.090)	(0.141)	(0.126)
Listing length	0.000	0.000	0.000	–0.000 +	–0.000	0.000	0.000	0.000	0.000
	(0.000)	(0.000)	(0.000)	(0.000)	+(0.000)	(0.000)	(0.000)	(0.000)	(0.000)
Sales concentration	–0.314	–0.285	–0.234	–0.203	–0.112	0.178	0.000	1.859	1.318
	(0.910)	(0.903)	(0.903)	(1.153)	(1.170)	(0.921)	(.)	(1.708)	(1.102)
	0.216 +	0.207 +	0.206 +	0.163	0.175*	0.166	0.387**	0.298 +	0.287 +

Prior commercialization	(0.114)	(0.122)	(0.114)	(0.103)	(0.087)	(0.103)	(0.130)	(0.174)	(0.166)
Generality		0.398*	0.574**	0.420*	0.725**			0.417*	0.841**
		(0.156)	(0.153)	(0.210)	(0.199)			(0.213)	(0.246)
Generality × Prior commercialization			−1.170**		−2.157**				−1.697**
			(0.333)		(0.482)				(0.407)
Technology importance × Prior commercialization							−0.031**		
							(0.009)		
Log likelihood	−336.02	−333.76	−330.60	−223.21	−220.06	−432.19	−428.58	−306.09	−301.43
Observations	199	199	199	139	139	256	256	195	195

$+p < .10$, $^{*}p < .05$, $^{**}p < .01$, robust standard errors.

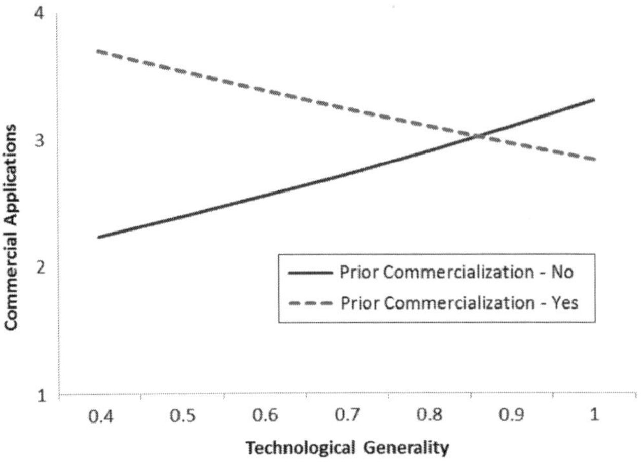

Fig. 2. Moderating Effect of "Prior Commercialization" (Technology Level).

already commercialized a technology internally. Also, we find (where possible) that in most (90%) cases, the application assigned on Yet2 is congruent with the business segments and, in their technology listings, firms explicitly mention the applications in which the technology was already commercialized to promote the technology. This suggests that firms do not systematically underreport those applications in which the technology was already commercialized, and hence, mitigates concerns that our results are driven by rent dissipation considerations (Fosfuri, 2006).

Robustness Tests: In order to ensure that our results are not driven by technology listings with just a few citations, we replicated our analysis for all technology listings with at least four or more citations. The results (reported in Models 4 and 5) are very similar to those reported in Models 2 and 3. Given that we exclude a large number of observations (with only 1 or 2 citations), we tried to find an alternative measure for fungibility and used an alternative approach including all available technology listings (256), which comprises those for which we cannot generate a generality measure (zero or one forward citation only). Given that important technologies (i.e., highly cited inventions) correspond closely with economic value (Harhoff et al., 1999; Shane, 2001), firms may have an incentive to apply them to a broad range of applications. The number of citations also reflects broad interest in the technology, which may suggest greater fungibility.

While not as close as *Generality*, *Technological Importance* (in the form of received citations) is an alternative proxy for fungibility, which we can capture for all technology listings on Yet2.com. As Models 6 and 7 demonstrate, we do not find a direct effect of *Technological Importance* on the number of applications. However, the moderating effect is very similar to the one observed for *Generality*. This gives us confidence that prior commercialization of a technology may indeed profoundly affect the way in which firms link technologies and applications in the market for technology. Finally, we excluded the 4 observations with 0 applications reported on Yet2. We redid our analysis deploying a zero truncated negative binomial model to account for the fact that we no longer have zero values for our dependent variable. Models 8 and 9 demonstrate very similar patterns to those previously observed.

Online Markets for Technology – Facilitating Linkages between Technologies and Applications?

Thus far, we have focused on firms participating in such markets to list their technologies and have used the market for technology setting to outline some of the inherent challenges of effectively linking technologies to applications. However, online knowledge markets connect and facilitate transactions between two pools of participants: on the one hand, they accommodate inventors listing technologies and, on the other, they assist those who seek to partner for and commercialize the inventions (Bakos, 1998; Dushnitsky & Klueter, 2010). Hence, such marketplaces may be able to facilitate revealing novel technology-application combinations for a technology-owning firm.

Online marketplaces are characterized by open networks and connectivity which allow participants to observe and communicate with distant and diverse constituencies (Amit & Zott, 2001; Bakos, 1997; Garicano & Kaplan, 2001). This offers access to a large pool of complementary knowledge, which could reveal application possibilities previously unconsidered by the firm. Put differently, it is likely that more applications are uncovered, the more diverse firms can engage and communicate with one another. In many cases, possible partners may have customers or have access to customers from industries previously unserved by a focal firm, which would further enable determining new technology-application combinations. Robert Hirsch (Dupont), on using Yet2.com, explained (Wood & Scott, 2004, p. 20): "But it's quite unlike a process where we know who the potential customers are. Often potential customers are from industries we would never normally have considered."

Another important advantage of using partners in online markets is that they, in contrast to the technology owner, are unencumbered by existing commercial routines or embedded competencies which, as we have mentioned, leads to challenges in linking technologies to applications. Extant research has suggested that firms are more likely to challenge their own status quo when they engage with outsiders (Gilbert, 2005). Hence, by involving outsiders through online marketplaces, firms may be more likely to challenge existing technology-application combinations and make it more likely that alternative applications will be considered. As an example, Chemcor, the durable glass Corning had produced for a variety of applications (phone booths, windshields, prison windows) had not had substantial success and many of the activities associated with the technology (sales, marketing) had been shut down. However, through their interactions and conversations with Apple, new potential uses (for iPhones) were revealed. As a consequence, the "Gorilla Glass" segment within Corning was introduced and experienced great success (e.g., a billion dollars in sales in 2013, according to the annual report).

Finally, engaging in a marketplace requires firms to systematically de-link the technology from the organization as they need to explain and codify that technology on its own merits, absent existing routines and commercial applications. These markets necessitate disclosure and codification such that each inventor has to provide a standardized written description of the invention to be listed on a marketplace (Dushnitsky & Klueter, 2010). When interacting with potential partners, firms must explain to outsiders the characteristics of the technology, without referencing existing organizational applications. This de-linking of technologies from the organization and its existing firm-specific applications and explaining the technology to an external party has noteworthy implications. Namely, it simplifies the representation of technological inventions and demonstrates their value beyond their firm-specific applications for the technology owner (Conti, Gambardella, & Novelli, 2013; Danneels, 2007). A quote from Yet2 exemplifies these benefits as "Yet2.com features functional abstracts written in plain English to communicate the potential applications and benefits of the technology". As the technology is further separated from the organization, it becomes easier to evaluate possible application opportunities than when the process would unfold internally. In a similar vein, researchers have highlighted the importance of structural separation when firms deal with technologies that require different commercial routines and business models (Chesbrough & Rosenbloom, 2002).

Given these underlying features, online markets for technology may be a way through which, over time, firms uncover novel applications for their technologies, and, hence, present a possible solution to the challenge of linking technologies to applications for inherently fungible technologies. As an example, in the pharmaceutical industry, there is already a great deal of repositioning of old drugs in partnership with firms with complementary knowledge in new business domains (Ashburn & Thor, 2004).

CONCLUSIONS

The challenges associated with deploying resources to growing businesses is of key importance to organizations (Penrose, 1959; Teece, 1982). This paper takes into account that a precondition for such deployment of technological resources to commercial applications is the awareness of possible linkages between technologies and applications in the first place. If firms are not aware of such linkages, they may consider one application for a technology but redeployment, that is, the withdrawal of resources from one business segment and the allocation of resource to another (Helfat & Eisenhardt, 2004; Sakhartov & Folta, 2014), cannot unfold.

In particular, we take the perspective of incumbent firms that intend to grow by leveraging their resources and examine the number of commercial applications they consider feasible for their technologies. We take into account that both technological (i.e., inherent fungibility captured through technological generality) and organizational (prior commercialization, deployment in organizational routines) characteristics may shape the number of applications considered feasible for a focal technology. We study this question using a unique research context: online markets for technologies, where we observe firms listing technologies and assigning commercial applications to these technologies.

Our analysis of 199 patented inventions listed by technology owners on Yet2.com, one of the largest online technology marketplaces, offers important insights. We confirm prior studies that focused on the role of technological characteristics and, in particular, the technology's fungibility, that is, the potential to apply a technology to multiple commercial applications (Levinthal & Wu, 2010; Penrose, 1959; Teece, 1982). Our evidence suggests that technologies with high technological generality (a proxy for the technology's inherent fungibility) are associated with a larger number of perceived applications by firms. However, supporting the idea of challenges linking technologies to applications (Danneels, 2007; Maine & Garnsey, 2006), the relationship does not hold once a firm has already internally commercialized the technology. This demonstrates that once a technology is deployed in organizational routines (dedicated complementary assets, personnel), firms may find it challenging to identify a broad set of commercial applications for inherently fungible technologies. This finding is important as it suggests that the deployment of resources to new applications may fail to unfold, as firms are simply not aware of the underlying technology-application combination possibilities. In such cases, technologies likely are applied narrowly, which would preclude a firm from reaping the true benefits of their technological resources (DiMasi, Hansen, & Grabowski, 2003; Rivette & Kline, 2000).

Beyond the challenges, which we observe to link technologies to applications, we further theorize the way in which online markets for technologies may be a possible solution. These markets bring together strangers, thus constituting a sharp departure from accepted practices wherein transactions tend to materialize in one's internal, geographic area and social circle (e.g., Kirsch, Goldfarb, & Gera, 2009; Shane & Cable, 2002). We outline that once listed on a marketplace, the diversity and breadth of external partners, the influential role of outsiders and the unbundling of the technology from the organizational context likely can help expand the technology-application combinations technology owners consider feasible.

While our theory applies equally to synergy and redeployment, it is particularly applicable to a theory around redeployment because value derives from the flexibility to reallocate resources. If a firm does not know where it might reallocate, then one cannot derive intertemporal economies of scope. In particular, the study demonstrates important challenges, which come before the actual implementation costs for redeployment (Sakhartov & Folta, 2014). It indicates that firms already deploying technologies in commercial routines may face challenges once these technologies need to be shifted toward alternative domains. In particular, our study shows that redeployment may be much more difficult than initial deployment, which suggests that firms may be less effective when redeploying technologies to applications. In an entrepreneurial setting, the linkages between technologies and commercial markets tend to occur at the same time (Grégoire & Shepherd, 2012; Maine & Garnsey, 2006; Shane, 2000) but, in our context, firms try to deploy technologies that may already be deployed in commercial markets. Hence, our study may explain some of the advantages nascent firms have in moving toward new markets compared to established firms (Christensen & Rosenbloom, 1995; Foster, 1986).

Second, the study showcases markets for technology, not only as a possible research setting but also as tools with which firms can expand the range of applications for a given technology. This augments the idea that resources for redeployment need to be both fungible and non-tradable (Anand & Singh, 1997). Namely, redeployment opportunities may only be uncovered through the involvement of external partners. Hence, considering that firms may redeploy by combining resources with other firms may be an important area for future research and could complement studies on pure internal redeployment.

Despite these insights, several issues remain unaddressed. First, we need a better grasp of what technologies firms would put on online markets for technologies and for which they would engage with external partners to the ones they prefer to exclusively deploy in-house. Also, we need a better understanding of under which circumstances firms may fully depart from their resources and leave the deployment to another firm, as has been suggested in the literature on the redeployment following acquisitions (Capron, Dussauge, & Mitchell, 1998; Capron, Mitchell, & Swaminathan, 2001). Hence, future research needs to compare the market for internal deployment to the market for external liquidation and address market failures underlying those two alternatives.

Moreover, we need to better understand how the actual linkage of technology and applications unfolds. Our study does not capture these issues as we do not observe realized deals (and their pricing) or the implementation of redeployment internally (following the interaction on such markets). Future research, hence, needs to capture in which applications technologies are ultimately deployed and the prices firms pay when they share and combine their resources.

Overall, we believe that online markets for technology may provide an important research setting to more systematically examine how matches between technologies and applications ultimately unfold. It will be interesting to observe how firms will experiment with such markets and how learning about their own technologies and their potential applications occurs and what consequences that has for the deployment and redeployment of their resources to applications.

NOTES

1. A resource is a tangible or intangible asset that the firm owns, controls, or has access to and from which the firm can derive rents (Helfat & Peteraf, 2003).

2. Our focus in the paper is less on the actual redeployment, that is, the withdrawal of resources and their deployment in another business segment, than on the initial step of redeployment wherein firms link existing resources to applications. As such, our insights may also have implications for the "intratemporal economies" (i.e., synergy) in which resources are shared contemporaneously across market applications (Helfat & Eisenhardt, 2004).

3. Now GlaxoSmithKline.

4. While technology in the form of IP may be considered scale-free, the redeployment of such resources tend to entail changes in personnel, management as well as new competencies (e.g., new therapeutic areas). Hence, the bundle of resources which is associated with the redeployment less likely is scale-free.

5. The inventions listed on Yet2 include major inventions such as the Oncomouse by DuPont (Murray, Aghion, Dewatripont, Kolev, & Stern, 2009).

6. The use of standardized listings ensures that the technologies on the marketplace conform to some minimum quality.

7. Hence, studying how technology-owning firms engage in such markets provides a lens to see what technology-application matches they consider feasible and are aware of. Our assumption is that applications considered for a technology on online markets correlate with those of which organizations are internally aware.

8. All data were accessed from Yet2.com in February 2009. We could then use Yet2 data to gauge the number a months a technology was posted on the website, dating the earliest posting to circa 2003.

9. See robustness tests for the inclusion of the missing 57 observations.

10. An important concern is that firms may simply opt to assign all possible applications for their technologies. However, as Fig. 1 demonstrates, this is not the case and there is substantial within-firm heterogeneity in the number of applications considered. Moreover, there are possible costs of overreporting applications as technology listers are scrutinized by a possible partner, which leads to a reputational risk if a firm is unable to explain why it assigned a product application category. We also conduct additional robustness tests in our analysis to address this issue.

11. We followed Hall et al. (2001) and considered patents with at least two forward citations. This led to omitting 57 observations.

12. For technology listings with multiple patents, we used the average generality score. Results did not change using the maximum value for Generality.

13. We follow Hall et al. (2001) who systematically distinguished measures using backward citations (i.e., technology breadth) and forward citations (generality). It is noteworthy that the literature has seen a number of related proxies. Claims have been suggested as an alternative measure for the general nature of an invention (Lerner, 1994). However, as firms could artificially augment their number of claims, this measure can be noisy (Gambardella & Giarratana, 2013), and we only used it as a control. In a similar vein, technology breadth could be another alternative measure. However, technology breadth has been used for a range of other theoretical

constructs including firm search activities (Ahuja & Katila, 2004) or the breadth of property protection (Shane, 2001).

14. For technology listings with multiple patents, all patent-based variables were averaged.

15. We have eight firms in total in our sample. The majority of technology listings come from DuPont, Honeywell.

16. We did not theorize about the direct effect of prior commercialization and deployment in commercial routines. Our theoretical arguments only relate to how prior commercialization interacts with highly fungible technologies and the moderating role of commercial routines.

17. The downward slope when Prior Commercialization is 1 is likely driven by two effects. First, the direct effect of Prior Commercialization is marginally positive, so that a technology already commercialized internally, in general, has more applications than technologies which have not yet been commercialized internally. Second, we were only able to capture commercial routines through an indicator variable and, hence, lack a more fine-grained measure.

ACKNOWLEDGMENTS

The authors would like to thank the volume co-editors, Tim Folta, Connie Helfat and Samina Karim, for their guidance and insights. They also thank the Mack Institute for Innovation Management for their support.

REFERENCES

Ahuja, G., & Katila, R. (2004). Where do resources come from? The role of idiosyncratic situations. *Strategic Management Journal*, *25*(8–9), 887–907.

Ahuja, G., & Morris Lampert, C. (2001). Entrepreneurship in the large corporation: A longitudinal study of how established firms create breakthrough inventions. *Strategic Management Journal*, *22*(6–7), 521–543.

Amit, R., & Zott, C. (2001). Value creation in e-business. *Strategic Management Journal*, *22*(6–7), 493–520.

Anand, J., & Singh, H. (1997). Asset redeployment, acquisitions and corporate strategy in declining industries. *Strategic Management Journal*, *18*, 99–118.

Argyres, N., & Silverman, B. (2004). R&D, organization structure, and the development of corporate technological knowledge. *Strategic Management Journal*, *25*(8–9), 929.

Arora, A., & Gambardella, A. (2010). Ideas for rent: An overview of markets for technology. *Industrial and Corporate Change*, *19*(3), 775–803.

Ashburn, T. T., & Thor, K. B. (2004). Drug repositioning: Identifying and developing new uses for existing drugs. *Nature Reviews Drug Discovery*, *3*(8), 673–683.

Audia, P. G., Locke, E. A., & Smith, K. G. (2000). The paradox of success: An archival and a laboratory study of strategic persistence following radical environmental change. *Academy of Management Journal*, *43*(5), 837–853.

Bakos, J. Y. (1997). Reducing buyer search costs: Implications for electronic marketplaces. *Management Science*, *43*(12), 1676–1692.

Bakos, Y. (1998). The emerging role of electronic marketplaces on the internet. *Communications of the ACM*, *41*(8), 35–42.

Basalla, G. (1988). *The evolution of technology*. Cambridge: Cambridge University Press.

Cameron, A., & Trivedi, P. (1998). *Regression analysis of count data*. Cambridge: Cambridge University Press.

Capron, L., Dussauge, P., & Mitchell, W. (1998). Resource redeployment following horizontal acquisitions in Europe and North America, 1988–1992. *Strategic Management Journal*, *19*(7), 631–661.

Capron, L., Mitchell, W., & Swaminathan, A. (2001). Asset divestiture following horizontal acquisitions: A dynamic view. *Strategic Management Journal*, *22*(9), 817–844.

Chatterjee, S., Lubatkin, M. H., Schweiger, D. M., & Weber, Y. (1992). Cultural differences and shareholder value in related mergers: Linking equity and human capital. *Strategic Management Journal*, *13*(5), 319–334.

Chesbrough, H., & Rosenbloom, R. S. (2002). The role of the business model in capturing value from innovation: Evidence from Xerox corporation's technology spin-off companies. *Industrial and Corporate Change*, *11*(3), 529–555.

Christensen, C. M., & Rosenbloom, R. S. (1995). Explaining the attacker's advantage: Technological paradigms, organizational dynamics, and the value network. *Research Policy*, *24*, 233–257.

Conti, R., Gambardella, A., & Novelli, E. (2013). Research on markets for inventions and implications for R&D allocation strategies. *Academy of Management Annals*, *7*(1), 715–772.

Danneels, E. (2002). The dynamics of product innovation and firm competences. *Strategic Management Journal*, *23*(12), 1095–1121.

Danneels, E. (2007). The process of technological competence leveraging. *Strategic Management Journal*, *28*(5), 511.

DiMasi, J., Hansen, R., & Grabowski, H. (2003). The price of innovation: New estimates of drug development costs. *Journal of Health Economics*, *22*(2), 151–185.

DuPont. (2011). *DuPont Teflon*, Vol. 2011.

Dushnitsky, G., & Klueter, T. (2010). Is there an eBay for ideas? Insights from online knowledge marketplaces. *European Management Review*, *8*(1), 17–32.

Dushnitsky, G., & Klueter, T. (2011). Is there an eBay for ideas? Insights from online knowledge marketplaces. *European Management Review*, *8*(1), 17–32.

Fleming, L., & Sorenson, O. (2004). Science as a map in technological search. *Strategic Management Journal*, *25*(8–9), 909–928.

Fosfuri, A. (2006). The licensing dilemma: Understanding the determinants of the rate of technology licensing. *Strategic Management Journal*, *27*(12), 1141.

Foster, R. N. (1986). *Innovation: The attacker's advantage*. New York, NY: Summit Books.

Freeman, C., & Soete, L. (1997). *The economics of industrial innovation* (3rd ed.). London: Pinter Press.

Gambardella, A., & Giarratana, M. S. (2013). General technological capabilities, product market fragmentation, and markets for technology. *Research Policy*, *42*(2), 315–325.

Gambardella, A., Giuri, P., & Luzzi, A. (2007). The market for patents in Europe. *Research Policy*, *36*(8), 1163–1183.
Garicano, L., & Kaplan, S. N. (2001). The effects of business-to-business e-commerce on transaction costs. *The Journal of Industrial Economics*, *49*(4), 463–485.
Gilbert, C. G. (2005). Unbundling the structure of inertia: Resource versus routine rigidity. *Academy of Management Journal*, *5*(48), 741–763.
Grégoire, D. A., & Shepherd, D. A. (2012). Technology-market combinations and the identification of entrepreneurial opportunities: An investigation of the opportunity-individual nexus. *Academy of Management Journal*, *55*(4), 753–785.
Griliches, Z. (1990). Patent statistics as economic indicators: A survey. *Journal of Economic Literature*, *28*(4), 1661–1707.
Gruber, M., MacMillan, I. C., & Thompson, J. D. (2008). Look before you leap: Market opportunity identification in emerging technology firms. *Management Science*, *54*(9), 1652–1665.
Hall, B. H., & Trajtenberg, M. (2004). *Uncovering GPTs with patent data*. NBER Working Paper No. 10901. Cambridge, MA: National Bureau of Economic Research.
Hall, B., Jaffe, A., & Trajtenberg, M. (2001). *The NBER patent citations data file: Lessons, insights and methodological tools*. NBER Working Paper No. 8498. Cambridge, MA: National Bureau of Economic Research.
Harhoff, D., Narin, F., Scherer, F. M., & Vopel, K. (1999). Citation frequency and the value of patented inventions. *Review of Economics & Statistics*, *81*(3), 511–515.
Hartmann, M., & Hassan, A. (2006). Application of real options analysis for pharmaceutical R&D project valuation—Empirical results from a survey. *Research Policy*, *35*(3), 343–354.
Helfat, C. E., & Eisenhardt, K. M. (2004). Inter-temporal economies of scope, organizational modularity, and the dynamics of diversification. *Strategic Management Journal*, *25*(13), 1217–1232.
Helfat, C. E., & Peteraf, M. A. (2003). The dynamic resource-based view: Capability lifecycles. *Strategic Management Journal*, *24*(10), 997–1010.
Hill, C., & Rothaermel, F. (2003). The performance of incumbent firms in the face of radical technological innovation. *Academy of Management Review*, *28*(2), 257–274.
Itami, H., & Roehl, T. W. (1991). *Mobilizing invisible assets*. Cambridge, MA: Harvard University Press.
Kirsch, D., Goldfarb, B., & Gera, A. (2009). Form or substance: The role of business plans in venture capital decision making. *Strategic Management Journal*, *30*(5), 487–515.
Kline, S., & Rosenberg, N. (1986). An overview of innovation. In R. Landau & N. Rosenberg (Eds.), *The positive sum strategy: Harnessing technology for economic growth* (pp. 275–305). Washington, DC: The National Academic Press.
Leone, M. I., & Reichstein, T. (2012). Licensing-in fosters rapid invention! the effect of the grant-back clause and technological unfamiliarity. *Strategic Management Journal*, *33*(8), 965–985.
Lerner, J. (1994). The importance of patent scope: An empirical analysis. *The RAND Journal of Economics*, *25*(2), 319–333.
Levinthal, D., & Wu, B. (2010). Opportunity costs and non scale free capabilities: Profit maximization, corporate scope, and profit margins. *Strategic Management Journal*, *31*(7), 780–801.

Long, J. S., & Freese, J. (2006). *Regression models for categorical dependent variables using stata* (2nd ed.). College Park, TX: Stata Press.

Maine, E., & Garnsey, E. (2006). Commercializing generic technology: The case of advanced materials ventures. *Research Policy*, *35*(3), 375–393.

March, J., & Simon, H. (1958). *Organizations*. New York, NY: Wiley.

Murray, F., Aghion, P., Dewatripont, M., Kolev, J., & Stern, S. (2009). *Of mice and academics: Examining the effect of openness on innovation*. National Bureau of Economic Research Working Paper Series No. 14819.

Murray, F., & O'Mahony, S. (2007). Exploring the foundations of cumulative innovation: Implications for organization science. *Organization Science*, *18*(6), 1006–1021.

Nelson, R. R. (1990). Capitalism as an engine of progress. *Research Policy*, *19*(3), 193–214.

Nelson, R., & Winter, S. (1982). *An evolutionary theory of economic change*. Cambridge, MA: Belknap Press.

Nerkar, A., & Shane, S. (2007). Determinants of invention commercialization: An empirical examination of academically sourced inventions. *Strategic Management Journal*, *28*(11), 1155–1166.

Palomeras, N. (2007). An analysis of pure-revenue technology licensing. *Journal of Economics & Management Strategy*, *16*(4), 971–994.

Penrose, E. (1959). *The theory of the growth of the firm*. Oxford: Oxford University Press.

Prahalad, C. K., & Hamel, G. (1990). The core competence of the corporation. *Harvard Business Review*, *68*(4), 79–91.

Rivette, K., & Kline, D. (2000). Discovering new value in intellectual property. *Harvard Business Review*, *78*(1), 54–146.

Rosenkopf, L., & Nerkar, A. (2001). Beyond local search: Boundary-spanning, exploration, and impact in the optical disk industry. *Strategic Management Journal*, *22*(4), 287–306.

Sakhartov, A. V., & Folta, T. B. (2014). Resource relatedness, redeployability, and firm value. *Strategic Management Journal*, *35*(12), 1781–1797.

Schumpeter, J. (1934). *The theory of economic development: An inquiry into profits, capital, credit, interest, and the business cycle*. Cambridge, MA: Harvard University Press.

Shane, S. (2000). Prior knowledge and the discovery of entrepreneurial opportunities. *Organization Science*, *11*(4), 448–469.

Shane, S. (2001). Technological opportunities and new firm creation. *Management Science*, *47*(2), 205–220.

Shane, S., & Cable, D. (2002). Network ties, reputation, and the financing of new ventures. *Management Science*, *48*(3), 364–381.

Teece, D. (1982). Towards an economic theory of the multiproduct firm. *Journal of Economic Behavior & Organization*, *3*, 39–63.

Tripsas, M., & Gavetti, G. (2000). Capabilities, cognition and inertia: Evidence from digital imaging. *Strategic Management Journal*, *21*, 1147–1161.

Venkataraman, S. (1997). The distinctive domain of entrepreneurship research. *Advances in Entrepreneurship, Firm Emergence and Growth*, *3*(1), 119–138.

Wernerfelt, B. (1984). A resource-based view of the firm. *Strategic Management Journal*, *5*(2), 171–174.

Winter, S. G. (2000). Appropriating the gains from innovation. In G. Day & P. J. H. Schoemaker (Eds.), *Wharton on managing emerging technologies*. New York, NY: Wiley.

Wood, A., & Scott, A. (2004). Licensing activity is on the rise. *Chemical Week*, *166*(10), 20.

Yang, H., Phelps, C., & Steensma, H. K. (2010). Learning from what others have learned from you: The effects of knowledge spillovers on originating firms. *The Academy of Management Journal, 53*(2), 371–389.

Yet2.com. (2009). Yet2.com executive overview, Vol. 2009.

Zollo, M., Reuer, J., & Singh, H. (2002). Interorganizational routines and performance in strategic alliances. *Organization Science, 13*(6), 701–713.

RESOURCE RECONFIGURATION: LEARNING FROM PERFORMANCE FEEDBACK

Ari Dothan and Dovev Lavie

ABSTRACT

Resource reconfiguration enables firms to adapt in dynamic environments by supplementing, removing, recombining, or redeploying resources. Whereas prior research has underscored the merits of resource reconfiguration and the modes for implementing it, little is known about the antecedents of this practice. According to prior research, under given industry conditions, resource reconfiguration is prompted by a firm's corporate strategy and by characteristics of its knowledge assets. We complement this research by identifying learning from performance feedback as a fundamental driver of resource reconfiguration. We claim that performance decline relative to aspiration motivates the firm's investment in knowledge reconfiguration, and that this investment is reinforced by the munificence of complementary resources in its industry, although uncertainty about the availability of such resources limits that investment. Testing our conjectures with a sample of 248 electronics firms during the period 1993–2001, we reveal a clear distinction between exploitative reconfiguration, which combines existing knowledge elements, and

Resource Redeployment and Corporate Strategy
Advances in Strategic Management, Volume 35, 319–369

ISSN: 0742-3322/doi:10.1108/S0742-332220160000035011

exploratory reconfiguration, which incorporates new knowledge elements. We demonstrate that performance decline relative to aspiration motivates a shift from exploitative reconfiguration to exploratory reconfiguration. Moreover, munificence of complementary resources mitigates the tradeoff between exploratory and exploitative reconfigurations, whereas uncertainty weakens the motivation to engage in both types of reconfiguration, despite the performance gap. Nevertheless, codeployment, which extends the deployment of knowledge assets to additional domains, is more susceptible to uncertainty than redeployment, which withdraws those assets from their original domain and reallocates them to new domains. Our study contributes to emerging research on resource reconfiguration, extends the literature on learning from performance feedback, and advances research on balancing exploration and exploitation.

Keywords: Resource reconfiguration; resource redeployment; learning; performance feedback; exploration; exploitation

INTRODUCTION

Organizational change and adaptation are essential for firms' abilities to sustain their competitive advantages and survive in dynamic environments, such as those prevalent in technology-intensive industries. Firms nurture dynamic capabilities that enable them to modify their resource stocks in response to changing environmental conditions (Helfat, 1997; Teece, 2007). However, recent research has shifted focus from the question of whether a firm is able to adapt to an examination of the processes and means by which adaptation is achieved (Anand, 2004; Lavie, 2012). Such research refers to resource reconfiguration, defined as the set of processes for supplementing a firm's current resource stocks with new resources, removing resources from these stocks, recombining different resources in these stocks, or redeploying them for various uses within the firm (Karim & Mitchell, 2004). To reconfigure their resources, firms rely on multiple modes of operation, including internal development, exchange transactions, alliance formation, and acquisitions, which leverage both internal and external resources, as well as integrate existing resources with newly acquired resources (Capron & Mitchell, 2009, 2012; Karim & Mitchell, 2000).

Whereas prior research has underscored the implications of resource reconfiguration and the means by which firms pursue this practice, little is known about the antecedents of resource reconfiguration. What drives a firm's decision to reconfigure its resource stocks? Prior research has associated the tendency to engage in resource reconfiguration with industry conditions, such as munificence of resources in the firm's industry (Sirmon, Hitt, & Ireland, 2007; Yasai-Ardekani, 1989) and uncertainty about the availability of such resources (Sutcliffe & Zaheer, 1998). In an attempt to account for heterogeneity in firms' tendencies to engage in resource reconfiguration under given industry conditions, scholars have focused on the characteristics of a firm's knowledge assets, suggesting that highly dispersed and tacit knowledge, and context-specific routines, may impede detection of knowledge elements and increase their transfer cost, which reduces the likelihood of resource reconfiguration (Galunic & Rodan, 1998). Fungibility of resources and their relatedness can facilitate the sharing and redeployment of resources, and thus encourage their reconfiguration (Sakhartov & Folta, 2015). Another stream of research has associated resource reconfiguration with strategies for expanding or contracting firms' corporate scope, as firms enter businesses, exit them, or attempt to improve their industry positions (Karim & Capron, 2015).

Besides external industry conditions, knowledge characteristics, and firms' strategies that drive resource reconfiguration, we contend that the behavioral inclinations of managers (Levinthal, 2011) can motivate resource reconfiguration. Specifically, we assert that performance feedback (Greve, 1998b) can influence the motivation of managers to reconfigure their firms' resource stocks. Thus, we study how changes in a firm's performance relative to its managers' aspirations affect the reconfiguration of the firm's knowledge assets, which are considered the most critical resource in technology-driven industries (Grant, 1996b; Spender, 1996). The firm's knowledge includes codified know-how in the form of documents or blueprints as well as tacit knowledge.

We follow the distinction between exploration and exploitation (Levinthal & March, 1993) when considering both exploratory and exploitative resource reconfigurations. Exploitative reconfiguration involves integrating, leveraging, or redeploying internal resources that the firm has already used in the past. In contrast, exploratory reconfiguration involves incorporating external resources that the firm has not previously used, and integrating them with its internal resources.[1] The knowledge management literature identifies the processes that enable firms to acquire, integrate, maintain, deploy, transfer, and combine knowledge elements (Grant, 1996a; Miller, 2002). Firms innovate by recombining knowledge elements that they developed in the past with newly acquired knowledge elements

(Katila & Ahuja, 2002; Kogut & Zander, 1992). Accordingly, knowledge recombination is a form of resource reconfiguration in which the firm leverages existing knowledge and integrates it with new knowledge. Hence, we examine how performance feedback drives both exploratory and exploitative knowledge reconfiguration.

Specifically, we predict that a firm will increase its investment in knowledge reconfiguration as its performance falls relative to its performance aspiration. Additionally, we predict that munificence of complementary resources in the firm's industry will reinforce the motivation to invest in knowledge reconfiguration following a performance decline, whereas uncertainty about the availability of such resources will attenuate that investment. We test our hypotheses with panel data on 248 publicly traded U.S.-based electronics firms operating during the period 1993–2001. We conclude with a post hoc analysis that distinguishes redeployment from codeployment of knowledge assets. Redeployment involves withdrawing a resource that has been originally used in a particular domain and reallocating it to new domains. In contrast, codeployment involves extending the deployment of a resource to additional domains in the hope of gaining synergy.

Our findings confirm that a firm increases its investment in exploratory reconfiguration of knowledge assets when its performance falls below aspiration. Nevertheless, at the same time, the firm reduces its investment in exploitative reconfiguration of knowledge assets in response to that performance decline. The shift from exploitative to exploratory reconfiguration is attributed to the tradeoff between exploration and exploitation (Lavie, Stettner, & Tushman, 2010) and to the riskier nature of exploration. Our findings further reveal that munificence of complementary resources, such as human resources, reinforces the tendency to invest in exploratory reconfiguration of knowledge assets following performance decline, but weakens the decline in exploitative reconfiguration, as it attenuates the tradeoff between exploration and exploitation. Finally, uncertainty about the availability of complementary resources restricts both exploratory and exploitative reconfigurations. This effect is more prevalent in codeployment than in redeployment of knowledge assets, since complementary resources that are non-scale-free restrict codeployment.

Our study contributes to the resource reconfiguration literature (Karim & Capron, 2015) by uncovering the role of performance feedback in driving resource reconfiguration. In addition, we introduce the important distinction between exploratory and exploitative reconfigurations and demonstrate the tradeoff between them. In particular, we reveal how a decline in performance relative to aspiration motivates a shift from reliance on existing knowledge elements to the riskier introduction of new knowledge elements. In this sense, we also contribute to the literature on exploration and exploitation (Levinthal & March, 1993) by indicating how performance feedback tilts the balance between these activities (Lavie et al., 2010). Moreover, to the best of our knowledge, this is the first study to introduce an empirical measure of resource redeployment that tracks the extent to which a resource is deployed in domains other than the domain in which it was first used. Prior research has captured this construct indirectly by inferring it from product market entry (Anand, 2004). Finally, we advance research on learning from performance feedback (Greve, 2003b) by underscoring its implications for resource reconfiguration, which serves as a precursor to various strategic endeavors observed by prior research, and by uncovering some environmental contingencies that serve as boundary conditions for these implications.

THEORY

Performance Feedback as a Driver of Resource Reconfiguration

Prior research on the antecedents of resource reconfiguration has underscored the roles of environmental conditions, knowledge characteristics, and firms' strategies, without alluding to behavioral inclinations that can shape the motivation to initiate resource reconfiguration. Nevertheless, research on learning from performance feedback suggests that performance feedback can motivate various corporate activities such as product development, R&D investment, and acquisitions. We extend this research by arguing that performance feedback can motivate resource reconfiguration, which underlies these corporate development activities and restructuring decisions.

The literature on learning from performance feedback builds on the early work of Cyert and March (1963), who introduce the notion of problemistic search to describe the process by which decision makers seek solutions to emerging problems. Such a search is prompted when a firm performs below an aspiration level set based on its own experience or a benchmark relative to relevant firms in its environment. The performance aspiration represents an acceptable level of performance from the firm's standpoint (Schneider, 1992) and thus serves as a reference point. Failure to reach that aspiration level prompts a search for solutions that can improve performance. According to Cyert and March (1963), a firm searches for an expedient solution in the vicinity of its prior solutions, which entails adjusting existing practices. If such proximate solution and minor remedies fall short of solving the problem, however, the firm may extend its search for solutions beyond its past experience, and undertake major initiatives (Grinyer & McKiernan, 1990). The underlying argument is that deviance from the performance aspiration motivates organizational search, risk taking, and corporate change (Shinkle, 2012). The gap between the firm's current performance and its performance aspiration is referred to as the performance gap (Park, 2007). Performance gaps are either positive, when performance exceeds the aspiration level, or negative, when performance falls below aspiration. It is mostly the latter that motivates corporate activities.

Managers assess their firm's current performance relative to their aspiration level, which represents the minimal outcome that is deemed satisfactory (Greve, 2003b). The performance aspiration typically combines historical aspiration based on the firm's past performance and social aspiration based on the performance of a reference group in the firm's industry (Fiegenbaum & Thomas, 1995), which offers a benchmark for desirable performance. Accordingly, a firm may follow the industry's leaders or compare its performance to that of other firms that are assumed to react similarly to environmental conditions. The better the firm's actual performance relative to its aspiration, the less motivated it is to engage in problemistic search and initiate corporate activities.[2]

Research on learning from performance feedback identifies the performance gap as an antecedent to a firm's propensity to undertake various corporate activities, including change in a firm's market position (Greve, 1998a; Park, 2007), repositioning within its strategic group (Schimmer & Brauer, 2012), R&D investment (Chen & Miller, 2007; Greve, 2003a), product innovation (Greve, 2003a, 2007; Yayavaram & Chen, 2015), acquisitions (Gaba & Bhattacharya, 2012; Iyer & Miller, 2008), and alliance formation (Baum, Rowley, Shipilov, & Chuang, 2005). These studies demonstrate that organizational changes are more likely when the firm's performance falls below aspiration than when it exceeds aspiration, resulting in a negative association between the probability of change and the extent of the performance gap. Since the aforementioned corporate activities entail resource reconfiguration, we expect performance decline relative to aspiration to facilitate reconfiguration.[3]

Indeed, the literature offers strong evidence of risky changes when performance falls below aspiration (Baum et al., 2005; Greve, 1998b). Such risk taking encourages firms to overcome organizational inertia and initiate bold actions (Audia & Greve, 2006) that entail resource reconfiguration. From a resource-based perspective, inertia results from the stickiness of knowledge assets (Anand, 2004; Szulanski & Jensen, 2004), or "core rigidities" (Leonard-Burton, 1992), which impede the firm's ability to dislodge from its current resource configuration (Lavie, 2006; Levinthal & March, 1993). When performance exceeds aspiration, both risk aversion and inertia attenuate the firm's tendency to invest in resource reconfiguration. Yet, when performance falls below aspiration, risk seeking motivates the firm to overcome inertial pressures and pursue resource reconfiguration. Although performance feedback cannot in and of itself alter the firm's core rigidities and organizational impediments, it reinforces the motivation to change the current resource configuration and prompts managers to overcome their cognitive constraints that prevent them from responding to environmental changes. When performance falls below aspiration, risk seeking is likely to overrule inertia, because inertia is ascribed to stable routines that are not susceptible to performance changes, whereas risk seeking increases as performance declines (Kahneman & Tversky, 1979).

We expect performance feedback to motivate resource reconfiguration, because managers believe that reconfiguration can improve their firm's performance by expanding activities (do more), contracting activities (do less), or fostering innovation (do something new) (Karim & Capron, 2015). A negative performance gap motivates a firm to seek solutions to organizational problems that currently undermine its performance (Greve, 2008). Such solutions often involve reconfiguration of existing knowledge and its recombination with newly acquired knowledge (Greve, 2003a). Hence, as performance falls below aspiration and increases the negative performance gap, the firm is likely to reconfigure its knowledge assets in order to facilitate restructuring of its corporate activities. Both exploratory and exploitative reconfigurations are essential for firms in technology-driven industries. Regardless of its nature, knowledge reconfiguration enables a firm to restructure or alter its corporate boundaries in response to performance feedback (Gaba & Joseph, 2013). Restructuring can increase managerial efficiency and effectiveness (Bowman & Singh, 1993), but it entails absorbing newly acquired knowledge and recombining existing knowledge (Karim & Kaul, 2015).

In particular, exploitative knowledge reconfiguration involves integrating, leveraging, or redeploying knowledge elements that the firm has used in the past. These processes involve mobilizing knowledge assets within the firm, coordinating the bundling of knowledge elements, and deploying the resulting configurations for routine use (Sirmon et al., 2007). For example, Corning's development of fiber optics evolved from its established expertise in specialty glass (Cattani, 2006). Similarly, Canon's technological achievements in copiers and cameras resulted from integrating its existing knowledge in electronics and optical devices (Prahalad & Hamel, 1990). A firm invests in an exploitative reconfiguration under the assumption that by refining and leveraging its existing knowledge, it can enhance efficiency. Accordingly, performance feedback is likely to reinforce local search, refinement of existing knowledge, and redeployment of that knowledge. A firm that reacts to performance feedback by investing in an exploitative reconfiguration can potentially improve efficiency by enhancing productivity and generating economies of scale and scope (Katila & Ahuja, 2002). Exploitative reconfiguration often entails transferring or sharing existing knowledge across the firm's units, and developing specialized skills in established technologies that can be used in multiple products or applications (Smith & Tushman, 2005).

In contrast, exploratory knowledge reconfiguration involves incorporating external knowledge elements that the firm has not previously used and integrating them with existing knowledge elements. For example, IBM's development of the electronic computer combined newly acquired knowhow in vacuum tubes and wiring with IBM's established skills in component integration (Usselman, 1993). Hence, performance feedback can motivate exploratory reconfiguration, which entails creating or incorporating new knowledge elements (Levinthal & March, 1993) that offer prospective streams of income. Exploratory reconfiguration often involves reaching beyond the firm's boundaries in search of external knowledge (Karim & Kaul, 2015). The new knowledge can serve to develop technologies and applications, while enhancing the diversity of technical skills and the firm's ability to meet customer requirements. Exploratory reconfiguration creates opportunities for value creation and makes it difficult for competitors to imitate the firm's knowledge assets (Brown & Eisenhardt, 1997). A firm that reacts to performance feedback by investing in exploratory reconfiguration seeks performance improvement by spanning boundaries, searching, experimenting, and facilitating innovation and adaptation to environmental conditions (Rosenkopf & Nerkar, 2001). Exploratory reconfiguration represents a departure from the existing technological trajectory (Zhou & Wu, 2010). Therefore, when performance exceeds aspiration (positive performance gap), the firm's managers become risk averse and avoid an exploratory reconfiguration that entails incorporating new knowledge, which may be unproven, untested, expensive, or prone to errors and "glitches" (Hoopes & Postrel, 1999; Levinthal & March, 1993). As performance falls below aspiration (negative performance gap), however, the firm's managers are likely to assume greater risk and incorporate new knowledge elements (Greve, 2003b). In sum, a negative performance gap is likely to increase the firm's tendencies to pursue exploratory and exploitative knowledge reconfigurations.

> **H1.** The lower the firm's performance relative to aspiration, the greater the firm's investment in its (a) exploratory knowledge reconfiguration and (b) exploitative knowledge reconfiguration.

Performance Feedback and the Munificence of Complementary Resources

A firm's reaction to performance feedback is driven by managerial motivation, but such motivation may be contingent on environmental conditions. Addressing the need for more research on these contingencies (Shinkle, 2012), we investigate how munificence and uncertainty of complementary resources serve as boundary conditions for learning from performance feedback.

Complementary resources include upstream and downstream assets that can be used in conjunction with the firm's knowledge assets in order to enhance the value of innovations. These resources enable a firm to effectively cope with technological changes (Tripsas, 1997), perceive and interpret these changes, and shape its technological trajectory and its investment in knowledge assets (Wu, Wan, & Levinthal, 2014). By enhancing the feasibility of knowledge reconfiguration and by mitigating its riskiness, complementary resources – such as trained employees and production facilities – affect the likelihood that knowledge reconfiguration is successfully executed. For instance, skilled employees can support knowledge reconfiguration by serving as agents that insource external knowledge that they have developed or learned while working for their previous employer (Rosenkopf & Almeida, 2003). Newly hired employees can also contribute to new knowledge development, to interpreting and integrating different knowledge elements, or to commercializing the firm's innovations (Rothaermel & Hess, 2007). Therefore, the effectiveness of knowledge reconfiguration depends on the availability of non-scale-free resources such as human resources and physical assets that enable the firm to implement the reconfiguration. Thus, when deploying knowledge assets, firms have their employees make complementary investments in firm-specific human capital, such as learning proprietary technologies (Helfat, 1994; Wang, He, & Mahoney, 2009).

The importance of complementary resources for knowledge reconfiguration is exemplified by the case of Smith Corona, a leading manufacturer of typewriters that failed to reconfigure its knowledge assets following industry trends that rendered its product category obsolete. This failure has been ascribed to Smith Corona's inability to effectively leverage relevant distribution channels and complementary resources in electronics manufacturing (Danneels, 2010). In the U.S. petroleum industry, in contrast, complementary resources, such as expertise in oil refining R&D and synthetic fuels, available refinery assets, and stocks of coal, were related to firms' tendencies to reconfigure their knowledge assets and invest in coal gasification and liquefaction R&D (Helfat, 1997).

Therefore, managers' decision to reconfigure their firm's knowledge assets depends on the availability of complementary resources in the factor market. The abundance of needed resources in the firm's environment is referred to as resource munificence (Castrogiovanni, 1991; Dess & Beard, 1984). Resource munificence concerns the availability, richness, and affordability of a set of complementary resources that the firm can potentially obtain. It indicates the extent to which complementary resources are abundantly available in the firm's industry and can be accessed or acquired with little effort and at a relatively low cost.

The more munificent are complementary resources in the firm's industry, the more likely are the firm's managers to willingly invest in knowledge reconfiguration. Whereas a negative performance gap motivates risk taking and organizational change (Greve, 2003b), munificence of complementary resources increases the likelihood that risk taking pays off and knowledge reconfiguration is executed successfully. In munificent factor markets, firms face fewer resource constraints and limited competition for complementary resources (Schimmer & Brauer, 2012), which lowers the risk of knowledge reconfiguration. Munificence of complementary resources can not only mitigate risk but also assist the firm in coping with inertial pressures that create resistance to knowledge reconfiguration. Managers and employees are more likely to make an effort and commit to knowledge reconfiguration under the assumption that the implementation of this reconfiguration is unlikely to fail as a result of a shortage of essential complementary resources.

Accordingly, munificence of complementary resources increases the likelihood of successful knowledge reconfiguration, and thus reinforces the motivation to engage in knowledge reconfiguration following performance decline relative to aspiration. In particular, exploitative reconfiguration requires resources such as skilled employees that can contribute to the refinement of the firm's knowledge assets and to the commercialization of its technologies (March, 1991). To the extent that such resources are abundantly available, the firm is more likely to engage in exploitative reconfiguration following a performance decline. Similarly, exploratory reconfiguration entails various resources that the firm may not currently possess. In the pharmaceutical industry, for instance, such reconfiguration entails the hiring of star scientists and forming upstream alliances that can support innovation (Hess & Rothaermel, 2011). In the solar photovoltaic industry, the availability of complementary resources, such as manufacturing and distribution capabilities in the ecosystem, encourages the adoption of advanced technologies by firms entering that field (Kapoor & Furr, 2015). Hence, munificence of complementary resources increases the likelihood that exploratory reconfiguration is successfully executed, and thus encourages managers to assume the risk and invest in such reconfiguration following a performance decline relative to aspiration.

> **H2.** The greater the munificence of complementary resources, the greater the firm's investment in (a) exploratory knowledge reconfiguration and (b) exploitative knowledge reconfiguration, following a decline in performance relative to aspiration

Performance Feedback and the Uncertainty of Complementary Resources

The association between the performance gap and knowledge reconfiguration is contingent not only on the munificence of complementary resources in the firm's industry but also on uncertainty about the availability of such resources. Environmental uncertainty represents the extent to which industry conditions are unpredictable (Dess & Beard, 1984; Milliken, 1987). Such ambiguity precludes managers' ability to discern and foresee trends in their industry (Hrebiniak & Joyce, 1995; Jauch & Kraft, 1986). Uncertainty can be distinguished from mere instability, dynamism, or fast-paced change in an industry, which can be entirely predictable, and thus elicit no uncertainty (Anderson & Tushman, 2001). Under uncertainty, boundedly rational managers face difficulty in gathering and processing relevant information as well as in assessing the probability of changes in environmental conditions. Hence, under uncertainty, managers may experience anxiety, lose confidence, and become more risk averse (Schimmer & Brauer, 2012; Waldman, Ramírez, House, & Puranam, 2001). For example, in light of uncertainty about the prospects of electronic computer technology, NCR's managers were cautious and slow to adopt this technology despite their customers' requests to experiment with computerized retail solutions (Rosenbloom, 2000).

Uncertainty about the expected availability of complementary resources indicates the extent to which the future availability of these complementary resources is unpredictable. Such uncertainty may encourage prudent managers to conservatively assume that the availability of these resources will be restricted (Cohen et al., 1996). Consequently, the firm's managers may feel threatened by possible resource constraints, a feeling that can lead to organizational inertia and resistance to change. This uncertainty amplifies the perceived risk associated with knowledge reconfiguration, because the firm's managers cannot confidently ascertain that the needed complementary resources will be available to support the pursued knowledge reconfiguration. In this sense, uncertainty increases the hazard of failure and the perceived risk associated with knowledge reconfiguration.

Moreover, uncertainty about the availability of complementary resources makes it difficult to figure out the desirable knowledge configuration, because the value-maximizing configuration of knowledge depends in part on the amount and the kind of complementary resources available to support it (Lavie, 2006). As a result, managers may become less confident about the desired configuration of knowledge. Hence, under uncertainty, a firm may face increased risk of pursuing an organizational change that results in adaptation to ill-predicted environmental conditions (Rosenbloom & Christensen, 1994). Furthermore, uncertainty raises the concern that the pursued knowledge configuration may be fragile rather than enduring (Anderson & Tushman, 2001), which further restricts the expectancy of knowledge reconfiguration. Therefore, under uncertainty, firms are likely to withhold plans for knowledge reconfiguration, and to the extent that they decide to reconfigure knowledge assets, they may do so in a gradual, more evolutionary fashion rather than opt for a riskier transformation (Lavie, 2006). Overall, uncertainty about the availability of complementary resources increases the risk associated with knowledge reconfiguration and makes managers more risk averse. As a result, uncertainty reduces the motivation for knowledge reconfiguration in response to a performance gap.

In particular, uncertainty about the expected availability of complementary resources such as qualified employees may discourage the firm from engaging in exploitative reconfiguration of knowledge assets in response to an increasingly negative performance gap. Even though local search, refinement of existing knowledge, and its redeployment necessitate complementary resources that the firm may already possess, uncertainty about the firm's ability to replenish these resources may call for caution. Managers are likely to withhold exploitative reconfiguration and avoid the risk associated with it by restricting the modification of existing knowledge assets and favoring existing applications, despite the firm's deteriorating performance.

In the case of exploratory reconfiguration, there is even greater uncertainty about the prospects of reconfiguration, because the firm is expected to incorporate new knowledge and rely on complementary resources that it does not currently own or control. Complementary resources associated with exploration are often causally ambiguous (Lippman & Rumelt, 1982), so there is inherent uncertainty about their contribution to the firm's ability to effectively leverage its knowledge assets. When the availability of these needed resources is uncertain, it becomes riskier to pursue exploratory knowledge reconfiguration, which entails leveraging complementary resources with which the firm has limited familiarity or past experience. Therefore, uncertainty about the availability of complementary resources is expected to elicit risk aversion and to attenuate the firm's inclination to engage in exploratory reconfiguration in response to performance decline relative to aspiration. In fact, under uncertainty, the motivation of managers to pursue exploratory reconfiguration may be hampered even more than their motivation to invest in exploitative reconfiguration, which is considered less risky.

> **H3.** The greater the uncertainty about the availability of complementary resources, the lower the firm's investment in (a) exploratory knowledge reconfiguration, and (b) exploitative knowledge reconfiguration, following a decline in performance relative to aspiration.

RESEARCH METHODS

Table 1 summarizes the hypotheses and the underlying arguments. We tested the study's hypotheses with panel data on publicly traded firms that operated in the United States during the period 1993–2001 in the following industries: telephone and telegraph apparatus (SIC3661, 17.0%), radio and television broadcasting and communications (SIC3663, 21.2%), semiconductors and related devices (SIC3674, 51.8%), and electronics components (SIC3679, 10.0%). In these industry sectors, firms applied for at least three patents per year on average. Of the initial sample of 544 firms, 248 firms

Table 1. Summary of Hypotheses and Theoretical Arguments.

Hypotheses	Underlying Arguments
H1. Performance gap negatively affects knowledge reconfiguration	• Performance decline facilitates problemistic search • Negative framing of failure prompts risk taking • Failure motivates managers to overcome constraints and resist inertia • Managers reconfigure resources, hoping to improve performance
H2. Munificence of complementary resources strengthens the negative association between performance gap and knowledge reconfiguration	• Complementary resources enhance the feasibility of reconfiguration and support its implementation • Available complementary resources mitigate the risk of reconfiguration • Munificence helps overcome organizational resistance to change • Munificence increases managers' motivation to reconfigure resources
H3. Uncertainty of complementary resources weakens the negative association between performance gap and knowledge reconfiguration	• Uncertainty increases the perceived risk of resource reconfiguration • Managers become risk averse when the desired configuration is unknown and reconfiguration outcomes are unpredictable • Under uncertainty, managers assume restricted availability of complementary resources • Uncertainty encourages managers to withhold resource reconfiguration

remain after accounting for the lag structure in our models, excluding firms that did not apply for patents during at least two consecutive years, and treating missing data with listwise deletion. The sample includes small, specialized firms and large, diversified corporations, operating in various value chain activities, including the production of semiconductors and manufacturing of electronic components and communication systems. On average, a firm's age was 21.5 years, and it had 7,488 employees, \$1,941M in assets, \$166M in sales, \$225M in cash, and \$198M in long-term debt.

We extracted firm-level annual data from Compustat, including industry classification, assets, cash, sales, net income, long-term debt, and number of employees. The firm's incorporation date was extracted from the Mergent or Corporate Affiliations database. Industry-level data on the number of employees and capital expenditures was extracted from the Annual Survey of Manufacturers of the Census Bureau. Patent citation data was gathered from the National University of Singapore's database, with patents recorded based on the application year to reflect the time of knowledge creation. During the period 1993–2001, the sampled firms applied for 42,003 patents, which cited 933,616 prior patents. To measure the knowledge reconfiguration variables, the study's timeframe was extended, with citing patents tracked back to 1981 and cited patents starting in 1927.

We pooled the data at the firm-year level, which served as the unit of analysis. Following Miller and Chen (2004), 5% of the observations with the lowest performance figures were excluded, because according to threat-rigidity theory (Staw et al., 1981), these firms are survival-oriented and do not respond to performance feedback in patterns characterizing firms that are aspiration-oriented (Ocasio, 2011).[4] Accordingly, the final sample included 1,217 observations.

Dependent Variable – Knowledge Reconfiguration

The reconfiguration of knowledge assets includes exploratory and exploitative reconfiguration processes. An exploratory reconfiguration enhances the scope of the firm's knowledge base by incorporating new knowledge elements, whereas an exploitative reconfiguration enhances the depth of that knowledge base by incorporating existing knowledge elements (Katila & Ahuja, 2002). Accordingly, the extent of knowledge reconfiguration in a given year can be captured with annual changes in the scope and depth of the firm's knowledge base, as measured with backward patent citations that indicate knowledge flows (Rosenkopf & Nerkar, 2001; Wang et al., 2009). In line with prior research (Su & McNamara, 2012), we adopted Katila and Ahuja's (2002) depthscope algorithm for capturing the firm's exploitative and exploratory reconfigurations, which are correspondingly measured with the search depth and search scope formulas. The firm's exploitative reconfiguration is measured as the proportion of times that, on average, the patents that the firm applies for in year $t + 1$ cite patents that were already cited in the firm's patent applications during the preceding five years. This time window is in line with research on organizational memory decay that reveals depreciation in the value of knowledge in technology-driven industries (Argote, 1999).[5] Whereas the measure of exploitative reconfiguration indicates the combination of knowledge elements that the firm has used in the past, the measure of exploratory reconfiguration indicates incorporating new knowledge elements that the firm has not previously used. Accordingly, the firm's exploratory reconfiguration in year $t + 1$ is measured with the proportion of citations to patents that were not previously cited by the firm. The corresponding formulas take the forms:

$$\text{Exploitative reconfiguration}_{i,t+1} = \frac{\sum_{t-4}^{t} \text{Repetition count}_i}{\text{Total citations}_{i,t+1}}$$

and

$$\text{Exploratory reconfiguration}_{i,t+1} = \frac{\text{New citations}_{i,t+1}}{\text{Total citations}_{i,t+1}}.$$

The inherent tradeoff between exploration and exploitation (March, 1991) is not built into these measures, whose correlation may vary (Katila & Ahuja, 2002).

Independent Variable – Performance Gap

We calculate the performance gap by deducting the performance aspiration value from the firm's actual performance (Lant & Montgomery, 1987). We measure performance with the firm's return on assets (ROA), as commonly used in resource-based research (Ndofor, Sirmon, & He, 2011) and in research on learning from performance feedback (Audia & Greve, 2006). This measure is preferred to measures such as return on equity that are susceptible to differences in firms' capital structure (Coombs & Bierly, 2006).

Following prior research (Bromiley, 1991), we operationalize the firm's aspiration as a weighted linear combination of historical aspiration based on the firm's past performance, and social aspiration based on the performance of other firms in its relevant reference group. In line with Greve (2003b), the firm's performance aspiration takes the form:

$$A_{i,t} = a_1 \times S_{i,t} + (1 - a_1) \times \text{HA}_{i,t}$$

where $A_{i,t}$ is the total performance aspiration of firm i in year t, $S_{i,t}$ is social aspiration, and $\text{HA}_{i,t}$ is historical aspiration, with a_1 as a weight that varies between 0 and 1, indicating the relative importance of social versus historical aspirations. Furthermore, firms whose performance exceeds the industry's median performance are likely to aspire to a higher performance level (Joseph & Gaba, 2015). Therefore, we use the industry's median performance as the reference point for social aspiration below the firm's aspiration level (Fiegenbaum & Thomas, 1988; Uotila, Maula, Keil, & Zahra, 2009) and the industry leaders' performance as the reference point above that level (Joseph & Gaba, 2015). The leaders' performance is operationalized as the 90th percentile of performance (ROA) measured for a subset of firms, out of the 544 publicly traded electronics firms that operate in the firm's four-digit SIC industry sector. The historical performance aspiration is calculated as $HA_{i,t} = a_2 \times HA_{i,t-1} + (1 - a_2) \times P_{i,t-1}$ (Greve, 2003b), with a_2 being a weight ranging between 0 and 1 that indicates the carryover from the prior year's aspiration level to the current aspiration level (Greve, 2003b), and $P_{i,t-1}$ being firm *i*'s performance (ROA) in year $t - 1$.

Because a_1 and a_2 are unknown, we estimate them using a "grid search" in which estimates are derived by running the full models for both exploratory and exploitative reconfigurations, with different values of a_1 and a_2 ranging from 0.1 to 0.9, and then selecting the values that yield the best fit statistics (Greve, 2003b). The resulting weights were $a_1 = 0.5$ and $a_2 = 0.9$ for the exploratory reconfiguration equation, and $a_1 = 0.1$ and $a_2 = 0.9$ for the exploitative reconfiguration equation. These estimated weights suggest that social aspiration plays a more central role in motivating a firm's exploratory reconfiguration, whereas historical aspiration is more influential in shaping the firm's exploitative reconfiguration. The dominance of historical aspiration in exploitative reconfiguration can be ascribed to the tendency of firms to seek straightforward solutions in the vicinity of their previously adopted solutions (Greve, 1998b). Conversely, when pursuing exploratory reconfiguration, the firm cannot rely on previously adopted solutions, and instead benchmarks relative to relevant firms in its industry (Anderson, Covin, & Slevin, 2009).

We calculate the firm's performance gap as $PG_{i,t} = P_{i,t} - A_{i,t}$, where $PG_{i,t}$ is the performance gap of firm *i* at year *t*, and $A_{i,t}$ is the performance aspiration level at year *t*. We split the performance gap measure into two variables using a spline function in order to assess its effect below and above the aspiration level. This procedure accounts for a firm's risk-proneness and increased motivation to change its behavior when performance falls below aspiration versus its risk aversion and thus weaker motivation to change behavior when its performance exceeds its aspiration level. A spline function captures the corresponding change in slope around that "kink" or "threshold" level that represents an inversion point between two types of behavior (Greve, 2003b; Sakhartov & Folta, 2013). Accordingly, the *performance gap below aspiration* equals performance minus aspiration for all observations in which firm *i*'s performance falls below its aspiration level, and it equals zero otherwise. The *performance gap above aspiration* equals performance minus aspiration for all observations in which firm *i*'s performance exceeds its aspiration level, and it equals zero otherwise.

Moderator – Munificence of Complementary Resources

The munificence of complementary resources in the firm's environment indicates the extent to which such resources are affordable and can be obtained with little effort. In knowledge-driven industries, the complementary resources most relevant to a firm's knowledge assets are human resources (Brown & Linden, 2009; Song, 2002). Firms in the electronics industry seek to recruit skilled employees in order to develop their knowledge assets. Some employees (2.7% of the employees in our sample are inventors) take part in exploratory reconfiguration of knowledge by introducing knowledge that they acquired and developed while working for various employers prior to joining their current firm (Rosenkopf & Almeida, 2003). Most of the employees contribute to exploitative reconfiguration by introducing new innovations based on the firm's existing knowledge (Ahuja & Katila, 2004) as well as by refining and commercializing existing technologies, and engaging in the manufacturing and sales of products embedding the firm's existing knowledge assets.[6] We capture the availability of employees in the electronics industry using a measure of four-year average growth in the number of employees in the firm's industry sector, as reported in the Annual Survey of Manufacturers.[7] *Resource munificence* is thus operationalized as the regression coefficient b_1 in the equation: $E_t = b_0 + b_1 \times t + \alpha_t$, where E_t is the total number of employees that operate in the corresponding four-digit SIC industry sector during timeframe t, with t corresponding to a moving window of the past four years, and α_t indicating the residual (Boyd, 1995; He & Huang, 2011; Keats & Hitt, 1988).[8]

Moderator – Uncertainty of Complementary Resources

For the aforementioned reasons, human resources are the most relevant complementary resource when studying knowledge reconfiguration in the electronics industry. Uncertainty about the expected availability of employees influences firms' decisions to invest in knowledge reconfiguration. We measure this uncertainty as the standard error in the above-mentioned regression of the number of employees (E_t) on t, per four-digit SIC segment

(Keats & Hitt, 1988). This standard error reflects instability in the availability of employees in particular sectors of the electronics industry.

Control Variables

We include several control variables that may influence the firm's tendency to undertake knowledge reconfiguration. Firm-level controls include the firm's size, solvency, and age. Firm size, measured as the natural logarithm of the firm's sales, can motivate a shift from exploratory to exploitative reconfiguration (Lavie et al., 2010). Firm solvency is measured as the natural logarithm of the firm's cash divided by its long-term debt. This measure represents unabsorbed slack that can facilitate investment in exploratory reconfiguration (Singh, 1986). Firm age is measured as the difference between the current year and the year of the firm's incorporation. A firm is expected to shift from exploratory to exploitative reconfiguration as it matures (Levitt & March, 1988). The firm's exploratory and exploitative reconfigurations may also be interdependent as a result of tradeoffs between its efforts to explore versus exploit (Lavie et al., 2010). Thus, we include the firm's concurrent exploratory reconfiguration when predicting exploitative reconfiguration, and vice versa. Additional controls include the munificence and uncertainty of complementary resources in the firm's industry sector, which may directly influence the firm's tendency to engage in exploratory and exploitative reconfiguration of knowledge assets (Sirmon et al., 2007; Sutcliffe & Zaheer, 1998). We account for the firm's acquisitions by incorporating patents of acquired subsidiaries in the knowledge reconfiguration variables. Intertemporal trends are controlled for by incorporating year dummies. Remaining interfirm heterogeneity is controlled with firm fixed effects.

Analysis

We test our hypotheses by estimating generalized least squares (GLS) models for panel data using firm and year fixed effects, and correcting for autocorrelation (Ahuja & Katila, 2004). Thus, we specify an error structure robust to heteroscedasticity within panels and a uniform first-order autocorrelation AR(1) coefficient, which is common across panels.

Because exploratory and exploitative reconfigurations are observed only for firms that file patent applications, we use a selection model (Hamilton & Nickerson, 2003; Shaver, 1998) to correct for a firm's tendency to apply for patents in a given year. In this first-stage model, we rely on the extended sample of 383 firms, which includes 2,358 observations, part of which belong to firms that did not apply for patents in certain years, and predict a firm *i*'s probability of applying for patents in year *t*. We run a probit model with this variable serving as the dependent variable. The independent variables in this model include firm size, age (Boh, Evaristo, & Ouderkirk, 2014; Macher & Boerner, 2012), solvency (Vissa, Greve, & Chen, 2010), the cumulative number of patents that the firm had applied for in the past five years (Macher & Boerner, 2012), and the level of capital invested in its industry sector (Mudambi & Swift, 2014). The latter two variables serve as the exclusion restriction variables that are excluded from the second-stage models. Finally, we control for inter-temporal trends using year dummies. Based on this first-stage model, we calculate the inverse Mills ratio (λ_t), which serves as an additional control variable in the second-stage models for estimating the exploratory and exploitative reconfigurations. These second-stage models are estimated using the aforementioned GLS specification, taking the following form:

$$\begin{aligned}\text{Exploratory reconfiguration}_{i,t+1} = {} & \beta_1 \times \text{Performance gap below}_{i,t} + \beta_2 \times \text{Performance gap above}_{i,t} + \\ & \beta_3 \times \text{Munificence}_{i,t} + \beta_4 \times \text{Uncertainty}_{i,t} + \\ & \beta_5 \times \text{Munificence}_{i,t} \times \text{Performance gap below}_{i,t} + \\ & \beta_6 \times \text{Munificence}_{i,t} \times \text{Performance gap above}_{i,t} + \\ & \beta_7 \times \text{Uncertainty}_{i,t} \times \text{Performance gap below}_{i,t} + \\ & \beta_8 \times \text{Uncertainty}_{i,t} \times \text{Performance gap above}_{i,t} + \\ & \beta_9 \times \text{Exploitative reconfiguration}_{i,t+1} + \beta_{10} \times \text{Size}_{i,t} + \\ & \beta_{11} \times \text{Age}_{i,t} + \beta_{12} \times \text{Solvency}_{i,t} + \beta_{13} \times \lambda_{i,t} + \beta_m \times T_t + \xi_i + \nu_{it}\end{aligned}$$

where $\lambda_{i,t}$ is the inverse Mills ratio, T_t are the year fixed effects, ξ_i are the firm fixed effects, and ν_{it} is an error term with a zero mean that is homoscedastic and uncorrelated with the regressors and the fixed error term. A corresponding model is specified for exploitative reconfiguration. The one-year lag between the dependent and independent variables and controls is in line with prior research on performance feedback (Vidal & Mitchell, 2015; Vissa et al., 2010).

Table 2. Descriptive Statistics and Pairwise Correlations for the First-Stage Model ($N = 2{,}358$).

Variable	Mean	Std. Dev.	Min	Max	1	2	3	4	5
1 Probability of patents$_t$	0.530	0.499	0.000	1.000					
2 Firm size$_{t-1}$	4.240	2.094	−3.863	10.534	0.425***				
3 Firm solvency$_{t-1}$	4.646	7.140	−10.778	20.889	0.031†	−0.141***			
4 Firm age$_{t-1}$	20.436	17.924	0.000	135.000	0.045	0.380***	−0.189***		
5 Cumulative number of patents$_{t-1}$	112.609	855.713	0.000	12714.000	0.188***	0.455***	−0.105***	0.339***	
6 Capital invested in industry sector$_{t-1}$	4.849	4.714	0.594	14.583	0.256***	0.125***	−0.006	−0.191***	0.007

***$p < 0.001$, †$p < 0.1$.

Table 3. Descriptive Statistics and Pairwise Correlations for the Second-Stage Model ($N = 1{,}217$).

Variable	Mean	St. Dev.	Min	Max.	1	2	$3_{Explore}$	$3_{Exploit}$	$4_{Explore}$	$4_{Exploit}$	5
1 Exploratory reconfiguration$_{t+1}$	0.747	0.259	0.000	1.000							
2 Exploitative reconfiguration$_{t+1}$	0.646	1.153	0.000	12.536	−0.681***						
3 Performance gap below (explore)$_t$	−0.054	0.147	−2.243	0.000	0.009	0.002					
3 Performance gap below (exploit)$_t$	−0.050	0.138	−2.342	0.000	0.006	0.010	0.907***				
4 Performance gap above (explore)$_t$	0.073	0.303	0.000	5.717	−0.031	0.040	0.088	0.086			
4 Performance gap above (exploit)$_t$	0.093	0.544	−0.017	10.891	−0.044	0.049	0.060	0.063	0.098***		
5 Performance$_t$	0.015	0.251	−2.568	4.256	0.043	−0.045	0.722***	0.560***	0.148***	−0.004	
6 Historical aspiration$_t$	−0.033	0.694	−13.389	0.685	0.062*	−0.072*	0.009*	−0.052	−0.877***	−0.951***	0.251***
7 Social aspiration (median)$_t$	0.042	0.081	−0.074	0.449	0.023	−0.055*	−0.149***	−0.040	−0.050	−0.028	0.049†
8 Social aspiration (leader)$_t$	0.161	0.033	0.080	0.221	0.010	0.006	−0.068*	−0.028	−0.067*	−0.072†	0.078**
9 Firm size$_t$	5.112	1.984	−1.414	10.534	−0.020	0.014	0.295***	0.197***	−0.092**	−0.122***	0.322***
10 Firm solvency$_t$	4.802	7.172	−10.778	20.390	−0.037	0.087**	−0.029	−0.059†	0.032	0.009	0.074**
11 Firm age$_t$	21.457	20.096	0.000	135.000	−0.014	−0.017	0.135***	0.107***	−0.048*	−0.067*	0.137***
12 Resource munificence$_t$	4.441	4.987	−6.100	13.461	−0.008	0.055**	0.014	−0.001	0.022	0.023	0.027
13 Resource uncertainty$_t$	2.578	1.578	0.604	6.919	−0.012	0.025	0.068*	0.037	0.019	0.025	−0.020
14 λ_t	−0.424	0.465	−1.800	0.000	−0.281***	0.272***	0.156*	0.125***	−0.040	−0.045	0.124***
15 Redeployment$_{t+1}$	0.406	0.768	0.000	9.543	−0.513***	0.616***	0.020	0.024	0.012	0.012	0.017
16 Codeployment$_{t+1}$	0.150	0.157	0.000	0.852	−0.627***	0.624***	0.009	0.054	−0.024	0.002	−0.037

Variable	6	7	8	9	10	11	12	13	14	15
7 Social aspiration (median)$_t$	0.039									
8 Social aspiration (leader)$_t$	0.104***	0.486***								
9 Firm size$_t$	0.182***	−0.044	−0.043							
10 Firm solvency$_t$	0.041	0.016	0.082*	−0.228***						
11 Firm age$_t$	0.083***	−0.079**	−0.23***	0.520***	−0.209***					
12 Resource munificence$_t$	−0.008	−0.148***	0.099***	−0.010	0.043	−0.014				
13 Resource uncertainty$_t$	−0.056	−0.303***	−0.327***	0.023	−0.071*	0.087**	0.236***			
14 λ_t	0.070†	0.017	0.178***	0.567***	−0.005	0.139***	0.043	−0.004		
15 Redeployment$_{t+1}$	0.007	0.023	0.092**	0.101***	0.007*	−0.009	0.069*	0.004	0.260***	
16 Codeployment$_{t+1}$	−0.043	0.021	0.000†	0.062	−0.017	−0.015	0.084*	0.000	0.309***	0.661***

Two sets of variables are included for performance gap below and above aspirations. The first set is used in the exploratory reconfiguration model with weights $a_1 = 0.5$, $a_2 = 0.9$, and the second set is used in the exploitative reconfiguration model with weights $a_1 = 0.1$, $a_2 = 0.9$.
***$p < 0.001$, **$p < 0.01$, *$p < 0.05$, $^{\dagger}p < 0.1$.

RESULTS

Table 2 reports descriptive statistics and pairwise correlations for the first-stage model (reported in Table 4), whereas Table 3 reports the corresponding statistics for the second-stage models (reported in Tables 5–6). Note that the performance gap variables are calculated separately for the exploratory reconfiguration and exploitative reconfiguration models with the distinctive weights for historical aspirations and social aspirations. Correlations among explanatory variables that are included in the same models are relatively low, with the exception of the high negative correlation between exploratory reconfiguration and exploitative reconfiguration ($r = -0.681$, $p < 0.001$). This negative correlation is indicative of the concurrent tradeoff between exploration and exploitation (Lavie et al., 2010). We account for this tradeoff by controlling for one type of knowledge reconfiguration when assessing the firm's investment in the other type of knowledge reconfiguration. Table 4 details the results of the first-stage analysis for predicting the probability of patenting. These results suggest that

Table 4. First-Stage Probit Model for Probability of Patents.

Dependent Variable: Probability of Patents$_t$	Model 1
Year effects	Included
Firm size$_{t-1}$	0.642***
	(0.031)
Firm solvency$_{t-1}$	0.125
	(0.006)
Firm age$_{t-1}$	−0.317**
	(0.003)
Cumulative patents in past five years$_{t-1}$	124.351***
	(0.020)
Capital invested in industry sector$_{t-1}$	0.311**
	(0.000)
N firm-years	2,358
N firms	383
Degrees of freedom	13
χ^2	140.4

Standardized coefficients are reported. Standard errors in parentheses.
***$p < 0.001$, **$p < 0.01$, *$p < 0.05$, †$p < 0.1$.

the propensity to patent increases with the firm's size ($\beta = 0.642$, $p < 0.001$), the cumulative number of patents for which the firm applied in the past five years ($\beta = 124.351$, $p < 0.001$), and the amount of capital invested in its industry sector ($\beta = 0.311$, $p < 0.01$). In contrast, the propensity to patent decreases with firm age ($\beta = -0.317$, $p < 0.001$). These findings are mostly consistent with prior research (Boh et al., 2014; Macher & Boerner, 2012; Vissa et al., 2010). Based on this first-stage model, we calculate the inverse Mills ratio (λ_t), which corrects for the selection bias in the second-stage models. Indeed, this variable generates significant effects in the second-stage models, indicative of a selection bias in firms' propensities to patent.

Table 5 reports the results of GLS models for predicting exploratory reconfiguration, whereas Table 6 reports the corresponding results for exploitative reconfiguration. In Table 5, Model 2 is the baseline model that includes only the control variables. Model 3 adds the independent variable, with Models 4 and 5 each adding one of the interaction effects. Model 6 is the full model that serves for testing the hypotheses. In Table 6, Models 7–11 correspondingly report hierarchical regressions for the firm's exploitative reconfiguration, with Model 11 serving as the full model for testing the hypotheses.[9] According to Model 6, the extent of exploratory reconfiguration of knowledge assets increases with the firm's size ($\beta = 0.194$, $p < 0.001$) and solvency ($\beta = 0.063$, $p < 0.001$), but decreases with the simultaneous extent of exploitative reconfiguration of knowledge assets ($\beta = -0.696$, $p < 0.001$). Similarly, according to Model 11, the extent of exploitative reconfiguration increases with the firm's size ($\beta = 0.185$, $p < 0.001$) and solvency ($\beta = 0.028$, $p < 0.001$), but decreases with the simultaneous extent of exploratory reconfiguration ($\beta = -0.375$, $p < 0.001$) and munificence of complementary resources in the firm's industry sector ($\beta = -0.025$, $p < 0.001$). These findings suggest that as a firm grows and accumulates financial assets, it increases its investments in both exploratory and exploitative reconfigurations (Bourgeois, 1981; Nohria & Gulati, 1996), but in light of the inherent tradeoff between exploration and exploitation, increased investment in exploratory reconfiguration comes at the expense of exploitative reconfiguration, and vice versa (Lavie et al., 2010). The need for exploitative reconfiguration is also mitigated when affordable complementary resources that support the current knowledge configuration are abundantly available in the environment (Voss, Sirdeshmukh, & Voss, 2008).

In line with Hypothesis 1, a firm's investment in exploratory reconfiguration of knowledge assets declines as its actual performance increases

Table 5. Second-Stage GLS Panel Models for Exploratory Reconfiguration.

Dependent Variable: Exploratory Reconfiguration$_{t+1}$	Model 2	Model 3	Model 4	Model 5	Model 6
Constant	−0.035	−0.077	−0.085	−0.118	−0.102
Firm and year fixed effects	Included	Included	Included	Included	Included
λ_t	−0.138***	−0.142***	−0.141***	−0.150***	−0.143***
	(0.009)	(0.009)	(0.009)	(0.009)	(0.009)
Exploitative reconfiguration$_{t+1}$	−0.689***	−0.688***	−0.688***	−0.699***	−0.696***
	(0.004)	(0.004)	(0.004)	(0.004)	(0.004)
Firm size$_t$	0.154***	0.171***	0.169***	0.022***	0.194***
	(0.003)	(0.003)	(0.003)	(0.003)	(0.003)
Firm solvency$_t$	0.052***	0.064***	0.064***	0.063***	0.063***
	(0.000)	(0.000)	(0.000)	(0.000)	(0.000)
Firm age$_t$	1.273***	1.319***	1.339***	1.342***	1.330***
	(0.003)	(0.003)	(0.003)	(0.003)	(0.003)
Resource munificence$_t$	0.002	0.001	0.001	0.003	−0.000
	(0.000)	(0.000)	(0.000)	(0.000)	(0.000)
Resource uncertainty$_t$	−0.004	−0.004	−0.003	0.004	0.006
	(0.001)	(0.001)	(0.001)	(0.001)	(0.001)
Performance gap below$_t$		−0.014**	−0.014	−0.071***	−0.071***
		(0.010)	(0.020)	(0.028)	(0.025)
Performance gap above$_t$		−0.049***	−0.033***	−0.030*	−0.040†
		(0.009)	(0.019)	(0.012)	(0.021)
Resource munificence$_t$ × Performance gap below$_t$			−0.001		−0.035**
			(0.007)		(0.003)

Resource munificence$_t$ × Performance gap above$_t$			−0.017		0.005
			(0.002)		(0.003)
Resource uncertainty$_t$ × Performance gap below$_t$				0.056***	0.081***
				(0.007)	(0.011)
Resource uncertainty$_t$ × Performance gap above$_t$				−0.067***	−0.046
				(0.002)	(0.007)
AR(1) coefficient	−0.126	−0.130	−0.129	−0.124	−0.125
N firm-years	1,217	1,217	1,217	1,217	1,217
N firms	248	248	248	248	248
Degrees of freedom	262	264	266	266	268
χ^2	31,966	28,376	28,191	182,415	28,101
Wald test of equality of coefficients below/above: χ^2		1.740	0.010	10.830***	7.830***

Standardized coefficients are reported. Standard errors in parentheses.
***$p < 0.001$, **$p < 0.01$, *$p < 0.05$, †$p < 0.1$.

Table 6. Second-Stage GLS Panel Models for Exploitative Reconfiguration.

Dependent Variable	Exploitative Reconfiguration$_{t+1}$					Redeploy$_{t+1}$	Codeploy$_{t+1}$
	Model 7	Model 8	Model 9	Model 10	Model 11	Model 12	Model 13
Constant	−0.468	−0.128	−0.929	−0.165	−1.140	−0.340	0.164
Firm and year fixed effects	Included	Included	Included	Included	Included	Included	Included
λ_t	−0.038***	−0.023*	−0.032***	−0.029**	−0.030**	−0.017†	0.042*
	(0.021)	(0.024)	(0.022)	(0.025)	(0.025)	(0.018)	(0.006)
Exploratory reconfiguration$_{t+1}$	−0.399***	−0.388***	−0.395***	−0.384***	−0.375***	−0.217***	−0.377***
	(0.032)	(0.034)	(0.029)	(0.035)	(0.027)	(0.027)	(0.007)
Firm size$_t$	0.164***	0.110***	0.152***	0.110***	0.185***	0.115***	0.074*
	(0.006)	(0.010)	(0.010)	(0.011)	(0.011)	(0.008)	(0.003)
Firm solvency$_t$	0.023***	0.017**	0.032***	0.019**	0.028***	−0.048***	0.022†
	(0.001)	(0.001)	(0.001)	(0.001)	(0.001)	(0.001)	(0.000)
Firm age$_t$	0.751	0.685	0.972	0.110***	0.987	0.510*	0.665†
	(0.036)	(0.035)	(0.033)	(0.037)	(0.036)	(0.008)	(0.003)
Resource munificence$_t$	−0.021***	−0.018**	−0.018**	−0.017**	−0.025***	0.008	0.023**
	(0.001)	(0.001)	(0.001)	(0.001)	(0.002)	(0.001)	(0.000)
Resource uncertainty$_t$	0.010	0.002	0.002	0.006	0.010	−0.002	−0.003
	(0.004)	(0.004)	(0.004)	(0.005)	(0.005)	(0.003)	(0.001)
Performance gap below$_t$		0.000	0.053***	−0.008	0.033***	0.066***	0.008
		(0.029)	(0.032)	(0.085)	(0.077)	(0.084)	(0.019)
Performance gap above$_t$		−0.064**	−0.031	−0.008	−0.005	−0.001	−0.040†
		(0.053)	(0.048)	(0.063)	(0.065)	(0.050)	(0.020)

Resource munificence$_t$ × Performance gap below$_t$			−0.060***		−0.085***	−0.066***	−0.033†
			(0.005)		(0.009)	(0.010)	(0.002)
Resource munificence$_t$ × Performance gap above$_t$			−0.069***		−0.076***	0.001	0.055***
			(0.005)		(0.005)	(0.005)	(0.002)
Resource uncertainty$_t$ × Performance gap below$_t$				0.004	0.042**	0.006	0.017*
				(0.033)	(0.038)	(0.021)	(0.003)
Resource uncertainty$_t$ × Performance gap above$_t$				−0.113***	0.003	−0.003	−0.058***
				(0.011)	(0.016)	(0.017)	(0.006)
AR(1) coefficient	0.088	0.091	0.087	0.085	0.072	−0.123	−0.1504
N firm-years	1,217	1,217	1,217	1,217	1,217	1,053	1,053
N firms	248	248	248	248	248	217	217
Degrees of freedom	262	264	266	266	268	237	237
χ^2	17,659	20,341	47,833,439	15,732	155,790	65,616	40,687
Wald test of equality of coefficients below/above: χ^2		3.980***	96.008***	0.170	8.470***	12.12***	2.23

Standardized coefficients are reported. Standard errors in parentheses.
***$p < 0.001$, **$p < 0.01$, *$p < 0.05$, $^{\dagger}p < 0.1$.

relative to its performance aspiration. Nevertheless, this decline is significant when performance falls below aspiration ($\beta = -0.071, p < 0.001$) and becomes only marginally significant when performance exceeds aspiration ($\beta = -0.040, p < 0.1$). A Wald test reveals a significant difference between the coefficients of the performance gap below versus above the aspiration level ($\chi^2 = 7.830, p < 0.001$). The finding that firms are more motivated to invest in exploratory reconfiguration when performance falls below aspiration is consistent with prior research that has revealed that underperforming firms tend to innovate (Greve, 2007), form risky alliances with unfamiliar partners (Baum et al., 2005), and engage in vicarious learning rather than in learning from their own experience (Baum & Dahlin, 2007). The flatter slope of the performance gap above aspiration can be attributed to a firm's risk aversion in that range, as predicted by prospect theory (Kahneman & Tversky, 1979). When performance exceeds aspiration, a firm is less motivated to invest in changing its current position, because of managers' heightened beliefs in their infallibility and their desire to sustain their firm's superior position (Boyle & Shapira, 2011; Simon, 1991). This finding is in line with prior research that reports a less significant effect of the performance gap above aspiration (Baum et al., 2005; Schimmer & Brauer, 2012).[10]

Counter to Hypothesis 1, we find that when performance falls below aspiration, the firm's investment in exploitative reconfiguration increases as the firm's performance improves relative to its aspiration ($\beta = 0.033, p < 0.001$). A Wald test confirms a significant difference in coefficients of the performance gap below versus above the aspiration level ($\chi^2 = 8.470, p < 0.001$). This finding can be explained by the fact that exploitative reconfiguration involves reliance on the firm's existing knowledge, whereas exploratory reconfiguration requires integrating external knowledge that is new to the firm. Because exploitative reconfiguration entails less risk than exploratory reconfiguration (Levinthal & March, 1993), the firm diverts investments from exploitative reconfiguration to exploratory reconfiguration once its performance falls below aspiration. The effect of this performance decline on exploitative reconfiguration is not merely weaker but rather opposite in direction to the effect on exploratory reconfiguration, because of the inherent tradeoff between the firm's efforts to explore versus exploit, as evidenced by the negative association between exploitative reconfiguration and exploratory reconfiguration ($\beta = -0.375, p < 0.001$). Indeed, a firm's exploratory reconfiguration often comes at the expense of exploitative reconfiguration (March, 1991). This tradeoff arises because of resource allocation constraints and the choice between maximizing short-term gains versus betting on long-term payoffs (Lavie et al., 2010). In sum, performance gap below aspiration motivates the undertaking of risk and investing in exploratory reconfiguration at the expense of exploitative reconfiguration, whereas performance increase above aspiration mitigates the incentive to invest in knowledge reconfiguration altogether.

Fig. 1 depicts the results of Models 6 and 11, which correspondingly report the effects of the performance gap on exploratory and exploitative reconfigurations. This figure illustrates the investments in reconfiguration below versus above the aspiration level for performance gap ranging between one standard deviation below the mean and one standard deviation above the mean, while holding all other variables at their mean levels.

In line with Hypothesis 2, the munificence of complementary resources in the firm's industry sector reinforces the firm's tendency to invest in exploratory reconfiguration as performance declines relative to aspiration (see Model 6). As expected, this moderation effect is significant only below aspiration ($\beta = -0.035$, $p < 0.01$). Furthermore, the munificence of complementary resources weakens the effect of the performance gap on the firm's investment in exploitative reconfiguration (see Model 11), both below the aspiration level ($\beta = -0.085$, $p < 0.001$) and above it ($\beta = -0.076$, $p < 0.001$). These findings are ascribed to the inherent tradeoff between exploration and exploitation, which generates conflicting effects on exploratory reconfiguration versus exploitative reconfiguration. Accordingly, as complementary resources in the firm's environment become more abundant,

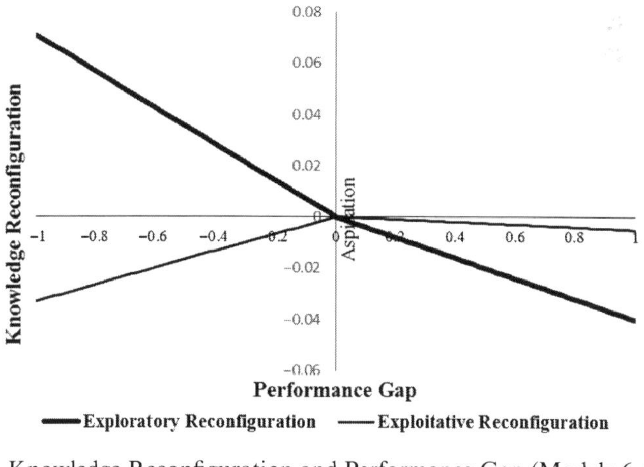

Fig. 1. Knowledge Reconfiguration and Performance Gap (Models 6 and 11).

the firm increases its investment in exploratory reconfiguration, but since this munificence also relaxes the resource allocation constraint and mitigates the tradeoff between exploratory and exploitative reconfigurations, the firm's investment in exploratory reconfiguration entails weaker decline in its investment in exploitative reconfiguration as performance falls relative to aspiration. Fig. 2 depicts the moderating effect of munificence, comparing the effects of performance gap on exploratory and exploitative reconfigurations when munificence is at one standard deviation below the mean

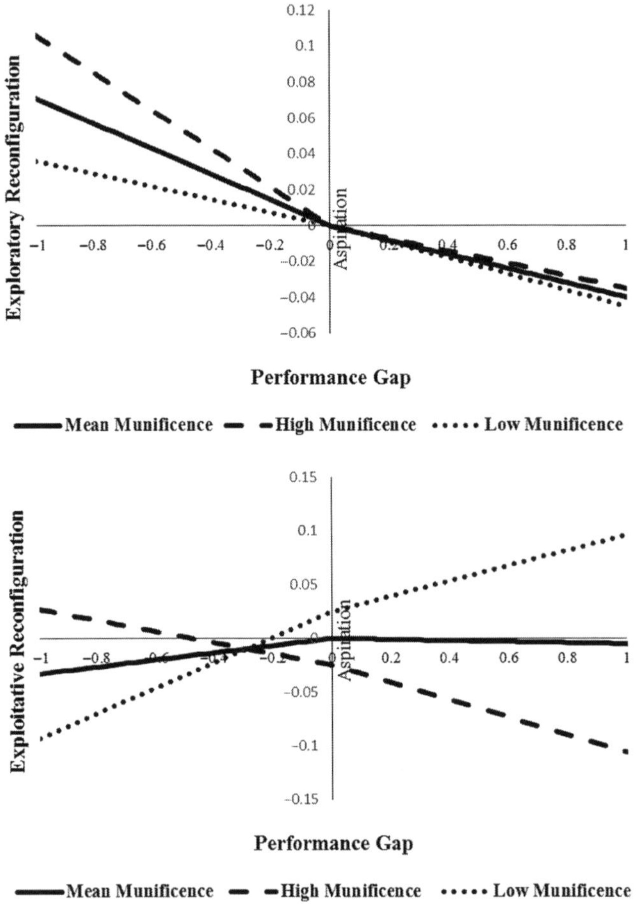

Fig. 2. Knowledge Reconfiguration and Performance Gap under Munificence.

(low munificence) versus one standard deviation above the mean (high munificence). It reveals how munificence prompts both exploratory and exploitative reconfigurations as performance falls below aspiration, although the incentive to engage in exploratory reconfiguration is stronger.

Finally, in line with Hypothesis 3 (Model 6), uncertainty about the availability of complementary resources restricts the firm's investment in both exploratory reconfiguration ($\beta = 0.081$, $p < 0.001$) and exploitative reconfiguration ($\beta = 0.042$, $p < 0.01$) as performance falls below aspiration. Still,

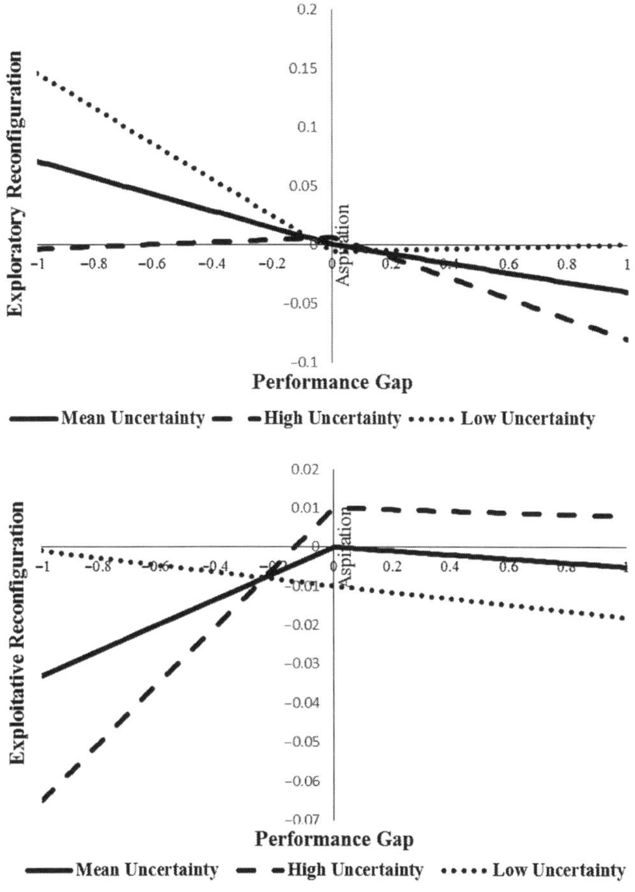

Fig. 3. Knowledge Reconfiguration and Performance Gap under Uncertainty.

Table 7. Summary of Findings.

Dependent Variable		Performance Gap H1 (−)	Munificence H2 (−)	Uncertainty H3 (+)
Exploratory reconfiguration	Below aspiration	−	−	+
	Above aspiration	−	n.s.	n.s.
Exploitative reconfiguration	Below aspiration	+	−	+
	Above aspiration	n.s.	−	n.s.

n.s., Not significant.

under uncertainty, the firm is likely to invest more in exploitative reconfiguration as performance improves relative to aspiration. However, once performance exceeds aspiration, the firm is less inclined to invest in either exploratory or exploitative reconfiguration. Fig. 3 illustrates these trends, comparing the effects of the performance gap on exploratory and exploitative reconfigurations for uncertainty at one standard deviation below the mean (low uncertainty) versus one standard deviation above the mean (high uncertainty). Table 7 summarizes our findings.

We conducted several auxiliary analyses to test the robustness of our findings. For instance, we calculated alternative measures of knowledge reconfiguration using three-, seven-, and 10-year timeframes instead of the five years assumed in the depthscope algorithm (Katila & Ahuja, 2002), obtaining consistent results. We also considered a two-year lag instead of the one-year lag between the dependent and independent variables, which produced less significant results, thus supporting our reported lag structure. In another analysis, we included the 5% of the observations with the lowest performance figures, and found consistent results for the effect of performance gap on exploratory reconfiguration, although the effect on exploitative reconfiguration became insignificant due to possible threat rigidity (Staw et al., 1981). Next, we operationalized munificence and uncertainty based on the capital invested in the industry segment and using a factor scale combining that measure with the original measure based on the number of employees, but our reported measures were superior. We believe that in the electronics industry the munificence of financial and physical assets is less relevant than that of human resources, for which the factor market is less efficient. In addition, we dropped the spline function and tested a linear effect of the performance gap on knowledge reconfiguration, finding support for the main effect, but the moderators became insignificant. In another analysis, we included an interaction of munificence and uncertainty, which turned out insignificant. Finally, we added controls, such as the lagged resource reconfiguration, to account for potential unobserved heterogeneity, which did not materially change our findings.

POST HOC ANALYSIS: CODEPLOYMENT VERSUS REDEPLOYMENT

Our findings reveal that performance feedback distinctively shapes firms' tendencies to engage in exploratory versus exploitative reconfigurations of knowledge. Nevertheless, exploitative reconfiguration, in which a firm integrates and leverages its existing resources, can serve multiple purposes. Besides deployment and integration, two of the primary purposes are *redeployment* and *codeployment*. A firm may *redeploy* its existing resource, which has been originally used in a particular domain, by withdrawing it from that domain and reallocating it to new domains wherein that resource serves other needs (Helfat & Eisenhardt, 2004). In addition, the firm may *codeploy* its existing resource by deploying it across multiple domains, with the hope that such extension will generate synergy (Sakhartov & Folta, 2014). Although redeployment is expected to be more straightforward in the case of scale-free resources such as knowledge, this process is still relevant given that a firm's ability to redeploy knowledge is constrained by the cost of developing new applications for that knowledge and by the availability of complementary resources that are non-scale-free, such as human resources. In order to gain further insights into how performance feedback motivates the firm's engagement in these two types of exploitative reconfiguration, we develop measures for knowledge redeployment and codeployment, and in auxiliary analysis consider them as alternative dependent variables.

The knowledge codeployment measure is based on Trajtenberg, Jaffe, and Henderson (1997) measure of generality, which captures the Herfindahl diversity in the technological fields of citing patents. Following Hall, Jaffe, and Trajtenberg (2001), we apply a bias correction, with the resulting measure taking the form:

$$\text{Codeployment}_{it} = \frac{1}{Pt}\sum_{p=1}^{Pt}\frac{1}{Rp}\sum_{r=1}^{Rpt}\left(\frac{N_{rpt}}{N_{rpt}-1}\right)\left[1-\sum_{k=1}^{Krpt}\left(\frac{N_k}{N_{rpt}}\right)^2\right]$$

where K_{rpt} is the number of unique classes of firm i patent applications citing patent r during the period between firm i's first citing of that patent until year t in which the firm applied for patent p, N_k is the number of times patent r was cited in class k, while N_{rpt} is the total number of times patent r was cited by firm i during that period; R_{pt} is the number of patents cited by patent p until year t, and P_t is the number of patents firm i has applied for in year t. Thus, knowledge codeployment captures the diversity of patent classes in which a firm has cited patents. In contrast, knowledge redeployment measures the ratio of the number of times a firm has cited patents outside the patent classes in which it first cited them to the number of times it cited these patents in the classes in which they were first cited. Formally:

$$\text{Redeployment}_{it} = \frac{1}{Pt}\sum_{p=1}^{Pt}\frac{1}{Rp}\sum_{r=1}^{Rpt}\left(\frac{N\text{out}_{rpt}}{N\text{in}_{rpt}}\right)$$

where $N\text{out}_{rpt}$ is the number of times between firm i's first citing of patent r and year t, in which the firm applied for patent p, that firm i cited patent r in patent classes other than the ones in which it first cited that patent; and $N\text{in}_{prt}$ is the number of times during that period that firm i cited patent r in the patent classes in which it first cited that patent. To compute these measures, we used the National Bureau of Economic Research (NBER) database (Trajtenberg et al., 1997), which provides information on the classes of citing patents. As a result of missing values, the sample size includes 1,053 firm-year observations. In particular, some patent categories that appear in the Singapore database, such as design patents and reissued patents, could not be traced in the NBER database.

Table 6 reports the results for redeployment (Model 12) and codeployment (Model 13), which are consistent with those reported for exploitative reconfiguration, with some nuances. For instance, as a firm improves its financial solvency, it tends to invest less in redeployment, and instead increases its tendency to codeploy knowledge assets. Additionally, munificence of complementary resources facilitates codeployment of knowledge assets, without influencing the propensity to redeploy these assets, probably because redeployment is considered riskier. With regard to Hypothesis 1, decline in performance below aspiration reduces the tendency to redeploy ($\beta = 0.066$, $p < 0.001$) but does not affect codeployment. In contrast, when performance exceeds aspiration, the tendency to codeploy declines marginally ($\beta = -0.040$, $p < 0.10$). Hence, performance decline below aspiration motivates a shift from redeployment of knowledge assets to exploratory reconfiguration, which entails greater risk taking and innovation; but when performance exceeds aspiration, the motivation to engage in any type of knowledge reconfiguration is reduced, including the propensity to codeploy.

With respect to Hypothesis 2, the munificence of complementary resources weakens the effect of the performance gap below aspiration on the firm's investment in redeployment ($\beta = -0.066$, $p < 0.001$). The moderation of the codeployment effect is weaker ($\beta = -0.033$, $p < 0.1$) but still in line with the reported result for exploitative reconfiguration. When performance exceeds aspiration, munificence mitigates the decline in codeployment ($\beta = 0.055$, $p < 0.001$) but does not affect redeployment, possibly because complementary resources that are non-scale-free restrict the firm's ability to extend the use of its knowledge assets across different domains, but do not constrain its ability to switch from one domain to another. For the same reason, uncertainty about the availability of complementary resources shapes the effect of the performance gap on codeployment without influencing the tendency to redeploy. Specifically, per Hypothesis 3, performance decline below aspiration accompanied by uncertainty about the availability of complementary resources discourages codeployment ($\beta = 0.017$, $p < 0.05$). In contrast, when performance exceeds aspiration, uncertainty reinforces the decline in codeployment ($\beta = -0.058$, $p < 0.001$).

DISCUSSION AND CONCLUSIONS

Prior research has underscored the role of resource reconfiguration in enabling firms to adapt to and cope with dynamic environments (Capron & Mitchell, 2009; Karim & Capron, 2015). This research has also identified various modes such as alliances and acquisitions that firms leverage in order to implement this reconfiguration (Capron & Mitchell, 2012). Nevertheless, firms vary in their tendencies to reconfigure resources, and little is known about the antecedents of this practice. Scholars have attributed the motivation to reconfigure resources to industry conditions such as munificence and uncertainty (Sirmon et al., 2007), to the characteristics of firms' knowledge assets (Galunic & Rodan, 1998), and to firms' strategies for changing their corporate scope (Capron, Mitchell, & Swaminathan, 2001; Helfat & Eisenhardt, 2004). However, we identify a fundamental driver that influences managers' motivation to invest in resource reconfiguration, namely performance feedback. This antecedent may underlie firms' corporate restructuring decisions (Bergh, 1997; Bowman & Singh, 1993; Kaul, 2012; Wiersema, 1995) and efforts to capitalize on emerging market opportunities (Chakrabarti, Vidal, & Mitchell, 2011).

Focusing on knowledge as the core asset of firms in knowledge-driven industries, our findings confirm that the motivation to reconfigure resources increases as performance falls below aspiration, in line with theories on learning from performance feedback (Greve, 2003b). However, our findings also reveal a clear distinction between exploratory and exploitative reconfigurations. Whereas exploitative reconfiguration involves redeploying and combining internal resources that the firm has used in the past, exploratory reconfiguration requires integrating these existing resources with external resources that are new to the firm. Evidently, these two types of reconfiguration are driven by distinctive motivations and entail tradeoffs. First, we found that exploitative reconfiguration is driven mainly by historical performance aspiration; that is, when deciding how much to invest in recombination of existing knowledge elements, managers react to the firm's performance relative to its past performance. In contrast, exploratory reconfiguration is driven to a greater extent by social aspiration; that is, when the firm's performance declines relative to that of its industry peers, the firm is motivated to absorb external knowledge and incorporate it in its new innovations. The dominance of historical aspiration in exploitative reconfiguration can be ascribed to the tendency to seek straightforward solutions in the vicinity of the firm's established solutions (Greve, 1998b). Conversely, exploratory reconfiguration entails a possible change in the firm's technological trajectory, which renders previously adopted solutions obsolete, so that the firm resorts to benchmarking relative to its industry reference group (Anderson et al., 2009).

More importantly, our findings reveal conflicting implications of a negative performance gap, that is, performance falling below aspiration, on a firm's tendencies to engage in exploratory reconfiguration versus exploitative reconfiguration. As performance falls below aspiration, the firm diverts its focus from exploitative reconfiguration to exploratory reconfiguration, which implies taking greater risks and generating more novel resource configurations. This finding is consistent with prior research that has demonstrated how decline in performance leads to greater risk taking (Lim & McCann, 2014) and experimentation in product innovation (Greve, 2007). The assumption is that disappointing performance is indicative of a deficiency in the firm's knowledge base, which calls for a more drastic approach for reconfiguration (Lavie, 2006), that is, exploratory reconfiguration. In contrast, given the inherent tradeoff between exploration and exploitation, the firm's investment in exploitative reconfiguration will be reduced following performance decline. Still, this reduction is more likely in redeployment than in codeployment, since redeployment is considered riskier, and thus serves as a closer substitute for exploratory reconfiguration.

With these findings, our study informs research on exploration and exploitation that has investigated the challenge of balancing these activities (March, 1991). Prior research has often advocated the simultaneous pursuit of exploration and exploitation, but uncovered heterogeneity in firms' efforts to strive toward such balance (Lavie et al., 2010). Our study uncovers one reason for this heterogeneity, namely managers' reaction to the gap between actual performance and their aspirations. When performance exceeds aspiration, the tension between exploration and exploitation becomes mute, and the firm restricts its efforts to reconfigure its knowledge. As performance falls below aspiration, however, the firm faces an increasing tradeoff between exploration and exploitation, which prompts exploratory reconfiguration at the expense of exploitative reconfiguration. By revealing how performance feedback tilts the balance between exploratory reconfiguration and exploitative reconfiguration, we enhance understanding of some of the factors that shape the balance between exploration and exploitation.

Moreover, our study advances research on resource reconfiguration and learning from performance feedback by uncovering some environmental contingencies that have not been sufficiently studied (Shinkle, 2012). Our findings reveal how uncertainty and munificence of complementary resources shape the effect of the performance gap on knowledge reconfiguration. Munificence of complementary resources, such as human resources, reinforces exploratory reconfiguration following a decline in performance relative to aspiration, while it also mitigates the tradeoff between exploration and exploitation, thus enabling the firm to simultaneously pursue exploratory reconfiguration and exploitative reconfiguration. These findings suggest that the motivation to invest in risky exploratory reconfiguration increases when affordable complementary resources are readily available in the industry. The availability of employees who can support R&D efforts increases the likelihood of successful reconfiguration, and thus enables the firm to invest in exploratory reconfiguration without jeopardizing its exploitative reconfiguration.

In contrast, as uncertainty about the future availability of these complementary resources increases, both exploratory reconfiguration and exploitative reconfiguration become riskier, which discourages managers from undertaking resource reconfiguration altogether. The effect of uncertainty is more prevalent in the case of codeployment as opposed to redeployment given that complementary resources that are non-scale-free, such as human resources, restrict codeployment. Scientists, engineers, and managers can be redeployed, but their scarcity constraints the extension of their assignments to new projects (Penrose, 1959). Instead of investing in reconfiguring its knowledge base, a firm is likely to be hesitant in its reaction to a failure or performance decline, and thus refrain from or defer knowledge reconfiguration altogether until the uncertainty is resolved (Eggers, 2012). Managerial prudence dictates that managers avoid costly investments (Koberg, 1987) despite the competitive challenges that the firm may face because of such delayed investments. Uncertainty about available resources not only makes it challenging for the firm to identify the desired resource reconfiguration, but also limits its ability to successfully execute such reconfiguration given that it is unclear whether needed complementary resources will become available (Lavie, 2006). Most prior research on learning from performance feedback is agnostic to environmental contingencies, yet in a recent study, Ben-Oz and Greve (2015) examine the effect of environmental dynamism on the association between performance gaps and potential versus realized absorptive capacity. Because dynamism comprises amplitude, frequency, and uncertainty of environmental change (Hannan & Freeman, 1977), our findings about uncertainty complement their study, which focused only on the amplitude and frequency of change.

Our study contributes to the literature on resource reconfiguration by shedding light on the heterogeneity in firms' inclinations to undertake resource reconfiguration under given industry conditions. We underscore motivational antecedents to firms' reconfiguration decisions and identify environmental contingencies that shape firms' motivations to reconfigure their resources. Our study extends recent research that has studied how performance feedback stimulates divestiture (Vidal & Mitchell, 2015) by highlighting its implications for other types of resource reconfiguration that entail knowledge recombination irrespective of the firm's organizational restructuring efforts. By focusing on the reconfiguration of knowledge assets, we complement research in strategic management that analyzes the implications of performance-related motives for firms' corporate restructuring decisions (Singh, 1993; Wiersema, 1995). Furthermore, our study advances recent research on resource reconfiguration (Karim & Capron, 2015) by distinguishing exploratory reconfiguration from exploitative reconfiguration. These two types of reconfiguration involve distinct processes for integrating and leveraging new knowledge elements versus existing knowledge elements. Because of their distinctive risk profiles and the inherent tradeoff between these processes (March, 1991), firms shift from exploitative to exploratory reconfiguration in response to performance decline relative to aspiration. Thus, we offer insights into the motivations of managers to pursue different types of resource reconfiguration. Moreover, although several studies have conceptualized redeployment and measured it in the product market, this is the first study that introduces a measure of resource redeployment that captures the extent to which a resource, such as knowledge asset, is deployed in domains other than the one in which it was first deployed. Hence, our measure can advance empirical research on resource redeployment.

Finally, by identifying resource reconfiguration as a consequence of learning from performance feedback, our study complements research that has considered the implications of performance feedback for corporate activities such as repositioning, innovation, acquisitions, alliance formation, and R&D investments. We contend that resource reconfiguration is a set of fundamental processes that underlie many of these corporate activities. For instance, our findings about the role of munificence and uncertainty in shaping the association between performance feedback and resource reconfiguration can explain a firm's divergence from its strategic group (Schimmer & Brauer, 2012).

Despite its conceptual and empirical contributions, our study is subject to several limitations. A limitation that is inherent to the behavioral theory of the firm (Cyert & March, 1963) concerns the generalization from individual behavior to corporate behavior. Our study assumes that firms react to feedback, take risks, and set aspiration levels, but such an analogy is not trivial given the complex human processes that bridge these two levels of analysis (Barney & Felin, 2013). Furthermore, as in most learning models, our study assumes a backward-looking process rather than one in which firms reconfigure resources in anticipation of future needs. Although the desirable configuration of resources and capabilities may be based on expectations (Lavie, 2006), the motivation to invest in resource reconfiguration is still driven by past performance. A related concern is that the theory explaining resource reconfiguration in response to performance feedback assumes risk propensity and organizational inertia, which remain latent variables in our study. Future research may consider multilevel research designs and directly measure these latent variables.

Another limitation of our study results from our limited focus on one type of core asset, namely knowledge, and one type of complementary resources, namely human resources. Clearly, resource reconfiguration may involve more complex combinations of tangible, intangible, and human assets (Agarwal & Helfat, 2009). Although our simplification enables us to isolate the effect of the performance gap from synergies associated with combinations of various resources, future research should consider whether performance feedback can affect potential synergies ascribed to different resource configurations. Furthermore, the effect of performance feedback on reconfiguration of scale-free resources, such as knowledge, may differ from its effect on reconfiguration of non-scale-free resources such as human resources, which often facilitate redeployment rather than codeployment. Additionally, the use of patent citations as a proxy for a firm's knowledge base may raise some concerns. We adopted this measure because of the knowledge-driven nature of the electronics industry. Patent citations indicate new technological developments, assuming that the firm is motivated to apply for patents. Yet it is unclear whether citations that were added by examiners are indicative of the firm's knowledge base. Moreover, the citations added by examiners may be firm-, industry-, and country-specific (Alcácer, Gittelman, & Sampat, 2009), and contingent, for instance, on certain organizational policies. To further refine our proposed measure of knowledge redeployment, future research may not only consider the static use of knowledge outside the domain in which it was first used by the firm, but also trace the evolving use of that knowledge in various domains over time. Additionally, future research may measure the firm's knowledge assets by relying on scientific publications as opposed to patents, even though patent citations are more appropriate in industrial settings (Roach & Cohen, 2013). Future research may also consider alternative types of resources in industries that are not technology-driven.

Furthermore, future research may consider the intensity of competition and market complexity as additional moderators that shape the process of learning from performance feedback. Changes in the competitive landscape may account for unobserved heterogeneity in firms' decisions to invest in resource reconfiguration. Finally, future research may seek to generalize the study's findings to other industries, which may experience a slower pace of innovation. Indeed, industry-level differences may explain why our findings about explorative reconfiguration differ from those reported by Greve (2007), who studied the relatively stable shipbuilding industry, and found that performance decline relative to aspiration motivates both exploration and exploitation. It is also possible that the tradeoff that we identify between exploration and exploitation is more evident in the factor market for knowledge than in the product market. Hence, future research should extend our investigation of resource reconfiguration to additional industries, markets, and countries.

In conclusion, our study contributes to resource-based research by relating resource reconfiguration to managers' responses to performance feedback, thus identifying an important antecedent of firms' decisions to initiate resource reconfiguration. We also advance emerging research on resource reconfiguration by introducing the important distinction between exploratory and exploitative reconfigurations, and demonstrating their corresponding reaction patterns, while accounting for their inherent trade-off. Finally, our study reveals how the interplay of behavioral inclinations and environmental conditions shapes a firm's motivation to reconfigure its resources.

NOTES

1. Although exploitative reconfiguration often relies on internal development while exploratory reconfiguration typically entails external sourcing (Capron & Mitchell, 2009), firms can engage in exploratory reconfiguration even without resorting to alliances or acquisitions – for instance, by hiring employees or licensing technologies. Firms can also acquire external resources and later redeploy and combine them with their internal resources (Grimpe & Kaiser, 2010).

2. Problemistic search differs from slack-induced search that is prompted by the availability of redundant resources that enable a firm to experiment without facing severe consequences of failure (Nohria & Gulati, 1996). A firm with abundant resources may allocate more resources to search for new solutions beyond those attainable by problemistic search.

3. The negative association between the performance gap and resource reconfiguration can be explained not only by the theory of problemistic search (Cyert & March, 1963) but also by prospect theory, which suggests that individuals give more weight to losses, so that their negative framing of problems encourages risk taking (Kahneman & Tversky, 1979). Both theories predict risk aversion when performance exceeds aspiration, and risk seeking when performance falls below aspiration. Some scholars note that performance below aspiration directs attention to the consequences of failure, which leads to risk aversion in the vicinity of bankruptcy (Lopes, 1987; Sitkin & Pablo, 1992). Such "threat rigidity" (Staw, Sanderlands, & Dutton, 1981) prevails only when managers shift from being aspiration-driven to being survival-focused.

4. Similar results were obtained when excluding observations with Altman z-scores lower than 1.8 (Miller & Chen, 2004). The z-score (Altman, 1968) proxies for the likelihood of bankruptcy, with lower values representing greater likelihood.

5. Auxiliary analysis using alternative time windows of three, seven, and 10 years yielded similar or less significant results.

6. In auxiliary analysis we considered alternative complementary resources such as investment of capital in manufacturing facilities and other physical assets as well as a factor scale combining the number of employees with the capital invested in the industry. These alternative measures generated less significant results. Data on the munificence of other complementary resources such as R&D investments were unavailable in the Annual Survey of Manufacturers.

7. Although the use of archival data for measuring resource munificence is common in strategy research, it entails the assumption that all firms in the industry conceive of munificence in a similar manner. Nevertheless, managers often react to perceived rather than to actual munificence, and perceive environmental attributes differently (Starbuck, 1976). Because of this complexity and the inability to rely on archival data for gathering longitudinal information on managers' cognitions, we used an objective measure of resource munificence.

8. Keats and Hitt (1988) suggest using a smoothing procedure that regresses the logarithm of the munificence measure on time, and calculating the annual munificence as the antilog of that line's slope. We obtained better results using a simpler procedure without smoothing, probably because during our study's timeframe, which preceded the economic crisis in 2001, the change in resource munificence in the electronics industry was progressive.

9. The VIF indices in the reported models range from 1.00 to 3.01, well below the threshold level (Kleinbaum, Kupper, Muller, & Nizam, 1998), thus mitigating concerns of multicollinearity.

10. Some studies predict risk taking when performance exceeds aspiration due to accumulated slack resources that can facilitate strategic change (Joseph & Gaba, 2015). Nevertheless, we control for slack resources with the financial solvency variable, which enables us to isolate the behavioral component of the firm's reaction to performance feedback.

ACKNOWLEDGMENT

We appreciate the feedback received from Peter Bamberger, Ido Erev, Moshe Farjoun, Henrich Greve, and Zur Shapira. Additional feedback was received from participants in the 3rd Israel Strategy Conference in Beer Sheva, 2009, the 6th Israel Strategy Conference in Jerusalem, 2015, the 15th Organization Science Winter Conference in Colorado, 2009, the Academy of Management conferences in Orlando, 2013, Philadelphia, 2014, and Anaheim, 2016, and the Advances in Strategic Management Conference in Strasbourg, 2015. We acknowledge the assistance and technical advice received from Uriel Stettner and the contribution of the late Avi Fiegenbaum, who guided Ari Dothan during the early phases of his dissertation research, which served as the basis for this paper.

REFERENCES

Agarwal, R., & Helfat, C. E. (2009). Strategic renewal of organizations. *Organization Science*, *20*(2), 281–293.

Ahuja, G., & Katila, R. (2004). Where do resources come from? The role of idiosyncratic situations. *Strategic Management Journal*, *25*(8–9), 887–907.

Alcácer, J., Gittelman, M., & Sampat, B. (2009). Applicant and examiner citations in U.S. patents: An overview and analysis. *Research Policy*, *38*(2), 415–427.

Altman, E. I. (1968). The prediction of corporate bankruptcy: A discriminant analysis. *Journal of Finance*, *23*(1), 193–194.

Anand, J. (2004). Redeployment of corporate resources: A study of acquisition strategies in the U.S. defense industries, 1978–1996. *Managerial and Decision Economics*, *25*, 383–400.

Anderson, B. S., Covin, J. G., & Slevin, D. P. (2009). Understanding the relationship between entrepreneurial orientation and strategic learning capability: An empirical investigation. *Strategic Entrepreneurship Journal*, *3*(3), 218–240.

Anderson, P., & Tushman, M. L. (2001). Organizational environments and industry exit: The effects of uncertainty, munificence and complexity. *Industrial and Corporate Change*, *10*(3), 675–711.

Argote, L. (1999). *Organizational learning: Creating, retaining and transferring knowledge*. Norwell, MA: Kluwer Academic Publishers.

Audia, P. G., & Greve, H. R. (2006). Less likely to fail: Low performance, firm size, and factory expansion in the shipbuilding industry. *Management Science*, *52*(1), 83–94.

Barney, J., & Felin, T. (2013). What are microfoundations? *Academy of Management Perspectives*, *27*(2), 138–155.

Baum, J. A. C., & Dahlin, K. (2007). Aspiration performance and railroads' patterns of experiential learning from train wrecks and crashes. *Organization Science*, *18*(3), 368–385.

Baum, J. A. C., Rowley, T. J., Shipilov, A. V., & Chuang, Y. T. (2005). Dancing with strangers: Aspiration level performance and the search for underwriting syndicate partners. *Administrative Science Quarterly*, *50*, 536–575.

Ben-Oz, C., & Greve, H. R. (2015). Short- and long-term performance feedback and absorptive capacity. *Journal of Management*, *41*(7), 1827–1853.

Bergh, D. D. (1997). Predicting divestiture of unrelated acquisitions: An integrative model of ex ante conditions. *Strategic Management Journal*, *18*(9), 715–731.

Boh, W. F., Evaristo, R., & Ouderkirk, A. (2014). Balancing breadth and depth of expertise for innovation: A 3M story. *Research Policy*, *43*(2), 349–366.

Bourgeois, J. L. (1981). On the measurement of organizational slack. *Academy of Management Review*, *6*(1), 29–39.

Bowman, E. H., & Singh, H. (1993). Corporate restructuring: Reconfiguring the firm. *Strategic Management Journal*, *14*(Special issue: Corporate Restructuring), 5–14.

Boyd, B. K. (1995). CEO duality and firm performance: A contingency model. *Strategic Management Journal*, *16*, 301–312.

Boyle, E., & Shapira, Z. (2011). The liability of leading: Battling aspiration and survival: Goals in the jeopardy! Tournament of champions. *Organization Science*, *23*(4), 1100–1114.

Bromiley, P. (1991). Testing a causal model of corporate risk taking and performance. *Academy of Management Journal*, *34*(1), 37–59.

Brown, C., & Linden, G. (2009). *Chips and change: How crisis reshapes the semiconductor industry*. Cambridge, MA: MIT Press.

Brown, S. I., & Eisenhardt, K. M. (1997). The art of continuous change: Linking complexity theory and time-paced evolution in relentlessly shifting organizations. *Administrative Science Quarterly*, *42*(1), 1–34.

Capron, L., & Mitchell, W. (2009). Selection capability: How capability gaps and internal social frictions affect internal and external strategic renewal. *Organization Science*, *20*(2), 294–312.

Capron, L., & Mitchell, W. (2012). *Build, borrow, or buy: Solving the growth dilemma*. Boston: Harvard Business School Publishing.

Capron, L., Mitchell, W., & Swaminathan, A. (2001). Asset divestiture following horizontal acquisitions: A dynamic view. *Strategic Management Journal*, *22*(9), 817–844.

Castrogiovanni, C. J. (1991). Environmental munificence: A theoretical assessment. *Academy of Management Review*, *16*(3), 542–565.

Cattani, G. (2006). Technological pre-adaptation, speciation, and emergence of new technologies: How Corning invented and developed fiber optics. *Industrial and Corporate Change*, *15*(2), 285–318.

Chakrabarti, A., Vidal, E., & Mitchell, W. (2011). Business transformation in heterogeneous environments: The impact of market development and firm strength on retrenchment and growth reconfiguration. *Global Strategy Journal*, *1*(1–2), 6–26.

Chen, W. R., & Miller, K. D. (2007). Situational, and institutional determinants of firms' R&D search intensity. *Strategic Management Journal*, *28*(4), 369–381.

Cohen, M. D., Burkhart, R., Dosi, G., Egidi, M., Marengo, L., Warglien, M., & Winter, S. G. (1996). Routines and other recurring action patterns of organizations: Contemporary research issues. *Industrial and Corporate Change*, *5*(3), 653–698.

Coombs, J. E., & Bierly, P. E. (2006). Measuring technological capability and performance. *R&D Management*, *36*(4), 421–438.

Cyert, R. M., & March, J. G. (1963). *A behavioral theory of the firm*. Englewood Cliffs, NJ: Prentice Hall.

Danneels, E. (2010). Trying to become a different type of company: Dynamic capability at Smith Corona. *Strategic Management Journal*, *32*(1), 1–31.

Dess, G. G., & Beard, D. W. (1984). Dimensions of organizational task environments. *Administrative Science Quarterly*, *29*(1), 52–73.

Eggers, J. P. (2012). Falling flat: Failed technologies and investment under uncertainty. *Administrative Science Quarterly*, *57*(1), 47–80.

Fiegenbaum, A., & Thomas, H. (1988). Attitudes toward risk and the risk–return paradox: Prospect theory explanations. *Academy of Management Journal*, *31*(1), 85–106.

Fiegenbaum, A., & Thomas, H. (1995). Strategic groups as reference groups: Theory, modeling, and empirical examination of industry and competitive strategy. *Strategic Management Journal*, *16*(6), 461–476.

Gaba, V., & Bhattacharya, S. (2012). Aspirations, innovation, and corporate venture capital: A behavioral perspective. *Strategic Entrepreneurship Journal*, *6*(2), 178–199.

Gaba, V., & Joseph, J. (2013). Corporate structure and performance feedback: Aspirations and adaptation in M-form firms. *Organization Science*, *24*(4), 1102–1119.

Galunic, C. D., & Rodan, S. (1998). Resource recombinations in the firm: Knowledge structures and the potential for Schumpeterian recombination. *Strategic Management Journal*, *19*(12), 1193–1201.

Grant, R. M. (1996a). Prospering in dynamically-competitive environments: Organizational capability as knowledge integration. *Organization Science*, *7*(4), 375–387.

Grant, R. M. (1996b). Toward a knowledge-based theory of the firm. *Strategic Management Journal*, *17*(Winter special issue), 109–122.

Greve, H. R. (1998a). Managerial cognition and the mimetic adoption of market positions: What you see is what you do. *Strategic Management Journal*, *19*(10), 967–988.

Greve, H. R. (1998b). Performance, aspirations, and risky organizational change. *Administrative Science Quarterly*, *43*, 58–86.

Greve, H. R. (2003a). A behavioral theory of R&D expenditures and innovations: Evidence from shipbuilding. *Academy of Management Journal*, *46*(6), 658–702.

Greve, H. R. (2003b). *Organizational learning from performance feedback: A behavioral perspective on innovation and change*. Cambridge: Cambridge University Press.

Greve, H. R. (2007). Exploration and exploitation in product innovation. *Industrial and Corporate Change*, *16*(5), 945–975.

Greve, H. R. (2008). A behavioral theory of firm growth: Sequential attention to size and performance goals. *Academy of Management Journal*, *51*(3), 476–494.

Grimpe, C., & Kaiser, U. (2010). Balancing internal and external knowledge acquisition: The gains and pains from R&D outsourcing. *Journal of Management Studies*, *47*(8), 1483–1509.

Grinyer, P., & McKiernan, P. (1990). Generating major change in stagnating companies. *Strategic Management Journal*, *11*, 131–146.

Hall, B. H., Jaffe, A. B., & Trajtenberg, M. (2001). *The NBER patent citation data file: Lessons, insights and methodological tools*. Working Paper No. 8498. National Bureau of Economic Research.

Hamilton, B. H., & Nickerson, J. A. (2003). Correcting for endogeneity in strategic management research. *Strategic Organization*, *1*(1), 51–78.

Hannan, M. T., & Freeman, J. (1977). The population ecology of organizations. *American Journal of Sociology*, *82*(5), 929–964.

He, J., & Huang, Z. (2011). Board informal hierarchy and firm financial performance: Exploring a tacit structure guiding boardroom interactions. *Academy of Management Journal*, *54*(6), 1119–1139.

Helfat, C. E. (1994). Evolutionary trajectories in petroleum firm R&D. *Management Science*, *40*(12), 1720–1747.

Helfat, C. E. (1997). Know-how and asset complementarity and dynamic capability accumulation: The case of R&D. *Strategic Management Journal*, *18*(5), 339–360.

Helfat, C. E., & Eisenhardt, K. M. (2004). Inter-temporal economies of scope, organizational modularity, and the dynamics of diversification. *Strategic Management Journal*, *25*(13), 1217–1232.

Hess, A. M., & Rothaermel, F. T. (2011). When are assets complementary? Star scientists, strategic alliances, and innovation in the pharmaceutical industry. *Strategic Management Journal*, *32*, 895–909.

Hoopes, D. G., & Postrel, S. (1999). Shared knowledge, "glitches," and product development performance. *Strategic Management Journal*, *20*(9), 837–865.

Hrebiniak, L. G., & Joyce, W. F. (1995). Organizational adaptation: Strategic choice and environmental dynamism. *Administrative Science Quarterly*, *20*, 336–349.

Iyer, D. N., & Miller, K. D. (2008). Performance feedback, slack, and the timing of acquisitions. *Academy of Management Journal*, *51*(4), 808–822.

Jauch, L. R., & Kraft, K. L. (1986). Strategic management of uncertainty. *Academy of Management Review*, *11*(4), 777–790.

Joseph, J., & Gaba, V. (2015). The fog of feedback: Ambiguity and firm responses to multiple aspiration levels. *Strategic Management Journal*, *36*, 1960–1978.

Kahneman, D., & Tversky, A. (1979). Prospect theory: An analysis of decision under risk. *Econometrica*, *47*(2), 263–291.

Kapoor, R., & Furr, N. R. (2015). Complementarities and competition: Unpacking the drivers of entrants' technology choices in the solar photovoltaic industry. *Strategic Management Journal*, *36*(3), 416–436.

Karim, S., & Capron, L. (2015). Editors' introduction to the virtual special issue on reconfiguration: Adding, redeploying, recombining and divesting resources and business units. *Strategic Management Journal.*

Karim, S., & Kaul, A. (2015). Structural recombination and innovation: Unlocking intraorganizational knowledge synergy through structural change. *Organization Science*, *26*(2), 439–455.

Karim, S., & Mitchell, W. (2000). Path-dependent and path-breaking change: Reconfiguring business resources following acquisitions in the U.S. medical sector, 1978–1995. *Strategic Management Journal*, *21*, 1061–1081.

Karim, S., & Mitchell, W. (2004). Innovating through acquisition and internal development: A quarter-century of boundary evolution at Johnson & Johnson. *Long Range Planning*, *37*(6), 525–547.

Katila, R., & Ahuja, G. (2002). Something old, something new: A longitudinal study of search behavior and new product introduction. *Academy of Management Journal*, *45*(2), 1183–1194.

Kaul, A. (2012). Technology and corporate scope: Firm and rival innovation as antecedents of corporate transactions. *Strategic Management Journal*, *33*(4), 347–367.

Keats, B., & Hitt, M. A. (1988). A causal model of linkages among environmental dimensions, macro organizational characteristics, and performance. *Academy of Management Journal*, *31*(3), 570–597.

Kleinbaum, D. G., Kupper, L. L., Muller, K. E., & Nizam, A. (1998). *Applied regression analysis and other multivariate methods* (3rd ed.). Pacific Grove, CA: Brooks/Cole Publishing.

Koberg, C. S. (1987). Resource scarcity, environmental uncertainty, and adaptive organizational behavior. *Academy of Management Journal*, *30*(4), 798–807.

Kogut, B., & Zander, U. (1992). Knowledge of the firm, combinative capabilities, and the replication of technology. *Organization Science*, *3*(3), 383–397.

Lant, T. K., & Montgomery, D. B. (1987). Learning from strategic success and failure. *Journal of Business Research*, *15*, 503–517.

Lavie, D. (2006). Capability reconfiguration: An analysis of incumbent responses to technological change. *Academy of Management Review*, *31*(1), 153–174.

Lavie, D. (2012). The case for a process theory of resource accumulation and deployment. *Strategic Organization*, *10*(3), 316–323.

Lavie, D., Stettner, U., & Tushman, M. L. (2010). Exploration and exploitation within and across organizations. *Academy of Management Annals*, *4*, 109–155.

Leonard-Burton, D. (1992). Core capabilities and core rigidities: A paradox in managing new product development. *Strategic Management Journal*, *13*(Special issue), 111–125.

Levinthal, D. A. (2011). A behavioral approach to strategy—What's the alternative? *Strategic Management Journal*, *32*(13), 1517–1523.

Levinthal, D. A., & March, J. G. (1993). The myopia of learning. *Strategic Management Journal*, *14*(Winter special issue), 95–112.
Levitt, B., & March, J. G. (1988). Organizational learning. *Annual Review of Sociology*, *14*, 319–340.
Lim, E. N. K., & McCann, B. T. (2014). Performance feedback and firm risk taking: The moderating effects of CEO and outside director stock options. *Organization Science*, *25*(1), 262–282.
Lippman, S. A., & Rumelt, R. P. (1982). Uncertain instability: An analysis of interfirm differences in efficiency under competition. *Bell Journal of Economics*, *13*(1), 418–438.
Lopes, L. L. (1987). Between hope and fear: The psychology of risk. *Advances in Experimental Social Psychology*, *20*, 255–295.
Macher, J. T., & Boerner, C. (2012). Technological development at the boundaries of the firm: A knowledge-based examination in drug development. *Strategic Management Journal*, *33*(9), 1016–1036.
March, J. G. (1991). Exploration and exploitation in organizational learning. *Organization Science*, *2*(1), 71–87.
Miller, K. D. (2002). Knowledge inventories and managerial myopia. *Strategic Management Journal*, *23*(8), 689–706.
Miller, K. D., & Chen, W. R. (2004). Variable organizational risk preferences: Tests of the March-Shapira model. *Academy of Management Journal*, *47*(1), 105–115.
Milliken, F. J. (1987). Three types of perceived uncertainty about the environment: State, effect, and response uncertainty. *Academy of Management Review*, *12*(1), 133–143.
Mudambi, R., & Swift, T. (2014). Knowing when to leap: Transitioning between exploitative and explorative R&D. *Strategic Management Journal*, *35*(1), 126–145.
Ndofor, H. A., Sirmon, D. G., & He, X. (2011). Firm resources, competitive actions and performance: Investigating a mediated model with evidence from in-vitro diagnostic study. *Strategic Management Journal*, *32*, 640–657.
Nohria, N., & Gulati, R. (1996). Is slack good or bad for innovation? *Academy of Management Journal*, *39*(5), 1245–1264.
Ocasio, W. (2011). Attention to attention. *Organization Science*, *22*(5), 1286–1296.
Park, K. M. (2007). Antecedents of convergence and divergence in strategic positioning: The effects of performance and aspiration on the direction of strategic change. *Organization Science*, *18*(3), 386–402.
Penrose, E. T. (1959). *The theory of the growth of the firm*. New York, NY: Oxford University Press.
Prahalad, C. K., & Hamel, G. (1990). The core competence of the corporation. *Harvard Business Review*, *68*(3), 79–91.
Roach, M., & Cohen, W. M. (2013). Lens or prism? Patent citations as a measure of knowledge flows from public research. *Management Science*, *59*(2), 504–525.
Rosenbloom, R. S. (2000). Leadership, capabilities, and technological change: The transformation of NCR in the electronic era. *Strategic Management Journal*, *21*(10–11), 1083–1103.
Rosenbloom, R. S., & Christensen, C. M. (1994). Technological discontinuities, organizational capabilities and strategic commitments. *Industrial and Corporate Change*, *3*, 655–685.
Rosenkopf, L., & Almeida, P. (2003). Overcoming local search through alliances and mobility. *Management Science*, *49*(6), 751–766.
Rosenkopf, L., & Nerkar, A. (2001). Beyond local search: Boundary spanning, exploration and impact in the optical disk industry. *Strategic Management Journal*, *22*(4), 287–306.

Rothaermel, F. T., & Hess, A. M. (2007). Building dynamic capabilities: Innovation driven by individual-, firm-, and network-level effects. *Organization Science*, *18*(6), 898–921.

Sakhartov, A. V., & Folta, T. B. (2013). Rationalizing organizational change: A need for comparative testing. *Organization Science*, *24*(4), 1140–1156.

Sakhartov, A. V., & Folta, T. B. (2014). Resource relatedness, redeployability, and firm value. *Strategic Management Journal*, *35*(12), 1781–1797.

Sakhartov, A. V., & Folta, T. B. (2015). Getting beyond relatedness as a driver of corporate value. *Strategic Management Journal*, *36*(13), 1939–1959.

Schimmer, M., & Brauer, M. (2012). Firm performance and aspiration levels as determinants of a firm's strategic repositioning within strategic group structures. *Strategic Organization*, *10*(4), 406–435.

Schneider, S. L. (1992). Framing and conflict: Aspiration level contingency, the status quo, and current theories of risky choice: Learning, memory, and cognition. *Journal of Experimental Psychology*, *18*(5), 1040–1057.

Shaver, M. (1998). Accounting for endogeneity when assessing strategy performance: Does entry mode choice affect FDI survival? *Management Science*, *44*(4), 571–585.

Shinkle, G. A. (2012). Organizational aspirations, reference points, and goals: Building on the past and aiming for the future. *Journal of Management*, *38*(1), 415–455.

Simon, H. A. (1991). Bounded rationality and organizational learning. *Organization Science*, *2*(1), 125–134.

Singh, H. (1993). Challenges in researching corporate restructuring. *Journal of Management Studies*, *30*(1), 147–172.

Singh, J. V. (1986). Performance, slack, and risk taking in organizational decision making. *Academy of Management Journal*, *29*(3), 562–585.

Sirmon, D. G., Hitt, M. A., & Ireland, R. D. (2007). Managing firm resources in dynamic environments to create value: Looking inside the black box. *Academy of Management Review*, *32*(1), 273–292.

Sitkin, S. B., & Pablo, A. L. (1992). Reconceptualizing the determinants of risk behavior. *Academy of Management Review*, *47*(1), 9–38.

Smith, W. K., & Tushman, M. L. (2005). Managing strategic contradictions: A top management model for managing innovation streams. *Organization Science*, *16*(5), 522–536.

Song, J. (2002). Firm capabilities and technology ladders: Sequential foreign direct investments of Japanese electronics firms in East Asia. *Strategic Management Journal*, *7*(23), 191–210.

Spender, J. C. (1996). Making knowledge the basis of a dynamic theory of the firm. *Strategic Management Journal*, *17*, 45–62.

Starbuck, W. H. (1976). Organizations and their environments. In M. D. Dunnette (Ed.), *Handbook of industrial and organizational psychology* (pp. 1069–1123). Chicago, IL: Rand McNally.

Staw, B. M., Sanderlands, L. E., & Dutton, J. E. (1981). Threat-rigidity effects in organizational behavior: A multilevel analysis. *Administrative Science Quarterly*, *26*(3), 501–524.

Su, P., & McNamara, P. (2012). Exploration and exploitation within and across intra-organisational domains and their reactions to firm-level failure. *Technology Analysis & Strategic Management*, *24*(2), 129–149.

Sutcliffe, K. M., & Zaheer, A. (1998). Uncertainty in the transaction environment. *Strategic Management Journal*, *19*, 1–23.

Szulanski, G., & Jensen, R. J. (2004). Overcoming stickiness: An empirical investigation of the role of the template in the replication of organizational routines. *Managerial and Decision Economics*, *25*, 347–363.

Teece, D. J. (2007). Explicating dynamic capabilities: The nature and microfoundations of (sustainable) enterprise performance. *Strategic Management Journal*, *28*, 1319–1350.

Trajtenberg, M., Jaffe, A., & Henderson, R. (1997). University versus corporate patents: A window on the basicness of invention. *Economics of Innovation and New Technology*, *5*(1), 19–50.

Tripsas, M. (1997). Unraveling the process of creative destruction: Complementary assets and incumbent survival in the typesetter industry. *Strategic Management Journal*, *18* (Summer special issue), 119–142.

Uotila, H., Maula, M., Keil, T., & Zahra, S. A. (2009). Exploration, exploitation, and financial performance: analysis of S&P 500 corporations. *Strategic Management Journal*, *30*, 221–231.

Usselman, S. W. (1993). IBM and its imitators: Organizational capabilities and the emergence of the international computer industry. *Business and Economic History*, *22*(3), 1–35.

Vidal, E., & Mitchell, W. (2015). Adding by subtracting: The relationship between performance feedback and resource reconfiguration through divestitures. *Organization Science*, *26*(4), 1101–1118.

Vissa, B., Greve, H. R., & Chen, W. R. (2010). Business group affiliation and firm search behavior in India: Responsiveness and focus of attention. *Organization Science*, *21*(3), 696–712.

Voss, G. B., Sirdeshmukh, D., & Voss, Z. G. (2008). The effects of slack resources and environmental threat on product exploration and exploitation. *Academy of Management Journal*, *51*(1), 147–164.

Waldman, D. A., Ramírez, G. G., House, R. J., & Puranam, P. (2001). Does leadership matter? CEO leadership attributes and profitability under conditions of perceived environmental uncertainty. *Academy of Management Journal*, *44*(1), 134–143.

Wang, H. C., He, J., & Mahoney, J. T. (2009). Firm-specific knowledge resources and competitive advantage: The roles of economic- and relationship-based employee governance mechanisms. *Strategic Management Journal*, *30*(12), 1265–1285.

Wiersema, M. F. (1995). Executive succession as an antecedent to corporate restructuring. *Human Resource Management*, *34*(1), 185–202.

Wu, B., Wan, Z., & Levinthal, D. A. (2014). Complementary assets as pipes and prisms: Innovation incentives and trajectory choices. *Strategic Management Journal*, *35*(9), 1257–1278.

Yasai-Ardekani, M. (1989). Effects of environmental scarcity and munificence on the relationship of context to organizational structure. *Academy of Management Journal*, *32*, 131–150.

Yayavaram, S., & Chen, W.-R. (2015). Changes in firm knowledge couplings and firm innovation performance: The moderating role of technological complexity. *Strategic Management Journal*, *36*(3), 377–396.

Zhou, K. Z., & Wu, F. (2010). Technological capability, strategic flexibility, and product innovation. *Strategic Management Journal*, *31*(5), 547–561.

THE IMPACT OF ABSORBED AND UNABSORBED SLACK ON FIRM PROFITABILITY: IMPLICATIONS FOR RESOURCE REDEPLOYMENT

Josep M. Argilés-Bosch, Josep Garcia-Blandon and Mónica Martinez-Blasco

ABSTRACT

This paper undertakes an empirical analysis of the impact of absorbed and unabsorbed slack, employing three different measures for each slack type, on firm profitability. We find that unabsorbed slack has a more favorable influence on future firm profitability than absorbed slack. While all the absorbed slack indicators have a significant negative influence on future profitability, the three unabsorbed slack indicators present positive, negative, and non-significant influences, respectively. The fewer constraints of unabsorbed slack on the redeployment to exploit new opportunities point to its comparative advantage over absorbed slack. We find evidence for the differential impact of absorbed versus unabsorbed slack on profitability in firms with lower levels of slack, which

Resource Redeployment and Corporate Strategy
Advances in Strategic Management, Volume 35, 371–395

ISSN: 0742-3322/doi:10.1108/S0742-332220160000035012

suggests firms prefer to withdraw resources from current business and redeploy them to develop new and more favorable business opportunities.

Keywords: Absorbed slack; unabsorbed slack; resource redeployment; profitability; financial performance

INTRODUCTION

Firms want to grow. There are well-known inducements to encourage firm growth, such as increasing demand for certain products; introducing technological changes that call for production on a larger scale; exploiting discoveries; taking advantage of opportunities to obtain a better market position; and, seeking protection against adverse environmental changes, etc. (see Penrose, 1995, pp. 65–66). Bercovitz and Mitchell (2007) claim that growth in both scale and scope enhances a business's long-term survival, owing to the greater availability of financial resources, organizational routines, and external ties. Indeed, there is a sizable body of research indicating that large firms and businesses tend to survive longer than smaller companies (Baum, 1996; Mitchell, 1994). Managers exploit resources to pursue their firms' general and, more specific, growth objectives, and to do so they first use existing resources. In this regard, Cyert and March (1956, p. 52) have defined this pool of excess resources, which enables firms to adjust to unexpected fluctuations, as "slack." Bourgeois (1981) similarly states that slack is a cushion of actual and potential resources that firms can use to adapt to internal and external pressures, counter threats and exploit opportunities. Despite claims that it is a somewhat nebulous construct (Daniel, Lohrke, Fornaciari, & Turner, 2004), slack serves as a useful indicator of a firm's resources. Likewise, slack can create opportunities for new investments, allowing managers to recognize opportunities and to recombine existing resources into new capabilities. Kaul (2012) found that new knowledge developed through innovation prompted a redeployment of scarce resources into previously unexplored areas of opportunity. In turn, new investments offer potential for better performance.

Financial resources are often needed to complement the redeployment of strategic resources. For example, resources may have to be adjusted for use in a new context, or additional resources may have to be acquired to complement the reallocated resources. In this sense, slack is closely associated with the availability of financial resources. Here, we investigate how slack affects firm profitability.

A distinction can be drawn between absorbed and unabsorbed slack in relation, respectively, to excess costs in organizations with low discretionary use, and uncommitted resources allowing greater managerial discretion. We expect they have different implications for resource redeployment and, hence profitability. On the one hand, absorbed slack is associated with constrained resources, which, precisely because of their constraints, are restricted in their use to the firm's current business and cannot be converted into alternative uses. The more specific a resource is, the lower its value when applied to its second-best use (Montgomery & Wernefelt, 1988). While absorbed slack can be readily used to expand current business, it is less suited to resource redeployment than unabsorbed slack. In contrast to absorbed slack, firms can more readily redeploy unabsorbed slack and commit it to use. While unabsorbed slack can also be used to expand extant business, what distinguishes it from absorbed slack is its comparatively greater potential for sharing and, consequently, for allowing synergies, as well as its comparatively greater potential for being applied to alternative businesses. In this respect, the distinction between absorbed and unabsorbed slack might provide some interesting insights to resource redeployment. Unabsorbed slack also provides more potential than absorbed slack for recombining resources in new ways.

The redeployment of resources can contribute to improving profitability by providing access to more profitable businesses than the current business. Moreover, the failure to exit a declining business in a timely fashion can degrade the overall performance of the firm (Sull, 1999), while firms may, through redeployment, benefit by exiting markets with declining opportunities and by taking advantage of new opportunities in other markets (Penrose, 1995). Redeployment of resources also underpins the reconfiguration of businesses, which in turn may fuel firm growth (Capron, Dussauge, & Mitchell, 1998; Seth, 1990). When current businesses are stagnating the firm can withdraw these resources to redeploy them in alternative businesses with higher marginal outcomes in terms of growth.

This study seeks to contribute to the analysis of the impact of slack on profitability, and to link slack with research in resource redeployment. We use three different indicators of both absorbed and unabsorbed slack and perform our study with a panel data for a sample of firms with at least 20 years of observations in COMPUSTAT. We find that unabsorbed slack has a more favorable impact on profitability than absorbed slack. While all the absorbed slack indicators present a significant negative influence on future profitability, the three unabsorbed slack indicators present positive, negative and non-significant influences, respectively. The fewer constraints on the redeployment of unabsorbed slack to exploit new opportunities, as well as to achieve synergy through resource sharing, point to its comparative advantage over absorbed slack. We find evidence for the differential impact of absorbed versus unabsorbed slack on profitability in firms with lower levels of slack, which suggests managers prefer to withdraw resources from current business and redeploy them to develop new business. However, there may be alternative explanations as to why slack impacts profitability, which we cannot rule out.

The rest of the paper is organized as follows: the next section outlines the research background and formulates the study's hypothesis. We then explain the research design and results, and end by offering our concluding remarks.

RESEARCH BACKGROUND AND HYPOTHESIS

Unabsorbed versus Absorbed Slack

Most authors draw a distinction between absorbed and unabsorbed slack (Lin, Cheng, & Liu, 2009; Tan & Peng, 2003). Alternative classifications of slack rely also on degrees of managerial resource use in relation to both types of slack (Bradley, Wiklund, & Shepherd, 2011a, 2011b; George, 2005). The most common and accepted difference between both types of slack relies on George's (2005) concepts of high-discretion and low-discretion managerial use, respectively. Absorbed slack is defined as excess costs of unused capacity with low discretionary use, while unabsorbed slack is uncommitted resources in an organization that managers have high discretion to redeploy and commit them to new uses (Huang & Li, 2012; Tan & Peng, 2003). The former is associated with excess resources that cannot be flexibly allocated to opportunistic ways that are unrelated to organizational routines, while the latter refers to flexible pool of unused resources that can be allocated to unpredictable opportunities (Mishina, Pollock, & Porac, 2004; Tan & Peng, 2003).

Likewise, we can distinguish between different degrees of resource constraints. The most constrained resources are restricted in use and can preferably be exploited for current business. They can be used to feed or expand current business, but given their limitations they hardly can be withdrawn from their current uses and redeployed to alternative uses. In contrast, less constrained resources are readily redeployed to new uses. Similarly, less constrained resources can be more easily shared with different businesses than more constrained resources. Fig. 1 illustrates these relationships.

Thus, absorbed slack is most closely associated with constrained resources, while unabsorbed slack is associated with unconstrained resources, allowing low and high discretionary uses, respectively. At the same time, there are different degrees of constraints affecting absorbed and unabsorbed slack. Finished products are a good example of the most constrained resources within a firm's absorbed slack. Once manufactured, they can almost exclusively be used to expand sales in current markets. Machines and equipment are another example of absorbed slack, but these resources are less constrained than finished products. While they can be used to manufacture current products (thus expanding current business), they can also be shared with newly designed, but related, markets and products, although they are less likely to be applied to completely new businesses. Similarly, while qualified personnel and managerial teams are more highly skilled and trained for their current commitments, they may also be

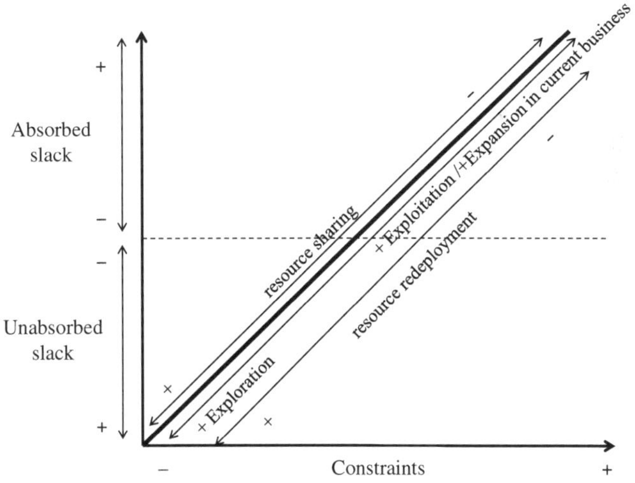

Fig. 1. Relationship between Slack and Resource Constraints.
Notes: The thick bold line represents the overall relationship between resource constraints and slack, while the thin lines represent specific relationships with respect to exploration/exploitation, resource sharing, and resource redeployment.

engaged on other assignments within the firm. Likewise, they can be trained to perform new business, but such redeployment often encounters greater difficulties. The lack of financial resources may prevent a firm from responding to new market opportunities, while access to financial resources can serve to alleviate the constraints on new ventures. Kraatz and Zajac (2001) found that greater financial resources allow firms to move into a new market as soon as opportunities arise. In this vein, financial resources – a typical example of unabsorbed slack – can be readily redeployed, and among such resources the equity-to-debt ratio is more readily redeployed than working capital, given that the former is a good indicator of the affordability of resources for long-term, new ventures, while the latter is a better indicator of short-term, more pressing commitments.

Absorbed and unabsorbed slack, therefore, are resources that can be devoted to expanding the existing business or to sharing, as well as to redeployment. Unabsorbed slack allows greater resource redeployment and synergies than absorbed slack, while the latter is less suited to redeployment. Finally, given that there are different gradations of absorbed slack, the less it is constrained the more it is suited to achieving synergies through resource sharing.

Implications of Slack on Profitability

Organizational theory holds that slack resources have a positive effect on firm performance (Daniel et al., 2004; George, 2005; Tan & Peng, 2003). According to the theory, a certain level of excess resources provides flexibility to experiment, take risks and undertake proactive initiatives. Firms use this slack to build capabilities that make them competitive while allowing them to make strategic choices. Slack acts as a buffer in periods of economic difficulties, facilitating adjustment in the face of unanticipated contingencies. Surplus resources make it easier for firms to pursue their projects. Thompson (1967) argued that slack provides a reactive bulwark against threats and facilitates proactive strategic initiatives. According to Sharfman, Wolf, Chase, and Tansik (1988), slack enables firms to survive in a turbulent environment. Although slack may entail a surplus cost, organizational theory considers that the benefits of slack outweigh its costs (Tan & Peng, 2003). Damanpour (1987) and Greve (2003) argued that slack has a positive effect on innovation. Firms with no surplus resources are more constrained in their dealings with operational issues. Managers and employees direct their efforts to addressing urgent matters and tend to rush orders. Coordination, planning, process improvement, innovation, market research, etc. are set aside, or may not be properly dealt with. However, the effect of slack on profitability is uncertain. According to Phan and Hill (1995) the use of scarce resources has an immediate positive impact on a firm's income, in the case of firms using their surplus resources, as well as reducing the amount of investment used for firm activity. The subsequent effect is an improvement in firm profitability through an increase in income and a reduction in the investment in resources (Starr & MacMillan, 1990). Sinclair, Klepper, and Cohen (2000) argued that firms with excess capacity have limited incentives to experiment. Stevenson and Jarillo (1990) suggested that resource slack entices managers to be administrative rather than entrepreneurial in their management approach. They become complacent and risk averse. Idle resources induce inefficiency. Baker and Nelson (2005) argued that firms with fewer resources are likely to leverage them efficiently. According to these authors, scarcity induces managers to improve their efficiency of use, while surplus resources induce waste and do not favor efficient use, thus reducing profitability.

Results from empirical research have found a positive relationship between slack and profitability (Peng, Li, Xie, & Su, 2010; Su, Xie, Wang, & Li, 2011; Vanacker, Collewaert, & Paeleman, 2013), a negative relationship (Subramanyam, Ramasubbu, & Krishnan, 2012), and also contradictory influences depending on the type of slack (George, 2005; Tan & Peng, 2003; Tan & Wang, 2010). Most previous research analyzed only a single (Love & Nohria, 2005; Mellahi & Wilkinson, 2010; O'Brien & Folta, 2009) or different measures of slack without considering the distinction between absorbed and unabsorbed (Bradley et al., 2011b; Mishina et al, 2004; Modi & Mishra, 2011; Tan, 2003), but those studies distinguishing between both types of slack (Huang & Li, 2012; Tan & Peng, 3002) did not focus on analyzing their differential effects on performance.

While the relationship between slack and profitability is uncertain, the differential effect of unabsorbed versus absorbed slack on profitability can be more precisely hypothesized. Helfat and Eisenhart (2004) explained the concept of inter-temporal economies of scope, discussing how resources from mature, declining, or defunct businesses can be reallocated quickly to more promising product-market opportunities. With respect to resource characteristics, we argue that unabsorbed slack has a differential advantage in terms of the opportunities for redeployment compared to absorbed slack. Matusaka (2001) argued that because organizational capabilities are at the source of a company's value, managers continuously search for better opportunities to ensure the survival of the firm, freeing up managerial resources and other productive factors from current uses to new businesses. Wealth creation depends in large measure on the identification of new opportunities and organizing effectively and efficiently to embrace them (Sirmon & Hitt, 2009; Teece, Pisano, & Shuen, 1997). In this vein, firms with unabsorbed slack are more ready to divert from current, unprofitable businesses to better opportunities, thus contributing more favorably to profitability than absorbed slack. We therefore formulate the following hypothesis:

Hypothesis. Unabsorbed slack has a more positive (or less negative) influence on future profitability than absorbed slack.

RESEARCH DESIGN

Equation and Dependent Variables

In this paper, we analyze the impact of a wide array of slack indicators on profitability. To do so we use the following equation, which formulates profitability at time $t + 1$ depending on different indicators of slack (SL) at time t, and controlling also for sales growth, size, industry profitability and growth, as well as for specific seasonal or temporal effects:

$$ROA_{i,t+1} = \alpha_0 + \sum_{j=1}^{J} \alpha_j \; SL_{i,t} + \alpha_s \; \frac{S_{i,t+1}}{S_{i,t}} + \alpha_z \; \log ASS_{i,t} + \alpha_r \; IPR_{i,t} + \alpha_c \; ISC_{i,t+1} + \sum_{t=1}^{T} \alpha_t \; Y_{i,t} + \varepsilon_{i,t} \qquad (1)$$

where all the variables refer to firm i in year t, S indicates sales, ASS is firm size measured as total assets, IPR indicates industry profitability, ISC represents the increase in industry sales with respect to the previous year, Y is a dummy variable indicating that an observation belongs to a given year (with value 1, and zero otherwise), j, s, z, r, and c are the subscripts for the estimators of slack, sales growth and size, industry profitability and the increase in sales, respectively, and ε is the error term. For the sake of simplicity, we use this last symbol to indicate the error term in all the equations in this paper.

We use return on assets (*ROA*) as an indicator of profitability, referring primarily to the economic profitability of firms and indicating how many dollars of earnings they derive from each dollar of assets they control. The indicator has been widely used in previous research (Daniel et al., 2004), and more recently in the work by Tan and Peng (2003), Tan and Wang (2010), and Modi and Mishra (2011), among others.

Measures of Absorbed and Unabsorbed Slack

As discussed, slack can be defined as the pool of resources in an organization that is in excess of the minimum necessary to produce a given level of organizational output. Extant research has identified different types of slack. George (2005), for example, distinguishes between high-discretion, low-discretion, and transient slack. Bradley et al. (2011a) employ indicators of potential, recoverable, and high-discretion slack, while Bradley et al. (2011b) use alternative measures of potential, absorbed and high-discretion slack. Tan and Peng (2003) and Huang and Li (2012) distinguish between absorbed and unabsorbed slack to refer, respectively, to excess costs in organizations with low discretionary use and uncommitted resources allowing greater managerial discretion. Unlike absorbed slack, firms can readily redeploy unabsorbed slack and commit it to use. This last distinction is the most commonly used and the most appropriate for our purposes here, given that it captures the constraints on the resources making up the slack. In order to include as wide an array of slack measures as possible in our study, we adopt three indicators for each slack type. Frequently employed elsewhere in the literature, for absorbed slack, we use the ratios of inventories to sales (*INVSL*), of property, plant and equipment (*PPE*) to sales (*PPESL*) and selling, general and administrative expenses (*SGA*) to sales (*SGASL*), while for unabsorbed slack, we use measures of financial slack, equity-to-debt ratio, and cash slack (*FINSL*, *EQDSL* and *CASHSL* respectively).

Inventories, *PPE*, and *SGA* have been previously and similarly used as measures of absorbed slack (Hendricks, Singha, & Zhang, 2009; Love & Nohria, 2005; Modi & Mishra, 2011). *FINSL* has been widely used in previous studies. In line with Mishina et al. (2004) and Bradley et al. (2011b), we define it here as the difference between working capital available and working capital required, and we take its relative value with respect to total assets. More precisely, we calculate it as a ratio of current assets less current liabilities to total assets. *EQDSL* has also been widely used in previous studies (Bradley et al., 2001a, 2011b; George, 2005; Vanacker et al., 2013). We calculate it as the ratio of stockholders equity to current liabilities and long-term debt. While the aforementioned authors describe it as potential or high-discretion slack, George (2005) uses the ratio of debt-to-equity as a measure of low-discretion slack. We consider it as allowing high discretionary use, given that the measure does not involve a specific asset or resource endowment. Vanacker et al. (2013), Bradley et al. (2011a), and George (2005) each use different measures of cash slack; here, we define *CASHSL* as cash and short-term investments to total assets.

We forward profitability to time $t + 1$ to capture more effectively the effects of slack and to help establish the direction of causality.

Control Variables

In the traditional model of cost behavior, costs are described as fixed and variable with respect to activity. Given that only variable costs are immediately related to changes in sales, the increase/decrease in sales in a given period significantly influences firm profitability (Anderson, Banker, & Janakiraman, 2003). We expect an immediate positive influence of sales growth on firm profitability.

Size is an important factor influencing firm performance. It is widely recognized that large firms enjoy certain advantages over small firms, including economies of scale (Alvarez & Crespi, 2003; Caves & Barton, 1990), more favorable access to the credit market and lower financing costs (Beck & Demirguc-Kunt, 2006; Martinelli, 1997), and more resources to afford quality-related investments (Noci, 1994). Large firms also have more resources to explore new opportunities. In contrast, the advantages of small firms are associated with their greater flexibility (You, 1995) and the fact that they tend to be less bureaucratic and so more likely to use their resources efficiently (Baker & Nelson, 2005). They also respond more quickly to changing circumstances (Knight & Cavusgil, 1996). As such, the influence of size on profitability is uncertain and so we use the logarithm of total assets.

Industry performance with respect to profitability is also likely to influence individual firm profitability. Industries with high growth rates or profits offer more opportunities (Gruca & Rego, 2005). We expect these variables to have a positive effect on the dependent variable in Eq. (1). Control dummy variables for years are also included in the equation.

Previous empirical research on slack employs diverse variable definitions and methodologies. While some use absolute measures of profitability as dependent variables, others use relative measures, which are combined with independent variables that measure slack in relative or absolute terms indistinctly, as well as being indexed to industry values in some cases, together with non-indexed values. In this paper, we seek to avoid any methodological flaws by defining variables in relative terms, standardizing them with year-industry means and standard deviations. However, we use non-standardized size values because these raw data allow us to make more appropriate comparisons, as well as the logarithmic transformation.

Sample

We use COMPUSTAT data for all American industrial firms (SIC codes 2 and 3) with data from 1979 to 2009 with at least twenty years of observations in the database. We prefer to use a sample that prioritizes firms that remain in the sample for the duration. Given that most of the firms remained in the sample for all the years in question, the results are reliable and not likely to be influenced by changes in the sample over time or by short-lived episodes of unusual firm performance. Although such firms might reveal interesting slack behavior, we consider that a sample of firms observed over a long period provides a more appropriate dynamic approach. We do not consider firms in the services industry because of their different cost structure and business approach. Table 1 shows our sample and descriptive statistics. We start with 37,730 year-data observations from 1,453 different firms. Table 1 presents means, medians, and year-data observations for the untransformed values of all the dependent and independent variables used in our study. The average *ROA* ratio for the available 35,797 observations in the whole period is 9.3%. Sales grew 15.8% on average for the available sample in the period, matched by a similar growth rate in *PPE*. The corresponding values for the remaining variables are also shown in Table 1.

Given the panel data structure of our sample, assets are converted into values for the most recent year in our sample, applying the US inflation rate. As discussed, we use the logarithm of these values as an independent variable in our study.

Substantial differences between the mean and median values of most variables, especially S_{t+1}/S_t, *PPESL*, *EQDSL*, *CASHSL*, PPE_{t+1}/PPE_t,

Table 1. Descriptive Statistics.

	Year-Data Observations	Mean	Median
ROA	35,797	0.09304	0.09770
S_{t+1}/S_t	35,777	1.15869	1.07002
PPE_{t+1}/PPE_t	35,698	1.16188	1.03755
ASS[a]	37,454	4300.72	296.00
Absorbed slack			
INVSL	37,369	0.22370	0.15214
PPESL	37,367	0.59664	0.21563
SGASL	35,298	0.24347	0.21917
Unabsorbed slack			
FINSL	36,848	0.27520	0.28393
EQDSL	36,918	2.07415	1.15805
CASHSL	36,762	0.12392	0.06567

Notes: *ROA* = return on assets, *S* = sales, *INVSL* = inventory slack, *PPESL* = property, plant and equipment slack, *SGASL* = selling, general and administration slack, *FINSL* = financial slack, *EQDSL* = equity-to-debt slack, *CASHSL* = cash slack, *PPE* = property, plant and equipment, and *ASS* = total assets.
[a]Constant values: $000.

and *ASS*, point to the presence of extreme values and hence the need to winsorize variables. We standardize all variables with mean and standard deviations of year and industry values, with two SIC digits. We also winsorize the top and bottom 1% of all standardized variables. However, all results remain largely unchanged with non-winsorized variables.

Given that not all the variables are available for all firms and years, as well as the delayed variables used, the sample size for our multivariate analyses ranges from 29,369 to 32,353 year-data observations with 1,420 firms (see Table 3).

Table 2 shows the Pearson correlations for the winsorized variables in our sample. While most correlations are significant at $p < 0.01$, the coefficients are not high. The highest value is 0.5385 (correlation between *FINSL* and *EQDSL*). Moreover, the highest variance inflation factor in all the subsequent estimations performed is comparatively low: 2.40 for *FINSL*. Therefore, estimations are not likely to be influenced by collinearity.

Table 2. Pearson Correlations.

	INVSL	*PPESL*	*SGASL*	*FINSL*	*EQDSL*	*CASHSL*	S_{t+1}/S_t	ln *ASS*	*IPR*	*ISC*	PPE_{t+1}/PPE_t
INVSL	1										
PPESL	0.0267***	1									
SGASL	0.1327***	−0.1343***	1								
FINSL	0.2243***	−0.2848***	0.1436***	1							
EQDSL	0.036***	−0.0247***	0.1059***	0.5385***	1						
CASHSL	−0.0344***	0.1107***	0.1889***	0.3517***	0.4362***	1					
S_{t+1}/S_t	0.0716***	0.0882***	0.0656***	0.0328***	0.0339***	0.1177***	1				
ln *ASS*	−0.1424***	0.1776***	−0.2345***	−0.2445***	−0.1876***	−0.0591***	−0.0675***	1			
IPR	0.0036	0.0035	0.0002	−0.0126**	0.004	0.0009	0.0003	0.0024	1		
ISC	−0.0007	−0.0086	−0.0023	0	−0.0067	−0.0066	−0.3157***	−0.0069	0.0230***	1	
PPE_{t+1}/PPE_t	−0.039***	−0.0735***	−0.0122**	0.1247***	0.0922***	0.096***	0.3816***	−0.0456***	0.0011	−0.0059	1

Notes: INVSL = inventory slack, PPESL = property, plant and equipment slack, SGASL = selling, general and administration slack, FINSL = financial slack, EQDSL = equity-to-debt slack, CASHSL = cash slack, S = sales, ASS = total assets, *IPR* = mean industry profitability, *ISC* = mean industry sales growth, and *PPE* = property, plant and equipment.

*, **, and *** indicate significance at the 10%, 5%, and 1% levels based on two-tailed tests, respectively.

Table 3. Impact of Slack at Time t on Profitability at Time $t + n$ (t-Statistics in Parentheses).

Variables	(1) ROA_{t+1}	(2) ROA_{t+3}
Absorbed slack		
INVSL	−0.247***	−0.155***
	(0.00662)	(0.00540)
PPESL	−0.201***	−0.156***
	(0.00751)	(0.00634)
SGASL	−0.391***	−0.260***
	(0.00759)	(0.00649)
Unabsorbed slack		
FINSL	0.108***	0.0379***
	(0.00674)	(0.00566)
EQDSL	−0.00886	−0.0503***
	(0.00660)	(0.00558)
CASHSL	−0.0992***	−0.0962***
	(0.00696)	(0.00582)
Control variables		
S_{t+1}/S_t (mean three years ahead for ROA_{t+3})	1.811***	2.642***
	(0.0394)	(0.0433)
log *ASS*	−0.0124	0.0827***
	(0.0145)	(0.0142)
IPR	−0.257	−0.131
	(0.157)	(0.130)
ISC	0.560***	0.911***
	(0.0191)	(0.0257)
Constant	−0.537***	−1.143***
	(0.0530)	(0.0556)
Observations	32,353	29,369
Number of firms	1,420	1,417
R-squared overall	0.1967	0.2010
Firm	Yes	Yes
Year	Yes	Yes

Table 3. *(Continued)*

Variables	(1) ROA_{t+1}	(2) ROA_{t+3}
Joint effects		
Absorbed slack ($\sum \alpha_j$)	−0.839***	−0.571***
Unabsorbed slack ($\sum \alpha_j$)	−0.00006	−0.1086***
Difference: absorbed − unabsorbed ($\sum \alpha_j$)	−0.83894***	−0.4624***

Notes: Standard errors in parentheses. Fixed effects estimations for Eq. (1) correcting for endogeneity (two-stage least-squares within estimator).
ROA = return on assets, *INVSL* = inventory slack, *PPESL* = property, plant and equipment slack, *SGASL* = selling, general and administration slack, *FINSL* = financial slack, *EQDSL* = equity-to-debt slack, *CASHSL* = cash slack, *S* = sales, *ASS* = total assets, *IPR* = mean industry profitability, *ISC* = mean industry sales growth, and α_j = coefficients of slack variables.
***$p < 0.01$, **$p < 0.05$, *$p < 0.1$.

RESULTS

Estimations of Eq. (1)

We perform panel data regressions on our sample, correcting for autocorrelation disturbances. The Hausman test rejects the null hypothesis of no correlation between individual effects and the explanatory variables. As the individual effects are correlated with the regressors in all the estimations, the random effects estimator is inconsistent, while the fixed effects estimator is consistent and efficient. We therefore perform panel data estimations with fixed effects.

Assuming that the results obtained with Eq. (1) might be biased, given that some of the covariates may be endogenous, we check for the presence of endogeneity. The equation includes sales growth as a control variable, influencing firm profitability, but in turn it also depends on an increase in investment in productive capacity. We, therefore, include PPE_{t+1}/PPE_t as an instrument for S_{t+1}/S_t in Eq. (1). As can be seen in Table 2, the Pearson correlation between the two variables is, as expected, positive (0.3816) and significant. The sales growth residuals dependent on this instrument, in the fixed effects estimation, is significant at $p < 0.01$ when included in Eq. (1), revealing the presence of expected endogenous disturbances. We then use the two-stage least-squares within estimator, available in STATA, for the fixed effects option.

Results are shown in Table 3. Column 1 displays estimations when the dependent variable is future profitability. The model estimated presents a significant goodness of fit, with an overall *R*-square of 19.67%. For the sake of simplicity, the coefficients for the year and firm dummies are not displayed. As far as the control variables are concerned, firm and industry sales growth have, as expected, significant positive influences on future profitability.

As for our variables of interest, absorbed slack has a significant (at $p <$ 0.01) and negative influence on profitability (see column 1 in Table 3), revealing the prevalence of the inefficiency effect. A plausible explanation for this prevalence is the need to apply increasing resources to remain competitive over time. The greater within-firm *R*-square value (0.3271) compared to the overall R-square value for this estimation provides further support for this explanation. The explanation is also in keeping with increasing globalization and greater exposure to foreign competition that reduce profitability (Ghosal, 2002; Katics & Petersen, 1995), and the subsequent need for complexity involving lower profitability (Banker, Potter, & Schroeder, 1995; Miller & Vollman, 1985) and for management innovations to avoid even greater reductions in profitability (Kinney & Wempe, 2002). Additionally, absorbed slack serves primarily for continuing to expand current business, and as such is detrimental to profitability. Our results suggest that few absorbed resources can actually be applied to create synergies through the sharing of resources with other businesses, and that they cannot be applied for redeployment in more profitable business. Absorbed slack is constrained and restricted to specific current uses. The coefficients for unabsorbed slack are significantly positive for *FINSL*, negative but not significant for *EQDSL* and significantly negative (−0.0992) for *CASHSL*, but they present values that are much less negative than the corresponding coefficients for absorbed slack (ranging from −0.201 to −0.391). Given that all the dependent and slack variables are standardized, the coefficients allow direct comparisons to be made between them. This table also displays the overall influence of absorbed and unabsorbed slack variables at time t on profitability at time $t + 1$. The sum of the coefficients of all the absorbed slack variables is −0.839 (significant at $p < 0.01$), which is considerably lower value than the corresponding sum of all the unabsorbed slack variables (−0.00006, non-significant at $p < 0.1$). The Wald test for the joint effect of both groups of variables reveals a significant (at $p < 0.01$) lower negative influence of unabsorbed slack on profitability than that of absorbed slack. The difference is significant (at $p < 0.01$) for all individual comparisons (nine out of nine) between the three indicators of absorbed and unabsorbed slack. These results support Hypothesis 1.

We also perform analyses on longer term future profitability. Assuming that converting organizational slack, and slack resources in general, into profitability might take much longer time than our analysis provides for at time $t + 1$, we analyze the impact of slack at time t on profitability at time $t + 3$. The results (see column 2 in Table 3) are largely similar to those reported in column 1. Together with firm and industry sales growth, size significantly influences higher profitability at time $t + 3$. Despite *EQDSL* has a significant negative influence on the dependent variable, again absorbed slack has a more negative influence on future profitability, considering all coefficients as well as the joint effect of both groups of slack. The sum of the coefficients of all the absorbed slack variables is −0.571, which is considerably lower value than the corresponding sum of all the unabsorbed slack variables (−0.1086). The Wald test for the joint effect of both groups of variables reveals a significant (at $p < 0.01$) lower negative influence of unabsorbed slack on profitability than that of absorbed slack. Again, the difference is significant (at $p < 0.01$) for all individual comparisons between the three indicators of absorbed and unabsorbed slack.

Additional Analysis

Capacity is an additional factor influencing business performance and resource redeployment. Redeployability is a property of a certain type of resource and, according to Sakhartov and Folta (2014), is only pertinent for resources of limited capacity. Given these considerations we wonder whether the amount of slack affects the effect of slack on profitability.

We distinguish firms with little slack using interaction variables of slack with a dummy variable *DL* indicating that the slack of a given firm is below the median industry-year (taking a value of 1 or 0 otherwise), with d indicating the subscript for these variables. We thus formulate the following enlarged model:

$$ROA_{i,t+1} = \alpha_0 + \sum_{j=1}^{J} \alpha_j \ SL_{i,t} + \sum_{j=1}^{D} \alpha_d \ DL_{i,t} \ SL_{i,t} + \ \alpha_s \ \frac{S_{i,t+1}}{S_{i,t}} + \alpha_z \ \log ASS_{i,t} + \alpha_r \ IPR_{i,t} + \alpha_c \ ISC_{i,t+1} + \sum_{t=1}^{T} \alpha_t \ Y_{i,t} + \varepsilon_{i,t} \tag{2}$$

Column 1 in Table 4 shows the results for the impact of slack at time t on profitability at time $t + 1$ with the full model, including the interaction variables for low slack levels. In two of the absorbed slack variables, resource scarcity stresses its negative impact on profitability. The exception is *SGASL*, which is a less constrained resource than *INVSL* and *PPESL*. *SGASL* is an indicator of the managerial and organizational resources that can be shared across businesses, and which are less likely to be used in redeployment. Firms with bottom-end managerial and organizational resources are more troubled by specific, daily operational tasks. An additional endowment of these resources allows organizational, planning and strategic activities, eventually enabling firms to explore new business opportunities as well as to share organizational capabilities across different current businesses, which eventually have a positive influence on profitability. For two of the unabsorbed slack variables, resource scarcity moderates the negative impact on profitability, with the *DL·FINSL* coefficient sign being negative and only significant at $p < 0.1$, and it also moderates the positive sign of *FINSL*. The overall impact on profitability is negative for absorbed slack (−0.915, significant at $p < 0.01$) and positive for unabsorbed slack (0.0971, significant at $p < 0.01$) in firms with below median slack considering the sum of all coefficients ($\alpha_j + \alpha_d$), as can be seen in Table 4. In all pairs of comparisons (nine out of nine) the effect is more favorable for unabsorbed than absorbed slack in these firms. Comparing only the interaction variables, this relationship holds for the joint effect of all variables (the total for the absorbed slack coefficients is −0.111, while for the unabsorbed slack is 0.1174), as well as for six out of nine pairs of comparisons at $p <$ 0.01 (and for seven out of nine pairs of comparisons at $p < 0.05$). However, there are no significant differences between the interaction variables of unabsorbed and absorbed slack on profitability for *INVSL* versus *FINSL* or for *SGASL* versus *EQDSL*.

Overall these results suggest that firms with scarce resources would be better advised to withdraw them from current unprofitable or unviable businesses and redeploy them in new opportunities, offering better profitability prospects. In the case of scarce constrained resources, firms with little slack are less likely to face environmental threats, and given the limitations of absorbed slack, they would be unable to redeploy these resources in order to exploit better opportunities. Firms with scarce non-constrained resources are also ill-equipped to develop new capabilities, but these resources would allow them to explore new opportunities. Given their scarcity, firms are better advised to break the inertia of their current business than are firms with plenty of resources. Firms endowed with plenty of

Table 4. Impact of Slack at Time *t* on Profitability at time $t + n$ (*t*-Statistics in Parentheses).

Variables	(1) ROA_{t+1}	(2) ROA_{t+3}
Absorbed slack		
INVSL	−0.221***	−0.152***
	(0.00816)	(0.00667)
DL·INVSL	−0.0680***	−0.00380
	(0.0167)	(0.0140)
PPESL	−0.163***	−0.126***
	(0.00869)	(0.00727)
DL·PPESL	−0.163***	−0.129***
	(0.0195)	(0.0166)
SGASL	−0.420***	−0.279***
	(0.00929)	(0.00795)
DL·SGASL	0.120***	0.0809***
	(0.0201)	(0.0170)
Unabsorbed slack		
FINSL	0.111***	0.0433***
	(0.0120)	(0.0101)
DL·FINSL	−0.0296*	−0.00847
	(0.0164)	(0.0137)
EQDSL	−0.0233***	−0.0388***
	(0.00738)	(0.00621)
DL·EQDSL	0.0834***	−0.0698***
	(0.0186)	(0.0157)
CASHSL	−0.108***	−0.106***
	(0.00754)	(0.00630)
DL·CASHSL	0.0636***	0.0617***
	(0.0197)	(0.0165)
Control variables		
S_{t+1}/S_t (mean three years ahead for ROA_{t+3})	1.772***	2.610***
	(0.0393)	(0.0430)
log *ASS*	−0.00430	0.0897***
	(0.0146)	(0.0142)
IPR	−0.238	−0.143
	(0.156)	(0.130)

Table 4. (*Continued*)

Variables	(1) ROA_{t+1}	(2) ROA_{t+3}
ISC	0.559***	0.922***
	(0.0191)	(0.0259)
Constant	−0.557***	−1.188***
	(0.0554)	(0.0579)
Observations	32,353	29,369
Number of firms	1,420	1,417
R-squared overall	0.2082	0.2082
Firm	Yes	Yes
Year	Yes	Yes
Joint effects		
Absorbed slack: low slack ($\sum\alpha_j + \sum\alpha_d$)	−0.915***	−0.6089***
Unabsorbed slack: low slack ($\sum\alpha_j + \sum\alpha_d$)	0.0971***	−0.1807***
Difference low slack: absorbed − unabsorbed ($\sum\alpha_j + \sum\alpha_d$)	1.0121***	−0.4282***
Absorbed slack: interaction variables ($\sum\alpha_d$)	−0.111***	−0.0519**
Unabsorbed slack: interaction variables ($\sum\alpha_d$)	0.1174***	−0.0165
Difference interaction variables: absorbed − unabsorbed ($\sum\alpha_d$)	−0.2284***	−0.0353

Notes: Standard errors in parentheses. Fixed effects estimations for Eq. (2) correcting for endogeneity (two-stage least-squares within estimator).
ROA = return on assets, *INVSL* = inventory slack, *PPESL* = property, plant and equipment slack, *SGASL* = selling, general and administration slack, *FINSL* = financial slack, *EQDSL* = equity-to-debt slack, *CASHSL* = cash slack, *S* = sales, *ASS* = total assets, *IPR* = mean industry profitability, *ISC* = mean industry sales growth (mean last three years when estimating ROA_{t+3}), α_j = coefficients of slack variables, and α_d = coefficients of interaction variables with slack.
***$p < 0.01$, **$p < 0.05$, *$p < 0.1$.

non-constrained resources are less likely to explore alternative businesses or even to explore them while at the same time maintaining their current business. Indeed, they would be more likely to maintain their current inefficiencies. Our results suggest that low levels of unabsorbed slack seem to have a moderating effect when the relationship between slack and profitability is negative. In fact, the joint effect of unabsorbed slack on profitability is positive in firms with low slack. Overall, the differential effects of both types of slack on profitability are greater for firms with less slack than for firms with more, which is presumably attributed to their differential suitability for redeployment. These results provide insights and hints on this assumption, but more in-depth research is needed on this issue.

Column 2 in Table 4 displays results for Eq. (2) when the dependent variable is profitability at time $t + 3$, which present some differences in the interaction variables. Overall, the distance between the influence of absorbed and unabsorbed slack on profitability is greater for firms with low slack levels, with respect to the whole sample, but it is non-significant.

CONCLUSIONS

In this paper, we have analyzed the impact of absorbed and unabsorbed slack, measured using three different indicators of each type, on future firm profitability. Absorbed and unabsorbed slack provide valuable indications as to the most likely redeployment of resources. Thus, absorbed slack is associated with resources whose use is largely restricted to current operations and business. As a result of these strict limitations these resources are less available than unabsorbed slack for redeployment in exploiting new opportunities. In contrast, there are fewer restrictions on the use of unabsorbed slack for these alternative uses. Accordingly, we have formulated a hypothesis concerning the differential effects of absorbed versus unabsorbed slack on firm profitability, which appear to be linked to their differential use for resource redeployment.

We find that absorbed slack has a negative influence on future profitability, which appears to reflect the need firms have to apply increasing amounts of resources to remain competitive over time, as well the difficulties they face to redeploy these resources to new uses. Indeed, the increasing levels of such resources required to maintain an on-going business are a source of inefficiency. At the same time, we find positive, negative, and non-significant relationships between unabsorbed slack and future profitability. In all instances, we find its influence to be more favorable, or less negative, than that of absorbed slack. This differential effect can be attributed to the greater possibilities for redeploying unabsorbed slack to more promising business opportunities, as well as to its ability to achieve synergies through resource sharing across different businesses.

We find evidence of the differential influences of absorbed versus unabsorbed slack on future profitability in firms with lower levels of slack. Our results suggest that given that firms with limited capacity are obliged to withdraw resources from current business and redeploy them to exploit more attractive opportunities, and that absorbed slack is more restricted for use in current business, firms with little unabsorbed slack deviate even further away from the inertia of current business. This comparatively beneficial effect may be attributed to the lower constraints on unabsorbed slack for redeployment to more favorable opportunities than those provided by current business, as well as to achieving synergies.

Our analysis presents several limitations. We use absorbed and unabsorbed slack as indicators of exploration and exploitation, expansion, sharing, and redeployment; however, we do not actually observe redeployment or synergy taking place, so our results are somewhat conjectural. There may indeed be other explanations as to why slack influences future profitability, which we cannot rule out. Future research is needed using precise measures of resource redeployment and synergy. Additionally, we do not take into account specific circumstances such as market stagnation, expansion, dynamism or munificence, nor diversification in related or unrelated businesses. Further research needs to address specific contexts and circumstances.

ACKNOWLEDGMENTS

We acknowledge the interesting and valuable comments and feedback received from all participants in the special conference on "Corporate strategy and resource redeployment" held in Strasbourg from November 1 to 3, 2015, and especially to Timothy Folta and Will Mitchell
Author biographies

REFERENCES

Alvarez, R., & Crespi, G. (2003). Determinants of technical efficiency in small firms. *Small Business Economics*, *20*, 233–244.

Anderson, M. C., Banker, R. D., & Janakiraman, S. (2003). Are selling, general and administrative costs sticky? *Journal of Accounting Research*, *41*, 47–63.

Baker, T., & Nelson, R. E. (2005). Creating something from nothing: Resource construction through entrepreneurial bricolage. *Administrative Science Quarterly*, *50*, 329–366.

Banker, R. D., Potter, G., & Schroeder, R. G. (1995). An empirical analysis of manufacturing overhead cost drivers. *Journal of Accounting and Economics*, *19*, 115–137.

Baum, J. A. C. (1996). Organizational ecology. In S. Clegg, C. Hardy, & W. Nord (Eds.), *Handbook of organization studies* (pp. 77–113). London: Sage.

Beck, T., & Demirguc-Kunt, A. (2006). Small and medium-size enterprises: Access to finance as a growth constraint. *Journal of Banking and Finance*, *30*, 2931–2943.

Bercovitz, J., & Mitchell, W. (2007). When is more better? The impact of business scale and scope on long-term business survival, while controlling for profitability. *Strategic Management Journal*, *28*, 61–79.

Bourgeois, L. (1981). On the measurement of organizational slack. *Academy of Management Review*, *6*, 29–39.

Bradley, S. W., Wiklund, J., & Shepherd, D. A. (2011a). The importance of slack for new organizations facing "tough" environments. *Journal of Management Studies*, *48*, 1071–1097.

Bradley, S. W., Wiklund, J., & Shepherd, D. A. (2011b). Swinging a double-edged sword: The effect of slack on entrepreneurial management and growth. *Journal of Business Venturing*, *26*, 537–554.

Capron, L., Dussauge, P., & Mitchell, W. (1998). Resource redeployment following horizontal acquisitions in Europe and North America, 1988–1992. *Strategic Management Journal*, *19*, 631–661.

Caves, R. E., & Barton, D. (1990). *Efficiency in US manufacturing industries*. Cambridge, MA: MIT Press.

Cyert, R., & March, J. (1956). Organizational factors in the theory of oligopoly. *Quarterly Journals of Economics*, *70*, 44–64.

Damanpour, F. (1987). The adoption of technological, administrative, and ancillary innovations: Impacts of organizational factors. *Journal of Management*, *13*, 675–688.

Daniel, F., Lohrke, F. T., Fornaciari, C. J., & Turner, R. A., Jr. (2004). Slack resources and firm performance: A meta-analysis. *Journal of Business Research*, *57*, 565–574.

George, G. (2005). Slack resources and the performance of privately held firms. *Academy of Management Journal*, *48*, 661–676.

Ghosal, V. (2002). Potential foreign competition in U.S. manufacturing. *International Journal of Industrial Organization*, *20*, 1461–1489.

Greve, H. R. (2003). *Organizational learning from performance feedback: A behavioral perspective on innovation and change*. Cambridge: Cambridge University Press.

Gruca, T. S., & Rego, L. L. (2005). Customer satisfaction, cash flow, and shareholder value. *Journal of Marketing*, *69*, 115–130.

Helfat, C. E., & Eisenhart, K. M. (2004). Inter-temporal economies of scope, organizational modularity, and the dynamics of diversification. *Strategic Management Journal*, *25*, 1217–1232.

Hendricks, K. B., Singha, V. R., & Zhang, R. (2009). The effects of operational slack, diversification, and vertical relatedness on the stock market reaction to supply chain disruptions. *Journal of Operations Management*, *27*, 233–246.

Huang, J. W., & Li, Y. H. (2012). Slack resources in team learning and project performance. *Journal of Business Research*, *65*, 381–388.

Katics, M. M., & Petersen, B. C. (1995). The effect of rising import competition on market power: A panel data study of U.S. manufacturing. *Journal of Industrial Economics*, *42*, 277–286.

Kaul, A. (2012). Technology and corporate scope: Firm and rival innovation as antecedents of corporate transactions. *Strategic Management Journal*, *33*, 347–367.

Kinney, M. R., & Wempe, W. F. (2002). Further evidence on the extent and origins of JIT's profitability effects. *Accounting Review*, *77*(1), 203–225.

Knight, G. A., & Cavusgil, S. T. (1996). The born global firm: A challenge to traditional internationalization theory. *Advances in International Marketing*, *8*, 11–26.

Kraatz, M. S., & Zajac, E. J. (2001). How organizational resources affect strategic change and performance in turbulent environments: Theory and evidence. *Organization Science*, *12*(5), 632–657.

Lin, W., Cheng, K., & Liu, Y. (2009). Organizational slack and firm's internationalization: A longitudinal study of high-technology firms. *Journal of World Business*, *44*(2), 397–406.

Love, E. G., & Nohria, N. (2005). Reducing slack: The performance consequences of downsizing by large industrial firms, 1997–93. *Strategic Management Journal*, *26*, 1087–1108.

Martinelli, C. (1997). Small firms, borrowing constraints, and reputation. *Journal of Economic Behavior and Organization*, *33*, 91–105.

Matusaka, J. G. (2001). Corporate diversification, value maximization, and organizational capabilities. *Journal of Business*, *74*(3), 409–431.

Mellahi, K., & Wilkinson, A. (2010). A study of the association between level of slack reduction following downsizing and innovation output. *Journal of Management Studies*, *47*, 483–508.

Miller, J. G., & Vollman, T. E. (1985). The hidden factory. *Harvard Business Review*, (September–October), 142–150.

Mishina, Y., Pollock, T. G., & Porac, J. F. (2004). Are more resources always better for growth? Resource stickiness in market and product expansion. *Strategic Management Journal*, *25*, 1179–1197.

Mitchell, W. (1994). The dynamics of evolving markets: The effects of business sales and age on dissolutions and divestitures. *Administrative Science Quarterly*, *39*(4), 575–602.

Modi, S. B., & Mishra, S. (2011). What drives financial performance – Resource efficiency or resource slack? Evidence from U.S. based manufacturing firms from 1991 to 2006. *Journal of Operations Management*, *29*, 254–273.

Montgomery, C. A., & Wernefelt, B. (1988). Diversification, Ricardian rents and Tobin's q. *Rand Journal of Economics*, *19*(4), 623–632.

Noci, G. (1994). Accounting and non-accounting measures of quality-based performances in small firms. *International Journal of Operations and Production Management*, *15*, 78–105.

O'Brien, J. P., & Folta, T. B. (2009). A transaction cost perspective on why, how, and when cash impacts firm performance. *Managerial and Decision Economics*, *30*(7), 465–479.

Peng, M. W., Li, Y., Xie, E., & Su, Z. (2010). CEO duality, organizational slack, and firm performance in China. *Asia Pacific Journal of Management*, *27*, 611–624.

Penrose, E. (1995). *The theory of the growth of the firm*. New York, NY: Wiley.

Phan, P., & Hill, C. (1995). Organizational restructuring and economic performance in leveraged buyouts: An ex-post study. *Academy of Management Journal*, *38*, 704–739.

Sakhartov, A. V., & Folta, T. B. (2014). Resource relatedness, redeployability, and firm value. *Strategic Management Journal*, *35*, 1781–1797.

Seth, A. (1990). Value creation in acquisitions: A re-examination of performance issues. *Strategic Management Journal*, *11*(2), 99–115.

Sharfman, M., Wolf, G., Chase, R., & Tansik, D. (1988). Antecedents of organizational slack. Academy of Management Review, *13*, 601–614.

Sinclair, G., Klepper, S., & Cohen, W. (2000). What's experience got to do with it? Sources of cost reduction in a large specialty chemicals producer. *Management Science*, *46*(1), 28–45.

Sirmon, D. G., & Hitt, M. A. (2009). Contingencies within dynamic managerial capabilities: Interdependent effects of resource investment and deployment on firm performance. *Strategic Management Journal*, *30*, 1375–1394.

Starr, J. E., & MacMillan, I. C. (1990). Resource cooptation via social contracting: Resource acquisition strategies for new ventures. *Strategic Management Journal*, *11*, 79–92.

Stevenson, H. H., & Jarillo, J. C. (1990). A paradigm of entrepreneurship: Entrepreneurial management. *Strategic Management Journal*, *11*(Special issue), 17–27.

Su, Z., Xie, E., Wang, D., & Li, Y. (2011). Entrepreneurial strategy making, resources, and firm performance: Evidence from China. *Small Business Economics*, *36*, 235–247.

Subramanyam, R., Ramasubbu, N., & Krishnan, M. S. (2012). In search of efficient flexibility: Effects of software component granularity on development effort, defects, and customization effort. *Information Systems Research*, *23*, 787–803.

Sull, D. M. (1999). The dynamics of standing still: Firestone tire & rubber and the radial revolution. *Business History Review*, *73*(3), 430–464.

Tan, J. (2003). Curvilinear relationship between organizational slack and firm performance: Evidence from Chinese state enterprises. *European Management Journal*, *21*(6), 740–749.

Tan, J., & Peng, M. W. (2003). Organizational slack and firm performance during economic transitions: Two studies from an emerging economy. *Strategic Management Journal*, *24*, 1249–1263.

Tan, J., & Wang, L. (2010). Flexibility-efficiency tradeoff and performance implications among Chinese SOEs. *Journal of Business Research*, *63*, 356–362.

Teece, D. J., Pisano, G., & Shuen, A. (1997). Dynamic capabilities and strategic management. *Strategic Management Journal*, *17*(7), 509–533.

Thompson, J. D. (1967). *Organizations in action*. New York, NY: McGraw-Hill.

Vanacker, T., Collewaert, V., & Paeleman, I. (2013). The relationship between slack resources and the performance of entrepreneurial firms: The role of venture capital and angel investors. *Journal of Management Studies*, *50*, 1070–1096.

You, J. (1995). Small firms in economic theory. *Cambridge Journal of Economics*, *19*, 441–462.

ABOUT THE AUTHORS

Gautam Ahuja <gahuja@umich.edu> is Harvey C. Fruehauf Professor of Business Administration and Professor of Strategy at the Ross School of Business, University of Michigan. His research interests focus on competitive analysis, innovation, globalization and the use of mergers, acquisitions and alliances in these contexts. His research has received several international awards from the top scholarly associations in the field. His publications have appeared in the major scholarly journals (*Administrative Science Quarterly*, *Organization Science*, *Strategic Management Journal*, *Academy of Management Review*, *Academy of Management Journal*). He has served as Associate/Senior Editor for several of the top academic journals.

Jaideep Anand is the William H. Davis Chair and Dean's Distinguished Professor of Strategy at the Fisher College of Business, Ohio State University. He earned a bachelor's in Mechanical Engineering from the Indian Institute of Technology, New Delhi, India, and master's and Ph.D. degrees in Strategy from the Wharton School, University of Pennsylvania. His interests include inter- and intra-firm redeployment of firm capabilities in different technological, corporate and international contexts. He is the recipient of numerous awards for his research, teaching, and service, and is currently the elected chair of the Academy of Management, IMD.

Josep M. Argilés-Bosch is currently Associate Professor of Accounting at the Universitat de Barcelona (Department of Business). He completed his Ph.D. in Economics and Business Administration at the Universitat Autònoma de Barcelona in 1998. His research interests' include management accounting, earnings management, resource valuation, and the effects of slack on firm performance, among others. He is author of academic articles published in accounting, business, management and economics journals, as well as books and book chapters on these topics. He has also 10 years of professional experience in control, management and financial accounting in multinational firms.

Joel Blit is Assistant Professor of Economics at the University of Waterloo and a Senior Fellow at the Centre for International Governance

Innovation. His research focuses on how firm organization influences knowledge flow and innovation, and whether intellectual property rights promote innovation.

Robert P. Bremner is a Ph.D. student at the Stanford Technology Ventures Program in the Department of Management Science & Engineering at Stanford University. Broadly, Bremner's research interests revolve around strategy in nascent industries and decision-making in new ventures. In this domain, he has focused on examining how firms manage interorganizational barriers to innovation and value creation, in addition to the implications of strategic moves on industry value and collaborative dynamics over time.

Ari Dothan is Adjunct Lecturer at the IDC (Interdisciplinary Center Herzliya). He received his Ph.D. in strategic management from the Technion- Israel Institute of Technology, Haifa. His research interests center on organizational learning from performance feedback, firm resources and capabilities, exploration and exploitation.

Gary Dushnitsky is Associate Professor of Strategy and Entrepreneurship at London Business School. He also serves as a Senior Fellow at the Mack Center for Technological Innovation at the Wharton School of the University of Pennsylvania. Dr Dushnitsky's work focuses on the economics of entrepreneurship and innovation. His research has appeared in leading academic journals, including *Organization Science*, the *Strategic Management Journal*, and *Nature Biotechnology*. Dr Dushnitsky serves as a senior editor at *Organization Science* and the *Strategic Entrepreneurship Journal*, and is an elected officer of the international Strategic Management Society.

Kathleen M. Eisenhardt is the Stanford W. Ascherman Professor of Strategy at Stanford University and co-director of the Stanford Technology Ventures Program. Eisenhardt's research sits at the nexus of strategy and organization theory where she focuses on high-velocity markets and technology-based firms. She is now studying innovation collaborations across firms, strategy as simple rules, and competitive interaction, particularly using multiple-case methods. Eisenhardt is also the co-author of Simple Rules: How to Thrive in a Complex World.

Timothy B. Folta is Professor and *Thomas John and Bette Wolff Family Chair of Strategic Entrepreneurship* at the School of Business, University of Connecticut; and Fellow in the University of Strasbourg Institute for

Advanced Study. His research and teaching both examine entrepreneurship and strategy for multi-business firms, analyzing how uncertainty affects decisions around entry, exit, and diversification. He has won a number of international awards for research, and serves as Associate Editor of *Strategic Entrepreneurship Journal* and on the Editorial Boards of *Strategic Management Journal*, *Strategy Science*, and *Journal of Business Venturing*.

Josep Garcia-Blandon is currently Full Professor of Accounting and Finance at the IQS School of Management, Universitat Ramon Llull in Barcelona. He completed his Ph.D. in Economics and Business Administration at the Universitat de Barcelona in 1997. He leads the Research Group on Corporate Governance at Universitat Ramon Llull. His research interests include the role of auditors, the ability of corporate governance codes to enhance corporate governance, resource valuation and the effects of slack on firm performance, among others. He has published numerous articles and book chapters and regularly participates in academic seminars and congresses on these topics.

Douglas P. Hannah is Assistant Professor of Management at the McCombs School of Business at the University of Texas at Austin. Hannah's research explores entrepreneurship and strategy in emerging industries and technology-based ecosystems, such as residential solar and healthcare. Key questions include how entrepreneurs identify and capture opportunities, form and maintain partnerships in evolving industries, and balance value creation and capture in uncertain and ambiguous settings.

Constance E. Helfat is the J. Brian Quinn Professor in Technology and Strategy at the Tuck School of Business at Dartmouth. Her research focuses on firm capabilities, technological innovation, and strategic change, with a particular interest in multi-business firms. She has also conducted research on corporate executives, including women executives. Professor Helfat is a Fellow of the Strategic Management Society, received the Distinguished Scholar Award from the Technology and Innovation Management Division of the Academy of Management, and serves as co-editor of the *Strategic Management Journal*.

Samina Karim is Associate Professor of Entrepreneurship and Innovation at Northeastern University's D'Amore-McKim School of Business. Her research is on corporate restructuring and organization design, acquisitions and alliances, and innovation through reconfiguration of resources and activities. Professor Karim is Chair for the Competitive Strategy Interest Group of the Strategic Management Society, and serves as a Senior Editor for the Journal of Organization Design and an Associate Editor for the Strategic Management Journal.

Hyunseob Kim is currently a Ph.D. Candidate in Strategic Management at Fisher College of Business, The Ohio State University. Before joining the program, he earned his BBA and MS degree at Seoul National University, and he worked for Korean Development Institute, a Korean governmental macroeconomic research institute. Hyunseob Kim is interested in topics related to how organizations adapt to changing environments and in the particular context of the competition between incumbents and latecomers. He focuses on the importance of resource allocation in the firm's strategy to identify opportunities and adapt to changing environments when they do not have sufficient capabilities.

Thomas Klueter <tmklueter@iese.edu> is Assistant Professor of Entrepreneurship at IESE Business School. Thomas received his Ph.D. from the University of Pennsylvania – Wharton School. His research lies lie at the intersection of corporate entrepreneurship and innovation. It focuses on how established and emerging firms manage technological change and the strategies firms pursue to develop and commercialize new technologies.

Dovev Lavie is Full Professor and Vice Dean at the Technion. He earned his Ph.D. at the Wharton School and served as an assistant professor at the University of Texas at Austin. His research focuses on alliance portfolios, balancing exploration and exploitation, and applications of the resource-based view in technology-intensive industries. His work has been published in leading journals. He is Associate Editor of the *Academy of Management Journal* and a Special Issue Editor at the *Strategic Management Journal*. He has also served on the boards of the *Strategic Management Journal*, *Academy of Management Review*, *Administrative Science Quarterly*, and *Organization Science*.

Gwendolyn K. Lee <glee@alum.mit.edu> is the Chester C. Holloway Professor at the University of Florida, Warrington College of Business Administration. She holds a Ph.D. in Business Administration from the University of California at Berkeley, and M.S. and B.S. degrees in Chemical Engineering from the Massachusetts Institute of Technology. Focusing on entry and exit dynamics, her research examines strategy for competition, cooperation, innovation and entrepreneurship. She is a member on the Editorial Review Boards of the *Academy of Management Journal*, and the *Strategic Management Journal*. She has served on the advisory board of the National Science Foundation, program on Science of Organization.

Christopher C. Liu is Assistant Professor of Strategy at Rotman/University of Toronto. His research explores spatial networks: how geography shapes communication patterns and market interactions. Empirical settings for his work have ranged from scientists working within a biotechnology firm to the US Senate Chamber. Chris also has a long-standing interest on scientists, innovation, and productivity. Chris received a Ph.D. in biology from MIT, and a DBA from HBS.

Shaohua Lu obtained her Ph.D. in Strategy from Fisher College of Business at the Ohio State University in 2015. She is now a visiting assistant professor at A.B. Freeman School of Business, Tulane University. Her research interests focus on adoption of new technology, strategic interactions, resource redeployment, and value appropriation. In particular, she applies her research to the U.S. electric utility sector and the renewable energy area.

Mónica Martinez-Blasco is Associate Professor at the IQS School of Management-Universitat Ramon Llull. She teaches principals of accounting in the Degree in Business Administration and advanced accounting topics in the Master of Auditing. She completed her Ph.D. in Economics and Business Administration at the Universitat Ramon Llull in 2004. Her research interests include accounting, auditing, and corporate governance, among others. She has contributed several book chapters in Spanish and English languages, and published various research articles in academic journals on these topics.

Luis L. Martins is Professor of Management and the Juanita Dreibelbis Fellow in Business at the McCombs School of Business at the University of Texas at Austin. He received his Ph.D. in management and organizational behavior from the Leonard N. Stern School of Business at New York University. His research bridges micro and macro aspects of organizations. He primarily studies managerial and organizational cognition, and in particular their roles in innovation, organizational change, and growth, as well as the dynamics of diversity in teams and organizations.

Patia J. McGrath is a Ph.D. candidate in Management at The Wharton School of the University of Pennsylvania, where she is part of the Strategy group. Her dissertation research focuses on organizational learning and its firm performance implications in the context of corporate divestiture.

Douglas J. Miller is Associate Professor of Management & Global Business at Rutgers Business School – Newark & New Brunswick, New Jersey, USA. He is a leading academic expert in Corporate Strategy, with highly cited research articles in *Strategic Management Journal* and *Academy of Management Journal* on vertical integration, diversification, and management of innovation in the multi-business firm. He earned his Ph.D. at The Ohio State University. A member of the editorial board of *Strategic Management Journal* for several years, Professor Miller also currently serves as Program Chair of the Corporate Strategy Interest Group of the Strategic Management Society.

Will Mitchell <William.Mitchell@Rotman.utoronto.ca> is the Anthony S. Fell Chair in New Technologies and Commercialization at the Rotman School of Management of the University of Toronto. He publishes actively in the strategy field, with an emphasis on business dynamics in developed and emerging markets, and teaches courses on related strategy topics in degree and executive programs. Will is a consulting editor for the *Strategic Management Journal* and a board member of Neuland Laboratories, Hyderabad, India.

Elena Novelli <novelli@city.ac.uk> is faculty member at Cass Business School. Her research focuses on the strategic management of knowledge, technology and innovation and the implications for firm performance. Her work has been published on international academic journals including the *Academy of Management Review*, the *Academy of Management Annals* and *Research Policy* and has been recognized by several grant and awards including the 2015 SMS Best Paper IG Knowledge and Innovation award and the ESRC Future Research Leaders grant. She is a member of the Editorial Review Board of the *Strategic Management Journal*, *Strategy Science* and the *Journal of Management Studies*.

Srikanth Parachuri <sup28@psu.edu> is Associate Professor in the Management & Organization Department of the Smeal College of Business, at The Pennsylvania State University. His research focuses primarily on two streams: knowledge workers and knowledge networks, and consequences of "momentous events." He serves on the editorial board of *Organization Science* and is a current Associate Editor for *Academy of Management Journal*. He has earned his Ph.D. from Columbia University, Master's degree in International Business from Indian Institute of Foreign Trade, New Delhi, and Bachelor's in Technology specializing in computer science from Regional Engineering College, Warangal, India.

Violina P. Rindova is the Captain Henry W. Simonsen Chair in Strategic Entrepreneurship at the Marshall School of Business, University of Southern California and the Research Director of the Lloyd Greif Center for Entrepreneurial Studies. Her research and teaching focus on the market and organizational processes through which firms create value, intangible assets, such as celebrity and reputation, and new market opportunities.

Harbir Singh is the Mack Professor of Management, Co-Director of the Mack Institute for Innovation Management, and Vice Dean for Global Initiatives at The Wharton School of the University of Pennsylvania. He has been the Chair of the Management Department at The Wharton School. His research interests include the development of world-class capabilities, and of sustainable competitive advantage. His research focuses on effective strategies for managing acquisitions and alliances, and on globalization of firms and markets. In addition, his teaching interests include the development of competitive advantage and management of acquisitions and alliances.

Hsiao-shan Yang is Economist and Data Scientist for a leading financial data provider in New York City. After receiving her Ph.D. in Economics from the State University of New York at Buffalo, she developed research in Strategic Management, patent law, and Industrial Organization economics in a post-doctoral position at the interdisciplinary Institute for Genomic Biology, at the University of Illinois at Urbana-Champaign.

Adrian Yeow is Senior Lecturer at SIM University where he teaches accounting information systems and digital marketing. Adrian has a Ph.D. from the R.H. School of Business, University of Maryland, College Park. His current research is focused on orchestration of organizational collaboration in integrated healthcare systems and the use of technology within such collaborations. Adrian is also interested in the role of dynamic capabilities in organizational growth and alignment of digital strategies.